IN THE SHADOW OF THE DOPE FIEND

IN THE SHADOW OF
THE DOPE FIEND

AMERICA'S WAR ON DRUGS

WILLIAM WEIR

Archon Books
1995

© 1995 William Weir. All rights reserved.
First published 1995 by Archon Books,
an imprint of The Shoe String Press, Inc.
North Haven, Connecticut 06473.

Library of Congress Cataloging-in-Publication Data

Weir, William, 1928–
    In the shadow of the dope fiend : America's war on drugs / by
William Weir.
        p.   cm.
    Includes bibliographical references and index.
    ISBN 0-208-02384-4 (alk. paper)
    1. Narcotics, Control of—United States—History.   2. Drug abuse—
United States—Prevention—History.   I. Title.
HV5825.W3834   1994
363.4'5'0973—dc20   94-28204
                                                                        CIP

The paper in this publication meets the
minimum requirements of American National
Standard for Information Sciences—
Permanence of Paper for Printed Library Materials,
ANSI Z39.48–1984. ⊗

Printed in the United States of America

Dedicated to the memory of Richmond Pearson Hobson—
war hero, congressman and creator of the Dope Fiend

CONTENTS

ACKNOWLEDGMENTS

Nobody, obviously, could write a book like this without help. It's partially based on centuries of research by people few of us, including me, have ever heard of. More of it is based on information gathered by reporters, sociologists, police officers, economists, and scientists and lawyers from all over the world. You'll find the names of many, but not all, of them in the notes and bibliography. All of their written works seem to be based on careful observation and logic. The persons I spoke with, some of whom certainly would not agree with all of my conclusions, were unfailingly polite and helpful. I am most grateful to all of them.

I owe a lot of thanks, too, to the people at The Shoe String Press, especially its president, Jim Thorpe. As usual they were always encouraging, and Jim, as usual, was a font of thought-provoking ideas.

Dale Salm and Valerie Schroth, managing editor and senior editor, respectively, of *Connecticut* magazine, deserve special thanks for getting me interested in drugs. So do Bill Taylor and Adria Henderson, private investigators, for getting me interested in the cloak-and-dagger aspects of international drug smuggling.

As always, my wife, Anne, read everything, contributed valuable ideas and put up with my hogging of the computer.

Guilford, Connecticut
May 25, 1994

INTRODUCTION

███

"A book about drugs?" a friend asked. "Do you have any practical experience?"

Well, I suppose my checkered career as a reformed smoker (of tobacco) and current status as a somewhat antisocial social drinker could be cited if this were a book about drugs as drugs. But it's not.

This book mumbles only enough about psychopharmacology to make other points clear. Nor is it either an ode to psychoactives or a compilation of horror stories. It is certainly not a how-to manual for getting high. But neither does it praise the heroic enforcers of drug laws. Alert readers will notice that I do not use the term "drug abuse." That is not from any affection for drugs but from a love of the English language. Although we've all heard of people kicking the habit, I've never heard of anyone slapping cocaine or stomping on heroin. People who use drugs to excess (and with some drugs and some people, almost any quantity is excessive) abuse themselves, not the drugs. But "self-abuse" sounds too much like masturbation (although both activities actually have much in common).

This is a history. A very unpleasant history of how the American people—and, to an extent, the whole world—have been manipulated by cynical politicians for their own gain. It describes the creation of a fantasy monster, the Dope Fiend, and how the Dope Fiend legend has been used to garner votes. It also tells how national leaders and their agents have aided and abetted those smuggling drugs into this country while they were denouncing drug use and declaring the War on Drugs. It also details the pernicious effects that so-called war has had on American life. On the side, it sketches a history of the modern American underworld and cites some of the alarming ways in which the Bill of Rights is being watered down.

None of this, of course, is based on "practical experience," in the sense of the author's personal experience. It is based on the experience and knowledge of some very smart people—some of whom have also demonstrated that they are very brave people—who have written and talked about what they know.

You'll meet them in the pages ahead.

PART ONE

BIRTH OF THE DOPE FIEND

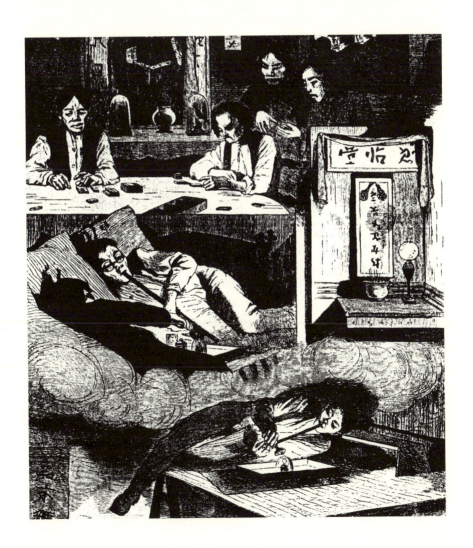

Reverse: Scene in an opium den in San Francisco's Chinatown, drawn by Winslow Homer for Harpers Magazine in 1874.

1

In the country of the Scythians, wrote Herodotus more than two thousand years ago, there is hemp, "a plant resembling flax, but much taller and coarser. It grows wild as well as under cultivation, and the Thracians make clothes from it very like linen ones—indeed, one must have some experience in these matters to be able to distinguish between the two."

The Scythians used hemp for something other than clothes, though, the Father of History wrote.

"On a framework of three sticks, meeting at the top, they stretch pieces of woollen cloth, taking care to get the joins as perfect as they can, and inside this little tent they put a dish with red-hot stones in it. Then they take some hemp seed, creep into the tent and throw the seed on to the hot stones. At once it begins to smoke, giving off a vapour unsurpassed by any vapour-bath one could find in Greece. The Scythians enjoy it so much that they howl with pleasure."

And so marijuana got its first mention in classical literature.

2

Inhaling smoke and howling with pleasure these days would seem to be odd behavior in anyone trying a marijuana cigarette. Most marijuana users act "cool" or "laid back" or just plain comatose. But the behavior of a person under the influence of a drug varies not only with the drug but with the person.

Take wine, a drug familiar to Herodotus, although he, like most modern imbibers, probably wouldn't consider it a drug. We're all familiar with persons who, when drunk, become aggressive, or weepy, or garrulous, or silent. The alcohol seems to reinforce an already established character trait. According to some experts, such as Richard H. Blum in *Society and Drugs: Drugs I: Social and Cultural Observations*, the user's expectation of the drug's effect and the user's surroundings also help determine the effects. In one set of experiments, persons given a "narcotic antagonist" that chemically blocks heroin still experienced the expected effect of the heroin dose. In another set, former drug users who had taken nothing experienced the effects of drugs when exposed to environments they remembered as settings for drug use. The Scythian junkies obviously expected to feel a noisy joy, even though marijuana is a depressant. Reinforcing one user's expectations was the fact that all his fellows were howling with pleasure.

Howling with pleasure is by no means inconsistent with use of a depressant. Alcohol is another depressant. And howling with pleasure, or something very like it, is among the memories of anyone who has ever been part of—or just heard—a convivial group of students, soldiers or whatever trying to sing after they've had too much beer.

3

Is alcohol a drug? Like marijuana, it's capable of intoxicating a user. Like cocaine, it can create an addiction in some people. Like LSD, it can cause wildly erratic behavior. Is it dangerous? Alcohol has killed far more people than all other drugs combined—with one exception. The exception is tobacco, which slays thousands upon thousands with lung cancer, emphysema and heart disease. According to the Centers for Disease Control, tobacco caused 430,000 deaths in 1992. The American Cancer Society says 418,000 die because of tobacco each year. A study published in November 1993 in the *Journal of the American Medical Association* reinforces those estimates. Dr. Michael J. McGinnis, director of the federal Office of Disease Prevention and Health Promotion, and Dr. William H. Foege, health policy fellow at the Carter Presidential Center in Atlanta and former director of the Centers for Disease Control, say that tobacco use led to about 30 percent of all cancer deaths and 21 percent of heart disease deaths. Overall, tobacco caused 19 percent of all deaths. The doctors said it is difficult to pinpoint causes of deaths, but a conservative estimate of deaths caused by tobacco in 1990 is 400,000. That makes tobacco the leading cause of all deaths in the

United States. Alcohol, McGinnis and Foege estimate, killed 100,000 in 1990.

Drugs are hard to define. If you said a drug is any chemical substance that when introduced into the body has an effect on it, that would be true of either cocaine or aspirin. It would also be true of bread or steak. To narrow the field to dangerous drugs, the effect might be described as "harmful." "Causing addiction" might also be added to the definition.

Even so, coffee could be included. Caffeine is a stimulant, and coffee is, for many people, mildly addicting. It can be dangerous for some persons, those with heart disease, for example. Most people, though, would have to drink it by the barrel to get into serious trouble.

Nicotine in its pure state is a deadly poison. Tobacco is a very mild stimulant, but like coffee, and unlike whiskey or barbiturates, it has no mind-altering properties unless used in gargantuan quantities. As mentioned above, though, it is extremely dangerous. It is also mildly addicting physically and powerfully addicting psychologically. It is, according to experts, more addictive than any of the currently illicit, or "dangerous," drugs. In other words, you have a greater chance of becoming "hooked" on trying your first tobacco cigarette than on trying your first vial of crack, your first snort of cocaine or your first shot of heroin. And the risk increases faster with each succeeding cigarette than with succeeding doses of other drugs.

Dangerous drugs could also be defined as harmful substances other people take. That's pretty much the unspoken definition held by most Americans. Let's look at these substances.

4

Opium: Opium is one of the oldest of the "hard" drugs. It is basically the gummy sap of the opium poppy. It can be eaten in its "raw" form or smoked after some processing. Mixed with an alcoholic beverage (flavored sherry, in its earliest form) it is called laudanum and can be drunk. In various doses, it can relieve pain, calm upset stomachs and prevent diarrhea. Introduced in an age when bleeding and blistering were the most common medical techniques, it was hailed as a wonder cure. Some time after its introduction to the West, in the Middle Ages, it was noticed that persons who used opium heavily for a long time often became extremely ill when they stopped using it. At that time, and for long afterward, it was commonly believed that withdrawal from opium might mean death for the addict. Death can occur when an extremely heavy user withdraws from alcohol—during the so-called DTs—but withdrawal from opium or its derivatives is seldom so severe.

The opium poppy seems to be native to the mountains in the southern Asian land mass, perhaps originating in modern Iran or Afghanistan. It requires the sort of moderate climate and clear, non-humid air found on the middle slopes of these mountains. Today, most opium is grown in a mountainous belt extending from Asian Turkey through Iran, Afghanistan, Pakistan, India and Burma, extending south into Thailand, Vietnam, Cambodia and Laos and north into southern China. There are many other places in the world where it can thrive, such as South and North America, including the United States. Mexico has long been a source of opium.

Opium's history goes back far before Herodotus' mention of the Scythian use of hemp. Some scholars believe it is the "lotus" mentioned in the *Odyssey* that will "lull all pain and anger, and bring forgetfulness of every sorrow." Certainly, its healing power was described by Hippocrates (466–377 B.C.), the Greek physician, and by the later Greek physician Galen (130–200 A.D.). The Chinese knew about it in the eighth century A.D.

During the nineteenth century, opium was used in many patent medicines sold over the counter in both drugstores and grocery stores. By that time, though, many of its medicinal functions were taken over by opiates, drugs refined from crude opium. One of the most important of these was . . .

Morphine. Morphine was developed in the nineteenth century and was extensively used in the American Civil War as a pain-reliever. The Civil War is sometimes cited as the beginning of widespread American use of narcotics (other than alcohol).

Morphine addiction acquired by wounded veterans of the war may have been a factor in American narcotics use. Another factor may have been the widespread use of opium as a cure for environmental illnesses involved in settling the West. Francis Parkman, in *The Oregon Trail*, tells of taking opium to counteract the dysentery he suffered in the desert. Rivers and lakes in "the unspoiled West" were seriously contaminated by a variety of alkalis and salts, including Epsom salts. And after settlement, the average doctor who went west was usually not the brightest of medical stars, even if he had graduated from medical school, as many had not. Western physicians relied far too much on opium and opiates. Still another factor was that in the United States, the states exercised whatever control there was of narcotics. There was a wide variety of laws, instead of the central control exercised in nations like Britain, France and Prussia. Finally, Americans have always prided themselves on their willingness to try something new, including new patent medicines. At any rate, U.S. importation of opium and opiates increased steadily throughout the nineteenth century. They were sold in general stores, grocery stores and drugstores. They were also sold by traveling medicine men who combined the arts of the showman and the con man and passed themselves off as medical authorities.

Morphine was widely hailed because it was so much more powerful than opium and easy to use with the newly invented hypodermic needle. Physicians noticed, however, that it was even more likely than opium to make addicts of its users. Late in the nineteenth century, the Bavarian chemical concern that introduced Bayer aspirin offered a substitute for morphine that was supposed to eliminate the earlier drug's undesirable side effects. The drug's trade name was . . .

Heroin. Heroin is a further refinement of opium, and it is usually injected, like morphine. As a pain-reliever, it is at least four times as effective as morphine. Unfortunately, it turned out to be even more addictive. It quickly became the "devil drug," to the general public, although heroin users are among the least aggressive druggies when under the influence. Heroin is so powerful the user seldom experiences the active high so common with alcohol or hashish intoxication. Heroin, nevertheless, developed such an evil reputation in the United States, that in spite of its medical effectiveness, doctors may not give it to a patient under any circumstances—not even to relieve the pain of someone dying of cancer. That has led to the creation of . . .

Methadone. Methadone is widely used in public clinics to help heroin addicts lead normal lives. Its effects are much like those of heroin. They last longer, though, so a single daily dose of methadone is enough to keep the most far-gone heroin addict functioning. The methadone high lasts longer than heroin's but is not so pleasurable, something that no doubt endears it to its "straight" advocates. The effects are so much like those of heroin because methadone is a kind of imitation heroin. Technically, it's called an opioid. The greatest reason for its existence is that its name is not heroin, which is specifically and totally banned from any legal use in the United States.

Like heroin, there's no legal use for another drug that is far less potent than any of the opiates or opioids . . .

Marijuana. "Mary Jane" has been around since before the Scythians, although it has not always been used as a drug. George Washington and all other law-abiding Virginia planters raised it before the Revolution. Its cultivation was required to ensure that there would be enough rope to manage the sails of the Royal Navy (and to hang the many felons, from pickpockets to murderers, eligible for capital punishment under English law). During World War II, it was also planted after sisal from the Philippines, the normal raw material for "hemp" rope, was cut off. It grows wild and thrives almost anywhere but the polar regions.

Cigarettes made from marijuana vary in strength, depending on what part of the plant is used. The flowering head is the strongest; the leaves, the weakest. Some marijuana is raised by a process called *sinsemilla*, which increases its potency. Compared with most other well-known illicit drugs, it isn't very potent, although it is intoxicating. Its ability to create addiction is also below most other drugs, including, of course, tobacco.

Marijuana has proven valuable for reducing the side effects of chemotherapy and also for relieving the pressure inside the eye caused by glaucoma. The ancient Egyptians used it to ease childbirth: The drug promotes contractions while easing pain. Until 1976, U.S. authorities, however, refused to see any redeeming value in marijuana. That year, they allowed people suffering from certain diseases, and who could find no relief from other drugs, to apply to the Federal Food and Drug Administration for permission to use marijuana. Permission was granted on a case-by-case basis. In 1992, the Bush Administration abolished even this mingy approval, saying marijuana could harm patients with weakened immune systems. At this writing, the Clinton Administration is taking another look at marijuana. In general, though, since 1935, doctors have been able to prescribe the very powerful and dangerous morphine, but never marijuana.

A derivative of marijuana, and perhaps the oldest "refined" drug is . . .

Hashish. Hashish, the juice of the marijuana plant, contains far more of the plant's intoxicating element, THC. It is also the origin of the word "assassin." In the eleventh century, a man named Hasan-e Sabbah and known as the Sheik el Jebel, or Old Man of the Mountains, founded a religious cult based on murder and extortion. He demanded money from notables all over the Near East and, when they did not pay, sent his followers to kill them. He kept his followers happy with large quantities of hashish. They were known to everyone else as *hashishin*, users of hashish, which became "assassin." The sheik's cult, minus murder, extortion and hashish, soldiers on as the branch of Islam headed by the Aga Khan.

Marijuana is a relatively weak sister among illicit drugs. Hashish is not. Neither is . . .

Cocaine. Cocaine is refined from the coca leaf, a mild intoxicant in use since prehistoric times by the natives of the Andes. Although almost all coca comes from South America, there's no reason why it could not be raised in most of the world. Like morphine and heroin, cocaine is a product of the chemical revolution of the nineteenth century. Technically, it is quite different from the opiates, marijuana and hashish. The other drugs are narcotics: They slow down the central nervous system. Cocaine is a stimulant: It speeds things up. A person on a cocaine high feels able to think more clearly, work longer, harder and more accurately and perform tasks normally beyond his strength. And, in fact, cocaine does liberate more of a person's energy. A user coming down from a cocaine high feels exhausted. That's because he has used up far more energy than he normally would. Sigmund Freud was one of a number of famous cocaine users before he decided he was doing himself more harm than good. The fictional Sherlock Holmes found that cocaine aided his analysis of clues. Besides a rush of energy, cocaine makes some people irritable and even produces a kind of temporary paranoia. Cocaine's effects are related to how much you take and how you take it.

One of cocaine's medicinal uses is as a local anesthetic. It once was also used to dry out nasal passages. In a heavy user, though, this effect can result in the destruction of tissue. Like all the other illicit drugs, cocaine is also an intoxicant. Someone on a cocaine high can develop a superman complex, which has the potential for all kinds of social harm. A variant of cocaine is . . .

Crack. Crack is cocaine processed so it can be smoked. Most co-caine is "snorted," although in the past it was often eaten or injected. Smoking gets the active ingredient into the body fastest, so crack provides a very fast, short-lasting but violent high. It is the most addictive of all the illicit drugs—almost as addictive as tobacco. It has been estimated that a first-time user has a one-in-six chance of becoming addicted. If those sound like good odds, remember that they are the same odds you get in Russian roulette. And losing can be just as disastrous.

There are dozens of other drugs used illicitly. One group includes medicines that may be legally prescribed—amphetamines, barbiturates, tranquilizers, etc.—that are acquired without prescriptions. Another group includes the synthetic drugs, the first of which was LSD. Then there are peyote, hallucinogenic mushrooms and the inhalants—airplane glue, Magic Marker fluid and gasoline. Prisoners in New York's jail, Rikers Island, were found to be smoking mace (the common kitchen spice, not the anti-mugger spray) to get high.

5

Two things all of these drugs have in common is that they can intoxicate, which is to say disorient the mind and disturb the reflexes, and they can create an addiction.

There are two kinds of addiction, physical and psychological. Of the two, physical addiction is usually by far the less dangerous. Medical people seem to have first become aware of this condition studying patients who had discontinued using opiates. Withdrawal symptoms include nausea, muscular pains and cramps, running nose and other symptoms of influenza. After a relatively short time, the symptoms become milder. They are completely gone in a matter of months. Because of several thousand years of experience with the sometimes fatal "cold turkey" withdrawal from alcohol addiction, though, physicians feared that opium addicts would die if suddenly cut off from their drug. This led to the idea of "drug maintenance" to keep addicts alive. "Maintenance" has been a feature of many drug control programs for the last hundred years.

Actually, most persons classed as addicts, including heroin addicts, cure themselves, and without "maintenance." During World War II, it became almost impossible to ship heroin or any other drug into the

United States. Authorities estimated that there were more than 200,000 heroin addicts in the country before the war. Using data compiled the same way, the same authorities estimated that there were only about 20,000 by V-J Day.

Breaking a serious cocaine addiction is tougher than breaking the heroin habit. Cocaine not only stimulates the central nervous system, it also stimulates the pleasure centers of the brain. When the stimulus is withdrawn, the pleasure centers react. When a user "crashes" from a powerful cocaine high, he is usually not only exhausted but depressed. Depression is so bad that a heavy crack user may find that he is incapable of experiencing any pleasure under any circumstances without his drug. It takes a lot of cocaine—even a pretty steady use of crack—to become addicted to this extent, but "coke" is an insidious drug: Addiction builds up without the user noticing anything. In the most extreme cases, withdrawal can be fatal.

The physical components of addiction are dramatic, as in the classic film *The Lost Weekend*, but the psychological component is harder to deal with for most people. Asked why she took heroin, a former addict said, "Because it makes you feel so good." This woman kicked her habit after a year at Connecticut's toughest residential rehabilitation center. Tobacco, as most former smokers can testify, has physical withdrawal symptoms. But compared with the symptoms of heroin or, especially, cocaine, withdrawal, they are laughable. By no means laughable, though, is the acute sense of insecurity a smoker feels when even the taste in his mouth tells him he must have a cigarette and none is available. Withdrawal from most drugs, except from a heavy cocaine (or crack) habit, produces symptoms not much worse than a severe case of flu. The physical symptoms, though, are not what makes users go on using. The fact is that after a few thousand years of dealing with addicts, the experts still aren't sure what causes addiction. That's why there are so many different types of treatment, almost all of which work for some people, but none of which works for all people.

Addiction to tobacco is easier to develop than to any other drug, and it is the cause of more deaths than any other drug, but it is not one of the illicit drugs on the lists of the Controlled Substances Act.

Alcohol, although it's second only to tobacco as a cause of death and is powerfully intoxicating and capable of creating one of the most serious forms of addiction, is not mentioned in the Controlled Sub-

stances Act either. There was an attempt to prohibit it—a 14–year period from which America has not yet recovered. We'll look at
Prohibition in more detail later.

If federal law seems inconsistent as applied to drugs, the various
state laws, considered as a whole, verge on the irrational. In Kansas and
Wyoming, for instance, a person arrested for possession of marijuana
for the first time, may be sentenced to a *maximum* of six months in
jail. In Alaska, until 1990, he wouldn't even have been arrested. But in
Texas, a person can be—and persons have been—sent to prison for
life.

Such inconsistency has characterized public dealings with drugs
since drugs first came to America.

2

Among the politically correct these days, it's common to assert that European "discoverers" brought all the world's evils upon the happy and peaceful inhabitants of the New World. And it's true that the white men did bring robbery, rape, murder, massacre, slavery and smallpox to the natives. But the natives, somewhat less happy and a lot less peaceful than often supposed, were quite familiar with robbery, rape, murder, massacre and slavery, although they couldn't perpetrate these crimes quite as efficiently as the newcomers. Some of their other customs, like cannibalism and human sacrifice on a vast scale, ran contrary to the conquerors' mores, so they had to give them up. True, smallpox was an evil the natives were quite unprepared for, but syphilis, which they gave in trade, found the Europeans equally unprepared.

The "noble savage," the unspoiled human living in a "state of nature," a conceit popularized by Jean Jacques Rousseau, eluded all the explorers and discoverers. The people they did find were seldom savage (in the anthropological sense) and never unspoiled. Particularly, they were no more innocent of drugs than any native of the Old World.

2

In both North and South America, the natives used tobacco. The Europeans took it back to their homeland, and from there it spread over the entire world—from the tundra of Iceland to the jungles of New Guinea. "The weed" was the New World's most significant contribution to the world drug pool, but it was hardly the only one. North American Indians used peyote and hallucinogenic mushrooms—substances that remained out of the mainstream until the 1960s. South American Indians

13

chewed the coca leaf, which, refined as cocaine, has been plaguing the world since the late nineteenth century.

According to legend, Indians were quite unused to alcohol and went wild after a few sips. Actually, Mexican Indians had been making mescal and pulque, alcoholic drinks consisting of the fermented juices of desert plants, long before Cortés. In the North, where Indians were not used to alcohol, the white men did, more than occasionally, get tribesmen drunk to take advantage of them.

If the English and French used alcohol to befuddle the Indians, the Spanish used another drug to keep them productive in spite of grueling hours and a meager diet. Coca leaf was a traditional comfort for the Andean peasants, and the Spanish made sure the Indians they had enslaved to work their mines had plenty of it. Perhaps coincidentally, perhaps not, cocaine later came to be identified in the public mind with the black ex-slaves of North America.

That, however, was far in the future. During the colonial period, the most important drugs were tobacco and alcohol. The major cash crop of the British North American colonies, particularly in the South, was tobacco. In the middle colonies, such as Pennsylvania, corn was more important, but it was bulky and hard to move over the miserable roads of the time. Western farmers, predominantly of Scottish and Irish descent, solved the problem by distilling their grain into whiskey, a drink invented by their ancestors. A much smaller load could bring much more money than corn.

Rum was another important item in the colonial economy. British sugar plantations in the West Indies shipped sugar cane to New England, where it was processed into rum. Yankee sea captains took the liquor to West Africa, where native chiefs took it in payment for slaves. The merchant sailors then sold the slaves in the West Indies and bought more sugar cane. Many a Yankee sea captain grew rich plying the "triangle trade." Rum was also important in trade with the Indians, although the French preferred to use brandy. (That may be one reason why the French had somewhat more success in enlisting the Indians in their struggle with the British for North America.)

3

All through the colonial period and long after the Revolutionary War, alcoholic drinks continued to be a major product. Taverns were the usual site for political meetings or other rallies. On the frontier, tea and coffee were scorned as "slops that won't stick to your ribs." Whiskey was the only drink for a man. In New England, rum was king. Yankees took a perverse pride in their ability to drink large quantities of the harsh local rum. During the Revolution, one test for a British spy was to give the suspect a "New Englander." If he could down this mixture of rum, water and molasses and seem to enjoy it, the colonists believed he couldn't be British.

Opium came into increasing use as the country filled up. It was sometimes eaten straight to ease pain or relieve intestinal distress. There was plenty of that, particularly during the move west. A diet of dried beans and salt pork, combined with alkali-and-salt-laced water in arid regions, did awful things to the digestive system. And in the West, where specialized medicines were hard to get, many physicians and medicine men relied on opium and opiates. Oliver Wendell Holmes, Sr., dean of the Harvard Medical School, declared just before the Civil War that "the constant prescription of opiates by certain physicians . . . has rendered the habitual use of that drug in that region [the West] very prevalent. . . . A frightful endemic demoralization betrays itself in the frequency with which the haggard features and drooping shoulders of the opium drunkards are met with in the street."

The Civil War gave another boost to drug use in the United States. Morphine, an opiate, had been developed during the chemical revolution of the nineteenth century. It was usually injected with a hypodermic needle, and it was a far more effective painkiller than opium. It was used extensively in the American Civil War. One by-product of the war was an increase in morphine addiction.

4

Opium, an opiate or cocaine was usually one of the active ingredients in a host of patent medicines sold in drugstores and groceries. The other was usually alcohol. These remedies, for every imaginable illness as well as simply to pep up the user, were aimed at and largely consumed by women, who were not welcome in those strongholds of masculinity, the saloons. Further, the lives of few women had any sort of intellectual stimulation. Poor women drudged at boring, repetitious tasks; middle-class women had servants and plenty of leisure time, but nothing to do with that time. Not surprisingly, a large number of both became addicted. Preachers and physicians of the day took this as evidence of woman's "weaker nature."

There had been a Chinese community in California since Gold Rush days. After the Civil War, California entrepreneurs imported large numbers of additional Chinese laborers to build the Central Pacific Railroad. The Chinese brought their opium pipes with them. Importation of smokable opium increased. Before long, the recreational use of opium began to catch on with the non-Chinese portion of the population. Although there were horror stories about the "opium dens," the Chinese were a notably peaceful and hardworking segment of the western population. Whenever they were involved in violence, it was as victims. And there was plenty of violence. Today, visitors to the Old Pueblo of Los Angeles can see the catacombs Chinese merchants dug beneath their stores so they wouldn't have to go out on the open street, where thugs and rowdies were always ready to attack them.

Anti-Chinese feeling was a constant undercurrent in the nineteenth century, especially strong during depressed times. Chinese were finally forbidden to enter the country. Then a number of states passed laws against opium, usually against opium dens rather than the drug itself. Apparently the legislators believed that if deprived of opium the Chinese would go back home.

"If the Chinaman cannot get along without his 'dope,' we can get along without him," declared the American Pharmaceutical Association's Committee on the Acquirement of the Drug Habit in 1902. The committee suspected, though, that not all opium smokers were Chinese. "The great increase in quantity of this special kind of opium [smoking opium] proves one of two thing or both: either our exclusion laws are being violated or the smoking of opium is largely practiced by others than Chinese."

Campaigns for American drug laws have often had an anti-minority component. The committee looked at two other repressed groups and the drug habit:

"The use of cocaine by unfortunate women generally, and by Negroes in certain parts of the country, is simply appalling. No idea of this can be had unless personally investigated. The police officers of these questionable districts tell us that the habitues are made madly wild by cocaine, which they have no difficulty at all in buying, sometimes being peddled from door to door but always adulterated with acetanilid [a painkiller used to treat fever, headache and rheumatism]."

A large number of women were undoubtedly addicted to cocaine. Cocaine, like opium, morphine and heroin, was a major component of the patent medicines consumed by women. No one, however, accused those women of wild, criminal behavior. It was different with blacks. People generally believed that cocaine gave blacks superhuman strength and endurance. It was even supposed to improve pistol marksmanship. Blacks crazed by cocaine, including that in Coca-Cola (until 1903), were supposed to be unfazed by .32-caliber revolver bullets. That legend led to a massive shift by police departments all over the country from .32- to .38-caliber revolvers.

But as David Musto points out, "So far, evidence does not suggest that cocaine caused a crime wave, but rather that anticipation of black rebellion inspired white alarm." The evidence does suggest that the supposed widespread addiction to cocaine among blacks was a fantasy. In 1914, a Georgia asylum reported that out of 2,100 consecutive admissions of blacks the previous five years, only two were cocaine users. This period, the very late nineteenth and early twentieth centuries, was the peak period for lynchings. The blacks, like the Chinese, appear to have been mainly the victims of violence rather than its initiators.

During the Great Depression, there was widespread unhappiness in the southwestern United States over Mexican agricultural laborers who were said to be taking jobs from Americans. That led to a campaign to ban marijuana, said to be an integral part of Mexican culture. It was also, according to such propaganda pieces as the film *Reefer Madness*, the "gateway drug" leading to hard drugs like heroin. And, as with cocaine, it was supposed to turn its users into monsters of superhuman strength and viciousness. So in 1937, marijuana was declared to be a dangerous drug. A new federal tax law made it illegal in practice for almost any use.

5

In 1874, an English chemist named C.R. Wright created heroin, a greatly enhanced form of morphine. Its painkilling capacity has been estimated as from four to ten times that of ordinary morphine. Wright decided it was too dangerous for medical use. In Germany, however, the Bayer company, part of the I.G. Farben cartel, decided otherwise. In 1898, Bayer introduced heroin as a new miracle drug. It was far more effective than morphine, Bayer said, and had none of the undesirable side effects (like addiction).

Cocaine, like heroin, was developed by a reputable German chemical company, E. Merck & Co. of Darmstadt in the late nineteenth century. It, too, was offered as a wonder drug. Sigmund Freud praised it as a cure for morphine and alcohol addiction. He wrote that the user had "absolutely no craving for further use of cocaine." After a couple of years of taking the drug himself, though, Freud apparently noticed a craving. After that, he stayed away from cocaine completely.

6

At the same time that modern chemistry was transforming ancient drugs, the industrial revolution was transforming ordinary lives. Farmers were turning into factory workers. The physical exertion of farm work was greater, but the pace of life was slower. There were no slack periods in a factory. The demands on nervous energy were greater; psychological stress was higher. Between 1850 and 1900, per capita consumption of sugar—a source of quick energy—increased fourfold in both England and the United States. American coffee consumption increased threefold. Between the 1840s and the 1890s, American consumption of opium—primarily in patent medicines—increased from 12 to 52 grains per capita. British sales of patent medicines increased sevenfold between 1850 and 1905.

One reason for this increased consumption of sugar, coffee and opium may have been, as Alfred McCoy suggests, the result of the increased tensions of urban life. Another may have been the change from a mainly subsistence economy to a money economy. The first situation would increase the urge for drugs; the second, the ability to buy them.

By 1896, drug addiction in the United States peaked at about 313,000, according to David T. Courtwright in *Dark Paradise: Opiate Addiction in America Before 1940*. Because there were no restrictions on opiates or other drugs in 1896, there was no reason to hide the importation of drugs. Courtwright's figures are probably more accurate than estimates of addiction in more recent times. All estimates of drug addiction depend on hospital admissions, court records, autopsies and a lot of extrapolation. In some of the modern estimates, as we'll see, the extrapolation is absolutely bizarre.

Considering the size of the population in 1896 (about 66,160,000), the addiction rate at that time was very high, even by current standards. It exceeds, in fact, the addiction rate in some current estimates. Except for the specious Negro-and-cocaine scare, however, there was nothing like today's plague of drug-related crime.

At the time, there were no national anti-narcotics or anti-cocaine laws. There were some state laws, but most of them were vitiated by two factors: (1) the patent-medicine lobby had managed to get exceptions for patent-medicines; and (2) a dealer in a state without drug laws could ship drugs into states where they were prohibited, and the state couldn't stop him, because that would be interfering with interstate commerce.

And at this time, states were more concerned about alcohol than narcotics or cocaine.

3

Between 1920 and 1933, it was illegal in the United States to manufacture, import or sell any alcoholic beverage. The period, known as Prohibition, is remembered today for the birth of organized crime on a grand scale, for the wholesale corruption of public officials and for machine gun battles on city streets. It did little, if anything, toward solving the problem of public drunkenness. It did result in murders—a thousand gang killings in Chicago and another thousand in New York, plus thousands more around the country during the period. And it created a tradition of American gangsterism that has continued to develop.

The most puzzling feature about Prohibition to people today is: Why did the United States, practically alone in the world, succumb to this madness?

2

National Prohibition had roots deep in the country's history. The first European settlers in what became the United States were almost all farmers. There were not many other ways to support yourself on the raw North American continent. With millions of acres of almost free land attracting settlers, farmers retained their predominance for centuries. In all that time, rural people never deviated from their belief that "God made the country; man made the cities." Some, though, suspected that the Devil had a hand in city building. Thomas Jefferson, a country gentleman, saw independent yeomen as the backbone of democracy. He hoped his country could avoid such centers of corruption as the teeming cities of Europe.

In the 1850s, America began to change. A lot of people, particularly in rural areas, didn't like what they saw. Irish and German Catholics were flooding into the land. The Irish, fleeing recurring famines, were destitute. Few of them had the money to buy farms, so they crowded into the cities. The famines finally ended, but later immigrants from that impoverished island were not much better off than the Irish of the first wave. The Germans, fleeing the results of the failed revolutions of 1848, were mostly solid, middle-class burghers. They had some money, but they spoke a strange language and huddled together in their own communities. Like the Irish, many of them were Papists, followers of that hierarch of evil, the Pope. Rural, native-born Americans were mostly evangelical Protestants. They watched these very foreign immigrants pouring into the country with apprehension. Would they be able to take political power and install Popish rule in the United States?

As the foreign-born population increased, so did their political clout. In the cities, the saloons were the basic units of political power. The saloon was the place all the workmen in the neighborhood would meet and discuss such matters as sports and elections over a glass of beer or a shot of whiskey. The saloon keeper was often his customers' link with the politicians at city hall.

Saloons were less important in the country. Not everyone abstained from alcohol for religious reasons. Farmers who didn't, though, made their own applejack and often their own whiskey. They tended to meet in churches and Grange halls. Rural saloons were not the inviting social clubs found in the cities. Business was poor in most of them. Except for some saloons in the mining and cattle boomtowns of the West, most rural saloons were little more than sparsely furnished shacks. Unpolished brass spittoons adorned floors covered with beer- and spit-soaked sawdust. Habitual drunks were always in attendance. In many saloons, so were prostitutes and crooked gamblers.

It was no surprise that rural people saw the saloon as the home of evil. And there actually were many abuses, even in the cities. In the cities, crooked politicians operated saloons and operated through saloons. Purchasing votes with free drinks was standard operating procedure in many places. Buying votes with booze was an old and unhallowed tradition, of course, but urban political leaders in the 1870s and 1880s raised the practice to new heights. Most saloon keepers, urban or rural, would sell drinks to their customers as long as they were able to stand up. From Maine to Colorado there were stories of farmers or ranchers who, full of liquor, dared to ride the ten miles to home through a blizzard and were never seen again.

Women were repelled by the saloons, which they saw as taking food from their families' mouths and posing all kinds of dangers to their menfolk. As the movement for women's suffrage gathered momentum, the "suffragettes" joined the evangelical Protestants, the nativists and the political reformers in opposing saloons. Less reputable allies quickly climbed on the bandwagon, including the Ku Klux Klan.

3

In 1851, Maine became the first state to outlaw alcoholic drinks. In the next four years, twelve more states followed suit. As the Civil War approached, though, slavery became the issue that dominated all discussion. People lost interest in banning liquor. Even more important, the U.S. Congress passed the Internal Revenue Act, placing a tax on alcoholic drinks to pay for the war. (The same emergency measure was used to pay off Revolutionary War debts.) There was no official encouragement of prohibition. Dry states became wet again.

After the war, rural people discovered that the problems that had bothered them in the '50s were still around. They had, in fact, gotten worse. Immigrants were still coming in, and now they included Italians, Jews and Slavs. These newcomers, unlike the Irish, couldn't speak English, and they were far less affluent than the Germans. They, too, were Roman Catholic or—even worse—Orthodox Catholic or Jewish. Scandinavians were coming in too, but they were Protestant and able to buy farms. Although no brass bands welcomed them, they were tolerated.

One thing most of the city-dwelling immigrants had in common was that they drank (the Jews, and to a lesser extent, the Italians, were exceptions). They met in city saloons run by friendly and helpful men with political connections. The saloon keepers found jobs for the unemployed and gave food and coal to the needy. The immigrants didn't know or much care what their political friends did in the wider world. The city saloons became the power bases of some of the most corrupt political machines in American history. This was the Gilded Age, the era of Boss Tweed and the crooked friends of President U.S. Grant. It was also the era of the robber barons, like Jay Gould, Jim Fiske, James Hill and Cornelius Vanderbilt—the financial and railroad moguls who were squeezing the honest farmers in the nation's hinterlands.

To the reformers, the nativists, the evangelicals and the feminists, the national malaise was a pattern of interlocked evils. Liquor let the politicians control the immigrants, who, the reformers were sure, had no idea of democracy. The politicians solicited bribes from the robber barons, who got their wealth by cheating the "good people" of the country.

Although the traditional drys, populist to the core, didn't admit it, they were joined by the big employers. Without saloons, the lower classes would work harder. Further, many employers now had to insure their employees against accidents: Sober employees had fewer accidents. And everybody admitted that too much liquor was unhealthy. By helping to close the saloons, the rich would actually be performing a philanthropic service. Another unlikely ally of the dry forces was a portion of the large breweries. These "shipping breweries" sold their product all over a region or all over the country. The states couldn't interfere with interstate commerce. And at the time, the federal government interpreted the interstate commerce clause in the Constitution so strictly it didn't think it could, either. If a state went dry, it would eliminate the big breweries' competition from the many local breweries. The big brewers were confident that somehow they would be able to sell their beer in the dry states.

4

Not all the "dry" states were very dry. Kansas, for example, alternated between being wet and dry. The reform movement had begun early there, a reaction to the notorious saloons in places like Abilene, Dodge City and Newton. But as a popular jingle of the day had it:

> Oh they say that drink's a sin
> In Kansas
> Oh they say that drink's a sin
> In Kansas
> Oh they say that drink's a sin
> So they guzzle all they kin
> And they throw it up agin
> In Kansas.

On March 10, 1881, Kansas officially went dry for the last time. It became the first state to make the prohibition of alcoholic drink part of its constitution, as well as one of its statutes. On March ll, the state's first speakeasy opened in the town of Manhattan. In a short time, though, nobody bothered to "speak easy." When Carrie Nation began her personal anti-saloon campaign in 1900, the first place she attacked was the very open bar of the Carey Hotel in Wichita. Other targets of her hatchet were equally conspicuous saloons in such Kansas cities as Topeka, Kiowa and Medicine Lodge.

As the movement grew, temperance advocates became more intemperate. They were no longer content with banning saloons: They wanted to eliminate all alcohol. Ironically, the heart of the movement was composed of fundamentalist Christians, who professed to believe every word in the Bible literally. Although drunkenness is denounced, wine is mentioned favorably in both the New and Old Testaments. It was the normal drink of everyone, and Jesus made water into wine during the wedding feast at Cana. Faced with this, the fundamentalists simply denied that Biblical wine was really wine. Dry propaganda built up into a drumroll. Drink led to insanity, venereal disease and murder. Drinking parents were sure to have deformed children. Drink was the worst of all evils. William Jennings Bryan, a professional presidential candidate and leading dry spokesman, hailed the murderous Pancho Villa as a "Sir Galahad" because he didn't drink.

5

One of the most vehement of the dry propagandists was Richmond Pearson Hobson, a naval hero of the Spanish-American War and a congressman from Alabama.

Hobson achieved hero status by volunteering to take an old hulk of a collier into Santiago harbor and scuttle it where the wreck could prevent the Spanish fleet from coming out. Hobson, a recent graduate of the U.S. Naval Academy, was convinced the Spanish gunners couldn't hit anything smaller than the ocean. He was wrong. His ship sank where it could do no harm. But even if Hobson's judgment was faulty, everyone admired his courage. Spanish Admiral Pascual Cervera personally fished the American officer out of the water.

Repatriated after the war and quickly promoted to captain, Hobson discovered that being a hero had made him a universal expert. He joined the anti-alcohol crusade and became its most vehement spokesman.

"Alcohol is killing our people at the rate of two thousand a day, every day of the year," Hobson told overflow audiences. He made up statistics as he spoke. "One out of five children of alcohol consumers is hopelessly insane"; or "Ninety-five percent of all acts and crimes of violence are committed by drunkards"; or "Nearly one half of all deaths that occur are due to alcohol." One classic Hobson assertion was "One hundred and twenty-five million white men today are wounded by alcohol." The captain apparently didn't much care what happened to black men or women of any color.

After Prohibition demonstrated that banning alcohol produced even greater evils than allowing it, Hobson became equally strong in his denunciation of opiates and cocaine, inventing impossible numbers of addicts to bolster his case. Before World War I, however, the great national concern was liquor. And, in truth, alcohol was causing far more social disruption than all other drugs.

The United States entered the twentieth century with a baffling mix of state drug laws and very little sentiment in favor of a national law.

A national law was coming, though. It would arrive well before the Eighteenth Amendment and the Volstead Act.

4

THE HEATHEN CHINEE

Americans liked Chinese. At least, they liked Chinese at a distance. Or, as one wag put it, they liked china—dishes, vases and other products of that ancient civilization—but not China or Chinese. Around the turn of the century, China's troubles, combined with the American triumph in the Spanish-American War, gave the United States its first national drug law. It happened like this:

Opium smoking was not an age-old Chinese custom. Although Chinese had known of opium since the eighth century, it was primarily used as a medicine. The Portuguese captured the opium trade between India and China from Indian and Arab mariners. Then they introduced another drug, tobacco, from their Brazilian colony. The Chinese, though, planted their own tobacco and smoked it in their pipes mixed with opium. For the first time, the drug was smoked instead of eaten or drunk. The Chinese imperial government recognized that opium addiction was both unhealthy and a subtle means of creating foreign domination. It banned opium. In the mid-nineteenth century, British merchants used the guns of Her Majesty's navy to force the Chinese to accept Indian opium. After the Opium Wars (1839–42 and 1856–58) addiction spread rapidly. In 1906, according to the imperial government, 27 percent of all Chinese men smoked opium. There was, however, no complaint that addiction was causing a high crime rate. The complaint was quite different.

One mandarin, recalling an expedition sent against rebellious mountain tribesmen in 1832, said that "great numbers of the soldiers were opium smokers; so that, although their numerical force was large there was hardly any force found among them."

Chinese nationalists late in the century were calling for the abolition of opium smoking, and the Dowager Empress of China tried to comply. The British refused to stop exporting opium, saying the drug was no more dangerous than alcohol. That may have been true, but it was no answer to the Chinese demand.

Meanwhile, Britain and all the other major European powers, plus Japan, had been extracting concessions from China, including foreign rule in areas of Shanghai. None of this pleased the United States. The U.S. had just become the world's foremost manufacturing power. China, the largest country in the world, was trying to modernize, and American business saw China as the greatest market on earth. The Europeans and Japanese looked as if they were gaining the inside track to this huge market.

2

Then the United States became involved in war with Spain. Nobody except the Spaniards expected Spain to win. (Spain's defeat created a Spanish literary movement, the Generation of 1898, much like the disillusioned Lost Generation that followed World War I.) Nobody, however, expected the Spanish defeat to be so swift and crushing. Dewey wiped out the Spanish Far East fleet in Manila Bay without losing a single American sailor. At Santiago, the Americans annihilated the rest of Spain's navy with the loss of only one man. The war was over in less than four months, and the only reason it took that long was American delays in organizing troops and moving them to Cuba.

It dawned on the rest of the world what should have been obvious after the Civil War. The United States was a great power. It could not be ignored. Like other great powers, the United States acquired colonies. The most important by far was the Philippine Islands, captured from Spain.

In the Philippines, the United States had its first experience with the kind of problems other colonial powers had been dealing with. One of them was opium. The islands had a large Chinese population, and the Chinese, as they had in California, brought opium with them. At first, the War Department, which was administering the islands, proposed to take over the old Spanish monopoly of opium, which had limited sales to Chinese. An outcry in Congress forced the army's Philippine Commission to prohibit opium (although it continued to be available up to the beginning of World War II). The U.S. government, then, was ready to lend a sympathetic ear to the Chinese government's complaints about opium. The Americans also wanted the Chinese to consider them friends so they could get into what they foresaw as a booming market. The exact opposite was happening. Disturbed by the Oriental Exclusion Act, Chinese nationalists began an embargo of U.S. products. The U.S. had to do something. The opium crisis offered an opportunity.

3

The British, under pressure from their own clergy, had modified their position on opium and were negotiating with the Chinese. The shift in the British position also had an economic motive: China was now growing its own opium and had become a major producer, making the Indian trade less profitable. At this point, the United States stepped into the dispute on the Chinese side.

President Theodore Roosevelt called for an international conference to discuss the Chinese situation and, he hoped, draft a treaty to halt the flow of opium into China. The call got a favorable response, although the British and Dutch insisted that the meeting be a commission, rather than a convention. That is, it could make recommendations but no binding agreements.

To represent the United States, Roosevelt appointed Dr. Hamilton Wright, a flamboyant Washington physician who was familiar with Malaya and the Philippines. Wright professed to be embarrassed because the United States, now the world leader in the anti-narcotics crusade, had no national drug law. (The other colonial powers had drug laws, but those were mostly laws setting up state monopolies in opium distribution.) Wright had adopted Maine as his home, and he was in full accord with the anti-liquor and anti-drug sentiments of the country's first prohibition state. Secretary of State Elihu Root joined Wright in pushing "to have legislation on this subject in time to save our face at the conference in Shanghai," as he put it in a letter to Rep. James S. Sherman. The act, banning the importation of opium suitable for smoking, passed in 1909, just in time for the meeting in Shanghai. The Shanghai Commission recommended ending all opium production and distribution except for medical purposes, but Wright was not satisfied. He appealed for an international conference that could produce a binding agreement. Meanwhile, he induced Rep. David Foster of Vermont to introduce legislation requiring records of the most minute quantities of opiates, cocaine, chloral hydrate and cannabis to be kept for tax purposes. Patent medicines were not exempted. Thanks to strong lobbying by the drug and medical industries, the Foster Bill was defeated.

4

Despite foot-dragging by the Netherlands, the Hague Conference got under way in 1912. The Netherlands was engaged in the opium traffic in the Dutch East Indies; France had an opium monopoly in Indochina; Portugal had an opium business in Macao; Japan had introduced morphine and hypodermic needles into China; Russia had a small poppy-farming industry, and Persia had an enormous one. Turkey, another poppy producer, was invited but did not come. Neither did Switzerland, Bolivia or Peru, all, in one way or another, deep in the legal drug trade. Siam, a major opium consumer, did come. Italy came only on condition that the conference study Indian hemp as well as other drugs.

Germany demanded to know how the conferees could be assured that, after having signed the convention, the United States would pass legislation implementing the treaty. The convention finally agreed on an anti-narcotics treaty, but specified that all governments in the world, not just those at the convention, must sign it before it could become effective. The convention met again in 1913, noted that there were still holdouts and agreed to hold a third meeting in 1914 if there were not unanimous consent among all nations before that. In 1914, it could consider putting the treaty in effect only among the signatories.

Wright, back home, had been working for a comprehensive national drug act like the defeated Foster Bill. It was, he argued, a moral obligation of the United States as the leader of the world crusade against narcotics. He hoped that an international treaty would make the law constitutional. The treaty looked as if it might never come to pass, so he tried to get a law under the taxing power of the federal government. He was successful. The Harrison Act, named after its sponsor, Rep. Francis Burton Harrison of New York, incorporated many compromises, softening the Foster Bill and dropping the regulation of cannabis, but it was the first national law regulating the internal commerce in drugs. President Woodrow Wilson signed it December 14, 1914.

World War I had broken out that August. It would soon give the United States a mighty shove into a new kind of drug control—perhaps, after the Great Depression, the most wrenching peacetime experience the nation ever had.

5

Thanks to the rhetoric of Hobson and his fellow propagandists and especially thanks to the organizational genius of Wayne Wheeler, president and general counsel of the Anti-Saloon League, the dry forces steadily increased their strength. Before 1907, only three states were dry—Maine, North Dakota and the notoriously ambivalent Kansas. But in the next seven years, eleven more states joined the dry camp. The Anti-Saloon League can take most of the credit for this rise in dry sentiment.

Wheeler maintained an extensive speakers bureau, most of them—unlike Hobson—unpaid volunteers.

"We started off with about 20,000 speakers . . . all over the United States," Wheeler later recalled. "They spoke at every opportunity, at every sort of gathering. . . . During the final stages of the battle, there were approximately 50,000 trained speakers, volunteers and regulars, directing their fire on the wets from every village, town, city, county and state."

The league's printing plant ran three shifts a day churning out dry publications. League workers canvassed every election district "where there was a chance to elect a dry and waged as strong a fight as candidates have ever seen," Wheeler said.

Meanwhile, "to let Congress hear from the people back home," as the league president put it, letters, telegrams and petitions "rolled in by the tens of thousands."

The country had never seen such an intense lobbying campaign. In the elections of 1914, the drys "triumphed even beyond our hopes," Wheeler said. A solid majority of both houses of Congress was dry. Because of the limits on the powers of the federal government as understood then, the drys planned to amend the federal constitution to require prohibition of alcohol. It requires a two-thirds majority in each house to submit a proposed amendment to the states. The dry forces didn't have that, but Hobson introduced such an amendment in 1914 as a trial run. The House vote was 197 to 190 in favor. That wasn't enough, but it was a portent of things to come.

2

The propaganda continued, and the drys increased their strength in the elections of 1916. The wets helped them. Wet propaganda was so transparently self-serving the public ignored it. Wet tactics backfired. Two brewers' associations were indicted for conspiring to violate state and federal law through vote-buying, bribery and hidden control of newspapers. The brewers had decided to concentrate on the drinking portion of the population, especially the Germans. When war broke out, the German-American organizations the brewers financed were openly supporting the *Vaterland*. In a country where the press and most of the population were calling the Germans "Huns" and changing sauerkraut to "liberty cabbage," that did not help the wet cause.

Drys took advantage of the situation. Liquor and beer, they charged, were using grain that could have fed our starving friends in Europe. When the United States entered the war, dry propaganda became more strident. Beer became identified with Germany. That the English and Belgians consumed at least as much beer per capita as the Germans was ignored. Beer drinking was responsible for German cruelty, the drys charged. The German-surnamed brewers in the United States were said to be conspiring with the Central Powers to use alcohol to weaken the will and destroy the efficiency of Americans and their armed forces.

The wets in Congress considered the submission of an amendment to the states inevitable. To become part of the Constitution, though, it would have to be ratified by thirty-six state legislatures. If the wets could hold majorities in one house of thirteen legislatures, they could kill the proposed amendment. They got the drys to agree to a seven-year deadline for ratification.

On December 18, 1917, the House voted to submit the amendment, already approved by the Senate, to the states. In Congress, dry supporters told their colleagues that the matter was too important for Congress to decide: It should be left up to the people in the states. In the state legislatures, disproportionately controlled by rural voters, they declared that any measure passed by more than two-thirds of the national Congress should not be rejected by a state legislature.

After Congress voted to submit the amendment to the states, dry senators and representatives pushed through a wartime prohibition act, relying on the federal government's wartime powers. It didn't bother them that when it went into effect, the armistice had already been signed.

Mississippi ratified the amendment almost immediately, on January 8, 1918. Scarcely more than a year later, on January 16, 1919, Nebraska approved the amendment, and it became law. Eventually every state but Connecticut and Rhode Island ratified the Eighteenth Amendment.

3

Congress immediately passed enabling legislation. Called the Volstead Act, after Rep. Andrew J. Volstead of Minnesota, who introduced it, the act was really written by Wayne Wheeler.

Surprisingly, President Woodrow Wilson, who previously seemed to favor the drys, vetoed the bill on the grounds that the war was over and there was no need for such legislation. It took the House less than two hours to override Wilson's veto. The Senate overrode it the next day.

The House Judiciary Committee did modify some of Wheeler's wilder clauses concerning search and seizure, soliciting orders for liquor and requiring local officers to report all arrests for drunkenness. Further amendments allowed possession of liquor in private homes and the sale of sacramental wine. Another amendment provided heavy penalties for the wrongful issue of search warrants. The Senate added more amendments to allow farmers and others to make light wine and hard cider at home, and to allow people to consume and store as much liquor as they wanted in "residences, apartments, hotels and similar places of abode."

The use of intoxicating drinks was, to use a modern term, "decriminalized." The manufacture, importation, sale and distribution of such beverages, however, was strictly forbidden, except that doctors were allowed to prescribe "medicinal" liquor. All intoxicating drink still in warehouses when the act took effect would be stored "in bond" for such legal uses as prescriptions.

The act defined "intoxicating" as any beverage containing one half of one percent alcohol by volume. That made possible the production of "near beer," something like the non-alcoholic beer of the 1990s. Manufacture of alcohol for industrial purposes was allowed with a permit.

4

Both the government and the public assumed that enforcement of national Prohibition would be easy. By 1920, 95 percent of the country's area and 65 percent of its population were dry by state or local law. The assumption that enforcement would be easy, though, overlooked the actual situation and ignored both chemistry and human nature.

Few dry states were bone-dry. Some allowed liquor to be imported for personal use. Others did so with restrictions on time and amount. Two states allowed homemade wine. One exempted both imported liquor and homemade wine from its prohibition law.

Further, alcohol is one of the easiest substances on earth to produce. Leave sweet cider or grape juice alone, and it automatically becomes hard cider or wine. Add some sugar and it becomes more potent cider or wine. The rural legislators who made national Prohibition possible understood that. They were taking care of their constituents, many of whom liked to start the day with a glass of hard cider. What may have been a surprise to many of them was the enormous increase in the tonnage of table grapes sold to consumers in the cities after Prohibition began. Portable stills, until then purchased only by amateur chemists, appeared in every hardware store for as little as five dollars apiece.

Many of the drinkers in the country were genuine alcohol addicts: They were not going to give up without a fight. Others found drinking such a pleasant habit they would ignore the law if they could do so easily.

There were plenty of people ready to help them.

The contiguous forty-eight states have approximately 12,000 miles of coast, 3,000 miles of river and lake front and 3,700 miles of land border. Neighboring countries immediately increased their importation of liquor from Europe. Between 1918 and 1922, Canadian importation of liquor from Britain increased sixfold. Mexican imports increased eightfold and West Indian imports nearly fivefold. Bahamian imports went from less than 1,000 gallons of liquor to 386,000 gallons. Bermuda in 1922 imported 40,000 gallons of spirits, up 39,000 gallons from its 1918 level.

Restaurateurs on the eastern seaboard and Gulf Coast suddenly developed an interest in boating. Many of them had fleets of fast speedboats that could dash out to freighters lying twelve miles offshore in "rum row," load up with liquor and speed back, evading the overworked Coast Guard. Fishermen found midnight excursions to rum row more remunerating than hauling in fish lines all day. There were a few attempts at hijacking, but bootlegging along rum row was mostly fun and games compared with what was going on in the rest of the country.

5

The economists Daniel Benjamin and Roger Miller point out that when a popular product is forbidden, criminals will take over its supply. The criminals, by definition, don't worry about breaking the law—they've been doing that for years. Further, because they have been doing it, they've learned how to evade the consequences and often have key persons in the justice system taking their bribes.

Dion O'Bannion of Chicago was a burglar and safecracker. Not only was he skilled at this trade, he had used his ill-gotten wealth to buy judges and police officers. When Prohibition came, he and his gang staked out the rich north side of Chicago as their territory and became bootleggers. There were, of course, potential competitors who tried to encroach on liquor sales in the Northside, but O'Bannion used merchandising techniques never taught at the Harvard Business School. "Dion O'Bannion is Chicago's arch criminal who has killed or seen to the killing of at least 25 men," said Chicago Police Chief Morgan Collins.

Another thief turned bootlegger was a young man named Arthur Flegenheimer but better known as Dutch Schultz. Schultz's base was the Bronx, but his clout came from control of the breweries in New

Jersey. He got the beer before the brewers could turn it into near beer and trucked it into Manhattan. Schultz used the same method of beating competitors as O'Bannion. One bootlegger who refused to yield his territory to Schultz was beaten almost to death by Schultz and his hoodlums. Then the gangsters tied an infected bandage over his eyes. When the ex-competitor recovered from his wounds, he was blind.

Not all bootleggers began their professional lives as thieves. Most of them operated territorial rackets, controlling loan-sharking, extortion, gambling and prostitution in depressed ethnic neighborhoods. That was the origin of Detroit's Purple Gang. Detroit proved to be a fortunate location. Because it's so easy to reach the Motor City from Canada, Detroit became the nation's liquor-smuggling capital. And liquor smuggling, like everything else illegal in Detroit, was controlled by the Purple Gang.

Bootlegging had, in fact, caused the gang to spread all over the city from the Jewish ghetto that had been its turf. Liquor was expensive—or it became so after monopolists like O'Bannion, Schultz and the Purples drove away their competitors. During Prohibition, a bottle of gin that cost a dollar in Windsor, Ontario, sold for six dollars in Detroit. Impoverished neighborhoods are not prime markets for expensive products. The Purple Gang and all the other bootlegging mobs targeted the posh downtown restaurants and gold-coast homes of their areas.

Competition for the downtown market could be severe. O'Bannion's greatest rival in Chicago was John Torrio. Torrio, a New Yorker, was brought to Chicago by his uncle "Big Jim" Colosimo to provide muscle for Colosimo's urban rackets, prostitution and loan-sharking. Big Jim turned a deaf ear to his nephew's plea that they branch out into bootlegging, so John imported another New Yorker, "Scarface" Al Capone. Capone killed Colosimo and became Torrio's enforcer. O'Bannion double-crossed Torrio on the sale of a brewery, and Torrio ordered the Northsider's murder. O'Bannion's successor, Hymie Weiss, attacked Torrio and almost killed him. Torrio was so shaken he gave the rackets to Capone and left the country. A major gang war erupted in Chicago—the first of what was to become an American phenomenon for decades. Weiss's Northsiders fought Capone's Southsiders, who were—at this time—allied with the Sicilian mob of the six Genna brothers. Weiss's most spectacular feat was machine-gunning Capone's headquarters in Cicero from a funeral cortege. Capone's most celebrated feat (after he had Weiss murdered) was having his gunmen machine-gun seven Northsiders in what became known as the St. Valentine's Day Massacre. Altogether, more than a thousand persons were killed in the Chicago gang wars in the 1920s. Capone emerged as the top thug in Chicago, controlling not only bootlegging but all the other urban rackets.

Ironically, the enforcement of Prohibition helped the big mobs. Smaller bootleggers didn't have the resources to evade the penalties for lawbreaking, so the Capones, Schultzes and Purples weren't bothered by nickel-and-dime competitors. And when the big crooks had established their monopolies, they could charge almost any price for their products.

The New York underworld in the early 1920s tended to look down on Chicago gangsters as uncivilized wild men. But during the last years of the '20s and through the '30s, the New Yorkers piled up as many corpses as their colleagues in Chicago in wars that were even more complicated. The end of Prohibition did not end the killing. All of the bootleggers had already branched out into urban rackets that did not require illegal booze. Dutch Schultz wiped out most of his rivals but let his ambition run away with his good sense. A Manhattan syndicate organized by his onetime friend Charles "Charley Lucky" Luciano put out a contract for his murder. Luciano, the greatest criminal organizer of the twentieth century, had taken over the Italian-American segment of the underworld through a couple of singularly successful pieces of treachery. With Schultz out of the way, he organized a nationwide criminal federation including all ethnic groups. After Schultz's murder, he became the most conspicuous crook in New York and the target of an ambitious prosecutor named Thomas E. Dewey. Dewey put Luciano in jail, but Lucky was to emerge a few years later to write one more chapter in America's criminal history.

6

What did Prohibition accomplish other than the creation of what we came to call Gangland?

In the beginning, it cut the consumption of alcohol by 20 to 30 percent, but by the end of the fourteen-year period, Americans were drinking as much as they ever had.

More important in a discussion of the prohibition of other drugs, it changed America's drinking habits. Before Prohibition, Americans drank far more beer than anything else. Big operators like O'Bannion, Schultz and Capone could run breweries. But for most bootleggers, beer was too bulky. When Prohibition began, beer consumption dropped sharply and made only modest recovery toward the end of the period. Wine consumption also dropped, but it then rose steadily so that by the repeal of Prohibition it was higher than it had been before 1920. Hard liquor demonstrated the same pattern to an even greater degree. The East Coast rumrunners cared only for hard liquor—especially whiskey—which packed a lot of alcohol in a small package. Whiskey shipments from Canada were the staple of the Purple Gang. *During the last five years of Prohibition, per capita consumption of hard liquor was higher than it had been during the sixty years before or since.* Because Americans were taking their alcohol in more concentrated form, there was, if anything, more drunkenness after Prohibition began than before—even during the early years when total alcohol consumption was down.

There was also, during Prohibition, an increase in the use of other illegal drugs, such as heroin, and still-legal drugs like marijuana.

Prohibition had a profound effect on the nation's homicide and attempted murder rates. According to the Census Bureau's *Historical Statistics of the United States*, the murder rate during Prohibition was 25 percent higher than in the years preceding 1920. With the repeal of Prohibition, the murder rate declined for eleven consecutive years.

Prohibition contributed to another cause of death—poisoning by alcohol substitutes and impure homemade drinks, or simply too much alcohol in too little time. In 1927 alone, 12,000 persons died of acute alcohol poisoning—alcohol overdose. The death rate from this cause was more than thirty times higher than it is today. Thousands more died or were blinded by substitutes or amateur-made bathtub gin and "white lightning." Between 1985 and 1988, the former Soviet Union tried a kind of semi-prohibition, making liquor extremely hard to get. The results resembled the "noble experiment." In the last full year of Gorbachev's prohibition, 40,000 Russians were poisoned, and 11,000 died.

The Soviet experiment had another effect that resembles a feature of the U.S. Drug War: The police were so busy keeping citizens from alcohol that the criminals ran wild. The larceny, assault and homicide rates all soared until vodka was again available.

Prohibition has been linked to a rise in the crime rate in India, too. "Bombay is known for decades for street dadas, street toughs," said Vasant Keshaorao Saraf, retired director general of police. "Then prohibition came in '49 and '50. And with that came the first rudimentary organized crime. Illicit distillation became an industry. A cartel-like thing came together."

There was an air of hope when Prohibition began but a feeling of disillusionment and disappointment when it ended. Richmond Pearson Hobson, however, did not hang his head. He had found a new target.

6

Well before Repeal, it had become obvious that Prohibition was a failure. For many people, that was emotionally crushing—a letdown so great it's hard to imagine today.

World War I had stirred up depths of hatred unknown in this country since the Civil War. Hatred so strong is not easily dissipated. With the end of the war, feeling against "the Hun" and the Kaiser had been redirected against an abstraction, Demon Rum, and the demon's supporters.

The older hatreds that led to Prohibition had not been forgotten, though. The wartime habit of hatred had merely reinforced them. Some of the nativists, the bigots and the upholders of rural values saw the failure of Prohibition as a betrayal, primarily by the cities. The cities were still growing, and now they were swollen not only by what the nativists saw as "the scum of Europe," but by blacks, who had begun leaving the farms to take factory jobs. Prohibition failed, the defenders of the Old Order believed, not because it was unworkable but because the forces of corruption were refusing to enforce the law.

That being the case, they thought, there was nothing to do but enforce the law—both as it was and as it should have been— themselves. The Ku Klux Klan was resurrected. The Klan in Kansas listed its targets in 1926:

> Every criminal, every gambler, every thug, every libertine, every girl-ruiner, every home-wrecker, every wife-beater, every dope-peddler, every moonshiner, every crooked politician, every pagan papist priest . . . every hyphenated-American, every lawless alien . . .

The Klan's method of law enforcement was a compound of native brutality and a viciousness born of frustration. "Uppity" blacks were tarred and feathered, flogged and sometimes killed. In Louisiana, five men were wired together and drowned. R.A. Patton reported a series of atrocities in Alabama: a black man who refused to sell his land to a white was whipped until he agreed to sell it for a fraction of its value; a "sassy" black woman was beaten and left in the woods, where she caught a fatal case of pneumonia; a white woman was beaten unconscious in her home because she had divorced her husband; a foreign-born man was flogged nearly to death because he married an "American" woman. Jews and Catholics were boycotted and shunned. In Birmingham, Alabama, a Klansman who killed a Catholic priest was acquitted. A Catholic church was burned down in Naperville, Illinois.

For a few years, white-sheeted Klansmen increased like fungi in a dank cellar. The Klan actually elected governors in Oregon and Oklahoma. It controlled the states of Indiana, Ohio, Texas, Arkansas, California and Colorado. Then David Stephenson, Grand Dragon of Indiana, was convicted of rape and murder. (That great foe of alcohol and drinkers had gotten drunk and raped a young woman, then apparently was trying to eat her alive when she escaped. She died from infection of the wounds his teeth had made.) The head of the Colorado Klan was imprisoned for income-tax evasion. Voters deserted the Klan in droves. In the northern states, the Ku Klux Klan, the last backlash of the rural revolt, was finished.

2

Richmond Pearson Hobson, however, was far from finished. Polemics against Demon Rum no longer roused the crowds, but Hobson found a new villain—the "dope fiend" and those who supplied him. He founded successively the International Narcotic Education Association, the World Conference on Narcotic Education and the World Narcotic Defense Association. As the best-known speaker of the Anti-Saloon League, Hobson was able to call on all the resources of the vast Prohibition establishment. Most drys, of course, were opposed to narcotics. But few of them—or of any other group, for that matter—had Hobson's imagination and talents as a rabble-rouser.

Hobson's particular target was heroin. Following is an excerpt from "The Living Dead," a radio broadcast he made in 1927:

To get this heroin supply, the addict will not only advocate public policies against the public welfare, but will lie, steal, rob, and if necessary, commit murder. Heroin addiction can be likened to a contagion. Suppose it were announced that there were more than a million lepers among our people. [That there were more than a million heroin addicts was a habitual Hobson claim. A report by Dr. Lawrence Kolb, Sr., and A.G. DuMez, both of the U.S. Public Health Service, indicated there were about 110,000.] Think what a shock the announcement would produce! Yet drug addiction is far more incurable than leprosy, far more tragic to its victims, and spreading like a moral and physical scourge.

There are symptoms breaking out all over our country and now breaking out in many parts of Europe which show that individual nations and the whole world is menaced by this appalling foe . . . marching . . . to the capture and destruction of the whole world.

Most of the daylight robberies, daring holdups, cruel murders and similar crimes of violence are now known to be committed chiefly by drug addicts, who constitute the primary cause of our alarming crime wave.

Drug addiction is more communicable and less curable than leprosy. Drug addicts are the principal carriers of vice diseases, and with their lowered resistance are incubators and carriers of the streptococcus, pneumococcus, the germ of flu, of tuberculosis, and other diseases.

Upon the issue hangs the perpetuation of civilization, the destiny of the world and the future of the human race.

Almost every statement in this short tirade is contrary to fact. Yet, although only a generation before the country had experienced a far higher drug addiction rate without any extraordinary violence, few questioned Hobson's thesis. And today the captain's words would strike many as quite reasonable. Hobson could have made Paul Joseph Goebbels green with envy.

Hobson recycled all his statements about the evils of alcohol and ascribed them to heroin. Like alcohol, heroin attacked "the top of the brain [and] since the upper brain is the physical basis of thought, feeling, judgment, self-control, and is the physical organ of the will, of the consciousness of God, of the sense of right and wrong, of ideas of justice, duty, love, mercy, self-sacrifice and all that makes character," therefore "the evolution of human life, the destiny of man and the will of God" were at stake.

Heroin caused crime not only because its addicts would steal and kill to get it, but because taking it aroused lusts to kill and rape and destroyed all inhibition. Black addicts, he asserted "degenerate to the level of the cannibal." Drugs not only turned people into monsters, Hobson said, "the addict has an insane desire to make addicts of others."

Hobson produced authorities like prison wardens who testified that they knew heroin caused crime because heroin addicts made up a large proportion of the prison population. A large proportion of the prison population *had* used heroin. But they had been arrested not for murder, rape, robbery or other crimes of violence, but for possessing heroin.

The former naval hero was so persuasive that, in addition to the organized drys, he got such groups as the National Federation of Women's Clubs, the Knights of Columbus, the Elks, the Moose and several Masonic orders to assist him in preaching the crusade against Demon Heroin. Hobson-authored material on drugs was used by American school systems. Even the American Medical Association joined the crusade. The AMA condemned heroin—that "German drug"—and said that it, the most powerful painkiller commonly available, could be replaced for medical purposes by morphine and codeine. Dr. Charles Richardson of the AMA testified that "Heroin contains double the action of morphine and cocaine," which is arrant nonsense—something like saying it is simultaneously wet and dry. Dr. Alexander Lambert, who helped develop a "cure" for addiction that sometimes proved to be fatal, supported Hobson's theory that heroin inspires crime; it "destroys the sense of responsibility to the herd."

In 1924, Congress passed a law banning heroin for *any* use in the United States.

3

Heroin became America's first "devil drug." That evil could be caused by a drug and not human will was an attractive theory to many people.

For example, it gave the police a marvelous excuse for being unable to cope with crime. In 1972, New York Police Commissioner Patrick V. Murphy testified:

> Local police agencies cannot . . . effectively stem the flow of narcotics into our cities, much less into the needle-ridden veins of hundreds of thousands of young people. Only the federal government is capable of making effective strides, through massive infusion of funds, to damming or diverting the ever-rising, devastating flood-tide from the poppy fields of the Middle East, South America and Indo-China into the bodies of pathetic victims in the United States.

In little more than a decade, heroin was joined by a second, much more unlikely, devil drug—marijuana.

Marijuana, or cannabis, had not been included in the Harrison Act, probably because of opposition from the pharmaceutical industry. It was widely used for corn plasters and veterinary medicine, but not in any internally taken medicines for humans. And in those days, nobody claimed that it caused any kind of a problem in the United States.

Then in 1920, Dr. Oscar Dowling, president of the Louisiana Board of Health, and John M. Parker, governor of Louisiana, asked that marijuana be restricted. Marijuana, Dr. Dowling said, was "a powerful narcotic, causing exhilaration, intoxication, delirious hallucinations." Governor Parker said the drug "seems to make them [its users] go crazy and wild." Gradually complaints about marijuana began to come from Louisiana, Texas and the southwestern states as far as California. The trickle of complaints increased to a flood during the Great Depression. Mexican farm laborers in the Southwest were seen as taking jobs from Americans. In the Southwest, feeling ran high against Mexicans and all things Mexican—such as marijuana.

"Marijuana, perhaps now the most insidious of our narcotics," wrote a prominent citizen of Sacramento to the *New York Times* in 1935, "is a direct by-product of unrestricted Mexican immigration. Easily grown, it has been asserted that it has recently been planted between the rows in a California penitentiary garden. Mexican peddlers have been caught distributing sample marijuana cigarettes to school children."

Horrible crimes were blamed on marijuana intoxication, and there was no attempt to conceal the bigotry in most of the complaints received by the newly formed Federal Bureau of Narcotics. "I wish I could show you what a small marijuana cigarette can do to one of our degenerate Spanish-speaking residents," wrote the editor of the Alamosa, Colorado, *Daily Courier* in 1936. "That's why our problem is so great: the greatest percentage of our population is composed of Spanish-speaking persons, most of whom are low mentally, because of social and racial conditions.

"While marijuana has figured in the greatest number of crimes in the past few years, officials fear it, not for what it has done, but for what it is capable of doing. They want to check it before an outbreak does occur."

Harry Anslinger, the first chief of the Bureau of Narcotics, wanted his agents to concentrate on "hard" drugs, like heroin, but he finally bowed to pressure from the Southwest. He bowed deeply. Anslinger never went into anything halfway. Not verbally, anyway. When he first took over his job, Anslinger began issuing statements on the almost unimaginable evils of narcotics—how sinister Orientals, for instance, used opium to entice "women of good families" into a life of prostitution. In the mid–30s, he asserted that marijuana use was responsible for "an epidemic of crimes committed by young people." He wrote a magazine article entitled "Marijuana: Assassin of Youth" and inspired the film (now viewed as high camp) *Reefer Madness*.

In 1937, Congress passed the Marijuana Act. Technically it was a tax act, but its provisions were such that it effectively banned marijuana for any use whatever except, in sterilized form, for canary food. For years afterward, one staple of popular entertainment was the marijuana-crazed villain, bent on evil, merciless and able to absorb countless bullets fired by defenders of law and order.

4

The same year the Marijuana Tax Act was passed, Capt. Richmond Pearson Hobson died. Almost single-handedly, he had created the "dope fiend," a propaganda masterwork that ranks with *The Protocols of the Learned Elders of Zion*. The concept has endured to this day.

In spite of all the horror stories and the real public fear of "dope-crazed fiends," until 1968 the Federal Bureau of Narcotics never had more than 330 agents, and most of them served in an administrative capacity. The fact is that there really wasn't that much drug-related crime.

All of that was about to change. It was to change because of what federal officials, acting from the best of intentions, did overseas.

PART TWO
THE COLD WAR

7

CHARLEY LUCKY AND THE FRENCH CONNECTION

If ever a criminal lived up to his underworld moniker, it was Salvatore Lucania. Lucania, who had changed his name to Charles Luciano, was a member of the Legs Diamond gang. He was, that is, until he had a falling out with the gang boss. Several of Diamond's hoodlums captured Luciano, hung him from a tree, stabbed him with ice picks, slashed him with razors and left him to die. But he didn't die. And he acquired his moniker, Charley Lucky (which the newspapers garbled to "Lucky Luciano").

A few years later, Luciano had a disagreement with another of his bosses, Giuseppe Masseria, who loved to call himself "boss of all bosses." Masseria was feuding with another boss, Salvatore Maranzano, in an inter-Italian squabble known as the Castellammarese War. Luciano called on Maranzano with a plan, then he visited two non-Italian bosses, Meyer Lansky and Dutch Schultz. Finally, he arranged a meeting with Masseria in a restaurant. When Charley Lucky excused himself to go to the bathroom, Bugsy Siegel, Lansky's partner, and three hoods from Maranzano's gang appeared and riddled "Joe the Boss."

Now supreme in the fractious Italian-American underworld, Maranzano created a new organization like the various secret societies Italian mobsters had brought over from the Old World. This, though, would not be rooted in Italian towns or regions. It would be for all Italians and their descendants, whether they came from Palermo or Milano. It had no name. In meetings, conducted in Italian, Maranzano simply referred to the organization as *cosa nostra* ("our thing").

Having seen Luciano in action, Maranzano, understandably, didn't trust him. He prudently decided to get rid of Charley Lucky. But he imprudently mentioned that to another mobster, and the word got back to Luciano. The lucky one once again called on his old friends, Schultz and Lansky, and once again set up a meeting with his boss. Maranzano, though, also dealt with gangsters not associated with "cosa nostra." He told Vinny (the Mad Mick) Coll that Luciano would be in his office the afternoon of September 10 and he would greatly appreciate it if the Mad Mick would arrange for Charley Lucky to have a stroke of bad luck. But half an hour before Luciano was to appear, four men who identified themselves as treasury agents walked into Maranzano's office. The "agents" were really Bo Weinberg, Dutch Schultz's chief lieutenant, and three gunmen who worked for one of Meyer Lansky's clients, Lepke Buchalter (who was later to found the mob called Murder, Inc.). Our Thing became Lucky's Thing.

The next day, bands of young Italian and non-Italian hoods assassinated old Italian ganglords ("mustache Petes," Luciano called them) all over the country. The "New Sicilian Vespers," as Luciano's admirers referred to it, had made the young Sicilian the country's first nationwide gang boss. The next step was to set up a national criminal federation that included gangsters of all ethnic groups. With his new prestige, that wasn't too difficult for Luciano. About the only holdout was his boyhood buddy, Dutch Schultz.

Schultz felt there was no need to be part of an organization. He could handle any problem himself. His major problem at this time was a special prosecutor, Thomas E. Dewey, who had convicted Schultz's Tammany connection and was now aiming at the Dutchman himself. Schultz decided to kill Dewey. Luciano persuaded his associates that Dewey's murder would create intolerable heat for all of them, so they made a contract with Murder, Inc., and Luciano became undisputed king of the hill.

That's what made Charley Lucky Dewey's new target. The ambitious prosecutor got Luciano convicted of ninety-one counts of extortion and compulsory prostitution. It looked as if Charley Lucky's luck had run out.

2

At the end of World War II, Dewey, now Governor of New York, pardoned Luciano, and the feds deported him to Italy. The reason for the pardon was said to be a reward for the services Luciano had performed for the U.S. government during the war. Just what those services were—if there were any — has never been revealed. One story has it that he guaranteed peace and no sabotage on the New York waterfront. But there was peace and no sabotage on the waterfronts of Philadelphia, New Orleans, Houston, Los Angeles, San Francisco and every other major port, where the imprisoned Luciano carried very little weight. Another story is that he got the Sicilian Mafia to cooperate with the Allies during the invasion of Sicily. Allied secret agents did contact Sicilian mafiosi before the invasion, but the help they got hardly decided the battle. It wasn't that the gangsters didn't want to help—Mussolini was their mortal enemy. Il Duce's police, though, had all but annihilated the Mafia, and they couldn't do much. Besides, they had no unified command, so Luciano would have had difficulty getting any kind of word to them. Cesare Mori, the leader of the Fascist anti-Mafia campaign, once explained the nature of his foes:

> It has happened in certain times and in certain districts that mafiosi habitually met in groups which had all the characteristics of true association, with regular and, of course, secret, statutes, concealed badges and marks of recognition, definite hierarchies and elections of chiefs; but these were exceptional cases . . . . [The Mafia is] a system of local oligarchies, closely interwoven, but each autonomous in its own district.

Charley Lucky had left Italy as a child. To him it was a country full of stupid peasants who couldn't speak English. When he got there, though, he saw a way to make a new fortune. His opportunity was spelled H-E-R-O-I-N.

3

Before he went to prison, Luciano had gotten his associates in the Italian "thing" into the drug business. Luciano himself got into drugs as a means of keeping the workers in his chain of brothels under control. The addicted prostitutes were too lethargic and too dependent on regular doses of heroin to cause trouble. The "mustache Petes" had always avoided drugs. Their reasons, of course, had nothing to do with morality. It was the same reason that had kept all but a few of the younger Italian-American bosses from getting deeply involved with bootleg liquor. Selling drugs was a federal offense. The federal government had thousands of frequently shifting law-enforcers and judges, which made it difficult to put in a decent fix. Luciano's nationwide organization made it easier.

In Sicily, Luciano contacted local mafiosi and explained the possibilities for exploiting the American market. The Mafia was rapidly reviving with help from the U.S. Army and the OSS. Vito Genovese, who fled the United States to avoid arrest, became a translator for Col. Charles Poletti, commander of the American Military Government unit and former lieutenant governor of New York. It made no difference that Genovese, after he fled the U.S., had joined the Fascist party and became an important man in Mussolini's regime. Don Calogero Vizzini, a high-ranking Sicilian mafioso, was treated as a VIP and appointed mayor of Villalba. He remained mayor even after he used his position to kill a rival. Mafiosi were chosen to replace the Fascist police.

In the north, an Italian resistance movement had sprung up. It fought the German occupiers and eventually killed the fleeing Mussolini. American officers, however, were afraid that the resistance had too much Communist influence. They cut back on supplies to the resistance fighters and increased aid to their pet mafiosi.

The mafiosi listened eagerly as Luciano told them about the United States. It was the richest country in the world, untouched by war. It was also the most populous country in the world after China, India and the Soviet Union (which had not yet shattered into fifteen independent republics, each far less populous than the United States). And it had the third-largest land mass in the world, after the U.S.S.R. and Canada, with long and virtually unguarded borders, making smuggling easy.

He probably did not tell them that at that time the United States had the lowest rate of heroin addiction in at least a century. The war had made it impossible to import heroin, and most of the addicts had cured themselves. At the end of the war, the federal Bureau of Narcotics, which usually erred on the high side, estimated that there were no more than 20,000 addicts in the country. With a population of approximately 150,000,000, that meant an addiction rate of .013 percent. The country had never been closer to totally wiping out heroin addiction.

Charley Lucky turned the tide.

The U.S. government gave him some help. In the two years after the war, it deported to Italy more than a hundred criminals who, like Luciano, had never become citizens. Lucky got a ready-made gang. With it, he was able to impose a sort of order on the mafiosi of Sicily and set up a network of smuggling routes across Europe and North Africa. The Mafia brought the raw opium from the poppy fields in Turkey to Lebanon, where it was turned into morphine base and shipped to Sicily, where it was processed into heroin.

To set up things on the American side, Luciano traveled to Cuba, where he was met by his longtime friend and associate, Meyer Lansky, and Lansky's assistant, Santo Trafficante, the "cosa nostra" chief in South Florida. Both were deeply involved in the pre-revolution Havana rackets. By 1952, the Narcotics Bureau estimated, the number of U.S. heroin addicts had tripled from its prewar low. It was then 60,000. At the time of Luciano's death in 1962, it was over 100,000.

The only hitch in Luciano's operation was that the Sicilian Mafia seemed to have trouble finding decent criminal chemists. Labs blew up; batches of heroin were botched, and Charley Lucky could see profits draining away. For help, he turned to another Mediterranean criminal group, the *Union Corse*, the conglomeration of Corsican criminal syndicates known to its members simply as *le milieu*.

The indefatigable Meyer Lansky seems to have been the man who convinced the Corsican milieu that it should join the American Mob and the Sicilian Mafia in the drug business. In 1949, he visited Luciano in Sicily, then proceeded to Switzerland, where he made certain arrangements with Swiss bankers. (Later, Lansky purchased a Swiss bank of his own, the Bank of Geneva.) From Switzerland, he journeyed to Marseille, where he had a series of discussions with leaders of the Corsican syndicates. After his return to the United States, French police found, in Marseille, the first heroin lab since before the war. The timing was good: Italy had begun cutting back its legal heroin production, which, siphoned off to the Mafia, had made up a substantial portion of the illicit heroin trade.

4

The Corsican milieu was in a good position to resume its involvement in the drug trade. Like the Mafia, it had benefited from American largesse after the war.

In 1947, a Communist-Socialist coalition dominated all organized labor in Marseille. The Communists called a general strike, which was enthusiastically adopted, because there were some gross inequities in the French economy. Taxes and transportation fees had risen, but workers' pay was frozen. The U.S. State Department, however, feared that the strike was an attempt by the Communists to seize political power. The brand-new CIA was convinced that the strike on the Marseille waterfront was intended to cripple the Marshall Plan. It began paying the Communists' main opposition, the Socialist Party, $1,000,000 a year to break the strike and keep the Communists out of power. In addition to using police to break up Communist rallies, the Socialists paid Corsican syndicate leaders to beat up strikers and protect strikebreakers imported from Italy. Antoine Guerini, a Corsican hoodlum who had also been an intelligence agent for OSS, received the most money from the Socialists. The CIA then contacted Guerini and other milieu leaders directly and furnished them weapons and money. By Christmas of 1947, the shipping strike was broken and the Corsican gangsters were glorying in new wealth and prestige.

In 1950, there was another strike. Fighting against the Viet Minh in what was then French Indochina had become serious. Ho Chi Minh, leader of the Viet Minh, was one of the founders of the French Communist Party, and the Communists organized a selective strike against all military shipments to Indochina. The CIA again found strike- breakers in Italy and again hired Guerini's hoods to beat up the pickets and escort the strikebreakers to work.

The Guerini clan remained top dogs in the Marseille underworld until the end of the 1960s and the early 1970s. They were supplanted by Marcel Francisci, who had more influence with the Gaullist government. Among his other services to Le Grand Charles, Francisci organized the *barbouzes*, the secret agents who ferreted out and secured the confessions of the right-wing terrorists who had attempted to assassinate de Gaulle. Also, members of the Francisci syndicate could always be relied upon to break up any anti-Gaullist rally. In return, the government gave Francisci's followers safe-conduct passes and looked the other way as they made heroin—as long as they didn't try to sell any in France. Some French intelligence officials got into the heroin business themselves. The arrest in New Jersey on April 8, 1971 of a retired French intelligence agent with forty-five kilos of heroin in his car led to the indictment of Col. Paul Fournier, one of the top agents in France's intelligence agency, the SDECE.

5

For many years the Corsicans refrained from selling in France. There was too much money to be made in the United States to tempt the Corsicans to open any new markets. The Corsicans, far more experienced smugglers than the Mafia, had taken over Luciano's smuggling routes to the United States. By 1965, the U.S. Federal Bureau of Narcotics estimated that the number of heroin addicts had risen to 150,000—more than a sevenfold increase since the end of the war.

In the '60s, after Luciano's death, the Sicilian Mafia began to fragment again. Some mafiosi began shipping heroin themselves, instead of going through the Corsicans. Then in 1967, the Turkish government, under pressure from the U.S., began to cut down opium production. By 1972, only four provinces, down from twenty-two, could grow poppies. U.S. heroin seizures dropped from 1,036 pounds in 1971 to 481 in 1973. To make matters worse, the Corsicans began selling heroin in France, which led to a ferocious crackdown by the French police.

In the United States, Lansky, the heir-apparent to Luciano's enterprises, went into semi-retirement and moved to Israel. His retainer, Santo Trafficante, Sr., was also getting along in years. The bulk of the U.S. Mob's heroin operations devolved on Trafficante's son, Santo, Jr., along with all Lansky's Caribbean enterprises. Santo, Jr., had been a loyal assistant to his father and Lansky. When, in 1957, Albert Anastasio, who had succeeded Lepke Buchalter as head of Murder, Inc., expressed an interest in opening a competing casino in Havana, Trafficante had a friendly talk with him. Anastasio was apparently not convinced. Three days later, he was murdered in a barber chair.

The Cuban revolution ruined the Mob's casino business in Havana, but it also resulted in the flight of thousands of Cubans, many of whom were absorbed into Trafficante's organization. For the first time, international drug trafficking included a large Latin American element.

The new organization, though, did not help the shortage of opium Trafficante's group was experiencing. He had to find a new source. So in 1968 he took a trip to the Far East.

8

When Santo Trafficante, Jr. went east, he visited three cities: Hong Kong, Saigon and Singapore.

Singapore was a mistake. It looked like a good choice, being a major world port and the link between mainland Asia and the populous Indonesian archipelago. Singapore was the hub of the trade routes serving India, China and Indonesia. None of those places, though, was now a large opium or opiate exporter. The word's greatest opium-raising area was in the mountainous "Golden Triangle" of Burma, Laos and Thailand. There were no roads to the landlocked Golden Triangle, and it was far from Singapore.

Hong Kong was a good choice: It had a thriving underworld and, since the Chinese revolution, some of the world's most skillful heroin chemists. But Hong Kong, like Singapore, was an island, and it had to import the raw opium for its heroin labs.

Saigon had the most potential of the cities Trafficante toured. There was a large Corsican colony there, and it included Corsican criminal syndicates, often blood relatives of members of the Marseille milieu. The Vietnam Corsicans had already begun shipping both opium and heroin to their cousins in France. There was also a large American presence, so Trafficante would not be dealing entirely with foreigners. Besides the military, there were entrepreneurs of all kinds, including American gangsters. There were also military gangsters, the "khaki mafia" of corrupt senior American NCOs who ran the military clubs and post exchanges. Heading the ring was William O. Wooldridge, who held the title Master Sergeant of the Army—a rank created for him—which made him the highest-ranking enlisted man in the U.S. Army. Wooldridge and his ring were master manipulators who could resist anything but temptation. Trafficante had a number of profitable discussions.

If it was a mistake to go to Singapore, it was a bigger mistake to miss Bangkok. The Thai capital also had an American presence, not nearly as large as Saigon's, of course, but different—CIA rather than army. Bangkok was the closest shipping port to the Golden Triangle, and the Thai police and military were at least as corrupt as any officials in South Vietnam. They controlled the illicit narcotics trade.

2

Narcotics had been an important feature of life in Southeast Asia for many generations, but until well after World War II, the area was notable as a consumer, not a producer. Production began about a century before, but for most of that time it was small scale. The history of opium and opiate production in Southeast Asia can be divided into several phases. Each phase was begun by war. Most of the wars involved the United States.

In the pre-colonial period, opium had been used in moderate amounts in the old Vietnam Empire and adjacent areas that later came under French control. In the colonial period, after their troops conquered Vietnam, Cambodia and Laos, the French government monopolized the distribution of opium. As opium sales produced revenue, the government actively promoted the drug's use. Most of the opium in what came to be known as French Indochina was imported from Persia (now Iran) and India. In Thailand, then called Siam, the opium was also imported, and distribution was also controlled by the government.

While the French were colonizing Indochina (and while the Americans were forcing the Indians into reservations), the Chinese were fighting colonial wars of their own. In Yunnan province, in southwestern China, imperial armies were attacking Muslim inhabitants and hill tribes, such as the Hmong and Yao nations. The Muslims and the hill peoples moved to Indochina, and the imperial government replaced them with ethnic Chinese. The hill tribes settled on the largely uninhabited mountains of Indochina and began raising poppies and harvesting opium, as they had in Yunnan. The Muslims carried the Hmong and Yao opium into the cities of Indochina with their mule caravans.

At first opium production was relatively modest, because the

French, having a monopoly of opium distribution, were able to buy low and sell high. Some smugglers did compete with them for opium to sell on the black market, but they couldn't be depended upon to buy regularly. The main crop of the hill farmers was rice. That was safe: If you couldn't sell it, you could eat it. Opium brought in a few piasters that could be used to purchase simple needs that couldn't be grown.

The end of World War II saw a new migration out of China, one quite different from the last. The Chinese Communists finally defeated the Nationalists, followers of Chiang Kai-shek's Kuomintang (KMT) party, in a civil war that began before World War II and continued, to some extent, all through it. Most of the Nationalist armed forces escaped to Taiwan, but the Eighth Army, commanded by General Li Mi, was driven out of Yunnan Province and into Burma (now Myanmar).

This had a heavy impact on the narcotics industry in Southeast Asia. At the time of the Communist victory, southern China was the world's largest producer of opium. Li Mi had sent tons of opium south on mule caravans escorted by KMT soldiers. When the Communists took over, they promptly plowed under all the opium, sent addicts to "re-education centers" and shot all those who refused to be re-educated. The Communist victory created a crisis for Southeast Asian addicts.

Once again, the American CIA stepped in. As had been the case in Marseille, or as it was with the OSS in Sicily, the U.S. agents had no desire to help the illicit drug industry. But that was the principal result of their intervention.

The United States wanted the KMT remnants to counterattack the Chinese Communists from Burma. Civil Air Transport (later Air America) planes airdropped CIA advisers, money, supplies and weapons to the KMT forces hiding in the Shan States—feudal mini-kingdoms in northeastern Burma. The effort was greatly increased after Communist Chinese troops crossed the Yalu River in Korea. And eventually, in June 1951, the Yunnan Province National Salvation Army invaded China. After less than a month in China, the KMT troops were routed and driven out. Two months later, Li Mi sent another force into Yunnan. It suffered the same fate. The CIA did not abandon its protégés, though. It built airports and flew in more supplies. Li Mi, in turn, began recruiting native troops into his army. Just a year after the last invasion, Li Mi struck again. He was no more successful. But the CIA still didn't give up.

With what appeared to be CIA support, and certainly with CIA-supplied weapons and CIA-financed mercenaries, Li Mi launched an invasion of eastern Burma. After one skirmish with the Burmese Army, the Burmese government reported finding the bodies of three white men that bore no identification other than personal letters with Washington and New York addresses. Li Mi was not much more successful against the Burmese Army than he had been against the Chinese Communist army. He was strong enough, though, to dominate the hill tribes in eastern Burma and northern Thailand. In 1957, Elaine T. Lewis, an American missionary, reported from Burma:

> For many years there have been large numbers of Chinese Nationalist troops in the area demanding food and money from the people. The areas in which these troops operate are getting poorer and poorer and some villages are finding it necessary to flee.

The Burmese learned that the KMT army was not simply robbing the villages. It had gotten into the drug business. The Burmese found three morphine base refineries near a jungle airstrip. Under Burmese pressure, the bulk of the Kuomintang army moved into Laos, where its members were hired by the CIA for its covert operations in that country.

In both Burma and Laos, the KMT troops forced villagers to raise more opium, then took most of it as taxes. When the Chinese left, the Shan tribes didn't stop opium production. Native Shan chiefs became a new crop of opium warlords. One of them, Khun Sa, eventually became the most powerful opium warlord in Southeast Asia.

At first, the Chinese shipped only raw opium to Bangkok. Later, they established laboratories to produce morphine base and heroin. Thai opium-smokers bought much of the opium. The rest was converted to heroin in Bangkok or shipped to Hong Kong. In both Bangkok and Hong Kong, heroin production was in the hands of Chinese of the Chiu chau ethnic group, who ran most of the rackets in Southeast Asia. In Hong Kong, the Chiu chau had won an underworld war against the Green Gang, a criminal organization dating from the fifteenth century that had been forced out of Shanghai. The Hong Kong Chiu chau drug organizations then spread all over the area, from Burma to Singapore, but they made special efforts in Bangkok and Saigon. A certain

Huu Tim-heng even went to Laos, a wild, backwoods area that got its first boundaries and first government from the French colonizers. Huu started a Pepsi-Cola bottling plant in Vientiane, the Laotian capital, and made Prime Minister Souvanna Phouma's son president of the company. That got him generous financial support from the U.S. Agency for International Development. Huu never bottled any Pepsi, however. He used his company as a front for ordering large quantities of chemicals used to turn opium into heroin.

Despite its innocent intentions at the beginning of its involvement with Li Mi, the CIA had gotten deeper and deeper into the outlaw general's machinations.

In 1951, David M. Key, U.S. ambassador to Burma, cabled the State Department protesting "American participation in the KMT operations which have brought chaos to eastern Shan states and have been conducted in flagrant disregard [for] Burmese sovereignty." When his protest was ignored, he resigned.

The CIA was not only supporting Li's invasions of neutral countries and his pillaging of villages. It was helping him develop his narcotics business. Some Civil Air Transport pilots, after unloading supplies for Li, were loading their planes with opium and morphine and flying back to Bangkok.

Bangkok was the major destination of most of the KMT opium. That city was the headquarters of Gen. Phao Siyanan, chief of the Thailand national police. The Thais, seeking to secure their borders against the Communists in China and Burma, had made alliances with both the KMT and the hill tribes in those areas. To cement their alliances, they made CIA-supplied weapons available to both the KMT troops and the hill tribes, including the Shan warlords. CIA operatives had considered Phao the most reliable of the Thai anti-Communists and had so enriched him with subsidies and weapons that he became the most powerful man in Thailand. That made him the most powerful ally of Li Mi. Phao, importing huge amounts of opium and morphine into Thailand, became one of the kingpins of Southeast Asia's narcotics production. Under his sponsorship, production and exports reached new heights.

3

While Phao Siyanan, Thailand's guardian of law and order, was making millions in the now-illegal narcotics business, the French in neighboring Vietnam were having troubles.

World War II had brought little change in the life of a Hmong farmer. Until the end of the war, the French continued to act as puppets for the Japanese.

As World War II approached its end, the Japanese threw their French puppets into prison, established a Vietnamese republic and withdrew. After the war, the French, with major British assistance, returned. When their negotiations with Ho Chi Minh, leader of the Vietnamese nationalists, broke down, the first Vietnam War began. The French supported Bao Dai, their puppet emperor. The war was not popular in France, and Paris kept the French forces on a tight budget.

The French were not only operating on a shoestring, they were fighting a revolutionary enemy—the type of war they were neither equipped nor organized to fight. They had, however, a number of unorthodox young officers who proposed fighting the Viet Minh guerrillas with a counter-guerrilla war. Foremost among them was Maj. Roger Trinquier, a brilliant and imaginative but utterly ruthless and undemocratic soldier.

Trinquier began enlisting Vietnam's many factions—including bandits, religious cults and hill tribes—to fight the Viet Minh. Most of these people had no more love for the French than for the Viet Minh, but Trinquier was able to convince them it was to their advantage to side with France. Basically, his method was simple—bribery. Bribery was not simple, though, because the home government saw to it that he had no money to spare.

Trinquier ordered his agents to buy opium from the Hmong and other hill people at prices that were competitive with what the opium smugglers paid. (The old French opium monopoly, which had bought cheap and sold dear—encouraging the growth of a black market—had been abolished.) The army then sold the opium for a profit to the Binh Xuyen river pirates of Saigon and other gangsters. The gangsters sold the opium locally, exported it to other countries and sold a growing amount to heroin laboratories operated by members of Vietnam's large Corsican colony. The Corsicans, in turn, sold increasing amounts of heroin and morphine base to their compatriots in Marseille.

The Hmong poppy-growers, finding a ready and profitable market, expanded their production and agreed to serve in the mercenary armies Trinquier was training. The Binh Xuyen took over Saigon's underworld. Operating openly, they controlled, for a time, the city's government. The Cao Dai, Hoa Hao and other armed religious sects profited by receiving French weapons and French money, generated by the opium trade.

While the drug trade was developing in the Golden Triangle area of Burma, Laos and Thailand, the first Vietnam War ended. The French fortress at Dien Bien Phu fell, and an international meeting at Geneva agreed that Vietnam should be divided into two parts and a nationwide election should be held to determine whether Ho Chi Minh or Emperor Bao Dai should rule the country. The prospect of a victory by the Communist Ho horrified U.S. officials. The Americans supported Ngo Dinh Diem, Bao Dai's premier, in a coup d'état that resulted in a new South Vietnamese republic. As the Pentagon Papers put it, South Vietnam was "essentially the creation of the United States."

The Americans inherited the French role in Vietnam, and also the mess the French had left there.

Ngo Dinh Diem, the president of the new republic, controlled little more than the area around the capitol building in Saigon. The rest of the city was in the hands of the Binh Xuyen gangsters who had been given the city, block by block, by the French in return for driving out the Communist guerrillas. The Binh Xuyen method of fighting the Communists was the same as Trinquier's, bribery. They paid informants and turncoats from the profits they earned from Saigon's thriving narcotics, prostitution, gambling and extortion rackets. Outside the city, some areas were controlled by the Vietnamese Communists, nicknamed Viet Cong. More were owned by the Cao Dai and the Hao Hoa religious sects, aberrant varieties of Buddhism.

The sects had fairly large and well-equipped armies which they financed partly through extortion. Most of their financing, though, came from the French. It was relatively easy, then, for the CIA troubleshooter, Gen. Edward Lansdale, to line the sects up on the side of Diem and his South Vietnam army. The French were out, and Lansdale held the purse strings. The French secret service, though, still favored the Binh Xuyen. They encouraged the gangsters to resist Diem. The result was a bloody proxy war, with France and the United States using Vietnamese pawns. After most of downtown Saigon had been destroyed, the remnants of the Binh Xuyen were again hiding in the swamps outside of Saigon, their political power gone forever.

4

For a while, everything seemed to be going smoothly. Diem launched a vigorous anti-opium campaign. Then Viet Cong cells reappeared in Saigon. Diem's brother, Ngo Din Nhu, head of the secret police, decided he needed more money to build up a network of informers, like the one that had served the Binh Xuyen so well. He resurrected the opium trade. Nhu established contacts with the Chinese syndicates in Saigon's twin city, Cholon, and with the Corsican gangsters. The leading Corsican, Bonaventure "Rock" Francisci, began flying into the Golden Triangle and dropping narcotics in the settled parts of South Vietnam. Nhu's strategy worked. Once again, Communist activity in the capital disappeared. The underground anti-Communist war was financed by an extensive smuggling syndicate run by the president's brother. The narcotics trafficking was too extensive to be completely hidden. The Americans urged Nhu to institute reforms. He refused. They urged Diem to send his brother away. He refused. They contacted dissident elements in the army and arranged a coup. Diem, contrary to American wishes, was murdered.

Key man in the coup was French-born, Kansas-raised CIA agent Lucien Conein. Conein was an old Vietnam hand. As a paratrooper major on loan to the OSS, he had jumped into northern Vietnam in 1945 to act as liaison between the U.S. and French forces. Previously, he had jumped into occupied France in a team that included William Colby, future U.S. Director of Central Intelligence. In Vietnam (then French Indochina) Colby had met both Ho Chi Minh and Vo Nguyen Giap, military commander of the Viet Cong. He was a close friend of another colorful CIA agent, Ed Lansdale, who became the model for Lederer and Burdick's *The Ugly American* and Graham Greene's *The Quiet American*. Conein believed the high-handed Diem and his corrupt brother had lost the support of the Vietnamese people and had to go. He did not expect to get rid of narcotics, though. Conein, who hung around with the Corsicans, said of them, "From what I know of them, it will be absolutely impossible to cut off the dope traffic. You can cut it down, but you can never stop it unless you get to the growers in the hills."

When Conein left Vietnam, the Corsicans gave the CIA man a heavy gold medallion of the type used by syndicate leaders to identify themselves in *le milieu*. Engraved on the back is *Per Tu Amicu Conein*—"For Your Friendship, Conein." Later, "Black Luigi," as the Corsicans called him, became head of intelligence at the U.S. Bureau of Narcotics and Dangerous Drugs and later held a similar position in the newly formed Drug Enforcement Administration.

Nothing improved after Diem's fall. Leadership passed to a succession of South Vietnamese military officers who also controlled narcotics trafficking. In 1970, the business appeared to be controlled by three factions: (1) the Vietnamese Air Force under Air Vice-Marshal Nguyen Cao Ky; (2) the police, customs service and port authority, reporting to Premier Khiem Tran Tien; and (3) the army, navy and National Assembly, all led by President Nguyen Van Thieu.

The Hmong opium from Laos was flown directly into South Vietnam on South Vietnam government planes. Later, after the invasion of neutralist Cambodia, opium was carried on mules to that country and then flown or shipped into South Vietnam. Some of the ships belonged to the South Vietnamese Navy.

5

The most obvious change after the fall of Diem was the growth of the narcotics industry all through Southeast Asia. Phao fell from power in Thailand, but the shipment of opium and heroin continued to grow. Local generals squeezed out the Corsican smugglers in Laos. With control entirely in their hands, they shipped out more opium.

Then someone discovered a huge new market: the American GIs in Vietnam.

Suddenly, a new kind of heroin appeared on the market—the white, finely powdered variety called Number Four. Number Four dissolved in water easily and was ideal for injecting. It was like the most expensive heroin sold in the United States.

There were differences, though. A $2 vial in Saigon would sell for $100 in the States. And the heroin an addict bought stateside was far less pure. The heroin package sold by American street pushers might be only 25 to 50 percent heroin. The Saigon package was 95 percent pure.

A CIA report said that the production of Number Four heroin "appears to be due to the sudden increase in demand by a large and relatively affluent market in South Vietnam."

The report is disingenuous in the extreme. The "large and relatively affluent market" is, of course, the GIs. But the demand did not
arise spontaneously. The first Number Four appeared in late 1969,
pushed by civilian employees at the military bases, bar girls, prostitutes
and even children at roadside stands. By 1970, it was everywhere the
U.S. Army was. The demand, in short, had been created by the intensive, intrusive, high-pressure salesmanship of a highly coordinated sales
organization.

At first there were wild rumors, passed on by officials like Harry
Anslinger, former head of the Narcotics Bureau, that the ultimate supplier was either Communist China or North Vietnam. Communist
China had long since wiped out its opium crop. As for North Vietnam,
the U.S. Army provost marshal reported in 1971:

> The opium-growing areas of North Vietnam are concentrated
> in the mountainous northern provinces bordering China. Cul-
> tivation is closely controlled by the government and none of
> the crop is believed to be channeled illicitly into international
> markets. Much of it is probably converted into morphine and
> used for medical purposes.

The source of the heroin was the South Vietnam drug organization.
According to the provost marshal, the organization had four "zones,"
or tiers.

> Zone I, located at the top or apex of the pyramid, contains the
> financiers, or backers of the illicit drug traffic in all its forms.
> The people comprising this group may be high level, influen-
> tial political figures, government leaders or moneyed ethnic
> Chinese members of the criminal syndicates now flourishing in
> the Cholon sector of the City of Saigon. The members compris-
> ing this group are the powers behind the scenes who can ma-
> nipulate, foster, protect, and promote the illicit traffic in drugs.

At that time, the leader of Zone I was Gen. Nguyen Van Thieu,
president of South Vietnam.

His motive was simple greed. The Americans might be protecting
his country, but the GIs were spending an estimated $88 million a year
on heroin. In September 1970, a survey of 3,103 soldiers of the
Americal Division disclosed that 11.9 percent of them had tried heroin

since they came to Vietnam, and 6.6 percent were using it on a regular basis. By mid–1971, army medical authorities estimated that between 25,000 and 37,000 troops were heroin users.

The army set up rehabilitation programs for soldiers who were due to return to "the world." Theoretically, the soldier would have to pass a urine test before he shipped out. Actually, some GIs arranged for buddies to supply clean urine samples. And a soldier who flunked the test twice was declared to be "of negligible value to the United States Army," sent back to the States and discharged immediately. Even those with clean urine samples could well have been psychologically addicted. How many were actually addicted is hard to say. It is known, though, that heroin consumption in the United States registered a steep increase in the early '70s.

During this period, the CIA made every effort not to see any connection between the South Vietnamese leaders and the campaign to sell heroin to Americans. The State Department actively defended Thieu and Company. The U.S. Army's Criminal Investigation Division compiled detailed information on the role played by General Ngo Dzu, one of Thieu's closest associates. It sent the report to the U.S. embassy. The embassy ignored it. U.S. Rep. Robert H. Steele told a congressional subcommittee in July, 1971: "U.S. military authorities have provided Ambassador Bunker with hard intelligence that one of the chief traffickers is Gen. Ngo Dzu, the commander of II Corps." The senior U.S. adviser for II Corps replied to Steele's accusation: "There is no information available to me that in any shape, manner or fashion would substantiate the charges Congressman Steele has made."

The dope dealing continued, and GI addicts continued returning to the United States until the end of U.S. involvement in Vietnam.

Although nothing was done in Vietnam, the "GI heroin epidemic" caused a panic in the United States—a panic President Nixon called a "war on drugs."

9

Probably no man in history was more eager to be President of the United States than Richard M. Nixon. Certainly, only a few took office in more trying times. Racial riots were burning out the centers of large cities from Los Angeles to Newark. Assassins had taken the lives of Martin Luther King, Jr., the nation's greatest civil-rights leader, and of Robert F. Kennedy, who looked certain to be the Democratic nominee for president. The United States was involved in an increasingly unpopular war in Vietnam, and the Tet Offensive at the beginning of 1968 had convinced most Americans that the country's Vietnam policy was bankrupt. Antiwar sentiment had grown so strong that Nixon's predecessor, Lyndon B. Johnson, a fervent supporter of the war, had announced that he would not seek a second term.

Young people were creating special troubles. A continuing problem was the growth of violent juvenile gangs among the poorest youth in American cities. A new problem was an atmosphere of alienation and rebellion among the most privileged youth of the nation.

2

The gang problem was very old. The pre-Revolutionary "Boston Massacre" occurred on the date of a traditional annual mob fight between two Boston gangs. In New York, large gangs like the Plug Uglies, the Hudson Dusters and the complex of gangs collectively called the Five-Pointers waged feuds and committed robbery, assault and extortion from the early nineteenth century until well into the twentieth. Most other large cities had a similar gang problem. The same gangs stayed in existence for generations because they provided, according to sociologists Richard Cloward and Lloyd Ohlin of Columbia University, alternative opportunities for youths in depressed areas. In the days when "no Irish need apply"—at least no poor, uneducated Irish—the gangs gave an enterprising boy a way to get ahead in the world. As the depressed areas became more Jewish, then more Italian, the gangs remained. When Prohibition brought the gangs out of their ghettoes and into the city at large, gang members became criminal celebrities. Al Capone had been a Five-Pointer.

World War II changed the gang scene. There were massive population shifts as families moved to be near the booming defense industries. Old neighborhoods broke up, and the old criminal gangs disappeared. In their place were swarms of juveniles, too young for the service or factory work. With both parents in either the service or war work, many kids were left to shift for themselves. Typically, they were from the poorest families and lived in the most crowded areas of large cities. They found new "families" in the territorial gangs of their neighborhoods. They committed some petty crime, but the real reason for the gangs was brotherhood. And as nothing increases unity like a struggle against a known enemy, their most important activity was fighting other gangs.

Gang structure was quite formal. Most gangs had not only a leader but a "war chief," who arranged terms and locations of forthcoming battles with the war chiefs of other gangs. The gangs sometimes engaged in "rumbles"—pitched battles with other gangs. At other times, they went "stomping"—beating up individual members of rival gangs in disputed territory. Weapons included clubs, chains, knives, rocks and garbage cans dropped from rooftops. Some gangsters carried "zip guns," homemade .22-caliber pistols. As a last resort, a gang might use a store-bought .22-caliber rifle or a Molotov cocktail.

This is the gang culture, growing throughout the 1940s, that Leonard Bernstein celebrated in his musical, *West Side Story*. During the '50s and '60s, America embarked on an orgy of slum clearance. What remained of the old neighborhoods was often pulverized and replaced with public housing units containing a random mix of strangers. New gangs formed, providing one of the few stable elements in their areas. The average age of gang members increased. Jobs were no longer easy to obtain for unskilled kids.

Gang life put a premium on muscle and fighting skill. Those who had these qualities were able to achieve recognition, at least among their peers. Those who weren't good fighters often dropped out. They became "coolies," named for their "cool" lifestyle. Howard Finestone, a Chicago sociologist, described the coolie, whom he nicknamed "the cat." The cat and his fellow cats lived for "kicks." He avoided work and professed contempt for those who worked. He devoted himself to "hustling"—usually nonviolent, but almost always illegal, ways of making "bread" to pay for his kicks. He considered himself and his friends a nonworking elite instead of a bunch of losers. His main way of achieving kicks was through drugs, especially heroin. Thanks to the OSS, the CIA and Charley Lucky, heroin was becoming easier and easier to get.

In the late '50s, gang violence appeared to subside. Rumors had it that juvenile authorities were encouraging the young gangsters to use heroin to get their minds off fighting. The rumors were probably untrue, but it was true that drug use was increasing among gang members, as it was everywhere in America.

3

In the sixties, gang membership continued to grow. Aid to Families with Dependent Children, the principal form of welfare in the period, encouraged one-parent families. That encouraged more kids to seek "families" on the street. And gang members began selling, as well as using, drugs. At first, the principal motive of the seller was to get enough money to purchase drugs for his own use. Later, nonusing gangsters began setting up professional merchandising organizations. After a five-year study of gangs in the eighties, Dr. Carl F. Taylor, a Detroit sociologist, concluded that there are three types of youth gangs. At the bottom of the heap are the "scavenger gangs"—loosely organized groups of youths who hang out together and commit petty crime. Then there are the "territorial gangs"—highly organized groups that wear "colors," claim "turf" and feud with other gangs. The territorials may sell dope, but that's not their main purpose. Groups of territorial gangs often belong to federations, like the famous Crips and Bloods of Los Angeles. The third type of gang is what Taylor calls "corporate gangs." These are the groups that really deserve that favorite newspaper term "drug gangs." The members are very young—even their leaders are seldom out of their twenties. They control all the retailing in large areas and may sell directly or through street peddlers who often belong to territorial gangs. Their leaders often get their drugs directly from foreign suppliers.

The new drug gangs are partly the result of the postwar changes in American organized crime. Maranzano's Italian "thing" (*cosa nostra*) still exists. So does the multi-ethnic criminal federation Charley Lucky had put together. But, as had happened to the Irish and the Jews before them, new opportunities opened for Italian-Americans. Most top Italian gang leaders are old; none of them approaches the intellectual level of Luciano. Any new Lucianos have gone into business or the professions, where they make equal amounts of money and enjoy the respect of all citizens. The same is true of other leaders in the old "syndicate." They try to hold on to territory and sell franchises to newer criminal groups, relying on the reputation of "the Mafia" or "the Mob" to keep the upstarts in line. And increasingly they watch money and power slipping away from them.

It's no accident that the upstart criminals are recent immigrants, like the Russian mobsters of New York; despised minorities, like the African-Americans and Latin-Americans in hundreds of U.S. urban gangs, or both, like Chinese, Cuban, Haitian and Jamaican immigrants selling dope around the country. Nor is it odd that they are young. Crime, like soldiering, has traditionally been a young man's game. In the wild and woolly '20s and '30s, not even the top bosses reached senior-citizen status. Dutch Schultz was gunned down at thiry-four; Charley Lucky was in jail, his criminal federation already created, when he was thiry-nine.

Dr. Terry Williams, a New York sociologist, studied a drug gang in his city. The members of this organization, which Williams nicknamed "the Cocaine Kids," were all black or Latino teenagers under eighteen. Their leader, "Max," dealt directly with a Colombian who brought the cocaine from his country. The Colombian spoke no English, but Max spoke Spanish. In his dealings with this Colombian "drug lord," the teenage Max was by no means in an inferior position.

One result of drug-selling by the gangs has been a quantum jump in weaponry. The corporate gangs make enough money to purchase any kind of weapon they want. Almost all of their purchases are illegal, so it doesn't matter that some of their weapons, such as fully automatic submachine guns and rifles, are also illegal. The corporate gangs even have enough money to supply their allies in the territorial gangs with firearms.

4

The gang scene today is far more sophisticated and dangerous than it was in Nixon's administration, but it was troubling even then. Even more troubling to Nixon, it seems, was the other youth movement, the "peaceniks" or "flower children."

The flower children belonged on the opposite end of the social scale from the gangsters. The bulk of them were in college, many of them in the most expensive and prestigious colleges in the country. They opposed the Vietnam War because, they said, it was unjust and colonialist. They also opposed it because they might end up in it. Opposition to the war drove them to oppose the values of the "establishment"—the values, that is, of the government, of the middle-class population, of their parents. Long hair drove their parents wild, so they avoided barbers. The middle-class population valued neatness, so the flower children wore scraggly beards and tattered clothes and washed only occasionally. The government considered drugs just about the worst of all evils, so the flower children "did" drugs.

The drug of choice was marijuana because it was cheap and relatively safe. Some, though, experimented with LSD—sometimes with horrific results. And a few tried heroin and cocaine.

The flower children, like the youth gangs, began before the Nixon Administration. But not much before—they became a significant part of the body politic in the Johnson Administration. Lyndon Johnson, who began his administration by declaring a war on poverty, became more and more obsessed with the war in Vietnam. Although plagued by pot-puffing peaceniks, Johnson didn't declare a war on drugs. Instead, as Robert Stutman, former agent in charge of the DEA office in New York, put it, Johnson "decided to use the drug issue and the FBN [Federal Bureau of Narcotics] agents to declare war on peace, on those activists opposed to the escalation of U.S. involvement in Southeast Asia. Rather than see the growing evidence of marijuana abuse as proof that drug use had taken root in the middle class, the administration decided it would try to prove that anyone opposed to Vietnam was a dope addict."

The bungling of Johnson's war on peace matched that of the war in Vietnam. The antiwar activists organized a mass sleep-in around the Washington Monument, to be followed the next day by a parade. They had all the permits they needed, but, Stutman wrote, "the Johnson administration ordered us to find a reason to revoke the permits."

Stutman and a number of other FBN agents were sent to mingle with the crowd. They would not carry official credentials. "Because," said a senior agent, "if you get in any trouble, we don't want you carrying badges." The reason was so that the authorities could deny that they had planted cops among the peace marchers to disrupt the operation. Instead of a badge, each agent would carry a bent penny. "And every cop in Washington, D.C., is going to know that there are undercover agents in there with those pennies bent in half."

The senior agent told the infiltrators to find evidence of drug use, then get out of the crowd before 8 A.M., when the mounted police would charge the crowd. The evidence would be used later to justify the charge.

Apparently the district cops and the agents got two different sets of instructions. Stutman and his partner, Steve Medwid, tried to leave at 6 A.M., but the police wouldn't let anyone through their cordon. They were holding the crowd in place so the mounted police could beat them up. In his book, *Dead on Delivery*, Stutman described the scene:

> So we start to walk out and we run into a cop, one of hundreds surrounding the perimeter.
>
> "Where you guys goin'?" he asked.
>
> "I got a bent penny," Medwid said.
>
> "I don't give a fuck if your penny's bent or not," the cop answered. Then he took a swing at us. Before he took another, we went back inside, where we waited for the horses to charge.
>
> When they came at 8 A.M. it was a horror. We and the 100,000 hippies were on the same side now, trying to get out of this cordon of horses and cops alive.

At the time, Stutman was a very young agent.

When demonstrating against the war, the pot-puffing flower children purposely tried to defy and shake up the establishment. They succeeded. Perhaps their greatest success was the horrendous three-day "police riot" in Chicago during the 1968 Democratic National Convention that followed Johnson's announcement that he would not seek another term. The most deadly demonstration took place in 1970, during Nixon's administration, at Kent State University in Ohio: The Ohio National Guard fired into a crowd of students and killed four of them.

Nixon was obviously less bothered by what juvenile gangsters in impoverished neighborhoods were doing than the antics of "the best and the brightest"—or at least the richest—of the nation's youth. They were attacking authority, challenging the right of the government to make war, giving aid and comfort to the Communist enemy. And they were defiantly blowing marijuana smoke in the face of the establishment. Like Johnson, Nixon attempted to label all war protesters as dope addicts, as well as Communists or Communist-sympathizers.

Then the president got the news from Vietnam. American soldiers were hooked on drugs. The only salvation for the country, he believed, was to make war on drugs—and druggies.

We'll look at the results of that war a little later. First, though, let's examine a few more Cold War developments.

10

On January 27, 1980, in Australia, a New South Wales state policeman noticed a Mercedes parked on a country road a little west of Sidney. In it was a dead body holding a rifle in a way that looked as if a suicide had occurred. The man was identified as Frank Nugan, a Sidney banker.

As Australian authorities investigated the death, a strange story began to unfold. Nugan, with an American named Michael Hand, was one of the founders of the Nugan Hand Bank. There was a third, very silent, partner, a somewhat mysterious American named Bernard Houghton. Alan Parks, a retired U.S. Air Force officer, told *Wall Street Journal* reporter Jonathan Kwitny that Houghton and Hand were involved with something called Project 404 that is still classified. Houghton was a pilot who would "fly anything," Parks said.

"The Golden Triangle, that's where he got his opium from. There was one flight, he flew in slot machines. He did some deals over in India."

There was no doubt that Houghton had great influence with both American and Australian officials. The Australian Commonwealth-New South Wales Joint Task Force investigating the Nugan Hand Bank reported that Houghton was "part of the intelligence community" in Southeast Asia before coming to Australia. His friends Down Under included John Walker, the CIA Australian station chief from 1973 to 1975; Sir Robert Askin, premier of New South Wales; and Abraham Saffron, Sidney's leading gangster.

The Nugan Hand bank opened in 1973 with five dollars in paid-up capital but claiming a million dollars. Through dizzying financial footwork and outright fraud, it was able to stay in business for seven years and open branches worldwide. It laundered money for gangsters and financed arms sales to southern Africa and drug trafficking from wherever drugs were produced. During its active life, Sidney experienced a significant narcotics problem for the first time. Soon after the bank began operations, a Sidney lawyer, Ivan Judd, told an Australian narcotics investigator named Russ Kenny that he had learned from a client that her employer, Kermit "Bud" King, a former CIA pilot, was flying drugs for Nugan Hand. Soon after that, King mysteriously fell from the tenth-floor window of his apartment.

According to the Joint Task Force report, "By 1977, Nugan Hand was well established in drug activity." Another official report, by the Australian Royal Commission inquiring into drug trafficking, stated that Nugan Hand regularly moved money to points in Southeast Asia to cover the cost of heroin shipped to Australia and on to the United States.

At the time of Nugan's death, the bank had an international branch chartered on the Cayman Islands and an array of officers that included Adm. Earl Yates, retired chief strategist of the U.S. Pacific Command; Gen. Edwin Black, former commander of U.S. forces in Thailand; Gen. Leroy J. Manor, former chief of staff of the U.S. Pacific Command; Dr. Guy Pauker, Asia expert for the Rand Corporation; Walter McDonald, retired CIA deputy director for economic research; Dale Holmgren, former chairman of the CIA airline, Civil Air Transport; and last, but certainly not least, William Colby, retired U.S. Director of Central Intelligence.

Prominent among the friends of Houghton and Hand and involved in the affairs of the bank, was a coterie of former U.S. intelligence officers, including Theodore Shackley, former CIA station chief in Laos; Thomas Clines, his former deputy; and Edwin Wilson, a rogue contract agent later accused of gun running to Libya and freelance assassination. This group, with others, would later be identified by a leading civil-rights lawyer as "the Enterprise" and unsuccessfully sued under the Racketeer Influenced and Corrupt Organization (RICO) statute.

Wilson is now in prison, because an ex-CIA agent named Kevin Mulcahy blew the whistle on him. Mulcahy was then murdered. Before he died, though, he told the *National Times* of Sidney that the CIA used Nugan Hand "for shifting money for various covert operations around the globe."

Everything collapsed after Nugan's death, which, ironically, may have been caused by problems involving his family's fruit farm rather than the bank. The CIA, though, went on operating covertly "around the globe." One covert project shifted the opium production problem from the Golden Triangle to South Asia.

2

In December 1979, the Soviet Union sent troops into Afghanistan to replace the pro-Soviet government in Kabul with an even more pro-Soviet government. A simmering rebellion in the hinterlands broke into a boil.

An outraged President Jimmy Carter decided to step up shipments of weapons to the rebels, called *mujaheddin* (fighters for the faith, or soldiers of the holy war). Carter had been helping to arm anti-Communist elements in Afghanistan even before the open Soviet invasion. As the U.S. and the U.S.S.R. were officially at peace, the weapons shipments had to be done clandestinely. The CIA, therefore, was in charge. (Carter's successor, Ronald Reagan, was less interested in keeping covert operations covert if he could gain political advantage by talking about them. He later would take credit for having initiated the shipments. His campaign organization, then, was able to accuse Carter of being "a wimp," and imply that he was guilty of that most grievous political sin, being "soft on Communism.")

Dr. David Musto, Yale University psychiatrist and historian of drug regulation, had misgivings about how the aid would be administered. Afghanistan was one of the world's leading opium producers and consumers. If the United States wasn't careful, it could give the drug trade in South Asia the same sort of boost it gave narcotics in Southeast Asia. Musto was a member of the White House Strategy Council on Drug Abuse, and he had reason not to trust the CIA.

A little earlier, the CIA had given the council a briefing on the cocaine industry in Colombia. Musto prepared for the meeting by getting World Bank figures on the role of the U.S. dollar in the cocaine trade. He asked about the economics of cocaine, and the agency specialists replied with what Musto knew from his data to be a direct lie. Confronted with the World Bank figures, the CIA representatives took back their answer without an apology. Musto complained to the White House but got no response.

The Afghanistan operation disturbed him. "I told the council that we were going to Afghanistan to support the opium growers in their rebellion against the Soviets," he recalled. "Shouldn't we try to avoid what we had done in Laos? Shouldn't we try to pay the growers if they will eradicate their opium production? There was silence."

Sure enough, heroin from Afghanistan and Pakistan began flooding into the United States. Drug-related deaths in New York City increased 77 percent. Musto and another physician on the drug council, Dr. Joyce H. Lowinson, wrote an op-ed piece in the *New York Times*. They expressed worry about the growing of opium poppies by the rebel tribesmen.

"Are we erring in befriending these tribes as we did in Laos when Air America (chartered by the Central Intelligence Agency) helped transport crude opium from certain tribal areas?" they asked. They noted that drug production in Afghanistan and Pakistan had increased, although they could not prove a direct relationship with the CIA. "On the streets, this drug [heroin] is more potent, cheaper and more available than at any time in the last twenty years." They concluded that "this crisis is bound to worsen."

3

Agents of the Drug Enforcement Administration noticed an increase in South Asian heroin at about the same time as the Soviet invasion. The unsettled conditions in the Middle East encouraged increased opium production by the lack of government regulation and the desire of restive tribesmen to get the cash to buy modern arms. Early in 1979, the Ayatollah Ruhollah Khomeini had replaced the U.S. friend, Shah Mohammed Reza Palavi. The Ayatollah had no warm feelings for the United States, which he named "The Great Satan." He certainly was not going to prevent dope exportation to the United States. Pakistan was friendly enough, but it was in continual turmoil, especially after a military coup overthrew the government in 1977. And in Afghanistan, rebels had, of course, been arming even before the Soviet invasion.

At a press conference held at about the same time as the Soviet invasion, Gordon Fink, the DEA's assistant intelligence administrator, mentioned the "concern and frustration the DEA is finding in dealing with the problem . . . due mainly to lack of control and intelligence at the source points, namely Pakistan, Afghanistan and Iran."

DEA Special Agent Ernie Staples, just arrived from the Middle East, said, "Europe at present is being flooded with Middle Eastern heroin."

In Europe, the Corsican milieu and the Sicilian Mafia revived their heroin operations and started shipping to the Gambino and Sollena organized crime families in the United States. The European heroin was competing now with South Asian heroin shipped directly to the United States. The old American Mob was getting new competition, too. Black syndicates in Harlem, which for several years had been importing heroin from Southeast Asia, began buying new supplies from Pakistan and Afghanistan. Heroin prices dropped and sales increased as "H" became plentiful. By 1983, the *New York Times* reported, Pakistan and Afghanistan were supplying 85 to 90 percent of all the heroin sold in New York City.

In spite of the DEA's concern, Iranian heroin was not much found in the United States. Iran's poppy harvest did increase, and its heroin production zoomed, but it was all absorbed internally. In spite of occasional reports of the execution of numbers of persons said to be drug traffickers, Iran has one of the highest—if not the highest—rates of addiction of any nation in the world. What the production increase meant was that Iran no longer had to import opium and heroin from Afghanistan and the Afghan-Pakistan borderlands. Afghanistan and Pakistan were left with a surplus of dope. That, they sent to the United States.

4

When revolt broke out in Afghanistan, opium production took another leap. More acres were planted with opium poppies to raise cash for the war. "We must grow and sell opium to fight our holy war against the Russian nonbelievers," explained the brother of Mullah Nasim Akhundzda, a fundamentalist Muslim cleric, resistance fighter and the largest opium-grower in Afghanistan.

Mullah Nasim's greatest rival in the ranks of the resistance fighters was a man named Gulbuddin Hekmatyar. Hekmatyar was also a Muslim fundamentalist. As an engineering student, he founded something called the Muslim Brotherhood, led student demonstrations and sent followers to throw acid in the faces of women who refused to wear the veil. He raised a mercenary force to fight the liberal prime minister, Mohammed Daud. His troops were armed by Pakistan, which feared that Daud, a member of the Pushtun (Pathan) ethnic group, would try to annex Pushtun-inhabited areas of Pakistan to Afghanistan. Hekmatyar was defeated and fled to Pakistan, where he became the favorite Afghan of Inter-Service Intelligence (ISI), Pakistan's CIA.

When the CIA began its project of arming the Afghan resistance, it approached the ISI. The ISI introduced the agents to Hekmatyar, who all through the war got the bulk of U.S. aid. Recently, the U.S. government has expressed concern that some of the 2,000 Stinger ground-to-air missiles and launchers it gave to Hekmatyar may be used by Muslim fundamentalist terrorists to shoot down American airliners.

Hekmatyar was only one of a large number of guerrilla leaders, many of whom had much larger followings. But thanks to the CIA, he was the best armed. He used his weapons not only to fight the Russians but to acquire more opium land from other Afghans. He and Mullah Nasim fought an indecisive war when Hekmatyar attempted to seize the Mullah's land in the fertile Helmand Valley. Hekmatyar already had six heroin factories nearby. Nasim was killed, but Hekmatyar didn't get the land.

Although Hekmatyar was the ISI's pet, he didn't get all the CIA weapons. And all the guerrillas who got CIA weapons also got protection. As in Southeast Asia, if the CIA didn't know who was in the narcotics business, it would have been a very poor intelligence agency. But it said nothing to either the U.S. DEA or the Pakistani authorities. The DEA refused to meddle in anything that had CIA protection. And the Pakistani military made millions protecting Afghan and Pakistani dope dealers who shipped their products through Pakistan. Some of the heroin was even transported in Pakistan Army trucks. Pakistani Gen. Fazle Haq, commander of the Northwest Frontier province (and de facto director of the Afghan resistance), made several *billion* dollars during the war.

What might have happened had the DEA put pressure on the Pakistani authorities is shown by the case of Raza Qureshi, who was arrested in Norway with 3.5 kilograms of heroin. Qureshi, to get a lighter sentence, told what he knew. A Norwegian detective, Oyvind Olsen, flew to Pakistan and confirmed Qureshi's story. Norway's public prosecutor filed charges against three Pakistani heroin barons in September 1985. Pakistan's Federal Investigative Agency arrested them. On one man, Hamid Hasnain, a bank president, the agents found the personal financial records of President Mohammed Zia ul-Haq. Hasnain was a personal friend of the president and managed his finances. On the night of the arrest, Zia's wife called from Egypt, where she was vacationing, and demanded Hasnain's release. He was not released, and he stood trial in Pakistan. During the trial, he screamed death threats at Qureshi, the chief prosecution witness. When it looked as if the conclusion of the trial might be delayed, Norway lodged a formal protest. Hasnain was convicted and sent to prison.

All this happened in spite of the fact that when it comes to international clout, Norway ranks only slightly higher than Luxembourg.

Pakistani dealers shipped Middle Eastern heroin to both Europe and the United States. But there was too much. They couldn't get rid of it all in foreign markets. So they sold the rest to their own people. In 1980, there were an estimated 5,000 heroin users in Pakistan. Three years later, there were 70,000. And in 1986, there were more than 1.3 million. Pakistan's Narcotics Control Board called the situation "completely out of control."

Narcotics has become a Frankenstein's monster for Pakistan. The warlike Pushtun tribes of Pakistan's Northwest Frontier, having expanded their opium plantings, are not ready to cut back. They were a formidable foe when they had only single-shot rifles. Now, thanks to the war, they have automatic rifles, machine-guns, mortars, rocket-launchers, ground-to-ground and ground-to-air missiles and anti-aircraft guns.

"The government cannot stop us from growing poppy," said one Pushtun farmer. "We are one force, and united, and if they come to us with their planes, we will shoot them down."

And even if the government could destroy all the opium in Pakistan, the enormous Afghan crop could be easily smuggled across the mountainous, sparsely populated border.

5

The United States government, of course, denied that any of its allies were involved with drugs—even though the allies themselves admitted it.

The drug situation in many parts of the world is curious. Untouched by the propaganda of Richmond Hobson, heroin, cocaine and similar substances do not pose the moral issue they do for most Americans. To the Hmong and Pushtun tribesmen, opium is a cash crop which, for some mysterious reasons, governments say is illegal, although they cut themselves in on the profits. And the reason their governments have declared these drugs illegal is something most Americans don't understand—their own country's influence.

The United States is an enormous country. It's the world's third largest in population and third largest in area. It is without any question the world's richest. This powerful American influence is not a post-World War II development. It's been a fact for a century. When the United States campaigns as long and hard for something as it has for the banning of opiates and cocaine, it gets results — even if the results are laws that are widely ignored.

In our country, though, the dope fiend image is alive and well. Government officials believe they can't afford to admit that our allies are in the business of creating more dope fiends. Still less can they admit that because they ally themselves with dope dealers, those dealers are automatically protected.

But they won't stop working with drug traffickers in covert operations. Traffickers, by their nature, are always in covert operations. Nobody knows the territory better. This has been true for many years in Latin America.

And in Latin America, U.S. involvement with illicit drugs has been more intimate than in other parts of the world, and attempts to cover up that intimacy far more strenuous. Denials have come not from almost-anonymous functionaries in the CIA and the State Department but from officials in the highest levels of government. Nor has the whitewash stopped with denials. Cover-up methods have included character assassination, malicious prosecution and murder.

11

In national politics, as in the territorial street gang milieu, nothing strengthens leadership like an external threat. For decades, American leaders were able to rally the populace against the threat of international Communism. Then Richard Nixon decided to recognize the biggest Communist power, China. His aim was probably to split the Communist bloc headed by the Soviet Union. A desire for a new market may have been a secondary aim. Nixon may also have wanted to end the supreme silliness of pretending that a nation of a billion people did not exist. But the act did reduce the perceived Communist threat by offering friendship to the only large Communist nation we've ever seriously fought.

Then, during the administration of Ronald Reagan, the Communist world began to change. Reagan held friendly talks with Mikhail Gorbachev, who led what Reagan had called "the evil empire." During the administration of George Bush, the Soviet Union itself broke up. The Warsaw Pact countries of Eastern Europe changed from "captive nations" to independent, and sometimes even democratic, republics.

The end of the Cold War brought all kinds of problems for Americans—from writers of spy thrillers to builders of nuclear submarines. Seriously affected were military leaders, the "intelligence community" and the presidency itself.

As the Evil Empire turned benign, Ronald Reagan discerned a new threat that would preserve some of the old values. Polls in the early '80s showed that the American public saw illegal drugs as the greatest threat to the country. And although the Soviet Union might be reforming, there were unregenerate Communist subversives and guerrillas everywhere, especially in Latin America. The Carter Administration was notably cool to the revolutionary Sandinistas who had seized power in Nicaragua and turned to the U.S.S.R. for support. Reagan was positively frigid. He saw Nicaragua as a Communist beachhead on the American mainland.

The U.S. public might not get excited about a leftist government that had ousted a brutal dictator in a country with a population the size of Connecticut's. But suppose it and other leftist countries were linked with drugs?

As Spitz Channell and Richard Miller, two conservative fund-raisers, put it, "the chance to have a single issue with which no one can publicly disagree is irresistible."

In a *Military Review* article, Col. John D. Waghelstein of the U.S Army Special Forces wrote:

> Congress would find it difficult to stand in the way of support-
> ing our allies with the training, advice and security assistance
> necessary to do the job. Those church and academic groups
> that have slavishly supported insurgency in Latin America
> would find themselves on the wrong side of the moral issue.

Ronald Reagan kicked off the campaign to explain the narcoterrorist threat. The president said, "The link between the governments of such Soviet allies as Cuba and Nicaragua and international narcotics trafficking and terrorism is becoming increasingly clear. These twin evils—narcotics trafficking and terrorism—represent the most insidious and dangerous threats to the hemisphere today."

Events were to prove that Reagan was at least half right. He made only one error.

He put the narcoterrorists on the wrong side.

2

The situation began to develop soon after the Cuban revolution, when Santo Trafficante, Jr. added scores of Cuban exiles to his organization. Not long after that, both Trafficante and the Cubans were co-opted by a bigger organization—the Central Intelligence Agency. The CIA approached Trafficante and a couple of other Mob types, Sam Giancana and John Roselli, to tell them it would be a great service to their country if they could arrange the assassination of Fidel Castro. Some thirty-three plans for assassinating or embarrassing Castro were devised: His daily milkshake would be poisoned; he would smoke a poisoned cigar; he would be given an exploding seashell. In one scenario, some daring soul would sprinkle a powder on his boots that would make his beard fall out while he spoke on television. While some of the country's biggest mobsters were thus demonstrating the fatuousness of the supposedly all-powerful Mafia, Trafficante's Cubans joined more of their exiled countrymen in the military organization that would launch the Bay of Pigs fiasco.

The CIA's performance over the years may indicate a lack of some desirable qualities. One quality it did not lack, though, was persistence. After the Bay of Pigs failure, Cuban exiles, with the agency's encouragement, continued to launch commando raids on their homeland. They killed few military personnel but a lot of civilians. Some of their actions could only be described as stark terrorism. The exiles formed an organization, CORU (Commando of United Revolutionary Organizations), to coordinate attacks. In the first ten months of CORU's existence, its agents set off some 50 bombs in Miami, New York, Venezuela, Panama, Argentina and Mexico. One bomb went off in a Cuban airliner, killing all 73 passengers, including the Cuban Olympic fencing team. Luis Posada Carriles, an agent of both the CIA and the Venezuelan DISIP, was arrested in Venezuela for the bombing. When arrested, he was carrying papers that linked him to the assassination of former Chilean ambassador Orlando Letelier in Washington a month before the airliner bomb. He quietly walked out of jail under mysterious circumstances. Years later, another exile, Ricardo Morales, would claim that he had planned the airliner bombing at the Cia's request.

After he became president, Lyndon Johnson said he was ending "the damned Murder, Inc. down there in the Caribbean" that the Kennedys had been running. Their CIA subsidies curtailed, the Cuban exiles found new sources of money.

Those who had joined Trafficante had made important contacts in the United States, including people who knew how to make a profit from illegal goods. Their CIA association led to other contacts in Latin America, including people who produced illegal goods. As they raided Castro's Cuba now, the exiles helped finance their operations by bringing heroin, cocaine and marijuana into the United States. And, as had happened to the smugglers in Vietnam and Pakistan, the fact that they were helping the CIA gave them protection.

Some of the smuggling organizations themselves had powerful friends. A heavy contributor to CORU, for instance, was the World Finance Corporation, a financial conglomerate and drug-trafficking front associated with the Trafficante organization. According to a congressional staff report, the company engaged in "a large body of criminal activity, including aspects of political corruption, gun-running, as well as narcotics trafficking on an international level." WFC's friends included members of the Miami circle of Richard Nixon and Bebe Rebozo as well as the Washington and Atlanta associates of Jimmy Carter. That does not mean, of course, that either president was directly influenced by the WFC, or that either was even aware of the organization's existence. Nevertheless, WFC had some interesting connections. Its founder, Guillermo Hernández Cartaya, served on the board of Jefferson Savings and Loan, founded by then-Senator Lloyd Bentsen, Jr., his father and his brother Donald. In 1976, two years after he took a seat on Jefferson's board, Hernández bought the S&L from Lloyd Bentsen, Sr. The senator said he had sold his share in the enterprise before it was associated with Hernández and did not know the man. Hernández was convicted of bank fraud in 1982. Previously, he and WFC had been investigated for narcotics violations and other crimes, but the investigation produced nothing more than an income tax indictment of Hernández. Assistant U.S. Attorney R. Jerome Sanford resigned in disgust because the CIA had quashed the narcotics investigation. Later, he tried to obtain the FBI's files on CIA connections with WFC but was refused on the grounds of national security. The CIA did acknowledge that it had twenty-four documents relating to World Finance. At least twelve WFC employees had been connected with the CIA, and one of Hernández's six co-founders was Walter Sterling Surrey, an OSS veteran described as "a charter member of the old boy network of U.S. intelligence." Dade County, Florida, investigated the WFC, and the head of the investigation said that one subsidiary of the conglomerate was "nothing but a CIA front."

On June 21, 1970, agents of the Bureau of Narcotics and Dangerous Drugs arrested Juan Restoy, a former Cuban congressman and veteran anti-Castro guerrilla who was also a veteran of the Trafficante organization; his partner, Mario Escandar, another guerrilla and career drug smuggler; and 150 other suspects in cities all over the U.S. The Justice Department said it had broken up "a nationwide ring of wholesalers handling 30 percent of all heroin sales and 75 to 80 percent of all cocaine sales in the United States." Restoy was killed in an attempt to escape, but the case against Escandar and the others was thrown out. Escandar then became an "untouchable" drug lord who used Miami detectives to arrest his enemies and collect his debts.

In October 1972, Richard Helms, director of central intelligence, loaned Lucien Conein to the BNDD. "Black Luigi," the Vietnam Corsicans' favorite American, established an intelligence unit in the Narcotics Bureau. Conein's Miami operation, called DEACON 1, concentrated not on drug dealers but on "extremist groups and terrorism of a political nature." DEACON 1 undoubtedly helped the CIA, but its intelligence did not contribute to convicting a single drug ring. Its activities, though, did lead the newly formed DEA to write regulations regarding "the level of drug trafficking permissible for an asset [an informant or agent]."

Most notorious of the factions in the CORU umbrella organization was the Cuban Nationalist Movement, which had strong links with the Chilean secret police as well as with the CIA. In 1978, two CNM members, Alvin Ross and Guillermo Novo, were arrested in Miami on suspicion of complicity in the Letelier murder. When arrested, Ross was carrying a large bag of cocaine. In Novo's company was a notorious drug dealer, Manuel Menéndez. Although wanted on federal drug charges, Menéndez was allowed to walk away because, supposedly, no one had checked his record. Menéndez was connected to a CIA-protected network in Mexico run by Alberto Sicilia Falcón, a Cuban exile. The Sicilia network had taken over the Latin American territory of Auguste Ricord, leader of the defunct Corsican group described in Robin Moore's *The French Connection*. Through most of the '70s, until the rise of the Colombian cocaine syndicates, cocaine smuggling was firmly in Cuban hands. Some of the still-unorganized Colombians managed to squeeze in, but Luciano's old federation was simply bypassed in the smuggling end of the operation, and frequently in the internal distribution end as well.

3

The Cubans went about their business relatively unnoticed. Such notoriety as they had came not from their drug dealings but from their raids on Cuba. (Or out of Cuba—one exile attack was a bazooka shot at the United Nations building in New York.) Most of the drug news in the early '70s concerned heroin addiction among the troops in Vietnam and the spread of heroin use in the United States.

When Ronald Reagan entered the White House, he refocused attention on Latin America, particularly on Nicaragua and its revolution. When Nicaraguan President Anastacio Somoza Debayle fled the country, members of the Nicaraguan National Guard also fled rather than face the wrath of the Sandinistas (named after Augusto Sandino, who had fought the American occupiers early in the century). These "Somocistas" ended up in Honduras, where they tried to organize a counterrevolutionary movement.

The right-wing military clique that was running Argentina offered to help them. Gen. Carlos Suárez Mason, head of Argentina's joint chiefs of staff, was a disciple of José López Rega, a Rasputin-like figure who was in charge of the police and ran the Argentine Anticommunist Alliance (death squad sponsors) after the second coming of Juan Perón. On the side, Lopez headed an extensive drug-trafficking network. When the Perón government was overthrown again, López Rega went into exile. Suárez Mason, however, continued to rise in the army. He became one of the most notorious practitioners in the late '70s of the "dirty war"—the kidnapping, torture, murder and disappearance of Argentine civilians. Like López Rega, he was a member of the infamous Italian Masonic Lodge P2 (*Propaganda Due*), which was involved with crooked banking and drug trafficking and was, according to Antonio Troccoli, Argentina's interior minister in 1986, "an enormous criminal conspiracy which aimed to take power in the country."

Suárez Mason was one of the prime movers of a coup that took place in Bolivia on July 17, 1980. Another prime mover, according to Michael Levine, a former middle-ranking DEA agent, was the CIA. The CIA, at this time, had no particular love for drug traffickers, but it hated leftist governments. It considered the Bolivian government leftist. The putsch (it included neo-Nazi German mercenaries) was called the "Cocaine Coup," because it was financed by Bolivia's leading coca growers, cocaine processors and smugglers. The new interior minister, Luis Arce Gómez, a cousin of Bolivia's top cocaine trafficker, Roberto Suárez, released convicted drug smugglers from prison and enlisted them in his paramilitary unit, led by Nazi war criminal Klaus Barbie. Barbie, known during World War II as the Butcher of Lyon, was an SS officer smuggled out of Germany by American intelligence. His South American storm troopers, *Los Novios de la Muerte*, composed of mercenaries from all over the western world, had spearheaded the Cocaine Coup and massacred scores of people, most of whom had nothing to do with the government being overthrown.

It's pleasant to record that both Arce Gómez and Barbie eventually fell from grace and were extradited—Arce Gómez to the United States and Barbie to France. Both are expected to end their lives in prison. It was not always thus. Just before the Cocaine Coup, DEA agents arrested José Roberto Gasser, whose father helped finance preparations for the coup, and Gasser's associate, Alfredo Gutierrez. Both were released without indictment. Michael Sullivan, U.S. attorney for Southern Florida, said he didn't have enough evidence to ask for an indictment, although Michael Levine, the street agent in charge of the case, had eyewitnesses and tape-recorded confessions. Levine reports that DEA headquarters people told him they didn't even have Suárez, Bolivia's "boss of all bosses" and leader of the traffickers behind the coup, in their computer files.

A month and a half after the Cocaine Coup, Suárez Mason (the Argentine general, not the Bolivian gangster) hosted a victory party at a meeting of the Latin American Anticommunist Confederation, known by its Spanish initials, CAL, an affiliate of the World Anti-Communist League. One of the guests was Roberto D'Aubuisson, the Salvadoran death squad leader who had allegedly ordered the assassination of Archbishop Oscar Romero six months previously.

The Argentine military had already trained many members of the Nicaraguan National Guard in the fine arts of torture and subversion repression. These connections and common membership in the CAL and the WACL made Argentina's connection with the exiled *contrarevolucionarios* (*Contras* for short) natural. The Reagan Administration was delighted to have Argentina take up the Contra cause. The United States could support the Argentinians and not be accused of intervening in the affairs of another American country. The Argentinians didn't need that much support. The Cocaine Coup gave them plenty of experience in financing a revolution with drug money. And the drug networks run by Cuban exiles had the same political interests as the Argentinians.

Meanwhile, a Sandinista hero, Edén Pastora Gómez, was having second thoughts about the government he was in. During the revolution, Pastora, who called himself *Commandante Cero* (Zero), had led a handful of men (and one woman, his second in command, twenty-two-year-old Dora Maria Tellez) into the national capitol. He captured the entire Somocista Chamber of Deputies. Somoza had to release all his Sandinista prisoners, pay the Sandinistas a half-million dollars (all the money available, Somoza said) and publish rebel communiqués. Pastora then went off to southern Nicaragua, where he opened the "Southern Front."

After the Sandinista triumph, Pastora was given a post in the government where he had little say on policy. Unlike the dominant faction of the Sandinistas, he was no Marxist. He grew dissatisfied, and in 1982, he quit the government and moved to the south, where he again opened a "Southern Front," using his old base, Costa Rica. Pastora's situation was to cause some problems for the Reagan Administration. After the United States took over aid to the Contras from Argentina, some members of the administration objected to giving aid to Pastora. The official reason for U.S. involvement at the time was to prevent the Sandinistas from sending guns to the rebels in El Salvador, and Pastora's position in southern Nicaragua (actually in Costa Rica) was nowhere near the border of El Salvador. The objectors were overruled, however, and Commandante Cero received CIA help for the next two years, until another problem appeared.

4

The Argentine-Contra operation went smoothly, although the Contras accomplished little, until the Falkland Islands War. Then the Argentine military learned that killing civilians provides little training for fighting an armed enemy. A smaller and less well-armed British force thoroughly trounced the Argentine army, navy and air force. The British tried to limit the damage their forces did, but they did have intelligence help from the United States. The U.S. administration wisely decided that however much the Argentinians agreed with it on Nicaragua, if the United States were involved in a war, the British would be infinitely more valuable allies. The Argentine generals and admirals were immediately deposed after the war. It seems that while some nations will put up with extended periods of tyranny, none will put up with leaders who have lost a war.

That led to a second phase in the sponsorship of the Contras. Now they received aid directly from the CIA. Duane "Dewey" Clarridge, chief of "the company's" Latin American operations, ran the show. The reason for aiding the Contras, according to Reagan Administration spokesmen, was to cut the supply of arms from the Sandinista government to the rebels in El Salvador. There was undoubtedly some gun-running on a small scale. Some weapons were intercepted. But they were intercepted by Salvadoran and Honduran police—not one gun was found by the Contras.

In fact, David MacMichael, the senior CIA analyst on the subject, stated publicly, "The whole picture that the Administration has presented of Salvadoran insurgent operations being planned, directed and supplied from Nicaragua is simply not true. There has not been a successful interdiction, or a verified report, of arms moving from Nicaragua to El Salvador since April, 1981."

The arms-interdiction excuse raised doubts in the United States. Besides, the Salvadoran government forces, which massacred hundreds of helpless peasants and a group of American nuns and their assistants, were not popular.

Then the CIA mined Nicaraguan harbors. Even Sen. Barry Goldwater, "Mr. Conservative," protested. He wrote to CIA chief William Casey, "I've been trying to figure out how I can most easily tell you my feelings about the discovery of the President having approved mining some of the harbors of Central America. It gets down to one, little, simple phrase: I am pissed off."

In 1984, Congress passed the first Boland Amendment, which forbade any government assistance to the Nicaraguan rebels. Direct control of the Contras by the CIA ended. In its place, the Contras got indirect control and assistance from a group coordinated by a young marine lieutenant colonel named Oliver North. North was a regular marine officer attached to the National Security Council, and many in his Contra-aiding organization were federal employees. The organization, though, was not part of the government. In 1986, a new Republican-dominated Congress heeded Ronald Reagan, who called the Contras "freedom fighters" and compared them to the United States' Founding Fathers. It reinstated government aid to the Contras.

Each phase of the Contra operation developed a relationship with different drug-smuggling networks. Or at least, with the heads of those networks—the so-called kingpins. When a kingpin was arrested or otherwise neutralized, his followers regrouped in a new network. For example, during the Argentine phase, the drug network headed by Aristides Sánchez sold drugs to finance the Nicaraguan rebels. As soon as the CIA took control, the Sanchez gang apparently lost its protection. It was broken in 1983, a month after the CIA installed Adolfo Calero as civilian head of the Northern Front Contras, by a major drug bust in San Francisco. It was replaced by another organization headed by Manuel Noriega, of Panama, and his Israeli confidant, Mike Harari, a former (perhaps) Mossad agent. Noriega, at the time, was a valued CIA asset. His involvement in the drug trade was largely for personal profit, rather than the good of the Contras, but the CIA tolerated his smuggling because of his other services. In the spring of 1984, the CIA cut off aid to Edén Pastora, who had refused to unite his forces with those of his former enemies, the Somocistas in the Northern Front. At the same time, the first Boland Amendment forbade U.S. government aid to the Contras. Noriega's network was replaced by that of George Morales, a Florida-based Colombian and indicted drug smuggler, who was nevertheless allowed to travel freely in the United States and abroad. Morales later said that after he was indicted, he had been approached by Octaviano César, a CIA operative, to aid in supplying the Contras. Morales did so both because he sympathized with the Contras and because he hoped his trial would be dropped or at least delayed. Morales and Floyd Carlton, a Panamanian who was Noriega's personal pilot, were arrested in 1986, after U.S. government aid to the Contras became legal. Oliver North changed the arrangements for Contra resupply. Replacing Morales was a group of Cuban exiles with strong CIA ties. Among them were Felipe Vidal, René Corvo, Francisco Chanes and Moises Nuñez. All were widely believed—and with good reason—to be dope dealers. Vidal would later play a sinister part in connection with the Southern Front.

The protection of these various factions of drug-runners was so blatant that the Senate Foreign Relations Committee Subcommittee on Terrorism, Narcotics and International Operations reported that not only was there "substantial evidence of drug smuggling through the war zones by individual Contras, Contra suppliers, Contra pilots, mercenaries who worked with the Contras and Contra supporters through-out the region," but U.S. officials were helping the smugglers, at least passively. "U.S. officials involved in Central America failed to address the drug issue for fear of jeopardizing the war efforts against Nicara-gua," the subcommittee's investigation showed. In each of the smug-gling cases the subcommittee looked into, it reported, "one or another agency of the U.S. Government had information either while it was oc-curring, or immediately thereafter." The reason appeared to be that "senior U.S. policy makers were not immune to the idea that drug money was a perfect solution to the Contras' funding problems."

5

The Reagan Administration made heroic efforts to keep the Contra-co-caine connection out of the public eye. Nevertheless, rumors were in-creasing. The administration was delighted, then, with the news from Colombia in March 1984. The Colombian syndicates had become in-creasingly powerful. Colombians had already, in 1979–80, fought a bloody war in Miami with Cuban exiles for the major share of the U.S. market.

Colombian police, aided by DEA-supplied beepers on ether barrels, raided an enormous cocaine lab in the jungle village of Tranquilandia. They were fired on by uniformed men, and after they landed from heli-copters, they reported they found evidence that Colombia's Marxist re-bels had been on the site. Destroying that much cocaine and cocaine processing equipment was, of course, welcome news. But what really made the administration rejoice was news of the cooperation between the drug smugglers and the guerrillas. The cocaine cartels in the past had been notably anti-guerrilla. After the guerrillas kidnapped Marta Ochoa, daughter of cocaine baron Fabio Ochoa in 1982, the trafficking families had contributed millions to establish an organization of profes-sional killers called *Muerte a Secuestradores*—"Death to Kidnappers." MAS promptly began killing guerrillas. The traffickers continued fund-ing MAS and later contributed to other right-wing death squads outside of Colombia. In 1983, the guerrillas raided a cocaine laboratory, seized eighteen people and four planes and held them for $450,000 ransom. Several days later, the hostages and two of the planes were freed by the Colombian Army.

U.S. Ambassador Lewis Tambs, an arch-conservative believer in a leftist-narcotics connection, loudly proclaimed that Tranquilandia proved it. Neither the DEA or even the CIA would fully support that conclusion, though. If there were, in fact, any guerrillas at Tranquilandia, it was probably an alliance of expedience between local leaders. The drug traffickers were probably paying local guerrillas for protection.

Then Barry Seal appeared.

6

Adler Berriman "Barry" Seal, also known as *El Gordo* (he weighed 300 pounds) and by a dozen other aliases, was one of the world's top drug pilots. He also ran one of the country's largest smuggling organizations. He owned several planes and had a stable of pilots. When he was twenty-six, Seal was the youngest airliner captain in the history of TWA. But ordinary flying was too dull for El Gordo. He craved thrills. He became a contract pilot for the CIA and was arrested in 1972 as he was about to take off in a plane loaded with explosives. The cargo, he said, was destined for Cuban exiles in Mexico. That adventure ended in a mistrial when two of the government witnesses failed to appear. Seal was fired by TWA and went to work full-time for the CIA. Still unable to resist a profitable sideline, he decided to take advantage of the enormous payoffs possible by flying drugs. (He could make as much as $1.5 million for a single run.) By 1977, he was a full-time doper, but training Contra pilots as a sideline.

In 1981, Jorge Ochoa, one of the Medellín Ochoas, contracted with Seal to handle transportation of his family's product. Seal charged $3,000 to $5,000 a kilogram just to move the coke from one place to another. The Ochoas thought he was worth it, though. Through his use of aliases, by making all calls from pay phones and general shiftiness, Seal managed his transportation empire for years without DEA agents suspecting that he was anything other than a run-of-the-mill drug pilot. Then he made a mistake and got convicted of smuggling a planeload of Quaaludes into the country. Facing ten years in prison, he tried to turn informer for the government.

Everyone in Miami and New Orleans knew Seal to be a consummate liar. Neither the DEA nor the U.S. attorneys would listen to him.

Out on appeal bond, Seal flew to Washington and telephoned the office of Vice President George Bush, Reagan's "drug czar." Seal was soon back in business. Bush, of course, was a former director of central intelligence. Seal's appeal to Bush and his later exploits in Nicaragua lend further credence to Leslie Cockburn's assertion that the drug pilot was "well known in the [drug] trade for his ties with the CIA."

He told the DEA that the Ochoas and Pablo Escobar Gaviria, who gloried in the nickname *El Padrino*—"the Godfather"—wanted him to fly 3,500 kilos (about 7,716 pounds) of cocaine to Louisiana. The dumbfounded DEA agents had never heard of such a large shipment. They were even more amazed when Seal told them he had already moved more than 30,000 kilos into the United States and had been paid $75 million. He told them the Ochoas wanted a big score to make up their losses at Tranquilandia and recoup thefts by the corrupt Bahamian police. The government agreed to take on Seal as an informant.

Seal flew to Colombia and, using his usual alias in that country, Ellis MacKenzie, visited Jorge Ochoa. As Seal later reported, Ochoa told him the family was planning to build an airstrip in Nicaragua so planes from Colombia could refuel. If they carried less fuel, they could carry more cocaine.

"You're dealing with Communists?" asked a horrified "MacKenzie."

"No, no, no. We are not Communists," Ochoa said. "We don't particularly like their political philosophy, but they serve our interests and we serve theirs."

According to the plan, Seal would fly the first 1,500 kilos to the United States. Then he would come back to the Nicaragua airstrip and pick up the next 2,000 kilos. Seal was to make the first flight in ten days.

Then there was a delay. In revenge for the Tranquilandia raid, the cartels had murdered Colombian Justice Minister Rodrigo Lara Bonilla. The government responded with more heat than the traffickers had ever known. All the leaders fled to Panama. Seal met them in Panama to refine plans for the 3,500–kilo shipment. The Ochoas and Escobar were there, along with Gonzalo Rodríguez Gacha, another top cartel leader, and a Nicaraguan who was introduced as Federico Vaughan. Vaughan said he was an assistant to Tomás Borge, the Sandinista interior minister.

Seal and Vaughan flew to Nicaragua, occupying distant seats on the same plane. Seal stayed at Vaughan's house, and the next day Vaughan took him to the airfield, carefully pointing out areas that it was forbidden to fly over. Seal returned to Panama and learned that the Colombians were planning to build a cocaine lab near the airstrip. Seal should first fly the 1,500 kilos to the States, Escobar said, then go to Peru and pick up 6,000 kilos of cocaine paste for the Nicaraguan lab.

At the Ochoas' airstrip, there was another mishap. It had been raining for several days, and Seal doubted he could get the heavily loaded plane into the air. Carlos Lehder, the cocaine biggie guarding the airstrip, pointed an automatic rifle at Seal's ample belly and told him to try. He tried. He crashed. He had to take a smaller plane with a lighter load and stop at Nicaragua for refueling.

He met Vaughan at the airstrip in Los Brasiles without trouble. Refueling took longer than he expected, and Seal got lost in the dark. A Sandinista anti-aircraft gun hit his plane, and he was forced down at the Augusto César Sandino Airport. Sandinista police arrested him. He asked for Vaughan and was allowed to make one phone call. He called the number Vaughan had given him, and the Nicaraguan official told him not to worry. The next day, Seal was out of detention and meeting Pablo Escobar in an hacienda near Managua. Vaughan had managed to get all the cocaine out of the downed plane and stored safely.

Seal went home and bought a big surplus C–123K military cargo plane. The DEA rigged it with hidden cameras. Back in Nicaragua, Seal snapped pictures of what he said was Vaughan and Escobar loading the plane. Seal took the plane back to Homestead Air Force Base, landing early in the morning of June 26, 1984, as arranged with the DEA. Under U.S. law, the DEA had to seize the cocaine. But if the Colombians learned that 700 kilos of cocaine had been seized, the DEA would lose its chance to lure the cocaine barons somewhere they could be arrested. What they did was to arrange an auto accident. A DEA car hit the van carrying the off-loaded cocaine, and local police ''discovered'' a load of cocaine in the van. The sting was undiscovered. Escobar talked to Seal on the telephone. On his next trip south, El Padrino asked, would Seal bring $1.5 million to pay off the Sandinistas for use of the airstrip? The DEA was jubilant. It looked like the beginning of the bust of the century.

Then Oliver North entered the scene.

The bumptious lieutenant colonel knew all about Seal's mission. When he heard Seal was taking a million and a half dollars to Escobar, he asked why the pilot couldn't land somewhere north of Managua and give it to the Contras instead. The DEA agents almost had apoplexy, and North withdrew the suggestion. But then he leaked the whole caper to the right-leaning *Washington Times*, adding that Seal had pictures of Escobar and Vaughan loading cocaine. Some suspicious parties, such as the Senate subcommittee chaired by Sen. John Kerry, of Massachusetts, thought that North was attempting to influence an impending Senate vote on Contra aid. At any rate, the DEA didn't get a chance to make the bust of the century, but Oliver North got some headlines supporting Reagan's commie-narcoterrorist thesis.

North's propaganda triumph was short-lived. First, the pictures showed two men, but that was all anyone could be sure of. Gen. Paul Gorman of the U.S. Southern Command, said they showed Vaughan and Ochoa. Richard Gregorie, the federal prosecutor who used Seal as a witness, said under oath they "caught Jorge Ochoa and Gonzalo Rodríguez Gacha loading cocaine onto an airplane." According to authors Peter Dale Scott and Jonathan Marshall, a "veteran of the Contra scene, who has proved reliable on other matters," said the pictures weren't even taken in Nicaragua but on an airstrip on Corn Island in the Caribbean.

Then there was trouble identifying who Federico Vaughan was. Although he apparently had some authority, he was not a top-ranking Sandinista. The CIA described him as "an aide to Borge" but offered no proof other than Vaughan's statement. Most troubling, the telephone number Seal used to call Vaughan was, according to a senatorial subcommittee investigating narcotics trafficking in Central America (the Kerry subcommittee) "a phone number controlled by the U.S. embassy since 1985, and by the U.S. and other foreign missions continuously since 1981."

Federico Vaughan appears to have been a CIA "asset."

Whoever Seal's camera may have caught, and wherever it may have caught them, one thing was clear. What he did would not please the Medellín cartel. On February 19, 1986, two Colombians walked up to Seal's white Cadillac in a Baton Rouge parking lot and riddled the thrill-loving pilot with a submachine gun. Barry Seal had had his last adventure.

While the Seal episode was coming to its gory end, a far bloodier and more mysterious series of events had begun in southern Nicaragua and was extending up into the United States.

12

It was a hot, sunny (as usual) morning on May 30, 1984 in San José, Costa Rica, when two dozen broadcasting and print journalists boarded a fleet of cars and jeeps and headed for the Nicaragua border. Edén Pastora had called a news conference at his camp over the border.

For the last few weeks, Pastora had been doing little but watching his army melt away. He had refused to put himself under the command of Adolfo Calero and Enrique Bermúdez, who led the Contras on the Northern Front. To make him change his mind, the CIA had been squeezing off his supplies. It was important to the Americans that he join the other Contras. His independence was a standing reminder that Enrique Bermúdez, military commander of the Northern Front, had been a colonel in Somoza's National Guard. In other words, that leader of "freedom fighters" had spent most of his career fighting freedom— killing protesters and torturing dissenters. Pastora's calling attention to that didn't help the Reagan Administration sell the idea of helping the Contras to the U.S. Congress or public. If Pastora didn't join by today, the CIA let it be known, he'd have to face the consequences. One of Pastora's lieutenants, Alfonso Robelo, had already defected to the Calero-Bermúdez faction, along with a majority of Pastora's troops.

The news conference, the journalists expected, would be to announce Pastora's decision. Nobody expected the independent "Commandante Cero" to join his old enemy, Bermúdez. But the Southern Front was already so fractured it was probably irrelevant to the Contra movement. Tony Avirgan, a freelance reporter/cameraman stringing for ABC News, was coming, but his wife, Martha Honey, was back in San José working on a story for the *New York Times* about the expiration of the CIA ultimatum to Pastora. Linda Frazier, who had just returned to journalism, represented the *Tico Times*, Costa Rica's English-language paper. Her husband, Joe, was on assignment in Managua, covering a story for a wire service. Their ten-year-old son was with a baby-sitter in San José. The press people were a fairly clubby group, except for Per Anker Hansen, a freelance Danish photographer who was working with a Swedish TV crew. The Swedish film maker tried to talk to him in Danish, but Hansen explained that he had been raised in Latin America and didn't know Danish. He spoke English and Spanish, but he spoke both with a marked foreign accent. Peter Torbiornsson, the Swedish filmmaker, said he talked to "Hansen" mostly in English and that "his Spanish was forced," as if he were trying to hide an accent. Hansen was something of a mystery. His wallet was always stuffed with U.S. $100 bills, and he knew nothing of the most popular Danish brands of beer. Hansen didn't mix well with the other reporters. He gave most of his attention to his camera and his big aluminum gadget case.

It was twilight when the journalists got in outboard-powered dugout canoes for the trip upriver to the jungle hamlet of La Penca. When they got to Pastora's hut, it had started to rain, and the guerrilla leader said it was too late. The journalists protested, and Pastora began explaining why he would not join. "The CIA will have to kill me first," he had told a television interviewer the day before.

Per Hansen put his gadget case on the floor near Pastora, snapped a few pictures, muttered something about his camera not working and backed away from the crowd.

There was a tremendous flash and a deafening bang.

"It was a human whirlwind. Blood splashed against the walls; people flew through the windows," recalled José Venegas, a Costa Rican photographer. "Someone screamed, 'Save me, help me, don't leave me here!' All I knew was that hell was there on the edge of the San Juan River."

After the explosion, there was a chorus of moans in the darkened, shattered hut. Eight persons, five of Pastora's men and three reporters, lay dead or mortally wounded. Twenty-six other soldiers and reporters were wounded. Pastora was only slightly wounded. His men rushed him away immediately. He gave no orders to help the other wounded.

Reid Miller, of the Associated Press, reported, "Many of Mr. Pastora's men stood with their rifles slung, offering no help to the wounded and seemingly stunned. Many of the wounded, like myself, had crawled or stumbled from the building and were sitting or lying on the muddy riverbank.''

Linda Frazier was not able to crawl. She lay on the floor, slowly bleeding to death.

"Linda Frazier was pulled from the house almost an hour after the explosion and laid on a blanket nearby," Miller wrote in his dispatch. "Mortally wounded, she was to lie there another two hours before help came—a doctor and two nurses dressed in the green fatigues of Mr. Pastora's Revolutionary Democratic Alliance [ARDE]. She and all the other wounded received an injection of antibiotics but little else. At one point I crawled over to her, unable to walk because of shrapnel wounds in my right leg. She took my hand, and I could see that she was talking to me, but I could not hear her words because the explosion had left me temporarily deaf.''

Tony Avirgan later recalled, "I was just sitting on a box, actually not far from where the bomb was planted, drinking a cup of coffee. And I mean, it's not even nice to think about, but one of the reasons I wasn't killed was because there was another journalist [Linda Frazier], a good friend, who was standing right in front of me and she took the major impact of the blast and she was killed. I remember it very clearly. . . . What was most horrible was not being able to help the other people who were injured and dying, to spend almost the whole night there just lying on the ground with others who were slowly dying next to me and just not being able to do anything for them.''

News of the bombing got out quickly. At 8 P.M. as Linda Frazier lay on the floor of the ruined house, San José television was reporting the attack. A helicopter delivery of rubber boats and medical supplies could have saved Frazier's life. But the American embassy sent no help. John Hull, who had U.S. and Costa Rican citizenship and who owned a huge ranch on the border, was famous for his hospitality to Contras. But even though he had two airplanes, he sent no help. Hull blamed the weather, but the rain had stopped by midnight. Rob Owen, Oliver North's representative, was meeting with Hull, but he claimed he hadn't even heard about the bombing.

Owen later testified that at about 3:30 A.M., three of Pastora's men woke Hull and asked him to pick up the wounded. Hull called a man identified as Phil Holtz, who advised him not to go. At 5 A.M., Owen testified, Hull called Bill Crone, another American who had a plane available, and asked him not to go "because it may be a trap, or I might get in trouble, or something."

Sometime the following morning, rescue personnel arrived and began to take the wounded to the hospital in Ciudad Quesada. Tony Avirgan had a mangled right hand, "a big hole ripped out of my side," numerous wounds from bomb fragments and severe burns over much of his body. He was incapacitated for two months.

Per Anker Hansen was outside, "to take a leak," he said, when the bomb went off. He showed no signs of injury. When he appeared at the hospital, though, he had two shallow cuts on his arms. He sat in a wheelchair asking everyone he saw for information about Pastora's condition. Then he went back to San José and disappeared.

Even before her husband recovered, Martha Honey began investigating the bombing. Avirgan joined her as soon as he was able to.

Before they could even start, U.S. officials, Costa Rican security officers, Contra leaders and agents of Manuel Antonio Noriega were offering explanations. Stories appeared in the press blaming the Sandinistas, the Basque separatist group *Euzkadi Ta Azkatasuna* (ETA), the German Red Army Faction, the Italian Red Brigades and even the victims of the bombing. Arturo Cruz, Jr., son of a major Contra leader who was being paid by both the State Department and the White House and was the boyfriend of Oliver North's secretary, Fawn Hall, called Linda Frazier the ETA agent who had planted the bomb. The U.S. ambassador to Costa Rica, Curtin Winsor, Jr., implied that Avirgan was involved in the bomb plot.

"Other diplomats, not myself, of course, are saying that Tony has ties to the ETA," said Winsor. No other diplomats were saying anything of the kind. Because of that remark by America's chief representative in Costa Rica, Avirgan was not flown to the United States for treatment for many days after the bombing. Later, an unnamed U.S. official told the *New York Times*, "The ETA [involvement] was launched on the streets to cause confusion."

No one seemed to ask these officials what the Spanish Basques could gain by planting a bomb 4,000 miles from their homeland in a place where local troubles blotted out any possible concerns about Europe.

"A year's worth of interviews with more than one hundred people in Central and South America, failed to uncover the bomber's name or many of the details of the plot," Avirgan and Honey wrote later in the *Nation*. "We did, however, gather proof that U.S. officials and Costa Rican security officers planted stories in the press, pinning the blame on the Sandinistas and the Basque separatist organization, Euzkadi Ta Azkatasuna (E.T.A.). A number of leads also pointed to Central Intelligence Agency participation in the bombing. Several current or former CIA agents and informants—including a high-ranking Uruguayan police officer and a Cuban from Miami—told us that the agency was behind it." In their investigation, the journalists reported, several names came up repeatedly. Among them were John Hull, Felipe Vidal and "a high-ranking official in the Costa Rican Ministry of Public Security."

Costa Rican authorities, meanwhile, identified the bomber as the supposed Danish photographer, Per Anker Hansen. There was a Per Anker Hansen in Copenhagen who had recently had his passport stolen. Who "Hansen" in Costa Rica was, though, remained a mystery.

"After analyzing a voice recording of a man later identified as the bomber," Avirgan and Honey wrote, "made by journalists on the scene, linguists concluded that he was not a native Spanish speaker, and several speculated that he was either a Libyan or an Israeli."

As the disinformation campaign about the bombing proceeded, U.S. officials seemed to have suddenly learned that Pastora had been exporting drugs to the United States. They made no mention, though, of John Hull, whose ranch was the base for all shipments to and from Pastora's jungle headquarters.

2

While Tony Avirgan and Martha Honey were trying to find out who had murdered their friends in La Penca, five young men, a Frenchman, two Englishmen and two Americans, were en route to Costa Rica. They were mercenaries. The Britons, experienced soldiers of fortune, were recruited by a man named Frank Camper, who operated a "mercenary clearinghouse" in Alabama. Camper sent them to Tom Posey, who ran something called Civilian Military Assistance, which ostensibly sent "humanitarian" aid to the Contras. The Frenchman was sent to Posey by a Bostonian named James Keyes, who had served in the OSS and in the CIA under George Bush, with whom he said he was still in contact. One of the Americans was Robert Thompson, a Florida state trooper who usually wore mirror sunglasses and boasted of his record in law enforcement and how tough he was. The second American was a youth named Steven Carr, who had always wanted to be a combat soldier and bitterly regretted that the Vietnam War had ended too early for him to have served.

Carr had flown to Costa Rica, looking for a way to join the Contras. He ran into a man named Bruce Jones, who owned a farm near Hull's. Jones gave Carr a list of people to look up in Miami. A little later, Jones told a writer for *Life* that he was a CIA operative. That boast got him thrown out of neutral Costa Rica.

Back in Miami, Carr met a group of Contra supporters, who put him to work. In March 1985, he and some other supporters collected six tons of weapons from safe houses in the Miami area, he later told CBS News. The man in charge of the operation was René Corvo, a Cuban exile nicknamed the "Poison Dwarf," who was generally believed to have CIA protection. At one of the safe houses, belonging to a shrimp importer named Francisco Chanes, Carr saw, in addition to guns, three kilos of cocaine.

Carr and the others loaded the guns, including several 60-mm. mortars, a .50-caliber machine gun and a 20-mm. automatic cannon, on a plane at Fort Lauderdale. Carr then boarded the plane. Thompson and Corvo were also on the plane, which landed at a military airfield in El Salvador. The plane proceeded on to Costa Rica, probably to John Hull's ranch. Carr, Thompson and Corvo waited a week, then also went to Hull's ranch. The two Englishmen, Peter Glibbery and John Davies, and the Frenchman, Claude Chaffard, were already there.

Peter Glibbery later said Hull was in charge of training a group of Contras on his land. He said he had met Hull, "an old guy . . . very standoffish" in Florida, and Hull had paid his passage and Chaffard's to Costa Rica with a credit card. (Hull later denied that, but the credit-card records showed he was lying.) Glibbery learned that he and the other mercenaries were at Hull's ranch to train the Nicaraguan rebels. Hull paid and supplied the group. After Corvo arrived, Glibbery reported, he and Hull had a dispute. Corvo wanted to attack the Sandinistas.

"Hull told him not to do it because of an upcoming vote in Congress," Glibbery later testified. "He told him the publicity would be bad [should any of the Americans get killed] and [would] blow the chances of $40 million." Corvo said he agreed. Then he ordered the raid anyhow.

Carr and Thompson were among the twenty or so raiders. They hit a village named La Esperanza (Hope). Corvo and half the force dashed for home, leaving Carr, Thompson and the rest, including a wounded man, to fend for themselves. According to various accounts, between thirty and seventy persons were killed at La Esperanza. The Sandinistas sent 200 soldiers in pursuit, and the Contras had to cross the Río Frío to get away. Glibbery told CBS News that "the first man on the boat wasn't the wounded man; it was René Corvo, leaving Carr and the wounded man to be the last men back across the river, which left a slightly pissed-off Carr even more fuming."

Carr rapidly became disillusioned about the Contra War. He told CBS News he remembered standing at one of Hull's five airstrips while he and the rancher watched bags of cocaine being loaded. (He wasn't the only one who saw Hull receive a shipment of cocaine. Jack Terrell, an American mercenary who surfaced later, testified to the same thing.)

Glibbery had misgivings too, although he was a hard-boiled mercenary, not an idealist like Carr. He knew Hull had high-level connections. Once a phone call came for Hull, and the rancher explained it was from a friend in the NSC.

"What's the NSC, John?" the Englishman asked.

"The National Security Council." Later Hull explained, "This guy on the NSC sends ten thousand dollars a month to my bank account in Miami, and God help me if the IRS ever finds out about it, because if they do, I'll never be able to explain where the money is coming from."

Steven Carr remembered the same call. He later told CBS News that Hull said his friend at the National Security Council had asked him if he were involved in drug trafficking, because the FBI believed he was and was investigating him. "For God's sake, John," said the friend, "tell us if you are, because we can do something about it."

"The thing about John Hull," Glibbery later told CBS reporters, "is that he only opens his mouth to change feet. He's the wrong guy for the job."

Hull's involvement with drugs was not a well-kept secret. Shortly after the La Penca bombing, three Cuban exiles, Orlando Ponce, Marcellino Rodríguez and José Sosa, came to Costa Rica to join Hull's force. They stayed for three weeks of training. Then, disillusioned by what they saw, they returned to the United States. They reported that cocaine was being shipped to the United States from Hull's ranch in shrimp containers by Francisco Chanes and Moises Dagoberto Nuñez, operators of the alleged CIA proprietary, Ocean Hunter, and other shrimp importing companies.

Hull did not say what he told his friend at the NSC about drugs. In 1987, Pat Korten, a Justice Department spokesman, did admit that Hull was a suspected drug trafficker. According to George Morales, Hull was paid $300,000 for each flight carrying military supplies to his ranch. The pilots would then pick up drugs for the return flight. Gary Betzner, a crop-duster-turned-drug-pilot who worked for George Morales, told CBS News he made two flights to Hull's ranch and returned with 500 kilos of cocaine for each trip. When he landed, Betzner said, "People that were hired by John Hull or working for him would load the aircraft. In both cases, John Hull was there." Of the cocaine he flew back, Betzner was allowed to keep twenty kilos to sell himself. Earlier, Betzner had flown some of the mines that were used to mine the Nicaraguan harbors. In payment, he was allowed to fill his plane with marijuana and sell it when he reentered the United States.

Betzner said the cocaine sent to the United States was to be used to buy more weapons. "It wasn't the private guns [weapons donated by Contra supporters] that were important; it was what was coming back," he said. "That [proceeds from the cocaine sales] could buy much larger and better and more sophisticated weapons, and it was unaccounted-for cash."

Once, when looking over a stock of weapons, Glibbery told Hull he had found some claymore mines, which, if not exactly "sophisticated" are hardly the kind of thing you find at the local hardware store. They are designed to project a hail of steel balls in the direction of an enemy.

The rancher told him to leave them alone, because "we might need them for an embassy job later on." At the time, the remark meant nothing to Glibbery.

One time Glibbery found a powerful crossbow in a cupboard at Hull's house in San José. Hull said it belonged to Felipe Vidal, a young Cuban who was a frequent visitor. Hull added, "I think he's a hit man." Carr called Vidal "Hull's pet bulldog."

Edén Pastora had some interesting comments about both Hull and

Vidal for CBS News. Of Vidal, he said, "He works for the CIA. One time we captured him [when the Cuban was poking around Pastora's positions without permission], and he started screaming that he was from the CIA."

Hull had transported and stored weapons and supplies for Pastora "for years," the guerrilla said. "The largest part of them came from the CIA." Then, when the CIA started to cut off Pastora, Hull would have nothing to do with him. Pastora suspected that Hull was behind the La Penca bombing. Joe Fernandez, CIA station chief in Costa Rica, warned Pastora not to touch Hull, because, Pastora recalled, Hull was CIA and was "responsible for the CIA in northern Costa Rica." At this time, because of the Boland amendments, it was utterly illegal for the CIA to have anything to do with the Contras in southern Nicaragua or Costa Rica.

Hull indignantly denied that he had any connection with the CIA. But the evidence mounted up, and in 1987, he admitted that he was a former CIA operative.

At dawn on April 25, 1985, the war ended for Glibbery, Carr and the other three "gringo" mercenaries. A group of Nicaraguan rural guardsmen led by a Colonel Badilla arrested them for the La Esperanza raid at a camp three miles from the Costa Rican border. The Costa Rican Civil Guards and the DIS, the intelligence service, were strongly pro-Contra. The Rural Guards were strongly in favor of Costa Rican neutrality. The mercenaries had the misfortune to encounter the wrong cops. Violation of Costa Rican neutrality carried a mandatory five-year sentence. After two months of eating rice and beans in a Third World jail, Carr and Glibbery started to tell their tale to anyone who would listen.

3

Jesús García was a guard at the jail in Miami. He was also a fervent Contra supporter. He was one of the men who helped René Corvo and Steven Carr gather and load the weapons for the March 6, 1985 flight that took Carr to Costa Rica. Then Corvo asked him to help with another project.

"They came to me with a plan to hit the American embassy in Costa Rica. They had an idea that this would start a war between Nicaragua and the United States," he said. Attending the meeting to plan the attack were, according to García, Tom Posey, Bruce Jones, René Corvo, John Hull, Steven Carr, Robert Thompson and another mercenary, Sam Hall. Hall displayed a blueprint of the U.S. embassy. According to the plan, a bomb would be set off outside the embassy. When the ambassador came out, a sniper would kill him.

At the time, both regular U.S. Army troops and U.S. National Guardsmen were training on the Honduras-Nicaragua border. Leslie Cockburn, at that time a producer for CBS News, said the troop dispositions had all the appearances of preparations for an invasion of Nicaragua.

Unknown to García, there was another reason to hit the U.S. embassy in Costa Rica. Curtin Winsor, Jr., the ambassador who had accused Tony Avirgan of ETA ties, had been transferred. To replace him, the State Department moved Lewis Tambs from Colombia. Tambs had been pressing for the extradition of the cocaine cartel leaders to the United States and otherwise making himself obnoxious to the drug lords. The Ochoa family put a million-dollar price on his head. If the Contras killed Tambs, they would give the United States an excuse to make war on the Sandinistas and they would also collect $1,000,000 from the drug lords.

García was happy to help ship arms, but, even though he was sure the plan for the embassy attack "was blessed from the White House," he wanted no part of it. That's what he told René Corvo, Tom Posey, Bruce Jones and the others, including Steven Carr and Robert Thompson. On July 2, 1985, García got a call from Tom Posey. Posey said he had a job for him in Central America. The next day, another Cuban exile, a gun dealer named Joe Coutín, called. García remembered Coutín as "Posey's right-hand man. He didn't know Coutín was also an FBI informant. Coutín told García to get an MAC submachine gun and a silencer and hold them for someone who would be en route to Honduras. A couple of weeks later, the traveler appeared and introduced himself as Major Alan Saum. Saum made a number of phone calls from García's house—three to Posey, one to someone in Honduras and one to Gen. Vernon Walters, U.S. ambassador to the United Nations and former deputy director of the CIA, in New York. Saum had a new proposal for García: a hit on the Soviet and Cuban embassies in Nicaragua. That was different. García agreed.

On August 13, 1985, Saum appeared at García's place with representatives of the Miami police and the FBI. He led them right to the submachine gun García had hidden. García was arrested for illegal possession of an automatic weapon and a silencer and for conspiracy to attack the embassies. He told his public defender, John Mattes, that he believed he had been set up because he knew about the plan to bomb the U.S. embassy and kill the ambassador. Coming from a felon convicted of planning to attack other embassies, his story would have little credence.

Mattes vigorously cross-examined Saum. The "major" had really been discharged from the marines as a private and said he was currently employed by the Honduras military intelligence. He admitted that he had helped Posey violate the Neutrality Act. Although Saum admitted committing felonies, the sympathies of Judge Clyde Atkins were obviously all with him and all against García.

Mattes vowed to get his client a new trial. He and an investigator, Ralph Maestri, began checking on all the details of García's story. They heard about Carr and Glibbery and their stories. A senior officer in Tom Posey's Civilian Military Assistance agreed to tell what he knew about his group's operations.

"We turned all that information over to the United States attorney's office," Mattes said. He began hearing that federal agents were investigating his information and that it all checked out.

Then the assistant U.S. attorney in charge of the case told Mattes that the Department of Justice "wasn't interested" in going forward with the case.

Mattes flew to Costa Rica and interviewed Carr and Glibbery. Carr had no problem talking about John Hull and the shipments of arms and drugs on his ranch. He appeared afraid, however, to talk about the "embassy job." Glibbery wasn't in on that discussion, but he did tell Mattes about Hull telling him to leave the claymores alone.

Mattes came back to Florida and gave the FBI the additional information he had uncovered. Two days later, at the U.S. attorney's office, Assistant U.S. Attorney Jeffrey D. Feldman told Mattes, "Get out. You're out. Stay out. You've crossed the line." If Mattes continued, Feldman said, he would be charged with obstructing justice. Mattes planned to present his new evidence at García's sentencing hearing. He never got the chance. The government postponed the hearing on the orders of D. Lowell Jensen, the senior deputy U.S. attorney general.

It seems that Joe Coutín, the FBI informant, also knew too much.

He was arrested for converting a semi-automatic weapon to full automatic. The weapon in question allegedly had been used to assassinate Barry Seal.

Joe's wife, Hilda, went to Mattes. She said her husband had applied through the correct channels and received permission to convert the gun. She also told Mattes everything she knew about the arms-and-dope-smuggling network. As she and Joe were both FBI informants, that was a lot. One of the persons who took part in high-level planning meetings, she said, was a man called Colonel Flaco ("Colonel Skinny," in English).

Flaco's real name was Jack Terrell, Mattes learned. He too was a mercenary. There were indications, though, that he had once been—or perhaps still was—associated with a U.S. military organization. At any rate, like Carr and Glibbery, he was ready to talk. His job in the Contra movement was organizing the anti-Sandinista Miskito Indians. He had joined the movement about the time the first Boland Amendment took effect. The idea that the movement was entirely composed of private citizens, unconnected with the government, amused him greatly.

"That would be like me going to South Africa tomorrow and saying, 'Give me a gun. I want to do my thing.' They'd laugh at you." Private citizens, he said, do not walk into a war if the government doesn't encourage it.

He had been brought into the effort of the FDN to form a new Southern Front, bypassing Pastora. The planners included Rob Owen, "Ollie North's bagman," as Terrell described him (Owen called himself a "foot soldier" in the struggle), Calero and Hull. Terrell said, "I'm thinking, you know, they've got 210 ragamuffin Contras that they're trying to put together to put in Costa Rica when you've [already] got a far greater organization in the area known as ARDE, led by Pastora."

Hull flew into a rage at Pastora's name. "You know this man's a Communist? He flies the Sandinista flag in his camp. He deals with the Sandinistas. He sells them ammunition."

Then, Terrell remembered, Hull said, "He's got to go."

"What do you mean, he's got to go?"

"We've got to kill him."

The plotters planned to have a group of Contras wearing Sandinista uniforms capture Pastora and publicly hang him.

At another meeting a few days later, the original planners were joined by Enrique Burmúdez, the military commander; Aristides Sán-chez, a high-ranking Contra (and drug smuggler); and Felipe Vidal (an-other drug trafficker). Outside was a man who looked to Terrell like an Arab. Vidal said the Arab's name was Amac Galil. During the meeting, Vidal said of Pastora, "We put a bomb under him the first time, but it didn't work because of bad timing."

4

While Terrell and the Contras were planning the second attempt on Pastora, Tony Avirgan and Martha Honey suddenly learned a lot about the first.

On March 29, 1985, a San José carpenter named Carlos Rojas Chin-chilla stopped into a bar after work. While he was sipping his beer, a young man sidled up to him.

"You must help me," he whispered to Rojas. "Hide me. I want to get away. I don't want to be involved any more with their things. They are going to dynamite the U.S. embassy and many innocent people will die."

The man said his name was David and that he was a Contra, one of a group living on the ranch of an North American named John Hull. He wanted to escape from his companions, who were scouting the Ameri-can embassy prior to a bomb attack. After he and his companions set off the bomb, he said, a professional assassin named Amac Galil would kill the ambassador. David believed he himself would be killed after the attack and dressed in a Sandinista uniform. He needed a place to hide and someone "on the outside" who could get word to his brother. David's brother, also a Contra, was on his way to Costa Rica to take part in the embassy attack. Carlos Rojas didn't want to get involved. He asked why David didn't go to the Costa Rican authorities. David said he was usually being watched by other Contras, and besides, a number of government security officials were cooperating with the Contras on Hull's ranch. Rojas told David he couldn't hide him in his house, but he urged the young man to stay in touch. David gave him a phone number where he could be reached.

On the face of it, this story sounds about as likely as a trout fisher-man hooking the Loch Ness monster in Lake Superior. But none of those involved in the telling had anything to gain. Avirgan and Honey, the journalists, sold the story to the *Nation*, but the proceeds of that sale were a small fraction of what they spent to send the Rojas family to Europe and safety. They stayed in Costa Rica and were the target of harassment and death threats. Rojas got only an opportunity to get himself killed, which almost happened. And David was killed, after torture, as Rob Owen reported to Oliver North. The story was corroborated by Jesús García, the Florida prison guard, who did not know and had never heard of David, Rojas, Avirgan or Honey.

Rojas kept the story to himself until he read about the arrest of Carr, Glibbery and the other mercenaries. That confirmed David's story that there were Contras on that ranch. Carlos told his wife what happened, and they decided they should tell some American. Rojas's wife was a hairdresser, and she had an American client. She told her. The American woman was the secretary of Martha Honey and Tony Avirgan.

Honey and Avirgan passed the story on to the U.S. embassy, which had no comment. Then they convinced Rojas to reestablish contact with David. Slowly, Rojas got more information from David and passed it on to the journalists. Rojas apparently convinced David, who was sure he'd be killed if he stayed with the Contras in a foreign country, that getting the details to the Americans was his only hope. David remembered the name of one North American visitor to Hull's ranch, Dewey Clarridge, the CIA's chief of Latin American operations. David said the Contras wanted to get rid of Pastora and include his army in a unified southern operation. He said the La Penca bomb plot had been worked out by Hull, Vidal and Corvo. The would-be assassin was the same Amac Galil, a Libyan posing as a Dane, who was to shoot Ambassador Tambs. He had been recruited in Chile by two Contra officials and a CIA man who pretended to be a journalist. David said some high-ranking Costa Rican security officers had helped the Pastora assassination attempt, and that Hull had managed to get Galil out of the country.

David also told about drug trafficking and specifically named John Hull, René Corvo and Felipe Vidal as being involved.

After David and Rojas had a meeting with Avirgan and Honey in July, a group of armed men grabbed the carpenter and the renegade Contra, forced them down on the floor of a jeep and drove to Hull's ranch. Hull wasn't there. The armed men left one to watch the prisoners and went looking for someone. David told Rojas that their captors were going to kill them. Then he kicked the guard in the crotch and both men ran. They eventually reached a phone. Rojas called Avirgan and asked him to pick them up, but David decided to keep on running. Avirgan and Honey later learned that he had been recaptured, tortured and killed.

On August 25, 1985, Rob Owen reported to Oliver North that an execution had taken place. "The internal investigation shows Chepón [a code name for Contra leader José Robelo] did order the torture and eventual execution. It was decided that Negro [Contra leader Fernando "El Negro" Chamorro, described elsewhere by Owen as a drunkard and leader of drug smugglers] should decide what punishment he deserves and was supposed to decide by Friday."

Avirgan, Honey and Rojas all received death threats. The journalists got Rojas and his family out of the country. Then they discovered they were under surveillance.

Martha Honey and two other women went to the American embassy and asked to talk to the DEA.

"We specifically asked to talk to people from the DEA, the Drug Enforcement Administration, because we had information that those who were harassing us were involved with cocaine trafficking," Honey told Leslie Cockburn. "We laid out to this DEA man what we had been suffering, expecting that as American citizens, which we all were, that we would be able to discuss with him what might be done. His response to us was, 'Well, ladies, my suggestion is that you find yourself a big friend and get a gun.' "

5

In spite of the noncooperation of the Justice Department and the embassy, by mid-1986 it looked as if the truth would come out. Avirgan and Honey were publishing a series of magazine articles. The plot to bomb the U.S. embassy in San José to force the United States into war and collect a million dollars from the cocaine cartels was just too outrageous to hide. And John Mattes's sister, who lived in Massachusetts, told one of her senators, a young activist named John Kerry, about her brother's frustrations. Kerry arranged to have a subcommittee of his senatorial committee, the Committee on Foreign Relations, investigate the matter.

Jeffrey Feldman, who had warned John Mattes to stay out of the case, went to Costa Rica to interview Carr. Although he told Carr he was after "the guns, the drugs and John Hull," Feldman did not appear friendly. After Carr told him he had been at John Hull's ranch house, Feldman threw Carr a pad of paper and a pencil and asked him to draw a floor plan of the ranch house.

"I was a carpenter; I can draw floor plans," Carr told Leslie Cockburn. "I drew him a floor plan of [the] house. And he was kind of upset about that, you know. I didn't understand it." Carr then told Feldman to look at the jail's visitors' book. Hull had to sign in when he visited Carr and Glibbery to persuade them to change their stories. (Carr eventually signed a recantation for a basket of food. Glibbery didn't.)

As the plot began to unravel, John Hull got nervous. He was in a strong position: He was a Costa Rican (as well as U.S.) citizen, rich and respected. His philanthropies had made him a community leader. He sued Honey and Avirgan for libel. The only witness the journalists were likely to have was Peter Glibbery, a foreign mercenary and therefore, almost by definition, the lowest kind of scum. Even the other mercenary, Carr, had recanted his testimony.

Carr was finally bailed out of jail by his family. Hull then bailed out the others, even Glibbery. That would show he had no hard feelings and was confident in his case. He tried to persuade Glibbery to come to his ranch, but the Briton stayed with Avirgan and Honey. John Davies, the other Briton, and Claude Chaffard, the Frenchman, went to San José and disappeared.

In spite of his recantation, Carr planned to testify against Hull, but he first checked in with the U.S. embassy, as the embassy had requested. Embassy officials, in violation of Costa Rican law, whisked him out of the country and back to the States.

Hull appeared confident as the trial, before a single judge, began. After Glibbery began to testify, his confidence appeared to falter. The Englishman calmly and matter-of-factly told of Hull's using his ranch to train guerrillas and his trafficking in arms and dope. He could not be shaken.

Then Hull got his first surprise. Mattes took the stand. Here was no disreputable mercenary but a respected U.S. lawyer with a booming voice and a polished courtroom manner. He told how his client, Jesús García, had been approached to help blow up the U.S. embassy in San

José and how he and the U.S. authorities had been investigating the network of which John Hull was a part.

Hull got a second surprise when "Colonel Flaco" appeared. Terrell coolly told about Hull's part in the plot to kill Pastora. Asked about Robert Thompson, Hull's only witness, Terrell explained that he was a mercenary, not a journalist, as Thompson claimed. He said that Thompson had complained to him about some of his duties at the ranch, such as guarding the large amounts of cocaine kept there.

When Thompson took the stand, he denied ever staying at Hull's ranch and said he knew the rancher only slightly. The Avirgans' lawyer then asked how he happened to be wearing Hull's jacket.

On May 17, 1986, the judge found for Avirgan and Honey.

Five months after the trial, on October 5, 1986, a plane dropping supplies to the Contras was shot down over Nicaragua. Interestingly, the plane was the same C-123K used by Barry Seal. Documents found on the plane indicated a long-standing involvement by the CIA in supplying the Contras. The only survivor of the crash, Eugene Hasenfus, spoke about the U.S. government-sponsored arms smuggling network in detail. U.S. officials began pointing fingers at other officials who, they said, had kept them in ignorance. The Kerry subcommittee in 1987 began looking into why the federal government had made a loan of $375,000 to a Contra supplier in 1984 that had not been repaid.

Two and a half years after the trial, in January 1989, Hull was arrested in Costa Rica for violating Costa Rica's neutrality and for drug trafficking. The charges were dropped under pressure from the United States. Costa Rica, hopelessly in debt, can ill afford to offend its giant neighbor and lose U.S. aid. Hull left the country. But the next year, after the U.S. invasion of Panama, Costa Rica accused the rancher of the attempted murder of Edén Pastora and indicted both Hull and Felipe Vidal for homicide. It issued an extradition order for Hull which U.S. authorities so far have studiously ignored.

Before Hull left Costa Rica for good, Jonathan Kwitny wrote, his saga took one more bizarre twist. A certain Guillermo Fernández-R., an editor for the Costa Rican newspaper *La Nación*, wrote a series on drug smuggling in his country. One of the people he questioned was John Hull. Later, on a trip to Washington, he found that Hull was on the same plane. The editor later learned that the rancher had called his secretary and asked about his travel arrangements. A retired U.S. Army colonel named Joseph Yurko, who owned a farm in Costa Rica, met him and Hull at the airport. The two Americans took Fernández-R. to Yurko's farm in Virginia, where he met Rob Owen. All three tried to persuade the editor to travel to Hull's farm in Indiana, where, they said, he could be "better informed." Hull and Yurko confirmed the chronology to Kwitny but said they were trying to help him, not intimidate him. Back in Washington, Fernández-R. met a man who called himself Mr. Glenn (and was really Glenn Robinette). "Mr. Glenn" also offered to help him. Later, in Costa Rica, Robinette again approached the editor and offered to install a security system for his home and newspaper.

Fernández-R. told Kwitny it was obvious they were trying to make a deal with him to keep him from printing something in his series.

When Kwitny published the story, Fernández-R. was in hiding.

After Hull fled, it looked as if the gothic structure the CIA had constructed in Central America was going to come crashing down on the heads of its builders.

But as Avirgan, Honey, Mattes and Kerry learned, in situations like this, appearances are deceiving.

13

Bodyguards, officials and reporters crowded the room in Miami's Sheraton River House May 29, 1986. All listened attentively as Adolfo Calero, civil leader of the Nicaraguan Contras, announced the formation of UNO (United Nicaraguan Opposition), an anti-Sandinista organization combining the Contra Northern Front with the Southern Front. When the questions began, the Rev. William Davis, S.J., who had press credentials showing he was a photographer from the Jesuit magazine *America*, asked Calero about a lawsuit that had just been filed against him by a public-interest law firm, the Christic Institute.

Calero said he had not had a chance to review the suit, so he had no comments on it yet.

"I have the complaint right here," Bill Davis said. "Here's your copy." He handed Calero a subpoena. Father Davis was really a legal investigator for the Christic Institute. And *America* runs no photographs.

After a second, Calero realized what he was holding. So did his bodyguards. They began to close in on the priest, but a bearded man they took to be a federal agent grabbed Davis roughly and hustled him through an exit. The bearded man was William Taylor, a private investigator employed by the institute. It took a few more seconds for Calero's people to realize that they had again been tricked. They dashed into the hotel parking garage, but Davis and Taylor got away after a chase through the parking ramps worthy of prime-time television.

Melodramatic as it was, this beginning of the Christic Institute suit was on a par with the rest of the case.

The Christic Institute is the creation of Daniel P. Sheehan, a legal Don Quixote who charges real giants instead of windmills. After graduating from Harvard Law School in 1970, Sheehan quickly became involved in a series of cases defending the Constitution and the rights of the underdog. Among his best-known cases are *United States v. New York Times*, defending the right of the newspaper to print the Pentagon Papers; *In Re Attica Prison Inmates v. Mancuso*, which reversed the official autopsy that claimed that forty-one inmates were killed by other inmates, whereas they were actually killed by the New York State Police; and, best-known of all, *Karen G. Silkwood v. Kerr McGee Nuclear Corporation*, a landmark environmental and civil rights case, in which he was chief counsel.

During the Silkwood case, Sheehan organized the Christic Institute (which, in spite of its name, is not a religious group) to help oppressed people who do not have access to first-class legal talent. While winning dismissal of criminal charges against Catholic church people who had been helping Salvadoran refugees obtain political asylum in the United States, Sheehan received a disturbing report. A Protestant minister told him that an FBI field agent said that one of his superiors warned that undocumented Central American refugees, including "known Communist terrorists," were being brought to this country by Catholic workers in the Sanctuary movement. These persons, said the FBI man, were "a potential threat to the national security of the United States in the event that President Reagan had to initiate direct military action by U.S. forces into Central America." The FBI agent warned the minister to stay clear of the Catholic Sanctuary workers. The minister knew the charge was untrue, and he thought Sheehan should be warned.

Troubled by the report, Sheehan began an investigation after successfully concluding the Sanctuary case. He contacted several investigators, including Bill Taylor. Taylor reported that on July 6, 1984, President Reagan had issued National Security Directive No. 52, directing the Federal Emergency Management Agency to "exercise civilian supervisory authority" over military personnel, state National Guard units and "State Defense Forces," military groups to be set up by state legislatures at the behest of FEMA, in the event the president chose to declare a "State of Domestic National Emergency" in connection with U.S. military operations in Central America. The code name of this military operation would be "Night Train."

Concurrent with the military operation, FEMA would "deputize" military personnel and National Guard troops in the United States. That was intended to make them civilians and avoid violation of the Posse Commitatus Act, which forbids using military personnel for domestic law enforcement. These troops (now honorary civilians, according to the planners) and the "State Defense Forces" would then round up an estimated 400,000 Central Americans and lock them up in ten detention centers until the "state of emergency" was over.

Sheehan continued investigating and got confirmation both from persons inside FEMA and from official FEMA documents. Another investigator confirmed that "State Defense Forces" had already been secretly established by the legislatures of Texas, Louisiana and Alabama. The existence of these forces was unknown to most of the people of their states, the investigator reported. They seemed to be known only to their members, all "survivalist" or *Soldier of Fortune* types." One group in the Texas State Defense Force, according to "Source #10," had been expelled from the Texas National Guard "for being too radically right-wing."

According to the affidavit Sheehan filed in federal court:

This investigation [of the Texas Defense Force] led him [Source #10] to a Louisiana State National Guard Colonel, Source #11. Source #10 informed me that this Louisiana State National Guard Colonel had informed Source #10 that the State Defense Force in Louisiana was—in the near future—(this being in May of 1984) going to be receiving a large quantity of small arms and ammunition "in some kind of war game activity" supervised by the Federal government—but that the State Defense Force in Louisiana "was only going to have to give back half of the arms and ammunition received in the war games. The half which were left with them were going to be smuggled out of the country to the Contras in Central America." This was to be achieved, according to the Colonel, by re-valuing the weapons, when in the field, from "manufacturer's value" to "replacement value" and then collecting the same dollar value, as was originally distributed at the outset of the war game.

Continuing his investigation, Sheehan turned up evidence that the Contras were being trained on U.S. soil, in violation of the Neutrality Act, and that there was a secret organization supplying military aid to the Contras, also a violation of the Neutrality Act. This organization was acquiring large quantities of U.S. military equipment, which had been conveniently declared surplus, apparently for the purpose. The organization then smuggled the equipment to the Contras.

A mercenary employed by the organization told Sheehan the equipment was flown to the Costa Rica ranch of John Hull. The mercenary also told the Christic Institute lawyer about Jesús García, Steven Carr, Peter Glibbery, Alan Saum and Joe Coutín. Sheehan visited these men and talked with John Mattes, Garcia's lawyer, who had already begun investigating the secret organization. What he heard convinced Sheehan that there was group of former federal intelligence operatives that had been in existence since the Bay of Pigs failure. This organization, he believed was actively aiding the Contras and also smuggling drugs into the United States.

One of Sheehan's legal specialties has been using two federal statutes to perform civil prosecutions of public interest cases. One is the Civil Rights Act. Sheehan used it to prosecute a civil case against a group of neo-Nazis and Klansmen who had murdered a number of Communist demonstrators and evaded criminal penalties. The other statute is the Racketeer Influenced and Corrupt Organizations (RICO) Act, which permits citizens to sue for damages against an organization with a record of ongoing criminal activity. All he needed was a plaintiff.

Then he heard about Avirgan and Honey. He flew to Costa Rica and helped them in their defense during John Hull's libel suit. Returning to the United States, he filed another suit in their behalf—a RICO lawsuit in federal court in Miami against John Hull and twenty-seven other men, among them Bruce Jones, René Corvo, Felipe Vidal, Moises Nuñez, Franciso Chanes, Amac Galil, Adolfo Calero, Robert Owen, Thomas Posey, Theodore Shackley, Thomas Clines, Jorge Ochoa and Pablo Escobar. This group, "The Enterprise," the lawsuit claimed, was responsible for the bombing at La Penca and the injuries to Avirgan. Because it had long been involved in smuggling narcotics and cocaine, violating the Neutrality Act and murdering inconvenient people, it was engaged in ongoing criminal activity. Sheehan began taking depositions under oath from scores of people and getting subpoenas for hundreds of documents.

The defendants asked federal Judge James Lawrence King to dismiss the case. The judge denied the request. The defendants got help from other quarters, though—from persons both high and low.

2

When Steven Carr arrived in the United States, he landed in Miami and immediately turned himself in as a probation violator. He had once been convicted of forging his mother's name on checks and had broken probation by going to Costa Rica. He was sent back home to Naples, Florida, for a six-month term in the local jail. Carr was delighted. He was home and buried in a jail with decent food and a television. He wanted to be as far as possible from everyone he knew in Central America. Before he left Costa Rica, he told CBS News, the people at the U.S. embassy told him that if he ever talked about where he had been and what he had done, they'd see that he spent the rest of his life in federal prison. Or they'd kill him.

Carr's presence in the Naples jail could not be kept a secret. He hadn't been long in his cell before investigators from the Kerry Subcommittee called on him. Then CBS News arrived. Carr's lawyer, Jerry Berry, tried to keep the reporters away.

"It took five hours at a corner table in the local Justice Department building's snack bar to convince Jerry Berry that Carr *had* to say something. It was his only insurance policy," Leslie Cockburn wrote later.

When he met the CBS team, Carr would not talk about how he got out of Costa Rica, but he did talk about the death threats he had received—from the embassy, from the Miami Contras and from John Hull. He talked about the cocaine at Hull's ranch. He did not talk about the meeting in Miami that plotted the attack on the U.S. embassy, even though Jesús García had testified that he was there. Carr did admit, though, that he had written to García saying he "would never kill Americans."

Carr grew nervous after he was released from jail. He heard that John Hull had convinced Costa Rican authorities to revoke Glibbery's bail, and that the English mercenary was now back in prison. Then he heard that Felipe Vidal, after his drug arrest in Costa Rica, had escaped to Miami. Carr became anxious to leave Florida. He had been worried about Vidal for a long time. When he was in the Costa Rican jail, he had written to his mother, "Just found out today; I'm supposed to be shot on my return to Fla. It seems a guy named Morgan/Felipe who worked for the FDN and John Hull has been given orders to shot [sic] me and Pete because we spoke out against John Hull. . . ." Vidal's code name was Morgan. Carr put a lot of distance between himself and Florida. It wasn't enough. His body was found in a driveway in Van Nuys, California, on December 13, 1986. The police officer who found the body reported, "decedent is a 27–year-old male who may have overdosed on cocaine . . . . I noticed decedent's eyes were dilated but found no tracks or trauma to the decedent. No paraphernalia was found and no drugs." A woman who lived at the house where Carr roomed said he came down from his room about 3:30 A.M., apparently drunk. He said he was going to get something from his car and collapsed in the driveway. He shook violently, foamed at the mouth and died. Carr was not a habitual needle user, as the police report indicated. But an autopsy back in Naples, Florida, disclosed recent marks of a needle injection behind the left elbow. That's hardly the most convenient spot to inject oneself, and few cocaine addicts these days use a needle anyway. Forcible injection, though, is obviously easier than trying to make a victim snort an overdose.

In April 1987, Peter Glibbery told John Mattes that John Hull, still trying to pressure him to sign a retraction of his earlier statements, shouted, "The CIA killed Steven Carr, and they can do the same to you."

3

No evidence linking a suspect with Carr's apparent murder was ever found. There was plenty of evidence, though, as to who was behind the effort to silence Jack Terrell. Terrell had already told *Boston Globe* reporter Ben Bradlee, Jr., about the meeting that planned Pastora's murder, and said that North's man, Rob Owen, was present. In a radio interview, Terrell said someone in Miami had offered him a million dollars to move some seafood into the United States. He said he "learned later that they were speaking of a cocaine operation disguised by imports of frozen fish from Costa Rica." He spoke to the media, to the Kerry subcommittee and to the Christic Institute. He would be the key witness in the Christic Institute's RICO lawsuit—the person whose testimony could tie North's organization to drug trafficking and illegal arms smuggling.

On May 13, 1986, Oliver North wrote in one of his notebooks, "19:30—Call from Rick Messick [an aide to Indiana Sen. Richard

Lugar]—Terrell told not to talk to FBI, Jonathan Winer." Jonathan Winer was a member of Senator Kerry's staff. Requesting a potential witness not to talk to him was legal. Requesting the same person not to talk to the FBI was criminal interference with a federal witness—a felony.

Among Oliver North's other positions, he was head of the Operations Sub-Group of the Terrorist Incident Working Group. The OSG had been created in January 1986, when President Reagan signed National Security Decision Directive No. 207. OSG was empowered to by-pass normal channels and issue orders directly to counterterrorist groups. As head of OSG, North received all FBI cables, including those related to drug trafficking and Neutrality Act investigations that implicated him. He could also order investigations of his own.

According to the sworn testimony of Robert Owen, Glenn Robinette, a private investigator employed by Tom Clines and Oliver North, reported "a mercenary by the name of Terrell" was contemplating the assassination of President Reagan. North hopped on this unfounded report to request an all-out investigation of "Colonel Skinny." He sent a memo to Adm. John Poindexter, his boss at NSC:

SUBJECT: Terrorist Threat: Terrel [sic]

Several months ago, a U.S. citizen named Jack Terrel became an active participant in the disinformation/active measures campaign against the Nicaraguan Democratic Resistance. Terrel's testimony was used in the Avirgan/Honey suit in Costa Rica and has been entered in the Florida law suit against Richard Secord *et al.* [the Christic Institute suit]. Terrel has appeared on various television "documentaries" alleging corruption, human rights abuses, drug running, arms smuggling and assassination attempts by the resistance and their supporters. Terrel has also been working closely with various Congressional staffs in preparing for hearings and inquiries regarding the role of U.S. Government officials in illegally supporting the Nicaraguan resistance.

After the "West 57th" piece by CBS two weeks ago, Project Democracy officials decided to use its security apparatus to determine how much Terrel actually knows about their operations. One of the security officers for Project Democracy

[Robinette] met several times with Terrel and evaluated him as "extremely dangerous" and possibly working for the security services of another country.

This afternoon, Associate FBI Director, Oliver Revell, called and asked for any information which we may have regarding Terrel in order to assist them in investigating his offer to assassinate the President of the United States [deletion]. The FBI now believes that Terrel may well be a paid agent of the Nicaraguan Intelligence Service (DGSE) or another hostile security service.

Mr. Revell has asked me to meet with the Project Democracy security officer who has been meeting with Terrel. A meeting has been arranged for this evening. The FBI has notified the Secret Service and is preparing a counterintelligence/counterterrorism operation plan for review by OSG-TIWG tomorrow.

It is interesting to note that Terrel has been part of what appears to be a much larger operation being conducted against our support for the Nicaraguan resistance. We have not pursued this investigation—which includes threatening phone calls to the managing editor of the *Washington Post*—because of its political implications. It would now appear that [deleted] of Terrel's activities, this may well be much more than a political campaign.

Poindexter asked North to write another memo addressed directly to the president. In this very confidential memo, North had nothing to say about assassination plots and foreign agents. He expressed his real concerns: Terrell was a potential anti-Contra witness before the Kerry subcommittee and in the Christic Institute RICO suit.

Beginning July 24, Terrell was placed under a full-scale FBI surveillance, although Oliver Revell seems to have had misgivings. He later told the *Wall Street Journal* that he was afraid North was running a "plumbers unit" from the White House to discredit political opponents. At the time, though, no misgivings were apparent. Not only was Terrell subjected to every conceivable kind of surveillance, but his associates in the International Center for Development Policy, a "peacenik" group, were subjected to interrogations, surveillance and at least one break-in.

Meanwhile, Jeffrey Feldman, who had warned Mattes to stay away from investigating the guns-and-drugs network, had become a believer. He launched an investigation into drug trafficking centered on René Corvo, the "Poison Dwarf." His attempts to call a grand jury were repeatedly postponed by Washington. The day after the Hasenfus crash, though, important people in the Justice Department felt that they ought to look as if they were doing something. Six months after Feldman had recommended it, a grand jury was to be convened.

The decision had two principal aims, neither of which was to send Corvo to jail. First, the Corvo investigation was now sub judice and no longer open to the Iran-Contra Select Subcommittees. Second, Jesús García and Jack Terrell were told that they were going to be indicted. A live bomb in front of García's house intimidated the former jail guard. Terrell took a job overseas and did not testify before the Kerry subcommittee. On his return to the United States, he was again warned that he could be indicted. On the advice of his lawyer, he declined to answer questions in the Christic Institute suit.

In addition to "encouraging" Terrell to leave the country, the Justice Department further hampered the Kerry subcommittee by refusing to turn over any of its material on the drugs-and-guns network. The subcommittee's only significant FBI memos came from John Mattes, who had obtained them through the legal process called discovery. Further, someone stole a document from the subcommittee's files. It was a staff memo, based on Terrell's revelations, that recommended investigation of "Violations of the Racketeering Influenced Corrupt Organization (RICO) Act and ongoing criminal enterprises by the Contras." The memo alleged the assassination plots against Pastora and Tambs and

> an on-going drug smuggling operation connecting Columbia [sic], Costa Rica, Nicaragua and the United States, in which contras and American supporters, with the apparent knowledge of the contra leadership, handled the transport of cocaine produced in Columbia, shipped to Costa Rica, processed in the region, transported to airstrips controlled by American supporters of the contras and contras, and distributed in the U.S. Allegations have also surfaced regarding other operations involving shrimp boats operating out of Texas, Louisiana and Florida.

The stolen memo went to the Justice Department, which then sent a copy to Feldman to aid in the prosecution of Terrell. Feldman resigned as assistant U.S. attorney in Miami and went before the Kerry subcommittee to tell it what happened. By that time, though, the investigation was all but over. Terrell's deposition was not included in the report, because he had not appeared for direct and cross-examination. The Kerry subcommittee wrote a report in December of 1988 but delayed issuing it until April, when the new Congress was in session. The report states that there is overwhelming evidence that the Contras and their supporters were engaged in smuggling cocaine to raise money for military equipment. It also specifically names Manuel Noriega as a smuggler and further reports that the U.S. government overlooked Noriega's crimes because it wanted his help against the Sandinistas. But because key witnesses had been silenced, the Kerry subcommittee could not recommend criminal prosecution under the RICO Act.

4

Terrell's absence also doomed the civil RICO case filed by the Christic Institute on behalf of Tony Avirgan and Martha Honey. In June 1988, Judge King granted a motion by the defendants, John Hull and the rest, for a summary judgment against Avirgan and Honey. Because of this judgment, apologists for the government have argued that the suit was groundless. That's really not true.

In his decision, the judge pointed out that the plaintiffs had to prove three things. The first thing is the existence of an ongoing criminal enterprise as defined in the RICO statute. The second is "causation"—a direct injury to the plaintiff because of such an enterprise. The third is the damages suffered by the plaintiff. The defendants moved for dismissal on the basis that the plaintiffs could not prove that they were connected to the La Penca bombing (causation) or that Avirgan's injuries were a result of their action (damages). Judge King ruled that the plaintiffs had failed to prove causation. He did not rule that they had failed to prove the existence of an ongoing criminal enterprise.

"What the judge did," John Mattes told the author, "he didn't say there was no evidence. He said that they failed to prove, with the evidence that they offered, certain aspects of their case. . . . He killed them on procedure, not necessarily on what the message was. . . . I've been investigating since 1985 a very narrow aspect of that—namely the United States involvement in Central America and with narco traffickers. My evidence parallels that of the Christic Institute regarding that period of time. . . . I can't speak of Nugan Hand Bank or Richard Nixon. I can speak about what happened in Central America between 1981 and the present."

While waiting for a decision by the federal Eleventh District Court of Appeals, Sheehan explained how the judge viewed his evidence:

"He [Judge King] entered a series of rulings saying that all our evidence was hearsay. We had the direct, sworn, videotaped testimony, for example, of Jack Terrell in that court down in Costa Rica, saying 'I was in a meeting with John Hull and Rob Owen and Adolfo Calero and the bomber, this guy Amac Galil, and Felipe Vidal,' and he listed the other guys that were there, and he said, 'Felipe Vidal, in their presence, turned to me and said, "We're the men who put the bomb under Edén Pastora, but it didn't work because of bad timing, and we want to hire you to carry out a second assassination attempt." ' And Judge King said that was hearsay. That's not hearsay. That's a direct criminal admission, testified under oath by an eyewitness to it. . . . And in fact, Terrell was a co-conspirator."

The problem was that Terrell refused to testify in the U.S. court, so the judge considered his videotaped testimony hearsay. After dismissing the case, he ordered the plaintiffs to pay all of the defendants' legal expenses. That came to $1,218,000, and King demanded a cash bond in that amount before the plaintiffs could appeal.

"He was clearly convinced that we would not be able to put that kind of a cash bond up," Sheehan said. "That would stop the appeal process, so that no matter how outrageous his ruling was, we'd never have a chance to appeal it."

Sheehan said the only other ruling like King's order that the plaintiffs put up this enormous bond was a case involving two huge oil companies.

Sheehan lost the appeal. Paying the legal expenses—lawyers' fees, transportation, etc.—almost bankrupted the Christic Institute. The institute had to leave its Washington headquarters and moved to Los Angeles.

In August 1993, Judge King, who nearly ruined the Christic Institute over a point of law, completely ignored a whole law—the Neutrality Act. He freed six men arrested by Bureau of Alcohol, Tobacco and Firearms agents on a boat loaded with hand grenades and pipe bombs. The men were about to leave for Cuba when arrested. In another case, the judge questioned whether anyone should be prosecuted under the Neutrality Act for attacks on Cuba.

"Did Congress have in mind a person who had intense convictions—patriotic in nature—but which could not have any direct possibility of harm [to Americans]?" he asked. His blanket approval apparently does not include persons with intense convictions—patriotic in nature—about the need to protect innocent Americans from harm by employees of their government.

5

In 1990, the Contra War ended. Violeta Barrios de Chamorro, neither a Contra nor a Sandinista, was elected president. To the end, the Contras never controlled a square foot of Nicaraguan soil. Their operations were commando raids launched from Honduras and Costa Rica. Nevertheless, hundreds of Nicaraguans lost their lives in the war; millions of American dollars were wasted. Reagan's obsession with Nicaragua led to the Iran-Contra scandal, which could have ended with impeachment.

Drug smuggling continued, although now without the encouragement of the federal government. Noriega's usefulness ended, and he was indicted. Then the government dusted off Operation Night Train (without the "State Defense Forces" and the concentration camps) and invaded Panama. Invading a country to arrest someone indicted for a crime has doubtful legality under international law (although when done by the United States, no one is likely to strenuously object). In any case, it didn't work. More cocaine has been coming through Panama since Noriega's fall than before.

In 1991, Col. James Sabow, a U.S. Marine Corps pilot, was found shot in the head in the backyard of his house at El Toro Marine Base in Southern California. Navy and marine investigators said he committed suicide with the shotgun found beside his body. His family refused to believe Sabow had killed himself. They hired Gene Wheaton, a private investigator with thirty years' experience in the military. Wheaton knew that families often refuse to believe a loved one is a suicide.

"It generally turns out that way [to be a suicide], so I didn't expect anything else," Wheaton told CBS News. When he saw the body, though, he changed his mind.

"The trajectory of the shotgun blast would have required the colonel to be a contortionist to have fired the shotgun himself," he said.

Even more suspicious, there were no fingerprints on the shotgun, not a single print. Navy and marine investigators said the heat of the shotgun "melted them away." Belief that such a thing could happen is unique to the investigators in this particular case. All other forensic-evidence specialists agree with the investigator who said, "Utter BS. Utter BS. If you're not wearing gloves, you're going to leave a fingerprint on a firearm." The body was not wearing gloves.

Sabow had been charged with using a government plane to transport personal property to his son in the state of Washington. The Corps wanted him to resign. Sabow wanted a court martial because, as a friend put it, "If all the naval aviators in the Navy and Marine Corps were put to the same standards as Colonel Sabow was, probably 92 percent of them would be charged with the same offense." The friend thought the idea that Sabow would commit suicide over the charge was ridiculous.

Gene Wheaton, the investigator, thinks the charge was an attempt to destroy Sabow's credibility. And when that didn't work, he was permanently silenced. What Sabow knew, Wheaton thinks, is that U.S. military planes were being used to bring drugs into the country. Flights were made, he said, "by covert operators who were flying weapons south into Central and South America, and they were protected on their return flights from customs inspections.

"If Colonel Sabow was murdered, he would have had to have known about the covert flights that were going south with the weapons and the covert flights that were coming back with the drugs and laundered drug money. He was going to demand a court martial which would publicly bring out the total covert operations that were going on in the military."

Tosh Plumlee, a former army pilot, told CBS's Bernard Goldberg that he flew drugs into this country while a civilian employee of the CIA. On at least three occasions, he flew drugs into military bases. He said he was paid $5,000 a flight. He said he got the planes from military bases. Some were civilian planes; some were military craft. He told

Goldberg he and a number of pilots were told the flights were part of a sting operations to get evidence so that drug lords could be arrested.

"They never went in and did one thing," Plumlee said. "That's when a lot of pilots began to turn. That's when a lot of pilots began to say 'What in the hell is happening here?' "

Plumlee said the flights were connected to the Contra War—sort of.

"They not only supply friendly forces, but they supply the enemy, too. This is a business for them." And there is no indication that they have gone out of business.

It seems that once initiated, a large-scale smuggling operation is even harder to stop than a war.

6

Each of this country's Cold War-inspired liaisons with dope dealers has resulted in a spurt in the consumption of narcotics or cocaine in this country. Was it worth it? Cold War successes have been few. Vietnam, where we exerted so much effort, is one of the few Communist countries left. The Russians in Afghanistan have been replaced by a gang of fundamentalist fanatics who sponsor such acts as the bombing of the World Trade Center. Nicaragua was a waste of lives, money and morals. Steven Carr is dead. James Sabow is dead. Tony Avirgan still suffers from the effects of the bombing. Danny Sheehan is almost ruined financially. John Hull and Felipe Vidal, wanted for homicide and drug trafficking, prosper. And Ollie North is one of the country's best paid-lecturers and just ran for the Senate, losing by a narrow margin.

A desire to promote the drug trade was not, of course, the reason for the U.S. government's involvement with the Nicaraguan Contras. But the fact that such involvement would—and did—greatly expand the drug trade was not, U.S. officials believed, a reason to limit that involvement. The drug trade was not merely a by-product of involvement. The sale of drugs was a key element in financing the Contra effort. The first Boland Amendment, in December 1982, prohibited the CIA or any other U.S. agency from using funds "for the purpose of overthrowing the Government of Nicaragua." The Reagan Administration was maintaining that it was helping the Contras only to inhibit arms flow to El Salvador, but it quickly became apparent that the Contras were not blockading, or even trying to blockade, El Salvador. So the administration began scrambling for donations from private U.S. citizens and foreign governments. The size of the contributions, especially those from the private sector, was greatly exaggerated. Most of the money raised went to the fund-raisers. Of the $10 million raised from U.S. citizens by Oliver North, Richard Miller and Spitz Channell, for instance, $1 million was used for pro-Contra publicity, and $2.7 million went to a Swiss bank account ostensibly set up for arms for the Contras. Most of the rest paid the salaries and expenses of Channel, Miller and their business associates. The second Boland Amendment, October 12, 1984, cut off all aid to the Contras. The squeeze got tighter. North's non-government "Enterprise" made a $6–million profit from the sale of TOW missiles to Iran. Only part of that profit went to the Contras. The joint House-Senate Committees investigating the Iran-Contra affair showed who really benefited from that complicated project:

> The decision to designate private parties—Secord and Hakim—to carry out the arms transactions had other ramifications. First, there was virtually no accounting for the profits from the arms deals. Even North claimed he did not know how Secord and Hakim actually spent the money committed to their custody. The Committees' investigation revealed that of the $16.1 million profit from the sales of arms to Iran, only about $3.8 million went to support the Contras (the amount representing the "diversion" [funds directly given to the Contras]). All told, the Enterprise received nearly $48 million from the sale of arms to the Contras and Iran, and in contributions directed to it by North. A total of $16.5 million was used to support the Contras or to purchase arms sold to (and paid for by) the Contras; $15.2 million was spent on Iran; Hakim, Secord and their associate, Thomas Clines, took $6.6 million in commissions and other profit distributions; almost $1 million went for other covert operations sponsored by North; $4.2 million was held in "reserves" for use in future operations; $1.2 million remained in Swiss bank accounts of the Enterprise; and several thousand dollars were used to pay for a security system at North's residence.

There were "contributions" from foreign countries too—Saudi Arabia pledged $32 million. But in this milieu, that's a piddling amount. Barry Seal claimed to have made $75 million himself trafficking in drugs. Running a war is a very expensive proposition. Without drug money, the Contras would not have been able to do even the little they did. So U.S. government agencies actively aided drug smugglers aiding the Contras (who in some cases were both smugglers and Contras).

And if the Contras were really planning to kill Ambassador Tambs to collect the Ochoas' bounty, the U.S. government, through its protégés, was involved in a conspiracy of mind-boggling criminality.

The drug trade was also the major reason for one of the most ruthless cover-ups in American history—one that involved libel, false prosecution and, apparently, murder. The American people have never been greatly disturbed by their fellow citizens or their government being involved in Latin American revolts. Pancho Villa had scores of American mercenaries in his army while he was receiving "most favored rebel" treatment from the U.S. government. American training of Cuban exiles before the Bay of Pigs invasion was hardly a secret. Many U.S. publications carried pictures and stories on the training camps. Conservative fund- raisers got large amounts of money for the Contras from American citizens. But the American people, raised with the image of the Dope Fiend, would never have stood for their government being involved with drug traffickers. So government officials tried to cover up that involvement by any means possible.

Just how extensively the CIA was involved with drugs may never be known. As this is being written, information is just being released indicating that the CIA set up an intelligence service in Haiti that promptly began smuggling cocaine into the United States. Also just released is the news that the CIA set up an anti-drug program in South America, which backfired resoundingly. In order to gain the confidence of Venezuelan drug traffickers, the agency says, its agents allowed a full ton of the traffickers' cocaine to enter the United States. The agency did not employ the kind of ruse the DEA did to seize the dope when Barry Seal flew a planeload in for the Ochoas and Escobar. *It allowed the cocaine to be sold to U.S. wholesalers, who then sold it to addicts who snorted or smoked it.* The agency now calls this poor judgment.

Some have defended the CIA's playing footsy with drug traffickers on the grounds that the agency was accepting a lesser evil in pursuit of a greater good (although, as we've seen, the good usually seems to have eluded the intelligence community and the rest of us). There is no way, though, to defend the means the agency has used to protect its relationship with the drug merchants. Inexcusable too is the blatant cynicism that underlies these operations. No matter how loudly the government proclaims its undying enmity toward drug trafficking, the traffickers know that if they help the right people, the government will look in another direction—or even give them a leg up—when they bring narcotics and cocaine into the country.

Unfortunately, this cynicism is not confined to foreign relations. In domestic affairs, governmental leaders have for years been demonstrating a profound cynicism about drug dealing. They have often shown far more interest in maintaining and increasing personal power than in ridding the country of drug addiction. And the ways they have of appearing to fight drugs have been undermining the social structure of the country.

PART THREE
THE DRUG WAR

Reverse: Agent of the Bureau of Alcohol, Tobacco and Firearms outside the Branch Davidian compound in Waco, Texas. *Bob Strong/Sipa Press*

14

At times, during election campaigns, U.S. voters can be excused for thinking that most candidates, regardless of what they are running for, really want to be heavyweight champion. Candidate X is going to be "tough on crime." Candidate Y is going to be "tough on drugs." Candidate Z is going to "make the tough decisions." The worst name you can call any candidate is "wimp." A wimp is anyone who is "soft" on anything undesirable, such as Communism, crime or illicit drug use.

Innumerable presidents have found that a way to get a quick boost in the popularity polls is to conduct a victorious war. Ronald Reagan bombed Libya, a country with the population of Connecticut and, except for oil wells operated by foreigners, almost no industry but camel grazing. That the bombing was really a botched assassination attempt made no difference. Reagan proved he was "tough." Then he invaded Grenada, a country with a population equal to New Haven's (about 1/25,500th of the U.S. population). Even though the supposedly heavily fortified prison was captured by a correspondent from *Time* magazine instead of the U.S. Army or Marine Corps, Reagan again emerged as a tough guy.

On the other hand, the failure of Jimmy Carter's poorly planned attempt to rescue the hostages held in Tehran wiped out his chances for reelection. If it had succeeded, the plan, which, unlike his successor's military ventures, was daring to the point of foolhardiness, would have left Reagan to be remembered only for such films as *Bedtime for Bonzo*. Neither president, of course, ran the slightest risk of physical harm. The remark of a World War II GI about Gen. George "Old Blood and Guts" Patton—"his guts and our blood"—applies far more to these presidents. But politicians learn how to look tough on the cheap.

The first step is to find a target almost everybody hates. The world is full of unpleasant leaders, ranging from Fidel Castro to Saddam Hussein. All you have to do is shine a spotlight on one of them. The spotlight may take a little effort, though, if the target is as unknown to the majority of Americans as Saddam Hussein was before George Bush told us he was another Hitler.

The best target of all is one everybody already knows and hates, like the Dope Fiend. The Dope Fiend is especially good, because he can be attacked by mayors and governors as well as presidents. In fact, the trend-setting anti-Dope Fiend campaign was launched by a governor. It apparently made no inroads on the treasury and it made the governor look like the toughest thing since Joe Louis. The governor was Nelson A. Rockefeller, of New York, heir to a family fortune founded by a drug-dealing great-grandfather.

2

The governor's great-grandfather William Avery "Big Bill" Rockefeller sold patent medicines and advertised himself as a "cancer specialist." At that time, almost all patent medicines contained opium, an opiate or cocaine. And of course, none of them could cure cancer. Business was good enough to let Big Bill give his son, John D. Rockefeller, Sr., enough capital to get a running start in the developing oil industry. John D. never stopped running. When the government finally caught up with him, he was refining 90 percent of the oil in the United States and two-thirds of the oil in the world.

The government broke up the Rockefeller monopoly, but John D., Jr. still had enough spare cash to bankroll much of the Prohibition movement and build Rockefeller Center in New York. He encouraged his son Nelson to go into public service.

Although a Republican, Nelson Rockefeller joined the Franklin Roosevelt Administration and was put in charge of U.S. propaganda to Latin America. He got the Treasury Department to exempt from taxation any U.S. corporations that cooperated with his propaganda effort. The cooperating corporations bought immense amounts of advertising in Latin American news media. At its peak during World War II, this advertising accounted for 40 percent of all the revenues the Latino media earned. That gave Rockefeller a long lever with which to steer

Latin American thought. Newspapers and radio stations that cooperated with Rockefeller's organization got that advertising largesse from the North American corporations. Those that didn't cooperate, didn't get advertising. And soon went out of business.

Nelson Rockefeller's wartime propaganda experience gave him a taste for what pioneer public-relations consultant Edward Bernays called "the engineering of consent." Rockefeller knew that to deliver propaganda effectively, you first have to know the mind of the audience. He had worked closely with George Gallup during the war. He did not sever the connection when, after serving in the Truman and Eisenhower administrations, he got into elective politics. He also learned that the media as a rule do not closely investigate any sensational claim that would make a good story. Rockefeller used his propaganda ability to create an image of himself as a liberal Republican. He picked up votes from both Republican upstate New York and liberal New York City.

The trouble was that he wanted more than merely governorship of what was then the largest of the United States. He wanted to be president. The liberal Republican image might play well in the country at large in the late '50s and early '60s, but it was not likely to impress the hard-core pols who would go to the Republican National Convention. At the 1964 National Convention, the delegates voted overwhelmingly for Barry Goldwater who was certainly a Republican, but certainly not a liberal Republican. Goldwater, in turn, was buried in the Lyndon Johnson landslide, showing that the general population still liked liberals.

3

Rockefeller's problem was finding a way to look conservative enough to be nominated, but liberal enough to be elected. He had to be a tough guy as well as a nice guy. Rockefeller consulted his pollsters and rediscovered the Dope Fiend. As Rockefeller later told the New York Legislature in 1973, "Every poll of public concern documents that the number one growing concern of the American people is crime and drugs—coupled with an all-pervasive fear for the safety of their person and property."

Crime and drugs—the dope-crazed criminal of Richmond Pearson

Hobson, robbing and murdering his way through life and spreading his addiction like a cancer in the body politic—had never died in the public mind. Nelson Rockefeller, the old propaganda master, set out to give the hobgoblin new life, and himself new responsibilities.

Like Captain Hobson's, Rockefeller's estimates of the addict population had no objective reality. He was more flexible than Hobson, though. If he wanted to terrify the population and the legislature into giving him additional power, he'd claim the addict population in New York was 150,000 or 200,000. When he wanted to show the efficiency of his anti-drug programs, the addict population would shrink to under 100,000. At one time, he estimated that addicts were responsible annually for more than a billion dollars' worth of thefts in New York. No publicity was given to the fact that the annual value of all reported and unrecovered thefts in New York City during Rockefeller's administration was never more than $100 million. Even Rockefeller's allies in the Hudson Institute reported, "No matter how we generate estimates of total value of property stolen in New York City, we cannot find any way of getting these estimates above $500 million a year—and only a part of this could be conceivably attributed to addicts."

Such cavils didn't stop Rockefeller. In his 1966 gubernatorial reelection campaign, he demanded "an all-out war on drugs and addiction." He pushed a law through the legislature making possible the involuntary confinement of drug addicts for treatment even if they had never been convicted of any crime. That there were practically no treatment centers for addicts in New York and no agreement among medical professionals as to what—if any—treatment could help them were minor details. There was not even agreement on what addiction was. Presumably people addicted to coffee or tobacco were liable to confinement under the "civil commitment" law. No matter. Rocky was showing that he was being tough on the "plague of drug addiction."

His Democratic opponent that year was Frank D. O'Connor, a former prosecutor who had put hundreds of criminals behind bars. When O'Connor called Rockefeller's "civil commitment" law "an election-year stunt" and "medically unsound," Rockefeller replied:

> Frank O'Connor's election would mean narcotics addicts would continue to be free to roam the street—to mug, snatch purses, to steal, even to murder, or to spread the deadly infec-

tion that afflicts them possibly to your own son or daughter. Half the crime in New York City is committed by narcotics addicts. My program—the program that Frank O'Connor pledges to scrap—will get addicts off the street for up to three years of treatment, aftercare and rehabilitation.

Rockefeller was reelected. The voters were terrified by what Rockefeller had been describing as a "reign of terror" by drug addicts in New York City. As a Democratic leader said after the election, "Parents are scared that their kids might get hooked and turn into addicts themselves; people want the addicts off the street, they don't care how you get them off."

Of course, they didn't get addicts off the street. Rockefeller's program, lacking treatment centers or even treatment, was totally unworkable. His newly created Narcotics Addiction Control Commission, which was to oversee the program, was filled with public-relations specialists rather than medical people.

As far as the public was concerned, though, Rockefeller was being "tough on drug addiction."

He wanted to get tougher. In December 1971, he wrote in the *New York Law Journal*:

How can we defeat drug abuse before it destroys America? I believe the answer lies in summoning the total commitment America has always demonstrated in times of national crisis. . . . Drug addiction represents a threat akin to war in its capacity to kill, enslave and imperil the nation's future: akin to cancer in spreading a deadly disease among us and equal to any other challenge we face in deserving all the brain power, man power, and resources necessary to overcome it.

As Rockefeller continued to whip up frenzy about the drug "reign of terror," his staff drew up plans for a "drug emergency." Under the plan, President Nixon and Mayor John Lindsay of New York would set up "emergency camps" and lock up all New York City addicts. As there was no way of positively identifying addicts, this plan was as unworkable as the "civil commitment" law. The aim of the plan, however, was not to lock up addicts. It was to show that Rockefeller was "tough on drugs and crime."

In 1973, Rockefeller got the legislature to pass the ultimate tough-guy law. Known as the "Attila the Hun law," it mandated life sentences for anyone—even as young as sixteen—who possessed a fraction of an ounce of heroin, amphetamines or LSD. The judge had no discretion. It also mandated a life sentence for anyone who ingested a hard drug before committing any number of crimes, including criminal mischief. Offenses that once meant no more than a fine or a few days in jail now meant prison for life if the suspect's urine showed traces of drugs.

Rockefeller, testifying before the U.S. Senate in 1975, justified the law by saying "about 135,000 addicts were robbing, mugging, murdering day in and day out for money to fix their habit." If that were true, New York City would have a total of around 49,275,000 robberies, muggings and murders a year, which would mean that the average New Yorker would be robbed, mugged or murdered seven times a year. Actually, the annual total of reported robberies, muggings and murders in the city was 110,000. There were, no doubt, more robberies and muggings than were reported (although they never approached 40,000,000), but murder is harder to ignore: Bodies attract attention. Rockefeller knew that if you proclaim a figure with enough authority, even a senator will believe it.

People on the firing line, in the police departments and the courts, knew that the Attila the Hun law would do more harm than good. So they quietly bypassed it whenever they could. And the drug peddlers took a countermeasure: They began recruiting children, who would come under the juvenile court, rather than the Attila the Hun law.

Unfortunately, mandatory sentencing proved to have an unholy attraction for politicians. It was adopted for drug offenses by both state and federal governments. We'll see later how it has been helping to destroy our society.

4

Mandatory sentencing had a strong attraction for President Richard Nixon and most of his staff. Before Nixon took office in 1968, the country was in the grip of a rising wave of street crime. Street crime—muggings, other robberies, assaults, rapes and murders—had never been of much concern to the federal government. The reason, of course, was that the feds could see little that they could do about the problem under the Constitution. Street crimes are almost all state offenses. Nixon, though, knew that crime was a major concern of voters, and he promised to do something about it.

During the campaign, he contented himself with vague references to how the legal system was being perverted by those who were more concerned with the rights of criminals than the rights of victims. He proposed no specific programs, primarily because he didn't know of any that would work. Then, at his election staff's urging, he focused on narcotics. He brought up the subject in a way he had almost patented, by reading a letter he had supposedly received from a nineteen-year-old drug addict in California. "Narcotics are a modern curse on America's youth," he asserted. Nixon implied, taking the trail blazed by Rockefeller, that narcotics are the prime cause of violent crime. One of his most frequent television commercials carried the message: "Crimes of violence in the United States have almost doubled in recent years . . . today a violent crime is committed every sixty seconds . . . a robbery every two and a half minutes . . . a mugging every six minutes . . . a murder every forty-three minutes . . . and it will get worse unless we take the offensive."

Once in office, the Nixon people saw that they had few offensive weapons. Egil Krogh, who was to become the point man in Nixon's law-and-order campaign, told writer Edward Jay Epstein that the administration discussed "symbolic strategies," such as harsh-sounding legislation that would have no effect on law enforcement. The ideas would make Nixon look "tough on crime." If Congress balked, it could be accused of being "soft on crime" or even "coddling criminals." Ideas like preventive detention, which had no chance of being enacted, were mentioned to increase the toughness factor.

One of the traditional federal strategies was to "declare war on the Mafia." In 1962, for instance, Attorney General Robert Kennedy sent a hundred FBI agents to Reading, Pennsylvania, after tipping off friendly journalists. There, this small army of G-men raided an otherwise quiet dice game. One of Nixon's bright young staffers came up with an idea to outdo the Kennedys. The FBI, he said, should make highly publicized raids and round up gamblers with "racketeer" (i.e., Italian) names. Even if they had to be released immediately, the publicity would show that the administration was fighting crime. That was too much even for Nixon, who was ardently wooing Italian-American voters.

As time went on, Nixon seemed to worry about becoming too

tough. He picked John Mitchell, the attorney general, to be the relentless, heartless nemesis of crime. About the same time, the results of the CIA's games with the heroin smugglers were beginning to have an impact on the United States. Troops from Vietnam, many of them regular heroin users, were returning in large numbers. In 1971, Nixon declared that he was launching an all-out war on the "scourge of narcotics." Inevitably, mandatory sentencing for drug offenders came up.

According to Krogh, Nixon himself brought it up at a cabinet meeting. Mitchell strongly objected. Mandatory sentences, he said, were "irrational" and "counterproductive." Nixon replied, "That's my position, and I cannot have it look as if I am weak or receding from a hard-line position." Mitchell continued to argue, and at last Nixon gave in. In this, the much-reviled Nixon showed better sense than most of his successors.

Mandatory sentencing is a way to "get tough on drugs" on both state and federal levels. Another method is that old favorite, "Put more cops on the street." That's been a promise of every president from Richard Nixon to Bill Clinton. The biggest trouble is that it's expensive. President Clinton, for example, promised 100,000 new police officers. His "police ROTC" plan, however, cut that figure in half. Although the 1994 Crime Law promised 100,000 more police officers, experts now say it will produce only about 20,000. Those additional cops have to be paid, and the federal government is not offering a permanent subsidy. After a few years, the cities will have to pick up the whole tab (and as the tab includes overtime, benefits and pensions, it will be steep). Nevertheless, more police has long been a popular solution to the drug problem. More police is tough, so it gets the lion's share of money appropriated to fight drugs. More treatment facilities is far less tough, and its appropriations testify to that. For many years, appropriations for fighting drugs have been roughly 70 percent for law enforcement and 30 percent for treatment, education and other means of prevention. The Clinton Administration's latest budget reduces the gap between law enforcement and other programs a hair. But only a hair. Treatment, as we'll see, is something of a problem, because there are several kinds of treatment, each only partially successful. The current emphasis on law enforcement, though, has done nothing to solve the treatment problem.

Another problem is: After you get those additional police on the street, what do you do with them? There are many approaches—simple saturation, organizing special narcotics squads and dispersing police stations throughout the city in "community policing" programs. Police Chief Nicholas Pastore, of New Haven, who served on national drug czar Lee Brown's advisory panel, is one of the country's leading advocates of community policing. He also has a fairly radical idea about what to do with drug users after they are arrested. He does not believe in decriminalizing drug use, but he thinks drug users should be sent to treatment centers instead of jail.

Most street crimes are matters for the states, not the federal government. The federal role in this kind of law enforcement is strictly limited, no matter what presidential candidates say. The feds, though, have ways to "get tough on drugs" not open to the states.

One way is to "tighten up our borders."

Although President Bill Clinton during his election campaign promised to make fundamental changes in the nation's war on drugs, most of the $13 billion federal budget for the drug war is still going to law enforcement. The only substantial change so far is a greater emphasis in the law enforcement program on interdiction and neutralizing the top drug "kingpins," especially the cocaine kings of Colombia.

Some proponents of increased interdiction concede that the job may be beyond the capacities of the Coast Guard, Customs Service and the Border Patrol. Their answer: Use the military.

We've been using the military for more than a decade, and the results are not encouraging. On June 15, 1988, Air Force Gen. Robert T. Herres, then vice chairman of the Joint Chiefs of Staff, told the Senate and House Armed Services Committees, "There is no practical way the Armed Forces of the United States can seal our borders." Barry Seal testified that he flew a hundred smuggling flights without ever being intercepted. And California Bureau of Narcotics Enforcement Special Agent Bennie Rincon said, "You win one; you lose twenty-three."

We'll take a closer look at the impossibility of sealing our borders in the next chapter, along with the related "tough guy" approach of interdicting cocaine, opium and marijuana crops in foreign countries. And we'll look at the use of military or covert operations against drug traffickers in foreign lands. That approach, not including the peculiar and unproductive expedition against Tony Noriega, has drawn support from a surprising range of opinion-makers.

15

In the United States, one of the national sports seems to be self-flagellation. We hear continually that Americans are the most violent nation, the most crime-ridden nation, the most drug-addicted nation.

None of these oft-repeated statements is true.

If you consider all kinds of violence—war, government-sponsored purges and factional mob violence, as well as individual crime—the U.S. homicide rate is piddling compared with the world average. It even lags behind Europe, where several wars and "ethnic cleansing" programs are underway at this writing. The overall individual crime rate does exceed that of Europe, but it's lower than that of most of the world. Precisely how much lower is hard to say, because statistics on reported crime in most countries—including several in Europe—are usually incomplete, if not mendacious. As for drug addiction, not even the most inflated estimates for the U.S. addiction rate approach conservative estimates for countries like Iran and Pakistan.

Estimates of drug addiction in the United States vary widely. The Bureau of Narcotics and Dangerous Drugs estimated the number of American addicts at 69,000 in 1969, 322,000 in 1970 and 560,000 in 1971. That would indicate a wild spurt in the addiction rate toward the end of the Vietnam War period but for one thing. All the estimates were based on the same data but used different statistical formulae for projecting the number of addicts. The numbers do not report new addicts that had been discovered. Joseph A. Greenwood, who devised the BNDD formula, explained it to Edward Jay Epstein.

"The estimate makes use of a technique similar to that by which the number of fish in a lake . . . is estimated," he said. Wildlife managers who want to know how many fish are in a lake catch a sample of fish and tag them. Then they put the fish back and wait long enough for them to distribute themselves randomly all around the lake. Then they catch another sample and count how many are tagged. If 10 percent of the second catch is tagged, the wildlife statisticians assume that the total population is ten times the number of fish in the second sample."

The BNDD statisticians compared the number of addicts reported in 1969 with the number reported in 1970 and checked to see how many in 1970 had previously been reported in 1969. The previously reported addicts were like the tagged fish. Fewer than one in five addicts in the 1970 "sample" had been reported in 1969. The BNDD then multiplied the 68,088 addicts reported in 1969 by 4.626 and estimated that there were 315,000 addicts. In 1971, using a slightly refined version of the "fish formula," the bureau found a ratio of one addict "tagged" in 1969 to 8.21 "untagged" addicts in the 1971 sample. That produced the staggering estimate of 559,000 addicts in 1972. The bureau then added a little to each estimate just in case they were short.

The formula makes no provision for addicts being cured, although, as we've seen, most addicts cure themselves. Even more basic is how the sample is "caught." In 1970, New York Police Commissioner Patrick Murphy decided to step up narcotics arrests. Each police officer received a day off for every drug bust he made. The number of reported drug addicts zoomed. But, as might be expected, all those arrests resulted in few convictions. The next year, Murphy eliminated the bonus days off. By 1972, the number of drug arrests was down more than 60 percent.

Deaths due to overdose is a somewhat more reliable way to estimate changes in the addiction rate. Even here, though, there are variables. Dr. Richard S. Wilbur, assistant secretary of defense for health, said the higher death rate from heroin after 1969 was at least partially due to the quality of heroin that could be purchased on the street. There was apparently a shortage of quinine, commonly used to dilute heroin. Of course, the Defense Department also wanted to minimize the effects of discharging large number of soldiers who had acquired a heroin habit in Vietnam.

The quality of the quinine substitute may have had less to do with the death rate than the Defense Department would like us to believe. The OD death rate reflects political factors. In 1985, before the flow of drugs from the Contra War hit its peak, the Drug Abuse Warning Network reported 643 deaths related to cocaine, compared with 1,315 associated with heroin. By 1990, after the end of the Contra War, DAWN reported 1,976 deaths related to heroin, but 2,483 related to cocaine. Most studies indicate that cocaine use peaked around 1989, but cocaine use continues at a much higher rate than before 1986. The reason for this is partially physical and psychological addiction. A more important reason is, as we'll see, the growth of a social phenomenon that might be called "the drug culture."

Besides the overdose death rate, the addiction rate may be measured is by comparing annual drug seizures by the authorities. In 1981, for instance, federal, state and local officers seized 1,937.8 kilos of illicit drugs. In 1985, they seized 24,654.9 kilos, and in 1990, 71,599.2. With one exception, the quantity of dope seized has increased every year. (The exception was 1989, when an incredible 21.4 tons of cocaine was seized in a single warehouse in California, resulting in a total seizure of 81,762.1 kilos.)

These figures might indicate increased efficiency of forces fighting the War on Drugs. There's one annoying fact, though. Drugs became increasingly available in spite of the seizures. The street value of a kilo of pure cocaine dropped from $70,000 in 1981 to $25,000 in 1990.

2

It seems likely, then, that there has been a considerable increase in drug addiction in the United States in the last decade. Just what the rate of addiction may be is impossible to say, but it's probably comparable to the addiction rate at the turn of the last century. While the United States is far from the most addicted nation in the world, the rate of addiction is higher than in any of what we call the "developed" countries. Most of the countries where the addiction rate exceeds that of the United States are source countries—places where opium, opiates and cocaine are produced. This country is certainly the major target of international drug traffickers.

There are several reasons why drug smugglers aim to sell here. One is the wealth of the country. There is more money available to buy drugs here than in any other country. Per capita wealth is higher here than in most countries. Even the poor here would be considered well-to-do in many countries. Per capita wealth multiplied by the size of the population puts the United States in a class by itself. Another reason is the absence of customs boundaries. The contiguous forty-eight states are about the same size as the whole of Europe. But in Europe, there are scores of boundaries, each guarded by customs officers. Even the European Community hasn't eliminated customs posts. In the United States you can travel the breadth of the continent without meeting a customs official.

Finally, as mentioned before, the length of the U.S. boundaries makes it impossible to guard every foot.

Every year, 118,000,000 automobiles cross the U.S. borders, while 574,000 planes fly over them and 177,000 boats and ships arrive here from foreign lands. Altogether, 422,000,000 people come to this country annually. Each of those vehicles, each of those persons, is a potential carrier of illicit drugs. Drugs don't take up much space. Heroin is worth more than its weight in $1,000 bills. The number of places a small quantity of heroin or cocaine could be hidden is virtually unlimited. Some drugs are even carried into the country inside the bodies of couriers who ingest sealed packages before they get on the U.S.-bound plane.

Giving even a cursory search to each arriving person and his or her baggage, each car, truck, bus or plane that crosses the border, each ship and boat that docks here after leaving another country is absolutely impossible. At one time, to put pressure on Mexico to eliminate its drug exporters, the Nixon Administration instituted Operation Intercept. The plan, devised by G. Gordon Liddy, deployed 2,000 Customs Service and Border Patrol officers at ports of entry along the Mexican border. Cars and trucks coming from Mexico were delayed up to six hours. During the three weeks it was in operation, 5,000,000 tourists crossed the border, but the guards found virtually no heroin, cocaine or marijuana. What the government did find was a vast amount of indignation from Mexican officials, so much that the operation was called off. (The administration, however, was pleased with the publicity "Intercept" received. It showed that Nixon was tough on drugs.)

To expand Operation Intercept to cover all ports of entry to the United States and to make it permanent would not only destroy the foreign tourist trade, it would keep most Americans from venturing outside the country: The majority of people held up by Intercept were Americans returning home. And such an operation, which would require far more guards than now available, would probably be as unsuccessful as Liddy's plan was in turning up drugs.

In spite of all the publicity about "mules" who swallow packages of narcotics, most of the heroin and cocaine that comes here is not carried in by individuals. It arrives on the decks of container ships. Approximately 8,000,000 of the big, sealed steel boxes called cargo containers arrive in the United States annually. San Pedro Harbor, the port of Los Angeles, receives 80,000 containers alone. The containers may be 40 feet long, 8 ½ feet wide and 8 feet high. One could hold enough heroin to supply all of the addicts in the United States for more than a year. The containers are not filled with heroin or cocaine, of course. At least we hope not. No such chock-full container has been found, but the customs people open only a sample (in Los Angeles, only 300 of the 80,000 containers are inspected), because searching one container takes about four days. Drugs can be hidden behind false walls, inside the twenty-four I-beams (each can hold 4 ½ kilos) or in the merchandise.

Take a typical shipment of 40,000 automobile tires from Asia. If just one of those tires were filled with heroin, it would be carrying $10,000,000 worth of illicit narcotics. A smuggler in South America could hide half a million dollars' worth of cocaine in a handful of plastic bananas concealed in a 20–ton shipment of the yellow fruit. One raid in Connecticut found a large quantity of cocaine concealed in a hollow aluminum ingot. Another found cocaine in large waterproof containers attached to the bottom of a ship. In New York, DEA agents found a load of charcoal that had been impregnated with liquid cocaine. Although it was invisible, the charcoal contained $25,000,000 worth of cocaine. Obviously, Customs Service agents are not going to X-ray every aluminum ingot that comes into the country or send frogmen to check out the bottom of each vessel that docks in the United States. Nor will DEA agents try to leach cocaine from every coal of imported charcoal. Some drug seizures are made as the result of intelligence from undercover tipsters; some are based on drug courier "profiles"—a practice we'll examine later; and some are the result of inspecting samples, like the 300 cargo containers selected from the 80,000 at Los Angeles. One reason Paco Chanes and his friends were so fond of shrimp boats is that if the refrigerated compartments that hold shrimp are opened for inspection, the shrimp will be ruined. Customs inspectors have to have a reasonable expectation of finding contraband before they start poking through heaps of frozen shrimp. In the late '80s, the Rand Corporation found that the federal government, by spending almost $6 billion on interdiction, had raised the street price of cocaine by only 4 percent more than it would otherwise have been. One expert quoted by Benjamin and Miller said searching for illegal drug imports makes looking for a needle in a haystack seem like child's play.

The government spends millions on devices to detect drug smugglers, but the smugglers are often able to counter them much less expensively. For example, drug pilots have learned they can evade radar with the help of simple highway "fuzz-busters." Drug smugglers usually get new technology, like anti-radar devices or secure communications, before the government agencies. They pay cash on the spot, while the government agencies spend time on paperwork. A veteran customs agent summed up the problem: "They are inherently flexible; we're not. That's why we always lose." According to Anthony Bocchichio, head of the DEA's technical operations unit, the smugglers get their technology cheaper too. Devices to counteract smugglers' innovations—such as the use of cellular phones to foil wire-tapping—usually cost ten to fifteen times what the innovation cost.

Then there's motivation. As one drug smuggler said:

There are places [along the shore] where the water is two feet deep and less, and the channels you have to use are unmarked. Now, a good doper knows those channels because he studies them. He's also making ten, twelve, fifteen thousand dollars—it depends on the load—for four hours work, and for that kind of money, he's expected to take the risk of getting it wrong. The guy chasing him is getting maybe a hundred bucks for a shift, on which he's going to pay tax, and if he hits that sandbank at sixty miles an hour he isn't going to collect his pension because he's going to be dead. Now, if you're in the Customs boat heading for the sandbank: Which way do you want to push the throttle?

The financial rewards of drug trafficking are enormous. An ounce of cocaine can be manufactured in the United States for about $50. Sold in a big city in diluted form, that same ounce will bring about $2,500. A dollar's worth of Mexican marijuana sells for $100 in the

United States. Part of this enormous increase in cost is caused by the risk, including compensation for daredevil pilots and small boat skippers. Another part is caused by the greed of monopolistic drug dealers who control their segments of the market with naked violence. As long as they can make the income they do from the drug trade, cutting off the flow of narcotics and cocaine into the country is a lost cause.

3

If we can't intercept illegal drugs at sea or as soon as they land in the United States, can we destroy them at the source?

Sometimes. But it takes unusual circumstances. In the late 1960s, the Nixon Administration began pressuring Turkey to make poppy cultivation illegal, except for a small opium crop to supply the pharmaceutical industry. In central Anatolia, poppies supply cooking oil, poppy leaves are eaten in salads, poppy husks feed the livestock and poppy stalks are used for food. And opium is a cash crop. The Turks resisted. Turkey, like most of the world, had not had the benefit of Richmond Pearson Hobson. Opium was a matter of economics, not morals. It was otherwise in the United States.

"To show you how seriously I view the matter," said a presidential assistant, according to Arthur Downey, a National Security Council staffer, "I intend to recommend to the President that unless we have an agreement, he should order the Sixth Fleet through the Dardanelles and shell Istanbul. They are committing naked aggression; why shouldn't we respond?"

Turkey is a member of NATO, and it depended on the United States for military equipment, especially as its relations with neighboring Greece, another NATO member, were distinctly unfriendly. In 1971, a military coup overthrew the government. The soldiers, unwilling to risk the loss of military hardware from the United States, agreed to cut back opium cultivation. The result, as we've seen, was a temporary shortage of raw material for the heroin factories in Sicily and Marseille.

Turkey, though, produced only 3 to 8 percent of the world's illicit opium. Far more was produced in India, but the United States had no lever on that country. In Iran, another major producer, the Shah was not to be pressured. Because of his country's oil fields and its proximity to the U.S.S.R., Washington aimed to keep the Iranian despot happy at all costs. Then there was the Golden Triangle, where Santo Trafficante, Jr., went to establish a new source of supply. And after a couple of years, Turkey went back to opium cultivation.

Country-by-country interdiction campaigns like the one aimed at Turkey illustrate the "balloon principle." You can press your finger against an inflated balloon, and it will collapse at that point. The rest of the balloon will expand, though, so the total volume remains the same. That's what happens in the drug world. Twenty-five square miles of poppy fields will supply all the heroin users in the United States with the dope they crave. The poppy will thrive not only in its native Eurasian highlands but in most of the world. At present, only about 1,000 square miles in the world are being used for coca production. That's 4/100th of 1 percent of the land suitable for coca growing in South America alone. And coca can be grown anywhere in the world that doesn't have freezing winters.

The U.S. government continues actively trying to get foreign governments to outlaw such plants as coca, the opium poppy and marijuana. But because no one outside of this country seriously thinks a drug trafficker is worse than a murderer, it hasn't had much luck. In Mexico and other countries, money and equipment earmarked for marijuana destruction has gone mostly to line the pockets and improve the lifestyle of government officials.

The United States did score one interesting coup in Mexico. It got Mexican planes to spray an herbicide on growing marijuana plants. The herbicide chosen was Paraquat. Paraquat is a poison. It slowly poisons the plants. But it quickly poisons people who smoke it. The herbicide had been chosen by the Mexican officials, so it isn't fair to blame our drug warriors. But if you buy the Dope Fiend image, mass poisoning of pot smokers may sound reasonable.

4

The work of the Drug Enforcement Administration in foreign countries is a tale of frustration. And in times of frustration, the spirit of the aide to President Nixon who wanted to bombard Istanbul, thrives. In 1986 President Ronald Reagan signed a directive calling drugs a national security threat. In 1989, soon after taking office, President George Bush followed with a secret national security decision directive greatly expanding the role of the military in fighting drugs and authorizing special military operations in drug-producing regions of Latin America. Defense Secretary Dick Cheney ordered commanders to develop plans for "operational support" of anti-drug actions in Latin America. Cheney called drugs "a direct threat to the sovereignty and security of our country" and vowed to establish "a more aggressive and robust" American military presence in the Andes. And by the end of the year, we invaded Panama.

This yearning for a military solution was not confined to the Bush Administration or the Republican party. Rep. Stephen Solarz of New York, a Democrat, said drugs are like missiles "fired at American cities," and we need a military plan to "knock out the enemy." Solarz had never been considered one of the intellectuals of the House, but Republican William Cohen, of Maine, a Senate intellectual who was a major critic of the Reagan Administration over the Iran-Contra operation, has said the only solution to the U.S. drug problem is to "go to the source" by "taking out the machine-gun nest."

Even liberal Democrat John Kerry, who did so much to uncover the CIA's dirty drug dealings in Central America, has called for sending in the troops to destroy the drug dealers.

"We should engage in joint military and paramilitary operations, with Congressional approval, including helicopter and air strikes on cocaine fields with processing centers," Kerry said in 1989. The final report of his subcommittee on Contra involvement with drugs defined drug trafficking as "a national security and foreign policy problem of significant proportions" and recommended that the government "consider how to utilize more effectively the . . . military options to neutralize the growing power of the cartels."

A year later, Kerry withdrew his recommendation, calling for a closer look at military options "before the body bags start coming back to this country." Kerry, a decorated combat veteran of Vietnam, knows a thing or two about war. Most of those calling for "surgical strikes" against the drug infrastructure, however, have witnessed neither combat nor surgery. Most surgical operations are pretty bloody.

Kerry's defection from the cause of making the War on Drugs a real war has not noticeably quieted the claque favoring military raids. Lawrence Korb, an assistant secretary of defense in the Reagan Administration, said the military themselves (at least the top officers) were thinking about joining the drug war.

"Getting help from the military on drugs used to be like pulling teeth," he said in 1989. "Now everybody's looking around to say, 'Hey, how can we justify these forces?' And the answer they're coming up with is drugs." One unidentified major general told a reporter, "With peace breaking out all over, it might give us something to do."

One recent proposal for military expeditions against foreign drug traffickers has come from Vincent T. Bugliosi, the Los Angeles prosecutor who helped send Charles Manson to prison.

Bugliosi proposes a quick raid, prepared in secret and without any consultation with Congress that might tip off the drug traffickers. He concedes that such an expedition has no constitutional basis, but points out that presidents all through the country's history have ordered military action on their own responsibility to save the nation from peril. And the epidemic of drug use, he says, has put the nation in serious danger.

He compares the threats to the United States by the Communists in Korea and Vietnam with the threat posed by the drug traffickers. "Whatever the merits of our military intervention were, certain realities have to be recognized. (1) The Communist aggression was thousands of miles from our shore. (2) The threat to us was indirect, speculative, and if it were to occur at all (i.e., the spread of Communism to our shores), was off in the distant future. With the Medellín cartel, their enormous crimes are being committed not only right here in this country, but at this very moment."

For some reason, selling a prohibited commodity to a willing buyer, which is the basic business of the Medellín cartel (and the Cali cartel), seems like a less "enormous crime" than the suppression of everyone's personal liberty (which is what the Communists tried to do in Korea and succeeded in doing in Vietnam). Maybe not, though, if you believe in the Dope Fiend.

In recommending a "surgical strike" against the drug lords of Colombia, Bugliosi concedes that the Colombian government "for reasons of sovereignty" would not give its consent. However, he believes, both the government and the Colombian people would secretly welcome such a move, because the Medellín and Cali cartels are a serious threat to civilized life in Colombia.

The raid, he says, would be "swift, very inexpensive and likely to succeed with probably no loss of American blood." It would not be like the Panama invasion, which killed hundreds of Panamanian civilians, vastly intensified anti-American feeling in that country and utterly failed to stem the flow of drugs. As a precedent, Bugliosi cites the 1916 pursuit of Pancho Villa. Villa had raided the town of Columbus, New Mexico, in an action that resulted in the deaths of seventeen Americans and almost two hundred Villistas (not seven and twenty-three, as Bugliosi reports). Bugliosi admits that the pursuit was called off because of the hostility of the Mexicans, among whom, he says, Villa was a folk hero.

Actually, Villa had lost his status as a folk hero many months before. At the time of the raid, he was a failed revolutionary whose troops were deserting at every opportunity. He had to resort to drafting troops. One of the draftees shot him during the pursuit, and Villa was out of action until long after General Pershing took his men back to the United States. Bugliosi is correct, however, when he says the hostility of the Mexicans caused the United States to cancel the pursuit. Ordinary Mexicans, who by this time had no use for Villa, were hostile. So was the Carranza government, even though Villa was a mortal enemy of everyone in it.

Somehow, many Americans seem unable to realize that the sight of foreign troops enforcing their law in your land is basically repugnant to any people. Unable to remember what happened in Mexico, we got into a similar mess in Somalia. Mohammed Farrah Aidid has injured far more people and caused far more damage in Somalia than Pancho Villa ever did in Mexico or Pablo Escobar and his associates ever did in Colombia. But as soon as American troops tried to capture Aidid, the United States seemed to become an enemy to the whole Somali people.

In short, an expedition against the Colombian drug lords would, even if successful, be neither short nor inexpensive. And if the expedition were successful and captured all of the Colombian "kingpins," what would happen?

Judging by what's happened in Central America, the kingpins would be immediately replaced by new kingpins. The death of Escobar in Medellín brought an interesting reaction from the U.S. press. Dozens of stories appeared pointing out that *El Padrino's* demise would not slow the flow of cocaine. All stories pointed out that the Cali syndicates, Medellín's great rival, now exported 80 percent of the cocaine sold in the United States. Considering the way the press and the DEA (from which the press generally gets its drug news) have concentrated on the Medellín drug lords, a reader might think Gilberto and Miguel Rodriguez Orejuela, José Santacruz Lodoño and the whole Cali cartel had suddenly sprung up out of the ground. Actually, Cali traffickers were selling cocaine here when Pablo Escobar was still stealing tombstones. There is no doubt that the Cali people ran a smoother operation. Money, not murder, was their prime weapon. As Scott and Marshall put it:

> Traffickers in Cali appear to have developed organized, institutional channels for importing cocaine into the United States, by (for example) corrupting corporate officers of at one major U.S. airline (Eastern). Their money launderers banked in Miami with a network of banks linked to both past CIA-drug bank scandals and to the State Department's "humanitarian assistance" to the Contras.
>
> There are other signs that, as former DEA agents and informants have alleged, the United States, even before Reagan, chose not to prosecute members of this International Connection [which included the Cali cartel] for political reasons. And the Reagan and Bush administrations appear to have used one member of the International Connection, Barry Seal, to blame the huge flow of cocaine into the United States on a "narcoterrorist" conspiracy, allegedly centered on the Medellín cartel and directed by Castro's Cuba and the Sandinistas of Nicaragua.

Scott and Marshall imply that the CIA was involved in shifting all blame for cocaine to Medellín. Certainly the CIA's drug-smuggling Cuban exile "assets" had reason to hate the Medellín mobsters. The "cocaine cowboys" from Medellín blasted the Cubans out of their cocaine monopoly in south Florida and took over most of that market. Then the violent Escobar took on the Cali people in New York. He lost that war and earned the enmity of the more powerful Cali cartel.

To get back to Bugliosi, the California attorney says people like the Ochoas and the late Pablo Escobar should be given the death penalty, which would deter other Colombians from trying to take their place. He does not explain why the death penalty would be a deterrent to

Colombians when it has never been a deterrent to any other people. And Escobar's death in the shoot-out in Medellin obviously has not deterred any other drug traffickers.

5

The most discouraging fact of all is that if all foreign drug importation could be stopped immediately, the United States would not be "drug free." At present, the most potent marijuana in the world, carefully cultivated "sinsemilla" pot, is produced right here in the U.S.A. American marijuana production has grown in quantity as well as quality. It has surpassed corn as the nation's leading cash crop. Home-grown pot now constitutes 20 to 30 percent of all the marijuana sold in the United States. The only reason it hasn't taken over the whole market is because it's still cheaper to grow marijuana in Mexico and smuggle it across the border than it is to raise it here.

Opium poppies could easily be grown in many U.S. states. But gathering opium is labor-intensive, so it's cheaper to harvest it in Pakistan or Laos than in Arizona or Arkansas. Coca is not promising either. It takes an enormous quantity of coca leaves to make a pound of cocaine. Cutting off imports might make the cultivation of both of these drugs economically attractive to many people, though.

More likely, ending the importation of traditional drugs would result in a boom in synthetic drugs. Even in the present situation, a number of criminal entrepreneurs are manufacturing methcathinone, nicknamed "cat." Cat was developed by Parke-Davis some forty years ago, but never sold because of its addictive properties. A couple of decades ago, it became a popular intoxicant in Russia. The center of its production now is Marquette County, in Michigan's Upper Peninsula, but cat factories have been located in all the Great Lakes states and even as far away as Seattle. It is supposed to produce a high more powerful than cocaine's, and it can be easily made with legal materials.

Another synthetic that's already carved out a niche in the drug market is methamphetamine hydrochloride, known as methedrine or, in its smokable form, crystal meth or ice. Methedrine was developed in Japan during World War II to give extra stamina to war workers and soldiers. When it was banned in postwar Japan, production shifted to South Korea. It is now being produced in the United States. Ice is similar to crack, except that it gives its user an eight-hour high, while the same quantity of crack results in twenty minutes of euphoria. The use of ice is already spreading rapidly. If cocaine were eliminated, ice would suffice.

Heroin addicts also have a synthetic to turn to. III-Methylfantanile can be manufactured in home laboratories from legal chemicals and is a hundred times more potent than heroin. It has already caused a number of deaths from overdoses.

If all foreign drugs were cut off, addicts would undoubtedly switch to home-grown drugs or locally-produced synthetics. And the Drug War would go on.

It's become increasingly clear to many that the War on Drugs is not likely stop drug use in this country. But the actual situation is even worse than that.

The Drug War is stimulating the market.

16

When sociologists began studying drug use in the inner cities during the 1950s, they started with a foregone conclusion: The drug user was "a double failure" who couldn't make it in the mainstream world and didn't have the talent for success in the underworld. That may have been true at one time. As the academics got to know real addicts, though, they had to change their opinions.

Instead of failures, they found that some of the most lively and enterprising of the ghetto youth were the first to use hard drugs. And they became role models for other kids. "A righteous dope fiend" was a term of respect. In the '60s, two anthropologists, Edward Preble and John Casey, published "Taking Care of Business: The Heroin User's Life on the Street," an article based on their observations of a number of New York addicts. Instead of being passive, withdrawn and inadequate, the authors wrote, their subjects were at least as busy as persons with steady jobs. And what they did was more interesting than most of the legitimate work their neighbors did. According to Preble and Casey:

> They are actively engaged in meaningful activities and relation-
> ships seven days a week. The brief moments of euphoria after
> each administration of a small amount of heroin constitute a
> small fraction of their daily lives. The rest of the time, they are
> aggressively pursuing a career that is exacting, challenging, ad-
> venturous and rewarding. . . . The heroin user is, in a way,
> like the compulsively hard-working business executive whose
> ostensible goal is the acquisition of money, but whose real sat-
> isfaction is in meeting the inordinate challenges he creates for
> himself.

One addict described his life this way: "When I'm at home with the bag safely in my pocket, and I haven't been caught stealing all day, and I didn't get beat [cheated] and the cops didn't get me—I feel like a working man coming home: he's worked hard, and he knows he's done something."

The lure of heroin, Preble and Casey concluded—and they are joined by other social scientists who have studied the ghetto environment—is not "in the effects of the drug on their minds and bodies; it lies in the gratification of accomplishing a series of challenging, exciting tasks, every day of the week."

In the upside-down world of the ghetto, anyone who could pull off enough scams, burglaries or other crimes to support a heavy habit was "a real hustling dope fiend" and the object of respect sometimes bordering on awe. He had to have connections: He needed to know where to fence stolen goods and where and when to buy his heroin. He had to have business sense, so the sellers and fences couldn't cheat him, and he had to have a "rep" so they wouldn't try to bully him. The size of his habit also showed how successful he was. The amount of dope he could afford was like someone else's Porsche, car telephone or gold chains.

In contrast, wrote the anthropologists:

Given the social conditions of the slums and their effects on family and individual development, the odds are strongly against the development of a legitimate, non-deviant career that is challenging and rewarding. The most common legitimate career is a menial job, with no future except in the periodic, statutory raises in the minimum wage level. If anyone could be called passive in the slums, it is not the heroin user, but the one who submits to, and accepts these conditions.

Another motive for the user, according to Preble and Casey, was "revenge" on the straight world for the "injustices and deprivations" of his life. The straight world held that drugs were evil and those who used them were wicked, so the ghetto dweller bought them to defy the straights. He got real satisfaction out of "outslicking" the police. "Drugs," one druggie told Preble and Casey, "is a hell of a game." Another told them that programs to provide heroin to addicts legally would take the "fun" out of heroin use.

The current War on Drugs, then, provides one of the major attractions of inner-city drug use.

2

It also greatly intensifies the harm that drugs do.

As alcohol consumption patterns during Prohibition showed, making a substance illegal results in a change from steady, moderate consumption to binges, from mild forms of the substance—beer—to potent forms—whiskey and gin. If the penalty for selling beer and selling whiskey is the same, the seller will concentrate on the more compact and more expensive whiskey. The same is true when there's little difference in penalties for the sale of marijuana and the sale of heroin or crack.

The War on Drugs makes narcotics and cocaine a hundred or more times more expensive than they would be if they could be purchased legitimately. In so doing, the "war" gives the "righteous dope fiend" a chance to display his wealth by using large quantities of drugs. His ghetto neighbors admire him for his business success. Taking heroin or cocaine in such quantities poses a grave danger of death by overdose. It certainly means genuine addiction in a very short time and completely broken health not much later. In the inverted values of the ghetto, though, the drug user shows his machismo, demonstrates that he's a "stand-up guy," by taking heavy doses of the most potent drugs.

Crack, a crystalline, smokable form of cocaine, could be called a product of the War on Drugs. It has the desirable characteristics for a contraband product of being compact and potent. It also appears to be cheap: A vial sells for around five dollars. The catch is that it produces a powerful but brief high that, as soon as it wears off, produces an immediate craving for another. "Crackheads" buy vials by the dozen.

During the '70s, some cocaine addicts discovered that by treating cocaine with ether, it could be made smokable. Smoking produced an instant high. The process of making "free-base," however was dangerous. Comedian Richard Prior was almost killed in a free-base explosion. Addicts began asking for ready-made free-base.

A gang of Dominican drug sellers in New York found that cocaine could be cooked with a chemical they called "comeback," a substance similar to lidocaine, and the result was smokable. Then they learned that they could substitute baking soda for some of the comeback. One ounce of cocaine, purchased for $1,200, will make from 600 to 1,000 vials of crack. Each vial will sell for $5, and the crack makers will also make a healthy profit. The profit is the only thing about crack that is healthy.

Besides adding to the carnage caused by the drugs themselves, the War on Drugs has created the "crack house"—an evil with many dimensions. Crack houses are operated by gangs or individuals with strong gang connections. They are abandoned buildings, because any property used in drug trafficking is liable to seizure. The crack house operator isn't risking his own property. To say that they are unsanitary is like saying Hitler didn't care for Jews. The floor are covered with excrement and vomit. The operator knows his customers will come anyway, so he doesn't bother to clean up. Crack increases sexual desire while it decreases ability to perform, so the operator welcomes prostitutes who will work for as little as $2 or a pipe of crack.

The ability of crack houses to spread disease in general is very high. Crack houses are credited with helping to revive tuberculosis, a disease once thought to be extinct in the United States. They're especially good at spreading sexually transmitted disease, or STD as public health officials now call it. Acquired Immune Deficiency Syndrome, AIDS, is, of course, one of these. Another is that ancient plague, syphilis, which is as fatal as ever if the person infected—like many crack house customers—has never heard of penicillin. In 1986, according to the Centers for Disease Control in Atlanta, there were fewer than 30,000 cases of syphilis in the United States. By 1990, there were more than 50,000. The incidence of the disease among black males increased 132 percent.

Most of the crack house prostitutes also have AIDS. Most of them got AIDS while shooting up heroin with infected needles. Injecting heroin, not homosexual activity, is the major cause of AIDS in many big U.S. cities. Heroin users often share needles, because the War on Drugs has made it almost impossible to obtain a hypodermic needle without a prescription. Some private organizations have begun distributing household bleach to addicts. Rinsing a needle with bleach kills the AIDS virus. A few localities have started needle exchanges in an effort to stem the spread of AIDS.

In Hong Kong, where there are no restrictions on needles, there is no drug-related AIDS. The French in 1988 began distributing hypodermic needles, and they say that has slowed the spread of AIDS. In the United States, the federal government opposes needle exchanges, because, the authorities say, that would encourage the injection of heroin and other drugs. Their position is much like that of the country's Catholic bishops, who say the distribution of condoms—also to stop AIDS—encourages sexual promiscuity. The bishops, though, seem to have a better case. No one is exchanging condoms. Those who get new needles are already injecting heroin.

Crack has produced a giant health problem even when no diseases are involved. The spread of crack has caused what physicians now call "crack babies," infants who have suffered cocaine poisoning as fetuses because of their mothers' use of crack. Crack babies are ten times more likely than normal babies to suffer sudden infant death syndrome (SIDS). Those who survive neither speak nor understand language as well as other children for the first five years of their lives. Some theorize that the children's innate language ability has been permanently destroyed. Hospital intensive care for crack babies can cost as much as $90,000. It can cost another $40,000 to overcome the learning difficulties of a child born to a crack-using mother—just to get the child ready for kindergarten.

3

According to the National Institute on Drug Abuse, drug use in the United States peaked around 1979 or 1980. At least, that's what the NIDA's National Household Survey on Drug Abuse shows. The survey is based on interviews with persons twelve and older in a sample of about 9,000 households. This survey, and a similar one taken annually of a sample of 16,000 to 17,000 high school seniors, has a couple of drawbacks as a valid indicator of drug use, though. First, it depends on respondents who had taken drugs truthfully admitting it. Most people would hesitate to admit such a thing, especially to a government agency. Second, and more important, it misses all the people who don't live in regular households. As the NIDA itself puts it, "Self-report surveys tap mainstream Americans with stable living arrangements."

The first drawback is the less important, because it's known that people lie about drug use. In several different studies, where respondents were asked to submit urine samples after they had answered questions about drug use, researchers found that between half and three-quarters of those who denied using drugs had drugs in their bodies. But if the sample is taken the same way, year after year, the proportion of liars should be the same. The surveys, therefore, are valid indicators of *trends* in drug use.

The trouble is that the self-report surveys show trends in drug use only in one segment of society—"mainstream Americans with stable living arrangements" and who stay in high school until their senior year. Another survey taken by the U.S. Department of Justice shows how the trends differ. This study samples convicted jail inmates. In 1983, 18.6 percent admitted taking a "major drug" (cocaine or crack, heroin, LSD, PCP or methadone) in the month before conviction. In 1989, 27.7 percent—an increase of 9.1 percent—admitted using.

All of which reinforces the contention of most experts that "casual" or "recreational" use of drugs among the middle class has been falling off for the last few years, but drug use has not fallen off among the underclass.

Government agencies, from the federal Department of Justice down to one-man city marshal offices have claimed this middle class drop-off shows some success for the War on Drugs. It might, if the War on Drugs had been waged in middle-class neighborhoods. But it hasn't. In 1989, about 40 percent of all who were arrested on drug charges were black, and most of them came from slum areas. Blacks are about 12.6 percent of the population. This has led to the belief that a huge disproportion of drug users are black. That's not true, either. As we've seen, "cat" is manufactured in Michigan's sparsely settled Upper Peninsula and other rural areas. "Ice" has similar rural roots, as does, of course, marijuana. As the economists Benjamin and Miller put it, "Inner city blacks consume their share of illegal drugs, but they can't—and don't—foot the bulk of the $100 billion illegal-drug bill in America. Most of America is white, and most of the illegal drugs in America are consumed by whites. The middle class is the largest income group in the United States, and it consumes the largest share of the illegal drugs in the United States."

Crack is usually considered the quintessential ghetto drug, but Dr. Arnold Washton, one of the first members of the "straight" world to discover crack, says, "It is a misrepresentation to think that the majority of people who use crack are black and Hispanic and live in urban ghettos. I will stand by the statement that the overwhelming majority of people who use crack in this country are middle-class employed people, and it includes, of course, all too many high school and college students."

Benjamin and Miller point out that 80 percent of the drug patients at the 7,000 treatment centers in the United States are white and that most of the estimated 35 to 40 million persons who have used one or more illegal drugs in the past year are white.

Monsignor Joseph Potter, of Bridgeport, Connecticut, had just finished speaking to the parents of a First Communion class in the affluent suburb of Ridgefield, telling about the poverty of his home parish. One of the fathers took him aside. "He said he knew every street I was talking about," the monsignor said, "because that was where he buys his drugs."

Potter and the Bridgeport police agree that it is people like the man from Ridgefield who are destroying the heart of Bridgeport. Their support of drug dealers have made the Long Island Sound city, which calls itself the "Park City," the murder capital of Connecticut.

If drug use among the middle class is falling off, it isn't because of the War on Drugs. It's falling off for the same reason cigarette sales have fallen off, exercise-machine sales are booming, and joggers are cluttering up city streets and rural lanes.

In the inner cities, where the War goes on with continued fury, drug use is still increasing. In 1982, according to the federal Bureau of Justice Statistics, there were 676,000 drug arrests; in 1987, 937,400; and in 1991, 1,010,000.

Where the War on Drugs is being waged, it has resulted in more and more arrests, more and longer jail sentences, bigger and bigger seizures. But it hasn't slowed down drug use.

4

The "righteous dope fiend" gets his kicks from beating the system—the system Uncle Sam calls the War on Drugs. "Boy George" Rivera got a lot more than kicks.

When George Rivera was arrested in 1989, he was barely twenty years old, but he had one of the biggest heroin-distributing organizations in New York. He owned a string of front corporations, one of which, the Tuxedo Corporation, owned a dozen Mercedes, Porsches and BMWs. He distributed cash bonuses, other gifts and free vacations to high-performing members of his empire. And he had a monopoly on heroin distribution in a large section of the the Bronx. To obtain his monopoly and keep it, he had committed, or ordered committed, more than a dozen murders.

The prohibition of heroin and other drugs had made possible Rivera's rise in the world. He had been working for another retailer until he met the Chinese wholesaler who supplied his boss. He promptly made his own deal with the Chinese and cut out his erstwhile boss. Anyone who got in his way died suddenly. Boy George bought his heroin for $85,000 a pound from the Chinese, a price wildly inflated by the illegality of heroin. His employees then cut the drug by adding an equal weight of milk sugar and quinine. Sold on the street, it *netted* Rivera's organization a profit of $150,000 a pound. Addicts either paid Boy George's price or they looked for another dealer. But Boy George owned all the dealers in that area.

Boy George was not unique. Arrested in the same year in Washington, D.C., Rayful Edmond III was four years older, but he, too, owned a string of legitimate businesses as well as real estate properties and a dozen expensive cars. At its peak, his organization was making $20 million a *month*. Every large city has its Boy Georges and its Rayful Edmonds. They are, as *Wall Street Journal* writer Joe Davidson, who wrote a feature on Edmond, learned, local heroes. Millions of young men in the inner cities of America yearn to take their places. Who would rather fry hamburgers at McDonald's or push a hand truck on New York's Seventh Avenue than tool around in a Mercedes, masterminding big deals on a mobile phone while a bevy of beautiful girls wait for your smile?

The way the Drug War has been fought created the Boy Georges and the Rayful Edmonds, just as the enforcement of Prohibition made possible the careers of Al Capone, Dutch Schultz and "Charley Lucky" Luciano.

Of course, there is only so much room at the top—or even, like Rivera and Edmond, the top of the bottom—in the drug food-chain. (Those at the top of the chain—such as the late Pablo Escobar and his rivals from Cali, the heads of the Chinese syndicates and the great landowners of Afghanistan—are among the world's richest billionaires.) But there's always a chance . . . . And that's why people buy lottery tickets. The street dealers, those who take the most risk, sometimes make little more than the minimum wage, but there's always the prospect of becoming another Boy George. The risk hardly has a chilling effect on street dealing. It's not that great. An estimated 35 to 40 million people break the drug laws annually, but only about 3 percent of them are caught. Those who go to jail find that while hardly desirable, prison isn't much worse than life in the ghetto as a "straight." Inmates get three fairly nutritious meals a day and a clean place to sleep. Not everyone in the inner city can say that. When you consider the conditions of inner city life, it becomes clear that only a person of fairly strong character can resist the opportunity to become a drug trafficker.

The War on Drugs provides the spice of danger that leads a ghetto youth to become a "righteous dope fiend." It also makes it possible for a smart kid with no education but a talent for violence to become a mini-drug lord.

There's still another way in which the War on Drugs has been stimulating the market. It's providing an education for aspiring drug dealers and dope addicts.

5

Three-quarters of all the people arrested in drug cases are charged with simple possession. Those who go to jail can broaden their horizons. Here they meet experienced drug users who know the best ways to make a buy and the best people to fence stolen property. They also meet shoplifters, burglars, con artists and contract killers—every variety of criminal. With no effort at all, an inmate can get an advanced degree in crime and even aspire to become a specialist. He can learn the best techniques for stealing a car, how to collect insurance by burning down buildings, where to get a gun whenever he needs one.

In short, there's a good chance that a person can go into jail as a simple drug user and come out prepared to support his habit in a comprehensive variety of illegal and violent ways.

He may even come out as a member of a gang. In fact, the chances are that he will. Gangs exist not only in our cities but in our prisons as well. In many prisons, a new inmate may feel obliged to join one or another gang for his own protection. Allegiances made in prison continue outside the walls, and vice versa.

According to Dan Stebbins, a Connecticut State Police lieutenant specializing in gang activity, "The connection between the streets and prisons is very tight. Gang members who join in prison remain in the gang when they go back to the street. There's a lot of correspondence, both written and over the phone, that assures them they will be taken care of either when they come in or get out."

We'll look at the gang situation more closely later.

That's just one of the problems that have been plaguing the criminal-justice system since the War on Drugs shifted into high gear. A major problem is the growth of violent crime. That's a problem that's both related and unrelated to the increase of drug use—and in a number of sometimes surprising ways.

17

Just about everyone today is convinced that drugs are the main cause of urban violence. Newspapers and broadcast media routinely describe the feuds of urban gangs—which they call "drug gangs"—as wars over drug markets. Any shooting of a black person is usually said to be the result of "a drug deal gone sour." In the fall of 1993, for example, a police captain in New Haven, Connecticut, described the shooting of a black bicyclist that way. The victim, though, belonged to an organization dedicated to *eliminating* drug use in the ghetto. The chief of police was also a member of that organization. The captain later apologized for his mistake. But how many other victims not known to police chiefs have been similarly accused of drug use or drug selling?

"Drive-by" shootings are also popularly supposed to be the results of feuds by "drug gangs." The August 2, 1993 issue of *Time* had a cover story on teenage shootings. One of the kids interviewed was a sixteen-year-old sophomore identified as "Doug." Doug is white, lives in a poor section of Omaha, Nebraska, and owns a sawed-off shotgun. He does not belong to a gang, and he is not involved with drugs. But he's done nine drive-by shootings.

"It's basically revenge, that sort of thing," he told *Time* writer Jon D. Hull. For instance, he admitted shooting up a truck that belonged to the boyfriend of a judge's daughter. That was "revenge" on the judge for having sentenced several of his friends. "I'm not actually aiming at anybody," he said. "But once my older brother missed a baby's head by a quarter of an inch." Sometimes the shootings have no reason. Describing a shooting at one house in his neighborhood, Doug said, "I saw this dog sitting on a couch in this big window above the front porch, so I just shot him. I'm not sure what kind of dog it was, but he fell out of the window and onto the porch. I could hear him yelping as we ran away."

The random violence the *Time* story described frequently has far more fatal results. It has become a major problem in the United States. In 1964, there were 7,990 murders and non-negligent homicides known to the police in the United States; in 1991, there were 21,505. There was a pretty steady progression until 1980, when the total reached 21,860. Since then it has been up and down, but never lower than 17,545. During the same period, use of illicit drugs increased at about the same rate. The decline in casual drug use by middle class people after 1980 is shown on the NIDA's self-reporting surveys. That decrease, though, has been made up for by the continued increase of drug consumption by poor people in the inner cities.

What's happened has been that the public has put two and two together and come up with five. Or maybe four-and-a-half, because drugs do have an influence on violence.

There's a lot of confusion between coincidence and cause-and-effect. For instance, if 27.7 percent of convicted jail inmates took a "major drug" within a month of the offense, does that mean that they committed the offense because they took the drug? In some cases, perhaps. But drugs are an important part of the criminal milieu, even in jails.

"If I'd have gone to jail . . . I would have done the same thing I did the last time. I would have got high and fought every day. I would have come out with new ways how to rob people, new ways how to get over," the inmate of a drug treatment center told the author. The man had been in jail often enough to qualify as an expert. In an environment where drugs are so prevalent, it's difficult not to use them. A user's habit may have nothing to do with his crime. Around 1900, the last period of peak addiction, there were plenty of people with drug habits, but the kind of individual street crime we have now was quite rare. There was a disgraceful amount of collective violence, such as lynchings, but nobody blamed that on drug addiction (although a lot of the participants were probably under the influence of that legal drug, alcohol).

On the other hand, in chapter 1, we saw that persons under the influence of drugs react in a variety of ways—often in the ways they are expected to react. If the common expectation is that drug use will lead to criminal behavior, drug use may well have helped cause some crimes.

Federal statistics, though, indicate that drug use is not a major source of homicide, and drug trafficking may not be, either, although that is doubtful. A study of murders in the seventy-five largest U.S. counties lists "Criminal Activity" as the cause of 22 percent of the murders. Of these, slightly less than half are due to criminal activity involving drugs. Another 16 percent are classed as "Felony Murder"—killing someone in the course of committing another felony such as robbery, rape, burglary or arson. ("Felony Murder" is a separate classification from "Criminal Activity," although any of the "Felony Murder" subcategories would seem to lay people to qualify as criminal activity.) The Bureau of Justice Statistics classifies 44 percent of the killings as the result of "Personal Conflicts." These include: Property Dispute, 18 percent; Love/Sex Dispute, 19 percent; Domestic Issues, 17 percent; Redress of Insult, 10 percent; On-Going Feud, 3 percent, and Dispute at Scene, 6 percent. Other causes include: Retaliation, 5 percent; Child Abuse, 3 percent; Premeditated Violence, 4 percent, and Other, 5 percent. Just what some of these classifications include and do not include is a bit mysterious. It's quite possible that drugs play a larger role in "Criminal Activities" and "Personal Conflicts" than is obvious to the police, or at least, to the statisticians. When a drug dealer kills a customer who tries to stiff him, there's certainly been a "property dispute." That's also true when a customer kills a dealer who sold him "bad dope." Disputes about who can sell drugs in a particular area often turn into "on-going feuds." A gang's decision to kill a business rival is obviously "premeditated violence." There is no violence more premeditated than the "trademark" murders committed by crack-selling Jamaican posses when they set up business in a new town.

The statistics are misleading in another way. They cover the entire United States, a nation of 255,000,000 people, most of whom don't live in the centers of major metropolitan areas like New York, Los Angeles or Chicago, or even Philadelphia, Detroit, Atlanta or Kansas City. Police in any big city will say that a large percentage of inner city homicides are related to the drug trade.

The statistics on murder and non-negligent homicide also contradict the widely disseminated statement that most murders are committed by the victim's "family and friends." Of the 21,505 homicides, 2,683 were committed by family members and 5,598 by "Acquaintances." "Friends," including boyfriends and girlfriends, committed 1,513, "Neighbors" committed 229, and "Strangers," 3,236. "Unknown Relationship," the vast majority of whom are probably strangers, committed 8,247 of these homicides. It should also be noted that "Acquaintances" includes drug buyers and their customers, members of rival gangs and persons with whom the victim has been involved in long-running feuds. In many cases, as might be expected, the victim was known to the assailant, although not necessarily well known or favorably known. When one person kills another, he often has a reason for disliking the victim.

The evidence indicates that while drug use and violence are increasing on parallel tracks, drug use does not necessarily cause violence. But the drug *trade*, which supplies the users, seems to be responsible for a substantial amount of the violence.

2

What causes the rest?

There are a lot of theories. One favored by many psychologists is that violent behavior in later life is caused by being raised in a violent household. As a matter of fact, just about all sociologists, criminologists, epidemiologists, probation officers, welfare workers, physicians, police officers, judges, youth workers and "gangologists" say that violence in the home is a major cause of violence in the community. If children learn from what they see at home that violence is the normal way to resolve disputes, that's what they'll use. One reason child-abusers are so generally hated in prisons, criminologists say, is that most prison inmates had themselves been abused children.

Violence witnessed while very young, according to the psychologists, has the most profound effect on later behavior. That's one reason why people living in countries where the government is very violent, as in the U.S.S.R. under Stalin or Argentina during the "dirty war" period, may not be particularly violent: Governments in those countries usually practice their violence out of public sight. In countries where the violence is open, as in Colombia during the last couple of decades of civil war, personal violence is usually widespread.

"I believe that if all the children born in America learned at home how to manage anger and aggression non-violently, our homicide and assault rates would decline by 50 percent—maybe even 75 percent," writes Dr. Deborah Prothrow-Stith, former Massachusetts commissioner of public health and now assistant dean at the Harvard School of Public Health.

Such unanimity of agreement is pretty strong evidence that violent families tend to produce violent children. But the question remains: Why is violence, indicated by the homicide rate in the last thirty years, *increasing*? Are the number of violent families increasing too? That seems not unlikely. But if so, why?

Another frequently cited reason—cited by Attorney General Janet Reno herself in October 1993—is violence in the movies and on television. Once again, there is a large bibliography of studies indicating that violence in the entertainment media tend to increase violent behavior among those who are entertained. And there are few, if any, studies that show it decreases violence.

Prothrow-Stith includes rap music in her indictment of the media. When rap songs have titles like "Fuck tha Police," lyrics that advocate machine-gunning unfaithful lovers, singers who promise to create a "bloodbath" and publishing companies called Ruthless Attack Muzick, it's easy to see her point.

According to psychologists, watching (or listening to) representations of violence builds up insensitivity, requiring ever more violent representations. Anyone comparing how violence is presented in movies a generation or two ago and how it is presented now can see the process. But some psychologists seem to go beyond common sense in their condemnation of entertainment, particularly television, violence. Dr. Brandon S. Centerwall, professor of epidemiology at the University of Washington, testifying on May 12, 1993, before the House Energy and Commerce Committee's Subcommittee on Telecommunications and Finance, said:

> The U.S. homicide has doubled since the 1950s. As a member of the Centers for Disease Control violence research team, my task was to determine why. A wide array of possibilities was examined—the "baby boom" effect, trends in urbanization, economic trends, trends in alcohol abuse, the role of capital punishment, the effects of civil unrest, the availability of firearms, exposure to television.

Over the course of seven years of investigation, each of these purported causes was tested in a variety of ways to see whether it could be eliminated as a credible contributor to the doubling of rates of violence in the U.S. And, one by one, each of them was invalidated except for television.

In his report, Centerwall compared homicide rates in the United States and Canada with the homicide rate in South Africa, where television was banned until 1975. Between 1945 and 1974, the homicide rate in the two North American countries rose more than 90 percent, while in South Africa, it declined 7 percent. After eight years of television, however, South Africa's homicide rate had increased 56 percent.

Centerwall's study was completed in 1989. In its conclusion, he says, "It is estimated that exposure to television is etiologically related to approximately one half of the homicides committed in the U.S., or approximately 10,000 homicides annually, and to a major proportion - perhaps one half—of rapes, assaults and other forms of inter-personal violence in the U.S."

It's hard to argue with a spokesman for the Centers for Disease Control. But it's also difficult to believe that 10,000 persons are murdered every year solely because of television. Particularly since there are studies of the pre- and post-TV violence rates of a couple of remote Canadian towns that got television late. The post-TV homicide rates were somewhat higher—but by no means double—the pre-TV rates. And it must be noted that Centerwall's South African study does not consider any changes in South African life except the introduction of television. The years 1975–83, though, saw the beginning of rioting, murder and massacre perpetrated by supporters of the African National Congress and the Inkatha Freedom Party. That violence was related to television the way the price of wheat in Kansas is related to the tides in the Bay of Fundy. Further, there is no television more violent than Japan's, and Japan has one of the world's lowest homicide rates.

What about the availability of firearms? In the last few years, there has been a flood of bills in state legislatures aimed at limiting access to firearms. Semiautomatic rifles that look like military automatic "assault rifles" are banned in some places. Semiautomatic rifles are banned in other places no matter what they look like. There are waiting periods before purchasing various types of guns or all types of guns. After 1934, purchasers of automatic weapons had to pay a heavy federal tax and put up with such state-imposed annoyances as unannounced inspections of the guns and ammunition. After 1986, sale of new automatic weapons to anyone outside of the military or the police was entirely forbidden. Both gun owners and manufacturers are subject to liability suits that would have been impossible a few years ago. Five of the largest discount chains in the country have discontinued selling firearms. Cities ranging in size from Morton Grove, Illinois to Washington, D.C., have banned the private possession of handguns.

In other words, there is a wide public perception that guns, especially handguns, are a problem. Some of this is due to distortion by advocates of "gun control" (which in many cases would be more accurately called "gun elimination"). These advocates compare, for instance, the rate of "gun murders" in the United States with the "gun murders" in certain other countries, as if murder is worse if it's noisy. Britain is a favorite subject for comparison, because it has stricter gun controls than the United States and a lower homicide rate (with any kind of weapon). Britain also had a lower homicide rate than the United States before it adopted gun controls. But that earlier British homicide rate was lower than the current British homicide rate *with gun controls*. Switzerland and Israel, countries with easy availablity of guns (in addition to the *required* possession of automatic weapons by most male citizens) and low private homicide rates, are seldom compared with the United States. Other gun-control advocates simply assume that all murders in the United States are committed with guns.

Nevertheless, the United States does have a higher homicide rate than any country in Europe but Russia (when the European country is not participating in a war or "ethnic cleansing"). It's also higher than the homicide rates of Canada, Australia, New Zealand or Japan. And about 60 percent of the U.S. homicides are committed with guns (although hardly any with the semiautomatic "assault rifle" look-alikes). Clearly, guns play some part in American murder. If nothing else, they make it easier to kill someone than most other methods.

With all the discussion of how guns may affect the American homicide rate, one question remains. Why is the homicide rate increasing at about the same rate gun availability is decreasing?

One study done by gun control advocates and published in the *New England Journal of Medicine* may contain a clue. It's not an obvious point, and it hints at an idea that is both ridiculous and repugnant. But if you examine the figures carefully, they point to an answer.

The study compared the homicide rates in the nearby cities of Seattle, Washington, and Vancouver, British Columbia, from 1980 through 1986. The cities are in the same part of North America and have similar population sizes. The Vancouver homicide rate with weapons other than guns (but including hands and feet) was about the same as that for Seattle. The gun homicide rate was much less. In 1976, Canada's Parliament had passed a federal law seriously limiting the availability of pistols and revolvers. Since the study was taken, the rate of non-gun murders in Vancouver has been increasing faster than Seattle's, but even so, the information appeared favorable to advocates of federal gun control. There was one catch: The gun homicide rate for Seattle's white inhabitants was about the same as it was for Vancouver's. Few blacks live in Vancouver.

3

That information could provide any aspiring neo-Nazi a chance to attempt a record-breaking jump to conclusion: that blacks are inherently more violent or more addicted to shooting people than whites. As we'll see, that's a conclusion that's as absurd as it is outrageous. Because it might lead some to such a conclusion, many consider the mere mention of the racial factor in the Seattle-Vancouver comparison to be politically incorrect. That may be why there has been so little analysis of it. There are plenty of reasons for this heavy black representation among murderers and murder victims. We'll examine them in a moment. First, though, let's look at some more statistics.

The statistics on murder in the seventy-five largest U.S. counties are broken down by race of the victims. They show little difference in the reason for the homicides. "Criminal Activity" was the reason 20 percent of the white victims and 24 percent of the black victims were killed. "Personal Conflict" accounted for the deaths of 42 percent of the whites and 45 percent of the blacks. Blacks are more likely to be killed in felony murders, and whites are more often killed in unknown circumstances. For obvious reasons, it's easier to count the victims than the perpetrators, but interracial murder is rare.

In 1992, blacks made up 12.6 percent of the population of the

United States, and whites, 83.8. Nevertheless, blacks made up half of the murder victims. The proportion has gone down only slightly since 1964, when 54 percent of the victims were black.

When looking at these figures, it's important to remember that half of the poor people in the United States are black, just like half the murder victims. Many studies have been taken that show poverty, not race, has a positive correlation with violence. Dr. William Julius Wilson and a team of sociologists at the University of Chicago have established that, as Prothrow-Stith puts it, "homicide rates soar in neighborhoods where men have no jobs or prospects, children are raised without fathers, and social institutions are in disarray." That's true for blacks, whites, Orientals and Hispanics of any race. To believe race is the deciding factor would mean expecting Dr. Prothrow-Stith, who is black, to be more violent than Dion O'Bannion, who was white.

For many years, an increasing number of blacks have been trapped in a situation of decreasing opportunities. Starting in the 1960s, manufacturing jobs, once the mainstay of the economy, began to be shipped out of the country. It was more profitable to have goods made in the Orient than in America. The blue-collar jobs that disappeared had offered a decent living and some opportunities to advance for millions of people. Replacing them, to some extent, were white-collar jobs in such fields as banking and the "information industry." These were unavailable to people without a fairly good education. Mere possession of a high school diploma wasn't enough. That left "service jobs" in fast-food restaurants, stores and cleaning crews. The pay in these places is usually at minimum wage level, and the employees are often classed as part-time so the employer won't have to pay benefits. When that was all that was available—and there weren't even enough of those jobs to go around—completing high school didn't seem worthwhile to many teenagers.

"If you've got an individual out there with no education, no skills and he doesn't know a damn thing about life except what he's learned on the street, employers don't want to talk to him," said Lt. Sam Beamon, of the Bridgeport, Connecticut, police. "He'll never be mainstreamed unless he gets struck by lightning."

This economic transformation changed the lives of everyone who had depended on factory work. Most of all, it changed the lives of that part of the black community.

In the early part of this century, Wilson points out, racially segregated housing was the rule in the United States. All blacks, rich and poor, lawyers and laborers, judges and junkies, lived in the same neighborhoods. As life became desegregated, well-to-do and middle-class blacks moved out of the ghettos, leaving the poorest and most disadvantaged. The result was a black underclass inhabiting depressed sections of our cities.

There's a white underclass too, of course. But it's easier to get out of it. A white person applying for a job at a white-run business (like the vast majority of businesses) doesn't encounter the instant distrust a black person does.

Government aid to the underclass consists mainly of Aid to Families with Dependent Children. Under current rules, AFDC penalizes two-parent families. The mother gets financial assistance only if there is no adult male capable of supporting the family in her home. The mother herself usually works "off the books" as a maid or at some other unskilled work. She has little time to care for her children. The kids, lacking family life and inspiration to better themselves, perpetuate and increase the underclass. The girls tend to get pregnant out of wedlock and go on welfare. In spite of common belief, this is not an exclusively black problem. It's true that a higher percentage of black girls have babies out of wedlock, but the *rate* at which this happens is increasing much faster for white girls. Here's how the percentages of unmarried births have increased: 1970, whites, 5.6 percent, blacks, 37.5 percent; 1980, whites, 10.2 percent, blacks, 55.5 percent; 1990, whites, 20.1 percent, blacks, 65.2 percent.

The boys join gangs. In the gangs, they learn values unlike those of most families. In *Manchild in the Promised Land*, Claude Brown describes the values of the street: "I was growing up now, and . . . I would soon be expected to kill a nigger if he mistreated me, like Rock, Bubba Williams and Dewdrop had. . . . I knew now that I had to keep up with those cats; If I didn't I would lose my respect in the neighborhood . . . I knew I was going to have to get a gun sooner or later and that I was going to have to make my new rep and take my place along with the bad niggers of the community."

Usually, the first step in combating gangs and "bad niggers" is to "put more cops on the street." What the cops do on the street, though, can add fuel to the fire. In Boston, after Charles Stuart killed his wife and said it was done by a black man, police began arresting young black men wholesale, sometimes partially strip-searching them on the street. That was not unusual in Boston. A teenager in Roxbury wrote:

> The police are like vicious dogs at times. The police come into black neighborhoods and snatch on kids, beat kids, cus [sic] you out, your mother and anybody else. How would you feel to get beaten or thrown in jail for nothing? That causes anger and frustration which leads to violence. Who are black people going to let their frustrations out on? White people? No! The police? No! They let their frustrations out on each other, and it is accepted. It is accepted in a way that not much happens if a black person shoots a black. Let a black shoot a white; it's a big situation.

The police are not so confident that a black won't shoot a cop. Some of the kids are heavily armed. Some of them are as young as twelve. The fear that any black male may be a potential assassin often makes police react brutally. In 1989, a black police officer was stopped in Long Beach, California, for a traffic violation. He was from another town and wasn't known to the cops who stopped him. What happened next resulted in a lawsuit. The black cop alleges the white cops beat him up and threw him through a plate-glass window.

Then there is Lorenzo Ricketts. Ricketts is a black Englishman, born in London of West Indian parents. He came to Hartford, Connecticut, started an auto-body shop and applied for citizenship. Anxious to improve life in his adopted land, he helped found a junior soccer league for Hartford kids. In addition to soccer, Ricketts said, "We've tried to teach them discipline. We're very strict about what we expect of our kids. And we've tried to get scholarships for them." Many of the soccer players have gone on to college—something very few of them would have done without Ricketts and his friends. To do still more, Ricketts went to the school system and offered to train children in the craft of bodywork. In short, he is anybody's idea of a public-spirited citizen.

On August 30, 1987, Lorenzo Ricketts was coaching his teams when a crowd of police in cars and on foot dashed on to the park where the soccer teams were playing. They were chasing a teenage boy who, Ricketts learned later, was suspected of having robbed the daughter of a state police officer. The boy fell, Ricketts said, and the police crowded

around him, beating him with clubs and kicking him. Ricketts said—
and except for the police, all of the dozen witnesses to the event back
him up—that he asked the officers why they were beating the kid. The
cops then began beating him. He was arrested on four counts of assaulting a police officer and inciting to riot and taken to a hospital. The
charges were dropped, but Ricketts's trip to the hospital was only the
first of many. He's had two operations to remove bone fragments from
a knee and repair a separated shoulder. Neither repair is complete. He
suffers from back pains and can no longer do any physical work. As this
is being written, his case too is in litigation.

There has always been an underclass in American cities, and they
have always been the targets of police violence. The reason is that at
any particular time, the ethnic group most strongly represented in the
underclass furnished the majority of the criminals. The Irish, fleeing
the incredible poverty of their homeland, came to an America where
their chances for advancement were only marginally better. The lucky
ones got to dig coal or lay railroad tracks, work that was long, hard and
dangerous for pay that was paltry. Most of the rest spent a lot of time
looking at signs that advised "No Irish Need Apply." Many men turned
to drink. More than a few turned to crime. In the 1880s, crime news in
New York and other eastern cities was almost exclusively about men
with names like Red Rocks Farrell, Googy Corcoran, Baboon Connolly,
Piker Ryan and Bull Hurley.

Jews today are respected as a group for their scholarship and their
philanthropy. Their ancestors are revered for their enterprise and hard
work. Around the turn of the century, though, the most notorious
member of the New York underworld was Harry Horowitz, alias Gyp
the Blood, who once seized an inoffensive stranger and broke his back
in three places to win a two-dollar bet. Gyp and his friends Lefty Louie
and Whitey Lewis were enforcers for Jack Zelig, who had taken over the
gang of Monk Eastman and led more than a hundred urban warriors.

After the Jews, Italians became the predominant group in the urban
underworld. That, of course, is well known. Not so well known is that
Italian dominance of organized crime has gone the way of Irish and
Jewish hegemony. As a result, Italian-Americans in all walks of life, but
particularly in politics, are still dogged by fools trying to discover their
"Mafia connections."

One reason for these cycles of criminality seems to be that the newest group in the country becomes the out-group. If, like the early Irish, you are ignorant, penniless, without experience in city life, and the object of centuries-old prejudice by the in-group, it's hard to get accepted. The same is true if, like the early Jews and Italians, you don't even speak the in-group's language. Without acceptance, it's hard to make a living. And that, to many people, makes crime an attractive alternative. What has helped all immigrant groups in the past has been the support of their families. That has been especially true of Orientals (although the recent influx from Hong Kong may be an exception). The first European immigrants, especially the demoralized Irish fleeing successive famines, tended to leave families behind. But family life soon reasserted itself among the immigrants. With it came stability.

African-Americans could be considered a new immigrant group, although their ancestors have lived in this country more than 300 years. Until fairly recently, the great majority of black people lived in rural areas of the South. Now most of them are in large cities. Although they were the target of ferocious discrimination in the past, discrimination against blacks today is probably milder than what the Irish immigrants suffered in the mid-nineteenth century. But today, the black underclass faces some hurdles that didn't confront the Irish. There are few jobs for unskilled people, and there will be fewer every year. Nor is there a frontier, where, like the Irish mother of Billy the Kid, they could homestead 160 acres. And neither the nineteenth-century Irish nor any other large European immigrant group had the "benefit" of Aid to Families with Dependent Children. As we've seen, AFDS has the effect of destroying families. Kids growing up without discipline may go to school, but they make education impossible. They may find jobs, but if they don't show up for work on time, they won't keep them. So everything gets worse, instead of better.

Life has not improved for the African-American underclass. The '80s were boom years, but the boom missed inner-city blacks. The average ghetto resident didn't have the education to take advantage of the new jobs offered. Instead of helping, the boom made things worse: The value of real estate went up, and so did rents. And although the economy was supposed to be booming, governments continued to withdraw services. And the heaviest cuts were in the ghettos. Sociologists Roderick and Deborah Wallace analyzed results of cutbacks in fire protection in the South Bronx. Between 1972 and 1976, they wrote,

"Some fifty New York firefighting units were either disbanded or re-moved, mainly from . . . overcrowded areas such as the South Bronx." At the same time, an arson boom began in the South Bronx, and thou-sands of poor people became refugees. That wasn't the worst, the Wal-laces found. As a result of the migration and disintegration of what was left of neighborhoods, tuberculosis, infant mortality, homicide and drug use all increased.

Drug use, as well as violence, is a product of this situation. And drug use blends with violence. The drug addict of the '80s and '90s is not as likely to get his kicks from nonviolent crime and evading detec-tion as the addict of the '60s and '70s. Today, addicts and non-addicts alike in the ghetto are likely to find pleasure in brutality.

Carl Taylor found that Detroit gangs, especially those in the drug business, had no compunction about using any kind of violence to keep business running smoothly. They didn't even consider that vio-lence.

"If somebody messes with your property," said one gangster, "then they need to be checked. I don't call that violence, that's just tightening your business up."

The gangsters did recognize that there were Zeros, though. A Zero is someone who has hit the pits of hopelessness. Zeros, one gang mem-ber said:

. . . don't care about nothing. They ain't afraid to die over any stupid thing . . . they like to rape babes, beat up people, and kill somebody for fun. . . . They just like to beast on whoever's around. Our crew enforces when people ill on them. But I think some of them boys [the Zeros] would beast on somebody for free.

A Zero told Taylor about himself:

I likes to bust heads. . . . You got to dog everybody or they gonna dog you. Doggin' is my specialty. I'm the dogmaster. I dogs men, boys, girls, bitches, my momma, teachers, police-men, policebitches, my momma's boyfriends, I'll just see some-body and start doggin' them in the street. Me and my boys like to crush mugs and kick ass at school. . . . [Another gang] tried to dog us at a house party last month. I got so pissed that I got me an Uzi from my cousin and went to one [of their houses] and sprayed that sucker. . . . I got put out of school for beasting on this teacher. . . . It took four security guards to stop me from killing that bitch. They put me in the youth home; big fucking deal. They called my old man. He said they could keep me. FUCK him, he ain't shit, he's a crackhead just like my ho-assed mammy. . . . I love to jump on preppies, punk-ass dudes, or preppy ho's, it don't matter. . . . I likes seeing little scared preppies when we beat on their asses. My crew is the beasting crew—crushing asses is our way of having fun.

The overall murder rate for the ten years from 1981 to 1991 has been fairly stable. That is not true of murder among juveniles, especially males in the age group of fourteen through seventeen. This is where the Zeros are found, along with the drug-selling gangsters who don't mind killing to "tighten your business up." There has been a steady increase in murders of and by teenage boys, both black and white. A higher proportion of both killers and victims is black, because a higher—and growing—proportion of blacks live in Zero-breeding conditions.

In the fourteen- to seventeen-year-old age group, there were 4.5 white victims per 100,000 in 1981 and 8.5 in 1991. The increase in black teenage victims was even worse—from 24.7 per 100,000 in 1981 to 65.9 in 1991. For some reason, statistics on juvenile murder seem more nearly complete: there are also figures on offenders. In 1981, in the 14 to 17 group, there were 8.2 white offenders and 51.2 black offenders per 100,000. In 1991, there were 13.6 whites and 111.8 blacks.

The increase in Zeros, obviously, has many causes. If the drug black market could be magically eliminated, there would still be murders and assaults. But not as many—especially in big cities, where the drug trade is a far more important cause of violence than in small towns and rural areas. Medical examiners in Washington, D.C., say that the bodies of 80 percent of the homicide victims there contain traces of cocaine. In New York, police say drug dealing plays a part in 40 percent of all homicides.

Violence in America has deeper and more tangled roots than simply the presence of illicit drugs. But drugs make a real contribution to the plague of violence. When people, like many ghetto youths, are already filled with a deep, unfocused anger, drug use alone can add to the carnage caused by the drug trade. Prothrow-Stith says cocaine is involved with unorganized crime and violence in two ways:

First, criminals like to use cocaine before committing crimes because it makes them feel brave, confident and in command. High on cocaine during the commission of a crime, adrenaline pumping through their bloodstreams, criminal offenders are likely to be buffeted by waves of aggressive impulses. That violence would occur in these circumstances is hardly surprising.

Second, cocaine's psychopharmacology predisposes users to commit violent acts. Cocaine is not a calming opiate like heroin. Heroin addicts desperate for a "fix" will commit violence to get money to buy drugs, but when they are high—and the heroin high lasts for three to four hours—heroin addicts pose little threat to anyone. Cocaine is different. Cocaine is a stimulant. It increases motor activity, and makes users jumpy, irritable and in some cases, paranoid. People who are high on coke see threats where none exist. Moreover, the alcohol that coke users consume may further distort their thinking and push them in the direction of violent action.

Violent acts resulting from these two causes may not be listed as drug-related by the statisticians.

Then there is organized crime. At one time, that meant to most people the "Mafia," bookies, prostitution, illegal gambling and loan sharks. Today it is much more complicated. And the most lucrative, as well as the most violent, part of it involves drugs. This part fuels much of the most lethal violence that occurs in street crime.

18

On November 1, 1993, twenty-three-year-old Robert Sheldon Brown, better known as "Cas" in South Central Los Angeles, was sentenced to thirty years in prison for one hundred seventy-five bank robberies—a record. The previous record-holder had robbed only sixty-four banks. Sentenced to twenty-five years with Brown was twenty-five-year-old Donzell Lamar Thompson, alias "C-Dog." The noteworthy thing about these young men was not the number of bank robberies they committed but how they committed them.

They robbed the banks by remote control. The actual robbers were groups of young teenagers, some as young as thirteen. These boys, Zeros or near-Zeros, got machine guns from Brown and Thompson, as well as training in the techniques of bank robbery. Brown, Thompson or both would supervise the operation from a distance. If all went well, they would meet their "henchmen" later to divide the loot. If the children ran into trouble, the adults would disappear.

Brown and Thompson have been called modern Fagins, after the character in Dickens's *Oliver Twist* who taught boys how to pick pockets. But compared with them, Fagin was a philanthropist.

The technique was for a group of kids to dash into the bank, some firing weapons into the ceiling while others carried pillowcases they would fill with money.

"Boys do not rob banks unless someone shows them how," wrote Assistant U.S. Attorneys John S. Wiley, Jr. and Michael R. Davis. "Brown and Thompson showed how. They took disadvantaged and miserable teenagers and turned them into felons of the most serious degree."

Brown's and Thompson's technique was extraordinarily dangerous, according to FBI agents involved with the case. "Excited boys with loaded guns and no sense of their own mortality created an unbeliev-able potential for violence," FBI agent William J. Rehder wrote in an affidavit. John Hoos, an FBI spokesman agreed. "They go in with auto-matic weapons and they are not afraid to use them," he said.

The kids took all the risk. There was plenty. Because they were so young and inexperienced, they often got caught. One fifteen-year-old fired at a police officer and was fatally shot. Brown and Thompson, though, stayed clear of danger. "They went through many disposable henchmen," said Wiley, the government attorney. "Brown used up a lot of henchmen," according to Rehder, the FBI agent. "Police cap-tured his workers on a regular basis. He needed steadily to replenish his supply."

Brown and Thompson belong to the Rollin' Sixties Crips, one of the many Los Angeles territorial gangs affiliated with the Crips or their rivals, the Bloods. The kids were often junior members of the Rollin' Sixties. Some came from other Crips gangs, and a few were "wan-nabes." Many of them, especially drivers of the getaway cars, were drug addicts. Brown and Thompson gave them drugs and some money for their services.

The appearance of the Zero—the teenage boy who has lost all hope and hates everyone—has added a new and frightening element to what we used to call "gangland." Given current economic and social condi-tions, there would probably be Zeros even if there were no illicit drugs. The drug traffic, though, gives the Zero an outlet for his antisocial urges, and—most important—the money made in the drug trade lets him be armed with the latest and most illegal weapons. As with Brown's and Thompson's baby bank robbers, the Zero's penchant for "beast-ing" is easily manipulated to serve cold-blooded operators who make most of the money and face little of the risk.

2

Occasionally, Zeros organize into what could be called Zero gangs. One such gang was the Clear Top Mobsters, formerly known as the Green Top Posse, of Bridgeport, Connecticut. The Clear Toppers were a genu-ine drug gang. The gang took its name from the color of the tops of the crack vials it sold. The Clear Top Mobsters controlled short stretches of Hallett and Shelton streets in Bridgeport. It's a small area, but their control, at the height of the gang's power, was virtually complete. At one point, they even set up toll booths to take a toll of all cars driving through their territory. One-tenth of all the homicides in the state of Connecticut in 1992 took place in the twelve blocks controlled by the Clear Toppers.

No street crime took place in the area without the gang's permission. The object was to provide a safe environment for suburbanites to enter and buy crack. Street peddlers were guarded by mobsters with automatic and semiautomatic rifles in windows overlooking the street. Not all the peddlers belonged to the gang, but they had to pay the gang to operate there. Any peddler who tried to cheat a customer died as quickly as any customer who tried to rob a peddler. On a good day, police say, there was a crack buy every minute in the gang's territory.

That would seem to indicate an orderly, if sinister environment. The Clear Toppers, though, were Zeros, and Zeros thrive on violence. "The shooting has been almost on a nightly basis ever since we opened the doors," said a developer who built a number of houses in the area. Lt. Dave Boston, who heads the Bridgeport police anti-gang unit, said of the Mobsters, "Almost all of those guys have been shot at one time or another." Most of them wore bullet-proof vests.

Unfortunately for the rest of the community, the Clear Toppers weren't very good shots. A clandestinely taped police video shows a Clear Topper trying to shoot out a streetlight. It takes nine shots from his rifle to hit a light a few feet above him. The unfortunate thing about this kind of marksmanship is that the shooters frequently miss their targets and hit about everything—and everybody—in the immediate vicinity. In December 1992, Steven and Jackie Rattley came close to losing their family. Their four children, aged three to ten, were up late planning a birthday party for the youngest boy. At about 11 P.M. shooting started. A bullet came through the wall and landed only 18 inches from the three-year-old's head.

"I just said, 'There they go again,'" Jackie Rattley recalled. "The kids scattered. They all ran to the back of the house. But the bullet holes were all over. You don't know where to run. When the policeman came, the first thing he said was, 'Do you have any problem with anybody?'"

When the officer heard that the Rattleys had no enemies, he said,

"Well, just pack your bags and go somewhere, because there's nothing we can do."

The Rattleys are still there. Most of their neighbors are long gone, though. One man who called the police to complain about the shooting found his car full of bullet holes. A short time later, his house burned down. A woman who complained to the mayor had her house perforated with bullets. She moved out immediately, leaving her refrigerator, which still has a bullet embedded in it.

No outsider not bent on buying crack entered the area.

"They beat more people than you could ever imagine," said Detective Pablo Otero. "Just stop them and beat them. But there's a reason. It's about control. They want to send a message about who controls the area."

Nine leaders of the Clear Top Mobsters have been arrested. But crack is still being sold in the area.

3

Control of a neighborhood, control of a state, control of a drug or control of all rackets—control is a continual source of trouble in Gangland.

As we've seen, Charley Lucky's criminal federation began losing its grip as drug trafficking grew. When a few American criminal families could deal with a few Corsican or Sicilian exporters, everything stayed under control. Then Chinese syndicates in Southeast Asia got into the act as exporters. The Chinese had more trouble with their suppliers than the European gangsters with theirs: Dealing with impoverished Turkish peasants is one thing; dealing with Shan warlords and predatory Thai and Vietnamese generals is another. The Southeast Asian exporters who profited were very tough guys. The Chinese wanted the best profit for their efforts. They'd sell to Trafficante's Mob connection in Saigon, or they'd go directly to the United States, whichever seemed more profitable at the time. The same thing was true of the Pakistanis—in spades. Men who successfully bargained with ferocious Pushtun tribal leaders were not impressed with American mobsters.

Then there were the Cubans and the Colombians. The Cubans at first worked through the Trafficante operation. But with an enormous Cuban exile colony in the United States, it was easy—and profitable—to bypass the established American distributors. And the Cubans had help from the CIA that Lansky, the Trafficantes and their associates couldn't even dream of. The Cubans were instrumental in the Contra support effort, as were, of course, the Nicaraguans. As we've seen, the stateside Contra support network was also neck-deep in cocaine distribution. Finally, there were the Colombians, who, like the Asian exporters, saw no reason why they shouldn't cut out the middleman.

One thing all of these Latins had in common: They were tough. Next to them, American, Sicilian and Corsican gangsters were teddy bears. The Cubans had been conducting a terrorist war against Castro since before the Bay of Pigs. The Nicaraguans were in the midst of a no-holds-barred civil war. The Colombians were products of a land undergoing the longest, bloodiest and most chaotic Latin American civil war since the Mexican Revolution of 1910–35. If they decided to kill someone, they often killed his whole family for good measure. The traditional American mobsters might break the legs of someone they felt needed a lesson. When they became exasperated, they might take him for a ride and discreetly murder him. The Latins had a lower level of exasperation. When they reached it, they were prone to mow the offender and all his friends down with machine guns during business hours in a crowded shopping mall.

Since the end of Prohibition, American crime had become more civilized. Our mobsters tried to avoid confrontation with the Spanish-speaking crazies. But there were more crazies on the way.

4

In 1980 Jamaica was in the midst of a bitter election campaign between Michael Manley and Edward Seaga. Bitter elections in Jamaica are not like bitter elections in the United States. In Jamaica, they're really bitter. Both sides hired thugs and gunmen to break up demonstrations and terrorize and intimidate supporters of the other side. One of Seaga's gunmen was a twenty-year-old Kingston lad named Delroy Edwards. His nickname was "Uzi." When Seaga was elected, he cracked down on all the thugs, both Manley's and his. Uzi Edwards and a lot of experienced Jamaican gunmen left for the United States.

Looking for something to do in his new country, Edwards started peddling marijuana. Then he discovered crack, at that time a little-known form of cocaine. The Colombians and Cubans almost had a lock on powder cocaine; black and white American gangs of various ethnic persuasions bought heroin from a variety of Asian and European suppliers. But nobody had started moving crack in a big way. Uzi found his niche. He started in Brooklyn, but he found there were too many competitors in New York. In 1986 he moved to virgin territory, Washington, D.C. The next year he branched out to Philadelphia and Baltimore. By that time he had a gang—a real drug gang—called the Rankers, with fifty members. By the time Edwards was convicted of forty-two counts of murder, kidnapping, assault and drug dealing, word of his success had spread back to Jamaica. Other Jamaican hoods crowded into planes for the United States. Like previous generations of immigrants, they were coming to the Land of Opportunity to make their fortune. This time in crack.

The Jamaican immigrants, most of them illegal, formed gangs called posses. A posse can have anywhere from twenty-five to several hundred members. The posses have some aspects of traditional territorial gangs. Mostly, though, they're business organizations. Their business is crack. Today, they control an estimated 40 percent of U.S. crack sales.

When Uzi Edwards started dealing crack, he bought his cocaine retail. As his organization grew, he worked out new arrangements with foreign exporters. The Colombian retailers didn't mind Uzi's competition at first, because he was, after all, buying from them. Later, he was too big for them to do anything about. When it came to violence, the Jamaicans didn't take a backseat to Colombians or anyone else. According to the U.S. Bureau of Alcohol, Tobacco and Firearms, the Jamaican posses have committed more than 1,000 murders since 1985.

There are dozens of Jamaican posses. The posses are independent, but they generally cooperate and respect each others' turf. From New York and Washington, they've spread up and down the East Coast and moved into the Midwest. Before the posses, crack dealing was generally done by a crowd of nickel-and-dime crooks who bought their cocaine from local street peddlers and cooked it at home. When they spread out, the posses took the path of least resistance. They moved into towns where crack was not controlled by any sort of strong organization.

When a posse is going to move into a town, it sends a member to scout the territory. The scout assesses the market and locates the potential competition. If the report is favorable, more posse members come to town and begin killing the local dealers. These "trademark" murders alert the local police that the Jamaicans are in town.

The murders aren't really necessary to insure the Jamaican monopolies. They just speed things up. Unlike the nickel-and-dime gangs, the posses get their cocaine direct from the exporters and move it to places where they're established. It's easy to price the small operations out of business. It's quicker, though, to scare them out by killing a few. One way the posses move crack is by airline, using couriers (overweight women are preferred) who can hide small amounts on their persons. Another way is simply to use the interstate highway system. Posse drivers carry considerable amounts of cocaine or crack while they obey all traffic laws. Thanks to the size and well-developed road net in the United States, the drivers have easy access to a quarter of a billion people without worrying about any customs checks. Using these methods, Jamaican posses moved into places ranging from small towns in western Wisconsin to major metropolitan areas like Kansas City, Missouri.

In Kansas City, the posses ran into trouble. In 1986, a federal organized-crime task force cracked down on the Jamaican crack merchants. Federal and local officers raided the fortress-like headquarters of the posse in downtown Kansas City. Federal court sent 178 of the Jamaicans to prison and deported 25 more. The Jamaican organization in Kansas City was smashed. The good news for Kansas City wasn't too cheery for Omaha and Des Moines, though. The remnants of the posse moved to those cities and opened shop.

And though the crack merchants were driven out of Kansas City, the crack addicts remained. That was an open invitation to two massive criminal organizations based on the West Coast, instead of the East Coast.

5

While the Jamaicans were organizing the eastern half of the country, two other criminal federations were active in the West. Both the Bloods and the Crips have been based in Los Angeles for many years. For more than thirty years, Los Angeles has had one of the most active street-gang milieus in the United States. Most Americans first became aware of the situation after the Watts riot in 1965, when such African-American gangs as the Businessmen took an active part in burning much of Los Angeles.

Some time after that, the gangs began to make alliances with other gangs and formed two rival federations, or supergangs, the Crips and the Bloods. The main activity of these two huge territorial gangs was fighting each other, although individual gang members also engaged in various types of theft and extortion. So did individual gangs. The Crips and the Bloods are not two enormous criminal monoliths like the "Mafia" or "La Cosa Nostra" of comic book writers and FBI publicists. Brown and Thompson were acting on their own, not on behalf of the Rollin' Sixties Crips. And the gang activities of the Rollin' Sixties Crips usually do not concern their allies, the East Coast Gangster Crips or any other Crips gangs.

For years, the member gangs of the Bloods and Crips were classic territorial fighting gangs, as the Mexican-American gangs in East Los Angeles still are. Because the African-American gangs had built-in al- lies—other Crips and other Bloods—their gang wars tended to be big- ger. But they were just very big territorial gangs. Then some of them discovered crack.

Like the Jamaicans, some of the Los Angeles gangs apparently worked out arrangements with cocaine exporters and began peddling crack in black areas of Los Angeles. From time to time, there were po- lice crackdowns on gang members, and well-known gangsters left the city for a while. Some went south, as far as San Diego; others went north, as far as Seattle. Out of home territory, they scouted the market for crack. Soon, there were branch offices of both the Crips and the Bloods all up and down the West Coast.

Branching out proved to be so profitable that the drug-selling Bloods and Crips began moving east. They found a fertile area for their operations.

In Kansas City, there was a large population of crackheads desper- ate to get their favorite drug. The Los Angeles gangsters already knew that. What they probably didn't expect, though, was that cities and towns in what its inhabitants call "the Heart of America" were filled with gang wannabes. In towns like Little Rock, Arkansas, or even cities like Denver, Colorado, the Angeleno gangsters impressed local kids the way emissaries from a superpower might impress provincial officials in a banana republic. They had no trouble recruiting members. Today, kids born and raised in Little Rock are selling crack and wearing the colors of either the Crips or the Bloods. They're also shooting other born-and-bred Little Rock kids who are wearing the other gang's colors.

To complicate things, there are now two more gangs in Little Rock, the Vice Lords and the Folks, both originally based in Chicago. Chicago and Detroit, both of which were wisely avoided by the Jamaicans in their westward move, have long gang traditions. Like the Los Angeles super-gangs, the gangs in Chicago and Detroit are branching out. The Chicagoans are, in general, colonizing the area south and southwest of the Windy City, and the Detroiters are concentrating on the eastern part of the Great Lakes states. Both the Chicagoans and Detroiters have branches much farther afield. The Latin Kings, the largest gang in Connecticut, originated in Chicago.

These inner-city gangs are loaded with Zeros. As they move out, they are learning that Zeros are not confined to multimillion-population metropolitan areas. They find kindred souls who suffer from the same hopelessness in cities of 50,000 or less. Wherever they go, crack use increases. So does murder.

The source of these killings is not so much crack intoxication as crack selling. Gangs are wiping out independent sellers. Rival gangs are fighting for territory. "Stick-up boys" are preying on street peddlers, who, they know, have no recourse to the law. Peddlers are shooting attempted robbers. Peddlers are shooting buyers who attempt to leave without paying. Buyers are shooting peddlers who sell them "bad dope." Because the drug trade is wholly without the law, its participants rely on the law of the gun.

Crack selling has gone from total anarchy, with "gangs" of one to three pushing home-cooked crack, to attempts by would-be monopolists to organize the trade. Today, you have something like the situation during Prohibition, when O'Bannion and Weiss were fighting Torrio and Capone for control of Chicago. In a sense, the Crips, the Bloods and the Jamaican posses are national gangs. In reality, though, they are loose federations of gangs who are not above a little intramural feuding. Anarchy is likely to be part of the crack scene for a long time, because it's so easy for anyone to buy cocaine from a retailer, cook it and make a profit. There are plenty of small-timers still around. And there are others, such as some motorcycle club members, who sell dope as a sideline.

6

Probably there will never be a single illicit drug empire in the United States. There are too many exporters selling too many varieties of dope. The heroin market is becoming a little more stable, especially in New York, where half of America's addicts live. The Chinese exporters are showing a preference for dealing with Chinese-American tongs. This is not merely a matter of blood being thicker than water. There are few federal agents of Chinese descent who are fluent in the dialects of southern China. The Chinese have their own enforcers too. Large numbers of young Chinese have come to the U.S. from Hong Kong, which is to be turned over to Communist China in the near future. Conditions on that overcrowded island have bred another crop of Zeros, some of whom have brought their violence here. Chinese youth gangs specialize in extorting money from Chinese businesses, but they also retail heroin and perform contract murders for the tongs and the exporting syndicates.

There are plenty of other groups involved in the New York heroin market, as the career of Boy George Rivera shows. Some of them are members of the traditional New York gangs, like the five Italian "families" and the West Side Irish mob called the "Westies." Others are newcomers, like the Russian and Cuban gangsters. The cocaine scene in New York is similar, but with Latinos instead of Chinese holding the biggest piece of the market.

7

During Prohibition, bootlegging liquor might have been called the key racket. The gangs committed all kinds of other crimes, but bootlegging was the biggest and steadiest cash producer. It even financed some of the other mob enterprises.

Since the end of Prohibition, the old mobs like the Italian "families" and the Westies have tried to develop substitutes for bootlegging. Luciano specialized in houses of prostitution. The old-fashioned whorehouses, however, have been almost driven out of the market by competition, which has grown with the increase in automobile ownership. On one end of the economic scale, there are the cut-rate streetwalkers; on the other, high-priced call girls who make house calls. And everywhere, there are amateurs who have sex for kicks. Another mainstay of the underworld used to be illegal gambling. Now, however, there is legalized gambling in Nevada and New Jersey and state lotteries almost everywhere and every Indian tribe in the country which hasn't already opened a casino is planning to. Loan-sharking, while never a major revenue producer like bootlegging, used to help fatten mob bank accounts. Now there are credit cards. During the '80s, some members of the Mob got involved with the savings and loan swindles, often, according to author Pete Brewton, helped by the CIA, which needed the Mob's cooperation in various Cold War adventures. Only a few old-line gangsters had the money and sophistication needed to make a profit from S&L scams, however. And in any case, the opportunities for this kind of crime have almost disappeared. The old Luciano federation needs a new key racket.

Illegal drugs is the new key racket. It makes far more money than any other criminal enterprise, and it finances other criminal activities. Drug profits purchase high-tech armaments for gangs, for instance. The lion's share of this key racket is in the hands of recent immigrants who are hard for the FBI and other agencies to infiltrate.

Prohibition created "gangland." The old gangland is fading away—not so much because of the FBI or any other police agency, but because the old rackets just aren't that profitable anymore. Now there's a new gangland, based on drug trafficking, that has been created and maintained by the War on Drugs.

19

On April 16, 1993, federal Judge Whitman Knapp, who headed a commission investigating the New York police force in the 1970s, announced that he would no longer preside over drug cases. He was joined by another respected federal judge in New York, Jack B. Weinstein.

The two judges were not alone. They merely made a public announcement of an action fifty other judges, out of a total of 680 federal judges, were already taking. Senior judges, like Knapp, Weinstein and the other fifty, are allowed to choose what kind of cases they will hear.

Knapp and Weinstein said they were taking the action to protest federal sentencing guidelines. The guidelines severely limit a judge's discretion. In most cases, they require a federal judge to sentence a convicted drug offender to prison, and they allow little leeway on the length of the sentence. To a large extent, the guidelines are a product of the desire by members of Congress to show their constituents that they are "tough on drugs" and against "coddling criminals." Knapp and Weinstein said that the federal government's emphasis on prison, and its neglect of prevention and treatment, have made the War on Drugs a failure.

"People think they can stop the drug traffic by putting people in jail and having terribly long sentences," Knapp said. "But, of course, it isn't true."

Judge Weinstein added, "The penalties have been increased enormously without having any impact. It's just a futile endeavor, a waste of the taxpayers' money."

Dissent in the federal judiciary with national drug policies has not been limited to some senior judges refusing to hear drug cases. A few judges have resigned rather than impose what they consider overly harsh sentences. Several others have called for the legalization of drugs.

One of these, federal Judge Robert W. Sweet, of New York, said, "The present policy of trying to prohibit drugs through criminal law is a mistake. It's a policy that is not working. It's not cutting down on drug use. The best way to do this is through education and treatment."

At the Federal Judicial Center in Washington, the director of this federal court research center, Judge William W. Schwarzer, said, "A lot of judges [who haven't made a public protest] feel the present system breeds injustice."

In an op-ed piece in the *New York Times*, Judge Knapp praised President Bill Clinton's selection of Lee Brown as director of the Office of National Drug Control but detailed the difficulties Brown faces.

"Each year," wrote Judge Knapp, "the Government has spent more on enforcing drug laws than it did the year before. Each year, more people have gone to jail for drug offenses.

"Yet each year there have been more drugs on the streets."

The judge said a famous economist had offered an explanation:

> Milton Friedman, the Nobel laureate economist, has a simple explanation for the upward spiral with which Mr. Brown must contend. Law enforcement temporarily reduces the drug supply and thus causes prices to rise. Higher prices draw new sources of supply and even new drugs into the market, resulting in more drugs on the street. The increased availability of drugs creates more addicts. The Government reacts with more vigorous enforcement, and the cycle starts anew.
>
> Mr. Friedman and those who share his views propose a straightforward way out of this discouraging spiral: Decriminalize drugs, thus eliminating the pressure on supply that creates an ever-bigger market. This, they contend, will reduce demand and reverse the cycle, much as a similar approach has cut into alcohol addiction.

Judge Knapp admitted he was not competent to evaluate Friedman's theory. His years on the federal bench, though, had convinced him that the current federal drug laws were a failure. He argued for what economists Daniel K. Benjamin and Roger Leroy Miller call "the Constitutional alternative"—giving drug control to the states, as was done with liquor. There are many possible approaches. If drugs were federally decriminalized, he wrote, the states "would have to decide whether to license drug retailers, distribute drugs through state agencies, or perhaps allow drugs only to be purchased with a physician's prescription."

Therefore:

> The variety, complexity and importance of these questions make it exceedingly clear that the Federal Government has no business being involved in any of them. What might be a hopeful solution in New York could be a disaster in Idaho, and only state legislatures and city governments, not Congress, can pass laws tailored to local needs.

> What did the nation do when it decided to get rid of the catastrophes spawned by Prohibition? It adopted the 21st Amendment, which excluded the [federal] Government from any role in regulation of alcoholic beverages and strengthened the powers of the states to deal with such matters.

> That is exactly what the Congress should do with respect to drugs. It should repeal all federal laws that prohibit or regulate their distribution or use and devise methods for helping the states to exercise their respective powers in these areas.

In addition to the failure of federal law to stop drugs and the futility of ever-longer sentences protested by Knapp and Weinstein, inflexible sentencing guidelines and mandatory sentences have given rise to a number of positive evils.

Perhaps the worst is prison overcrowding. In order to make room for nonviolent drug possessors, correction officials have been forced to release murderers, rapists and robbers.

Like judges forced to adhere to sentencing guidelines and mandatory sentences, prison officials have little discretion in the matter unless their state legislatures have adopted formulae for early release. The courts have ruled that at a certain point, overcrowding in a prison becomes "cruel and unusual punishment," which is prohibited by the U.S. Constitution. The basic guideline for early release is that those closest to the end of their sentence are released first. Prison administration is conducted under iron-clad rules. Judges can (unless laws prohibit it) decide the length of sentences. Wardens never can. The corrections officials try to give nonviolent offenders preference in early release. If a con artist and a rapist have the same length of sentence remaining, the con artist will be the one who walks. That, though, is about the limit of the prison officials' discretion.

A state may, by statute, give its correction officials a little more leeway, but not much. For example, a formula just recommended to the Connecticut legislature specifies that "Whenever the Department of Correction inmate population exceeds 110 percent of capacity for thirty consecutive days, the commissioner shall request the commission to declare an overcrowding emergency. If the commission finds that all available means of reducing the population have failed, they shall order the implementation of the Control Action Program, or CAP. Under the Program, the department shall rank all inmates sentenced to two years or less, based on the amount of time remaining until discharge date and begin releasing inmates until the population reaches 95 percent of capacity."

If that does not reduce the population to 95 percent, the department must then begin releasing inmates who have been sentenced to more than two years but who have been "voted favorably for parole." That means, said William Flower, the department spokesman, that if the parole board votes, as it frequently does, to approve an inmate's parole a few months hence, he can be released immediately.

So far, Flower says, his state's prison system has not reached 110 percent of capacity for thirty consecutive days, because another law has given the department authority to place inmates convicted of nonviolent crimes under community supervision if they have been sentenced to two years or less and have served 50 percent of their time.

There's a limit to even that discretion. A huge number of nonviolent offenders are drug offenders. Most of them have been sentenced under laws that prohibit any early release.

The effect of this situation is that an inoffensive pot smoker stays in jail while a murderer is released to resume preying on society.

This is not something that happens only occasionally. In Florida, almost 2,000 prisoners a months are released early.

The number of people imprisoned for drug offenses in Florida grew more than 500 percent from 1983 to 1988. About a third of all persons convicted of felonies there have been convicted of drug offenses. Florida is not unique. Drug convictions are the fastest-growing class of convictions all over the country. And the prison population is growing everywhere. A few years ago, the U.S. Sentencing Commission estimated that the federal prison population would double by the beginning of the new century—five years from now—and about half of all prisoners would be held for breaking the drug laws. In 1991, 58 percent of all federal prisoners were already serving time for drug offenses. When you remember that about 95 percent of all drug cases are not handled by the federal judicial system but by the states, you have an idea of the size of the problem.

"Early in the year [1993]," said Kevin Roberts, controlled-release officer of the Florida State Parole Commission, "almost all of our early releases were of violent offenders, and a lot of those taking up their bed space were just first-time drug users or couriers. What's the purpose of locking up a first-time user for 10 years? All you're doing is teaching him how to re-offend, and it's costing a lot of money and bed space. These guys need to be looked at in terms of rehabilitation."

Pat Sullivan, sheriff of Arapahoe County, Colorado, put his feelings about long sentences for nonviolent offenders more strongly early in 1993. Rep. Peggy Kerns of the Colorado legislature had introduced a bill that would reduce some sentences for drug offenses and other nonviolent crimes while increasing other sentences, such as for assaults on children. The bill was killed on a party-line vote in the Colorado House Judiciary Committee.

Sullivan, who has to accommodate prisoners in his increasingly overcrowded jail, lashed out at what he called the "outrageous political shenanigans" of the House Republicans.

"The House Judiciary Committee has torpedoed thousands of hours of work in the prison crisis at the halfway point in this session," the Republican sheriff wrote in a letter to the *Denver Post*. "The House Judiciary Committee has shafted the county property tax payers and county government in destroying the solution to the rapidly growing county jail backlog of state prisoners. . . . Maybe the House will wake up to its responsibility if they find 115 state prisoners handcuffed to their very stately chairs and desks in the House chamber. And I am just irate enough to do it."

Sullivan said the state paid him $9.27 a day for each state prisoner in the county jail, but housing each state prisoner cost the county $48.84 a day.

Protests against the current system are not confined to judges and county sheriffs. An American Bar Association panel early in 1992 reported that the U.S. criminal-justice system, because of its emphasis on drug offenses, is "on a fast track to collapse."

The number of adults in prison for drug offenses more than tripled from 1986 to 1991, largely because of mandatory sentences. According to the panel, the focus on drug offenses has meant less emphasis on violent crime. It's also taken money that might have been spent on schools and libraries and put it into prisons. Schools and libraries, Andrew L. Sonner, chief prosecutor of Montgomery County, Maryland, said, "have more to do with the prevention of crime than locking people up."

Sheriff Sullivan has already had to suspend a couple of his crime-prevention programs. In Arapahoe County, as in almost anywhere else in the United States, a huge percentage of prisoners is illiterate. An even larger percentage has no high school diploma. At least some of those persons may have turned to crime because they weren't qualified for anything else. Arapahoe County used to offer literacy and education programs. It can't now, because the classroom space is needed for beds.

Getting rid of mandatory sentences would seem to be a good idea, but according to qualified observers, it would be bad politics.

"While many Democrats are closet supporters of repealing minimum mandatories," columnist Jack Anderson wrote in August 1993, "most recognize that saying so publicly would be like handing the GOP a loaded assault weapon."

Sen. Phil Gramm, of Texas, summed up the Senate Republican position: "If the president's plan doesn't have minimum mandatories for drug thugs, then it's not a crime bill."

Like most senators, Gramm finds logic less important than looking "tough."

3

The federal sentencing guidelines are enormously complicated because they try to cover every possible situation. No set of rules, though, can take the place of a judge with common sense.

Robert Blanchette, of Voluntown, Connecticut, was arrested for growing marijuana plants. Blanchette's harvest wouldn't have produced much pot—at best, a few ounces per plant. If he were tried in a state court, he would probably have been put on probation. Under federal rules, however, the court had to consider each plant capable of producing more than two pounds of marijuana. That meant that Blanchette theoretically had almost a ton of marijuana, and he was sentenced to five years in federal prison.

The judge, Jose A. Cabranes, was not happy about the sentence. He wrote in his decision: "A sentence of five years is substantially more than is required to achieve any of the major purposes of a criminal sanction. Blanchette's incarceration for a period of five years will unnecessarily burden the federal prison system . . . yield no discernable benefit to society and yield no discernable benefit to the defendant."

Then there's Tonya Drake, a single mother trying to raise four small children on welfare payments. An acquaintance gave her $100 to post a package for him and told her to keep the change. Drake didn't know or care what was in the package; the money was manna from heaven. The package contained 232 grams of crack. Drake was arrested. She had no criminal record and no history of drug use, but under the sentencing guidelines, the judge had to sentence her to ten years in prison.

"That's just crazy," said Federal District Judge Richard Gadbois, Jr., "but there's nothing I can do about it."

On February 3, 1994, a man named Adam Carom stood outside the house of Charlene Troutman of New Haven, Connecticut, and fired a magazine full of bullets into the wall and a window. Police said Carom evidently had a dispute with some member of the household. He was not, however, enraged at either Troutman or her baby granddaughter. Those were the people he hit, though. The baby died. Carom was technically a state prisoner. He was supposed to be in prison until June 1995 but had been "released to the community" two years early to make room for new prisoners. Since he had never reported to a parole officer, he was technically an escaped prisoner. Carom had been convicted of a drug offense, but he was known to be violent. Four days after killing the baby, he and another escaped prisoner tried to hold up a drug dealer. The drug dealer began shooting, and the other man was wounded. Carom was not hurt, however, because he was wearing a bullet-proof vest. A bullet-proof vest costs betweem $400 and $700.

That's a lot of money unless you are in a business—like robbing drug dealers—in which you are likely to be shot.

One glaring trouble with drug sentencing as it's now done is that the more serious offenders often get the lighter sentences. The serious offenders usually have information they can trade for a lesser charge. The novice in drug trafficking who doesn't have information the prosecutors and police can use gets the "limit of the law."

Nicole Richardson, of Mobile, Alabama, was a high school student who had the bad luck to fall in love with a small-time dope dealer. A police informant who said he wanted to buy some LSD asked her where he could find her boyfriend. When she told him, both she and the boyfriend were arrested. She was charged with conspiracy to distribute the drug. Her boyfriend could tell the police where he got his LSD, so he was allowed to plead guilty to a lesser charge. He got five years. Richardson, now twenty, who had never actually engaged in drug trafficking, had no information. She wasn't allowed to "cop a plea." She got the mandatory ten years. She's still in prison, and her boyfriend is out on the street.

Most legislative advocates of long sentences would deny that they hold their views so they can look "tough" to their constituents. They would also deny that simple revenge is a motive. The principal reason for long sentences, they say, is that long sentences deter criminals. Deterrence is also the reason the 1994 federal crime bill specifies the death penalty for sixty separate federal crimes. The death penalty, its advocates claim, is the ultimate deterrent.

At least two countries—Singapore and Malaysia—have the death penalty for any drug trafficker. Run-of-the-mill drug users get either a public flogging or two years in a brutal "rehabilitation camp" that would make an American penal "boot camp" look like Club Med. In neither country, however, has the arrest rate for drug offenses slowed. Both countries are continuing to build gallows and expand their rehabilitation camps.

Because the majority of persons convicted of drug offenses come from the poorest parts of large cities, the deterrent effect of prison is not what we might expect. As pointed out before, prison has some advantages over life on the street. Moreover, for many inmates, a trip to prison is like a neighborhood reunion.

"The joint? Scared, worried about jail? No way, not the kid," a young Detroit drug dealer told researcher Carl Taylor. "The youth home is really down. If you get sent to the youth home, it ain't no big thing. . . . I ain't been to the big time, but when I do it will be cool. Everybody I know has been to Jack house [the Michigan state penitentiary in Jackson], three of my boys are doing a bit now. . . . Going away is just part of being out here. . . . Most of the time you know everybody in the home, so it's like being with your crew inside."

Some people even like prison, the kid told Taylor:

The big time is just there like the streets. . . . My brothers are inside Jack town, and they say the joint is just like the street. . . . Some dudes belong to the Muslims, some go with their homeboys, some just chill out. . . . You can get dope and anything you want in the joint.

Another dealer added the voice of experience:

Pussy, money, food, you want it? You could get anything if you had the paper [cash]. . . . A lot of dudes like prison because that's where all their boys is.

As might be expected, prison has not proved to be much of a deterrent.

"You have to realize that these individuals don't have the fear that most people have of going to prison," said Lt. Dan Stebbins, the Connecticut State Police gang specialist. "Some of them look forward to it. In some cases, prison is a better lifestyle than the one they had on the streets."

Sociologist Jeffrey Fagan found that whether those arrested for drug offenses were sent to prison or not had no bearing on their likelihood of being rearrested. Neither did the length of the sentence. "The severity of the criminal sanction," Fagan concluded, has little influence on "the likelihood of reoffending." In fact, Draconian sentencing seemed to affect drug dealers the wrong way. The longer the sentence, it turned out, the greater the chance that the offender would be rearrested for the same crime.

"They learn this trade [crime] as they go through the prison system," said Michael Sheahan, sheriff of Cook County, Illinois. "They start as drug offenders; they eventually become property offenders; and then they commit crimes against people."

Robert Gangi, executive director of the Correctional Association of New York, expressed the futility of the "lock-'em-up" theory of crime fighting.

"Building more prisons to address crime," he said, "is like building more graveyards to address a fatal disease."

There's another practical objection to mandatory sentences with no possibility of parole. According to the director of the Bureau of Prisons, these sentences have undermined prison discipline by removing the possibility of parole as a reward for good behavior.

The United States might benefit from the experience of Singapore and Malaysia, and also of two European countries, the Netherlands and Sweden.

The Netherlands has adopted a policy of de facto decriminalization for drug use. Drugs, even marijuana, are still illegal, but there is no attempt to prosecute small scale use, or even small scale dealing. The Dutch do prosecute large scale traffickers in what they call "drugs of unacceptable risk." The maximum penalty for the most unacceptable trafficking in drugs of unacceptable risk is twelve years in prison. Generally, though, the Dutch ignore sales and use of marijuana and try to reintegrate most drug users and small-time dealers into the mainstream by giving them the choice of treatment centers or prison.

If the Dutch are proud of their tolerance, the Swedes proclaim that they are tough on drug use. The Swedish idea of penalties, however, differs radically from the American. Possession is punished by fines, and the fines are scaled according to the culprit's ability to pay. The maximum sentence for a drug offense is ten years, but during a typical year—1985—it was imposed only once. During 1984, there were only eight sentences of more than five years. All of these were for trafficking in "a particularly large quantity" of drugs or for trafficking of "an especially dangerous or ruthless nature." "Normal" drug offenses draw sentences of up to three years and small-scale trafficking fines or imprisonment of up to six months. In both the Netherlands and Sweden, the recidivism rate is lower than it is in the United States, and in both countries drug use is declining.

Drug use continues to increase in the United States, according to some experts, because the chance of being caught is so slim. According to some estimates, 35 to 40 million American violate the drug laws every year. Less than 3 percent of that number is punished. The answer to this, according to some members of the "tough guy" school, is to hire more police and build more prisons.

But the United States has a larger percentage of its population imprisoned than almost any other country in the world. The annual cost of operating the prisons we have is $35 billion dollars. To expand the prison system enough to take care of all the drug offenders—more than thirty-three times—would cost more than a *trillion* dollars. And that's not counting the cost of the police needed to catch all the users and the judges, court officials and courtrooms needed to send them to prison.

4

One solution that appeals to both tough guys and liberals is the "boot camp." Boot camps are supposedly patterned after military basic training, which in the U.S. Navy and Marine Corps is conducted in what are called boot camps for new recruits, or "boots." The penal boot camps are designed to take care of first-time, nonviolent offenders. They are cheaper to operate than prisons and theoretically teach the inmates self-discipline. The first boot camp opened in Oklahoma in 1983, and the concept has grown increasingly popular with both state and federal legislators.

From one point of view, the notion seems bizarre. It aims to punish convicted felons by giving them the same treatment received by young people who have volunteered to serve their country. One would think that either the punishment isn't serious, or some of the services treat new recruits with gratuitous brutality.

Punishment, though, is the prime reason for penal boot camps, according to some of their most ardent proponents. One of these, Gov. Zell Miller, of Georgia, said, "Nobody can tell me from some ivory tower that if you take a kid, you kick him in the rear end, and it doesn't do any good." Professional correction officials often refer to boot camps as S.I. (shock incarceration).

Governor Miller, a former marine, is convinced boot camps instill self-discipline, and to support his contention he points to the many graduates of the Marine Corps who are model citizens. The argument overlooks the fact that most youths who enter the Marine Corps already have a healthy sense of self-discipline. There has never been any hard evidence that months of bullying by representative of an all-powerful

Corps made anyone a better warrior. In American history, the combat performance of the marines has been generally neither better nor worse than soldiers who have not had the benefit of marine boot camp. In world history, in fact, some troops with almost no externally imposed discipline have beaten superior numbers of disciplined regulars. Examples include the American militia in the Revolution and the Afrikaner irregulars in the first and second Boer wars (1881 and 1899–1902).

There's no evidence, either, that boot camps instill self-discipline. A study by Doris L. MacKenzie, a criminologist at the University of Maryland, shows that boot camp graduates are just a likely to be arrested again as former prison inmates. The General Accounting Office of the U.S. Congress reached a similar conclusion. But according to William Jenkins, Jr., the GAO's assistant director of justice issues, the report "died on the vine."

"It didn't tell them [the Congressmen] what they wanted to hear," Jenkins said. "Most people on the Hill believe that boot camps should be expanded."

The White House shares that view. President Clinton (who, of course, has no experience of either boot camps or basic training) is an enthusiastic booster of boot camps. Boot camps are a feature of Clinton's 1994 crime law.

The recidivism rates of boot camp graduates are usually a hair lower than for former prisoners—14.3 percent of former boot camp inmates are back in prison within six months in Louisiana, for instance, as opposed to 15.4 percent of former prisoners. Dr. MacKenzie does not find those figures significant. Further, they measure only the cream of the boot camp graduates. Convicts serving in boot camps may be discharged. In that case, they go directly to jail. The recidivism rates of failed boot campers is probably higher than that of the average prisoners. There are a lot of failed boot campers. They amount to 37 percent of the boot camp inmates in New York, 43 percent in Louisiana, 50 percent in Florida and 80 percent in Wisconsin. These large percentages of discharges mean that the supposed savings from the less-expensive boot camps are largely illusionary. A state has to have enough prisons to receive boot camp inmates who have been discharged. Further, says Dale Parent, who completed a mostly negative study of boot camps for the National Institutes of Justice, many of the youths sent to boot camps would have been put on probation if there were no boot camps. In effect, boot camps have increased correctional costs.

But as William Jenkins learned, these facts mean little to lawmakers who desire to take an insolent, disrespectful kid and vicariously "kick him in the rear end."

5

There's a much more sinister drawback to increasing sentences. If a drug dealer can get life in prison without possibility of parole, or if he can get the death penalty, what is he liable to do if he sees a police officer approaching him? The cop may be only planning to issue a traffic ticket, but the dealer knows that if he sees drugs in the car, it is the end of his life. The penalty for murder is no worse. How many cops have been murdered because of these circumstances is unknown. But there have been too many. And as penalties increase, there will be more.

As Benjamin and Miller point out, "*Raising* the penalties for drug dealing is equivalent to *lowering* the penalties on other crimes in the course of the illegal drug business. *The result is more intimidation, violence and lawlessness by drug dealers.*"

The same thing applies to penalties for use. If the penalty for smoking marijuana is a long prison sentence (in Texas, it's two years to life for possession), the pot smoker may take desperate measures to avoid capture. These measures could include murdering informers or police officers. Getting "tough on drugs" in this way means making things tough for everyone.

These are some of the problems associated with the long sentences that have become fashionable in the War on Drugs. There are a lot of other problems the "war" has caused.

20

Even if politicians had no desire to show how tough they are by "throwing the book" at drug offenders, the way the war is waged would still be a disaster for the justice system in the United States. There are just too many drug arrests and too many criminal cases involving drugs. The repercussions of this plethora of drug cases affects many aspects of life.

Both federal and state courts have enormous backlogs of drug cases. In 1990, the California State Judicial Council concluded that 60 to 65 percent of all criminal trials in that state were for drug offenses. Another 20 percent were for drug-related crimes. Some state judges have dockets with as many as 250 drug cases waiting for trial. Individual prosecutors may be simultaneously working on as many as 40 drug cases. In Washington, D.C., drug cases account for two-thirds of all felony cases. In the state of Washington, prosecutors have been deputizing volunteer prosecutors from the lawyers in their areas. This unique kind of pro bono work—pro bono prosecution—is not wildly successful. The volunteers are relatively young and inexperienced. They receive only three days' training before prosecuting cases. Their trial work is rarely supervised.

King County, Washington's largest county, has even had volunteer judges. When calling back retired judges didn't provide enough justices to hear Seattle's crushing backlog of drug cases, Charles B. Johnson, the presiding judge of King County Superior Court, appointed lawyers in private practice to act as temporary judges.

Temporary judges introduce a wild card into the criminal justice system. And using inexperienced volunteer prosecutors may mean that many persons who should be locked up are acquitted. On the other hand, public defenders say that many cases that would normally be plea-bargained go before a jury, which further adds to the backlog. If convicted, of course, those defendants would also receive much heavier sentences. In other words, the volunteer system increases the chances that serious criminals will go free and minor offenders will receive major sentences. Washington officials, though, are doing more to meet the drug-case overload than those in most other states.

In most states, the crush of cases has resulted in the mass production of plea bargaining. In some cases, plea bargaining is a way to mitigate the effects of overly harsh mandatory sentencing. The culprit is allowed to plead guilty to a lesser offense and receives a more appropriate sentence. More often, the prosecutor lets serious criminals plead guilty to lesser offenses because if he doesn't, most of his cases will never be tried.

In some urban centers, judges dispose of 70 to 100 plea-bargained cases a day. That presents a problem for the person who believes himself or herself to be innocent. If the case goes to trial, it will bog down the judge's schedule. That may annoy the judge. If the accused is found guilty—and innocent persons have been found guilty—he or she will not only be sentenced for a more serious offense but will be sentenced by an angry judge who may impose the maximum. The difference in sentences for persons originally charged with the *same* offense may be probation for one and twenty years in prison for the other. Federal sentencing guidelines were introduced to modify inequities caused by too much judicial discretion, but, as we've seen, they've introduced other problems, especially as the trend has been toward ever-higher minimum mandatory sentences.

State courts have suffered the most from the drug case overload, but federal courts are not immune. In some areas, federal officials even agree to take a share of the cases that might otherwise be tried in state courts. In Manhattan, everyone arrested on a particular day, called "federal day," is prosecuted in federal instead of state court. Most federal court officials are happy with this arrangement, because it shows that they are doing their part in the national crusade against drugs. These days, though, federal courts, like state courts, are beginning to show the strain of drug-case overload.

2

A decade ago, drug cases made up less than a quarter of all federal criminal trials. Now drug cases constitute more than half of them. And the proportion is still increasing. In some federal courts, 70 percent of all trial time is spent on drug cases. Benjamin and Miller point out that during one eight-month period, two federal judges responsible for hearing cases in nineteen Florida counties had not heard a single civil case. Almost 70 percent of the civil cases in federal courts nationwide have been pending for three years.

The right to a speedy trial on a criminal charge is guaranteed by the U.S. Constitution and the Speedy Trial Act. It is entirely proper that criminal cases take precedence. But the overload of criminal cases—most of them drug cases—means that justice in many noncriminal cases is unreasonably delayed. Every delay in a criminal case increases its cost. Lawyers have to be paid. Most major civil cases involve corporations, whose legal expenses are business expenses. Like all business expenses, these are met by raising the price of the product. So all Americans end up paying for delays in civil justice. Further, many of these civil cases involve vital environmental issues. These issues do not concern the health and safety of the snail darter and the spotted owl but of men, women and children. Benjamin and Miller cite the suit of the state of Florida against the Great Lakes Chemical Corporation. The state accused the corporation of contaminating the groundwater at twenty-two locations with carcinogenic chemicals, endangering tens of thousands of persons. The case had been waiting for months without trial because the courts were spending all their time on drug cases. Unfortunately, few lawyers are fanatically interested in expediting justice, because delays cause them no loss of money.

3

Time is a vital commodity in the justice system. Proper use of time is as important to police forces as it is to the courts. Nationwide, at least 25 percent of all police budgets is expended on drug-law enforcement. In large metropolitan areas, the expenditure on drug-law enforcement is much larger—half of the total budget or more. The drain on police personnel is even heavier. A survey by the Bureau of Justice Statistics found that 77 percent of local police and sheriff's officers have primary responsibility for drug-law enforcement in their jurisdictions, as do 69 percent of state police departments. Most of these officers (85 percent) belong to special drug units and almost all (91 percent) participate in multi-agency task forces. As we've seen, the largest number of drug arrests, by far, are for simple possession. (As Benjamin and Miller put it, "No more than 25 percent of Americans arrested for drugs are involved in 'trafficking,' and almost all of those are petty, small-time dealers. The remaining 75 percent of the arrests are for simple possession, often for marijuana.") So, during an unprecedented rise in the homicide rate of and by juveniles, police departments are expending a staggering proportion of their time and money busting pot smokers. Some of those arrested for simple possession may, of course, be guilty of far worse crimes. But even though Al Capone was imprisoned for income-tax evasion instead of multiple murder, the American criminal-justice system is not based on presumption of guilt. To the best of our knowledge, the vast majority of those arrested for possession are guilty only of possession.

The cops do, of course, try to arrest dealers. One popular method is the "sting." Until the arrival of Chief Nicholas Pastore and a new emphasis on community policing, stings were the usual way police fought the drug war on the streets of New Haven, Connecticut. The way the sting was conducted in New Haven, and still is in most U.S. cities, was that an undercover police officer would buy drugs from a street dealer. As soon as the money changed hands, undercover cops would erupt from doorways, cars and street corners to surround the dealer and arrest him and any customers nearby. The sting uses a lot of police officers to capture a few nickel-and-dime dealers and some unwary possessors.

Benjamin and Miller cite the case of Desmond Legister. Legister, a twenty-four-year-old drug dealer, was arrested in June 1989 after a five-week surveillance by eight New York police officers. Finally, one undercover officer approached him and asked for drugs. Legister agreed to take the officer's money, buy the drugs the officer wanted from his source and turn them over to the officer. When he turned over the drugs, he was arrested. When Legister's case came to trial a year later, each of the officers had to spend six days in court either testifying or waiting to testify. To convict this very minor dealer, the New York police had to spend 200 man-days, almost the equivalent of a full year's work by one officer.

Meanwhile, the murder rate keeps edging upward.

One answer, of course, is to hire enough cops to keep fighting the war on drugs and still control street crime. That answer prompts more questions: How many cops is enough? And what do you hire them with? Every city in the country is currently strapped for funds; some are on the edge of bankruptcy. The federal government is talking about giving the cities and states enough money to hire 100,000 new police officers. When you spread those 100,000 cops around a nation of 255,000,000, though, will there be enough to make a difference? There are 604,000 state, county and municipal police officers now. An increase of 100,000 would be less than 17 percent. According to the Bureau of Justice Statistics, "The total number of police and sheriffs' employees increased by 17% from 1986 and 1992, including a 35% increase by sheriffs' departments." During the same period, the crime rate, and especially the juvenile homicide rate, continued to rise.

It should not be forgotten, either, that the federal funds that would finance this sudden expansion of state and municipal police forces come from the same people who supply state and municipal funds.

It's not as if we weren't already spending money on drug-law enforcement. A fourth of all the money spent on all the municipal, county and state police agencies in the country is earmarked for drug-law enforcement. One federal agency, the Drug Enforcement Administration, is exclusively devoted to drug law enforcement. Another, the U.S. Customs Service, spends almost all its time and energy on the same subject. The U.S. Coast Guard spends more effort hunting down drug smugglers than anything else. Then there's the FBI, which never lets any federal crime escape its purview. In addition to all of this, there are the federal and state correctional systems, which will soon be used mostly to house drug offenders. When you add in all the elements, the officially announced federal budget for the War on Drugs is piddling compared with the real expense. The War on Drugs is costing the American taxpayer far more than the $12 billion officially announced for the federal War on Drugs in fiscal '92. It actually approaches $100 billion.

The real cost is higher still. These costs include crack babies and overdose deaths caused by the concentrated dosages that prohibiting a substance causes; AIDS from shared needles because new needles can't be obtained; the growth of crime and organized gangs; the financing of other crime and the arming of gangs from illegal drug profits; and the destruction of hope in inner cities by making urban ghettos the main target of the War on Drugs. These costs are not mere rhetoric, like the value politicians proclaim for life—"If only one life is saved, this measure will be worth the cost." (Actually, no measure taken by government can save a life; it can only prolong a life.) These costs can be measured in dollars—the dollars needed to treat crack babies, AIDS sufferers and victims of urban violence, the dollars stolen by criminals, and the dollars spent on additional law enforcement.

We started with the image of the Dope Fiend as described in Richmond Pearson Hobson's "The Living Dead." In America's imagination, Hobson transformed the unfortunate, usually curable, drug addict into a kind of vampire—a twentieth century Dracula. The way we, as a nation, have cracked down on this imaginary being has helped create another monster—the Zero. We have, in effect, begun with a concept from one of the world's classic horror stories, Dracula, and made reality of another, Frankenstein. And like Victor Frankenstein, we, through our government, have done all this from the best of intentions.

21

On Sunday, February 28, 1993, seventy-six federal agents climbed into cattle trucks, crawled under tarps on the truck beds and headed across the empty plains near Waco, Texas. Their destination was a desolate collection of shacks built of scrap lumber, plywood and, in one building, cinder blocks. It was the headquarters of a very strange religious group called the Branch Davidians. The agents wore military helmets and armor vests. They carried concussion grenades as well as guns. Their faces were covered with ski masks.

The agents had a warrant to search the compound, allegedly dubbed "Ranch Apocalypse" by the Branch Davidians—about sixty men and women and some forty children from North America, Europe, Japan and Australia. (Actually, the Davidians called their compound Mount Carmel, but the news media apparently thinks "Ranch Apocalypse" has more sex appeal. They've continued to use it.) The agents also had an arrest warrant for the leader of the Davidians, a former rock musician named Vernon Howell, who called himself David Koresh.

The warrant for Koresh accused him of converting semiautomatic rifles, which were legal, to full automatic rifles, which were not. The evidence for the charge was highly circumstantial: No one had ever seen one of the automatic weapons Koresh's group was supposed to possess. The warrant was based on the statement by a gun dealer that he had sold (legally) the Branch Davidians some parts which might be used to make the alleged conversions. No one had formally accused the Branch Davidians of assaulting anyone or even of disturbing the peace. Nevertheless seventy-six agents armed with hand grenades and guns didn't seem like enough firepower to the Bureau of Alcohol, Tobacco and Firearms leaders. They wanted helicopters. The BATF wanted to get them from the Texas National Guard, but under Texas law, the guard could lend equipment to civilian law enforcers only if it was needed to arrest drug traffickers. So the BATF agents told the guardsmen that Koresh's followers were operating a methamphetamine factory.

During more than 200 years of United States history, the custom and practice when serving a search warrant has been to knock on the door and tell whoever answers that you have a warrant. According to Charles Richards of the Associated Press:

> The battle began when federal agents hidden in livestock trailers stormed the main home of the sect. . . . Witnesses said the law officers stormed the compound's main home, throwing concussion grenades and screaming "Come out!" while three National Guard helicopters approached.

The agents later said that an agent had approached the front door and told an occupant he had the warrants; then the hidden agents jumped out and rushed the building. Whoever opened the door slammed it shut as the grenades began exploding. Even if this is what happened, it was a most unusual way to serve a search warrant and an arrest warrant for a nonviolent offense.

Months later, at the trial of the cult's survivors in San Antonio, agents admitted that they had rehearsed storming the compound for three days at a nearby military base, but they had never made any preparation for a peaceful entry.

Not surprisingly, the Branch Davidians returned fire. Few, if any, knew there were any warrants. All they could see was a gang of masked men throwing grenades and breaking into their buildings. Four federal agents were killed and sixteen wounded. Several cult members were also killed, including a two-year-old child.

At the trial, one of the agents, Timothy Gaborie, said that as the raid began, he shot a dog that was "barking offensively" and then ducked under a truck and emptied three pistol magazines in the direction of the compound without looking to see where he was shooting. He said he kept his head below the truck bed to avoid bullets from the compound. "I would just put it [the pistol] on the bed of the truck and empty my magazine," he said.

The BATF, later supplemented by the FBI, laid siege to the compound for almost two months. Press reports invariably described the flimsy, barracks-like shacks as Koresh's "fortress." The BATF blamed the local press for tipping off the Branch Davidians, and one agent actually filed suit against the *Waco Tribune-Herald* for warning the cultists. Inasmuch as the newspaper had apparently precipitated the raid by publishing a series, "The Sinful Messiah," which accused the Davidians of molesting children and stockpiling arms in preparation for the Apocalypse, the suit seemed ill-grounded. It turned out that the agents themselves had tipped off the news media, and a Davidian who struck up a conversation with members of a waiting TV crew got the idea that something was about to happen.

After fifty-one days, the federal task force, now commanded by the FBI, moved in. They sent National Guard tanks to punch holes in the flimsy walls and shoot in tear gas. The Davidians had gas masks, but masks lose their effectiveness in time. The federal agents said they expected the cult members to surrender in a short time. Instead, the compound burst into flames. Only nine members were able to get out.

Government spokesmen said the cult members had deliberately set the fire in a mass suicide. Six of the survivors, though, told their lawyers a different story. Although all were questioned separately, the stories jibed in every detail. The biggest tank, they said, did not merely punch a hole in a wall. It rammed the main building directly where a section had been built of cinder blocks and where the government believed Koresh was hiding. The tank smashed a door and an upright piano the Davidians were using to barricade the door. It also flattened a tank of propane, spraying its contents all over the building. The vibrations of the impact knocked over a number of camp lanterns the cult members had been using since their electricity had been turned off. The lamps ignited the propane.

In forty-five minutes, an estimated eighty-six persons were dead.

While "Mount Carmel" was being consumed in a firestorm, the federal officers kept fire engines from approaching it. They said they feared that snipers in the inferno would shoot the firefighters.

Federal authorities said that some of the first forty-six human remains found at the site showed evidence of having been shot. But Dr. Nizam Peerwani, head of the Tarrant County medical examiner's office in Fort Worth, said, "There is absolutely no evidence of that as far as we are concerned at this stage." Within a few days, however, the story of mass shootings was adopted by all news media.

Three weeks after the fiery end of Koresh and his followers, bulldozers rumbled across the burned ruins. Jack Zimmerman, lawyer for one of the dead cult members, protested.

"I guess what it does, it forever prevents any checking on the ATF's rendition that the fire was intentionally set," Zimmerman said.

Explaining the reason for the tank attack that led to the annihilation of the Branch Davidians, FBI spokesmen said, according to the Associated Press, "The decision was made only after federal agents were completely frustrated by unproductive negotiations and psychological experts said further talks would not lead to a resolution."

Attorney General Janet Reno said she authorized the attack because of reports of child abuse. White House spokespersons said child abuse inside the compound had been continuing. The FBI, however, said the only reasons it had for believing child abuse was going on were old (and unverified) reports and a psychiatrist's (absentee) opinion.

The main reason for the whole bloody mess, that began with a projected arrest for a nonviolent offense and ended with mass killing and the arrest of the survivors for murder, was that the Branch Davidians were different.

The authorities seem to believe that if they can convince the public that any person or group is different enough, they can get away with anything. That's particularly true if they can accuse the "oddballs" of dope trafficking, as they did by alleging that the Branch Davidians operated a methamphetamine factory.

In this case, they miscalculated. The jury in San Antonio refused to find any of the defendants guilty of murder or conspiracy to murder. It did convict five of the eleven of voluntary manslaughter, which according to federal Judge Walter S. Smith, Jr., is a killing "in the sudden heat of passion, caused by adequate provocation." One was convicted of possession of a grenade, and another of conspiracy to possess and aiding in the unlawful possession of a machine gun. The jury had convicted seven of carrying a firearm in the commission of a violent crime, but the judge threw out the convictions because the jury had acquitted all of the violent crime (conspiracy to murder). Two days later, those convictions were reinstated after government lawyers cited case law to show that a conviction is not necessary for a jury to find a defendant guilty of using a firearm in a crime. In other words, the jury can find a defendant guilty of using a firearm in a violent crime even if it found that there was no crime. The government lawyers had essentially lost their case, but they were doing their best to make the defendants pay.

2

An accusation of drug trafficking was a detail the BATF overlooked the year before its Branch Davidian raid. The earlier raid, which began August 21, 1992, was instigated by the BATF but carried out by the U.S. Marshals Service. The object of the bureau's attention this time was much smaller than in Waco. It was simply forty-four-year-old Randy Weaver and his family. Nobody, including nobody in the Bureau of Alcohol, Tobacco and Firearms, ever accused Weaver of any sort of involvement with drugs.

Randy Weaver was different in other ways. Radically different. He was a white separatist. He wanted nothing to do with blacks, Orientals, American Indians or even Jews. But then, he didn't want much to do with anybody. He and his wife, their four children and a boy they had almost adopted lived in a plywood shack in northern Idaho, near the Canadian border. They had no running water and no electricity except what they produced occasionally with a small generator. They kept a garden, hunted for subsistence and Weaver cut firewood for customers. His few friends were different too. They belonged to something called the Aryan Nation. They were neo-Nazis.

Neo-Nazis, for good reason, are not popular with most Americans. They aren't popular with the federal government, either. The feds, in fact, would dearly love to lock up the whole crew. But the Aryans were a clannish group. It was hard to infiltrate them. A BATF informer in the area had been trying to cultivate the Aryans without success. He did become a friend of Weaver, however. Then somebody got an idea: Randy Weaver could be used as an informer. So Weaver's "friend" asked if he could buy a couple of the subsistence hunter's shotguns. Weaver agreed. Then the "friend" said he wanted shorter barrels on the guns.

A shotgun with a barrel shorter than eighteen inches is illegal under federal law. Guns like this are illegal because they were widely used by gangsters during the '20s and '30s. They're not uncommon in rural areas, though. Western farmers and ranchers have found them handy to carry in a truck and effective for killing coyotes. Federal agents in western states usually handle several sawed-off shotgun cases every year. If the gun owner had been keeping the weapon to reduce the coyote population, the shotgun is confiscated, but usually not much else happens.

Weaver needed the money. He agreed to shorten the gun barrels. After he cut them, the barrels were 17 ¾ inches long, making them illegal by a quarter of an inch. Eight months later, two BATF agents told Weaver he had committed a federal crime. He didn't have to go to jail, though. If he would keep the government informed on what the Aryan Nation was doing, the government would forget the crime. He refused. Six months later, he was indicted and arrested. Out on bond, Weaver vowed to stay on his mountain and have nothing more to do with the government. He refused to appear in court.

On August 21, six federal marshals surrounded the cabin and moved up the hill. Weaver's yellow Lab began barking. Weaver, his fourteen-year-old son, Sam, and Kevin Harris, a youth living with the Weavers, thought the dog must be chasing a deer. They grabbed rifles and ran out. A marshal with an automatic military rifle shot the dog. Little (4 feet, 11 inches) Sammy was running up to the dog when the marshal's burst killed the animal. Startled, Sam fired his rifle in the direction the shots seemed to come from. A marshal fired again, hitting Sammy in the arm. The boy began to run.

Randy Weaver, looking for the dog in another area, heard the shots. He called to Sam.

"I'm coming, Dad," the boy yelled. The marshal fired again. A bullet hit Sammy in the back, killing him instantly.

Kevin Harris saw it all happen. He fired at where the shots seemed to have originated and ran back to the shack. His bullet hit and killed a marshal.

A police officer had been killed. Within days, the FBI, the Idaho State Police, sheriff's deputies and the Idaho National Guard all surrounded the Weaver cabin. They had armored personnel carriers, machine-guns and high-tech robots.

That night, the Weavers carried Sam's body back and left it in an outbuilding. The next day, Weaver, Harris and sixteen-year-old Sara Weaver went out to clean up the body. The federal agents opened fire and hit Weaver in the upper arm. Weaver's wife, Vicki, holding her ten-month-old baby, opened the door and held it open for her husband and the kids. The marshals were still firing. Harris was hit several times. Then a sniper's bullet hit Vicki Weaver, blowing half her head away and almost killing the baby at the same time.

Then, as they were to do in Waco, the FBI took over.

The FBI negotiating team brought up loudspeakers to communicate with the Weavers. Their "negotiation" techniques would strike most people as rather odd. According to Sara Weaver, "They'd come on real late at night and say, 'Come out and talk to us, Mrs. Weaver. How's the baby, Mrs. Weaver?' in a real smart-alecky voice."

At one point, Sara said, the FBI sent a robot to the door with a telephone so the Weavers could talk to them. But the robot also held a shotgun, which it pointed right at the door.

Eventually, the authorities got James "Bo" Gritz, Weaver's commanding officer when the recluse was in the Army Special Forces, to ask Weaver to give up. Weaver agreed to surrender on condition that the authorities ask Gerry Spence to defend him. Spence, a onetime cowboy and self-styled "country lawyer," lives in Wyoming, runs a ranch and has never lost a criminal case. Spence is considered one of the best, if not the best, trial lawyers in the country. Daniel Sheehan recruited him to handle courtroom matters in the Karen Silkwood case.

Spence agreed to talk with Weaver, but he was not eager to handle the case.

"My name is Gerry Spence," he told Weaver. "I'm the lawyer you've been told about. Before we begin to talk, I want you to understand that I do not share any of your political or religious beliefs. Many of my dearest friends are Jews. My daughter is married to a Jew. My sister is married to a black man. She has adopted a black child. I deplore what the Nazis stand for. If I defend you, I will not defend your political beliefs or your religious beliefs, but your rights as an American citizen to a fair trial.

"That's all I ask," Weaver replied.

When Spence heard Weaver's story, he agreed to take the case. During the trial, the government called fifty-six witnesses. Spence called none. He was confident that the government's witnesses had destroyed their own case. At one point, for instance, one of the U.S. marshals told of the elaborate preparations they had made to get Weaver out of his house. Spence asked if they had ever considered simply knocking on his door. The marshal said they hadn't.

The jury found Kevin Harris innocent of all charges, including murder. It found Randy Weaver innocent of eight felonies, including murder and the gun charge that started everything. It found him guilty only of failing to appear in court and of violating his bond conditions.

After the trial, Spence told the *New York Times*, "A jury today has said that you can't kill somebody just because you wear badges, then cover up those homicides by prosecuting the innocent."

That, of course, was before Waco.

3

What place do the Waco disaster and the Randy Weaver case have in a book on drug-law enforcement?

In Waco, the federal agents did publicly charge that the Branch Davidians were running a methamphetamine factory. That, though, proved to be merely a ploy, and lies by representatives of the federal government are hardly unusual. It did demonstrate that in Texas, as in most states—thanks to the Dope Fiend myth—drug offenders are considered worthy of the most ruthless enforcement tactics. The principal reason both cases are included, though, is to show how ruthless law enforcers can be when their targets are those most of society considers to be members of the lunatic fringe. It also shows how much the public will tolerate such ruthlessness if the targets are supposed to be involved with drugs. The Weaver case is one of the rare cases in which the law enforcers were *proven* in a courtroom to be in the wrong.

This ruthlessness is not merely a federal failing. A few years ago, another strange cult, known as MOVE, was the target of Philadelphia police. MOVE members were alleged to use drugs but not soap and water. Neighbors complained that they were noisy and filthy, and their building was unsanitary. They refused to be evicted. The police tried to move MOVE but ended up by dropping a bomb on their building. The building quickly became a roaring furnace, but the police, like the feds at Waco, kept the fire engines away. Most of the cult members burned up. Most of their neighbors, whose houses were ignited in the blaze, became homeless. For the first time in American history, dirtiness became a capital crime. And arson by the authorities was condoned. Unlike the Randy Weaver family, MOVE was never vindicated by a court.

One thing the cults had in common, and the Weavers did not, was the accusation that they used drugs. For cops who think they're commandos, the Dope Fiend has provided a handy excuse. The Branch Davidians, Weaver and MOVE got national attention, but in thousands of smaller cases, the civil rights of persons accused of drug use and trafficking are grossly abused all the time. We'll look at some cases a little later.

"Civil rights," applied to criminal cases, is a somewhat vague term that to many people merely connotes "something for lawyers to argue about." That attitude, of course, assumes that the police know who is guilty, and a trial is only to confirm their accusations.

The most important civil rights in this country are those founded in the Constitution of the United States. The part of the Constitution most concerned with civil rights is the Bill of Rights, the first ten amendments.

Today, knowledge of the Bill of Rights is not widespread. One result is that lawmakers, prosecutors and police often act as if it does not exist, particularly when drugs are concerned.

For the record, this is the Bill of Rights:

1. Congress shall make no law respecting an establishment of religion, or prohibiting the free exercise thereof; or abridging the freedom of speech or of the press; or the right of the people peaceably to assemble, and to petition the government for a redress of grievances.

2. A well-regulated militia being necessary for the security of a free state, the right of the people to keep and bear arms shall not be infringed.

3. No soldier shall, in time of peace, be quartered in any house without the consent of the owner, nor in time of war but in a manner prescribed by law.

4. The right of the people to be secure in their persons, houses, papers and effects, against unreasonable searches and seizures, shall not be violated, and no warrants shall issue but upon probable cause, supported by oath or affirmation, and particularly describing the place to be searched, and the persons or things to be seized.

5. No person shall be held to answer for a capital or other infamous crime unless on a presentment or indictment of a grand jury, except in cases arising in the land or naval forces, or in the militia, when in actual service, in time of war or public danger; nor shall any person be subject for the same offense to be twice put in jeopardy of life or limb; nor shall be compelled in any criminal case to be a witness against himself, nor be deprived of life, liberty or property, without due process of law; nor shall private property be taken for public use without just compensation.

6. In all criminal prosecutions, the accused shall enjoy the right to a speedy and public trial, by an impartial jury of the state and district wherein the crime shall have been committed, which district shall have been previously ascertained by law, and to be informed of the nature and cause of the accusation; to be confronted with the witnesses against him; to have compulsory process for obtaining witnesses in his favor, and to have the assistance of counsel for his defence.

7. In suits at common law, where the value in controversy shall exceed twenty dollars, the right of trial by jury shall be preserved, and no fact tried by a jury shall be otherwise re-examined by any court of the United States than according to the rules of the common law.

8. Excessive bail shall not be required, nor excessive fines imposed, nor cruel and unusual punishments inflicted.

9. The enumeration in the constitution of certain rights shall not be construed to deny or disparage others retained by the people.

10. The powers not delegated to the United States by the constitution, nor prohibited by it to the states, are reserved to the states respectively, or to the people.

4

Considering the flimsy basis for the raid on the Branch Davidians and the excessive force with which it was conducted, one could argue that it violated the spirit of the freedom-of-religion clauses of the First Amendment. And as the motivation for the Idaho raid that resulted in the violent death of Vicki and Sammy Weaver was to get the Aryan Nation, it would seem that reverence for the freedom-of-speech clause in the same amendment was not excessive among the federal officials. It's become an axiom for civil libertarians that the first attacks on the rights of individuals are aimed at the least powerful and most disreputable individuals among us. If successful, those attacks set precedents for the further restriction of the rest of us. Spence put it this way: "When the rights of our enemies have been wrested from them, our own rights have been lost as well, for the same rights serve both citizen and criminal."

Think about the rights supposedly guaranteed by the first ten amendments.

The First Amendment is probably the most zealously guarded: Both the press and the churches are powerful forces, and both are sensitive to their rights. But the churches were silent when the "oddball" church in Waco was attacked, and the press generally acted as a cheerleader for the federal forces in both Waco and Idaho.

The Second Amendment has recently become highly controversial. It would take another book to examine that controversy and the conflicts it engenders. One side holds that because it begins with the words "A well-regulated militia being necessary to the security of a free state," the amendment simply guarantees the states the right to keep militias. The other side says that because the rest of the amendment reads "the right of the *people* to keep and bear arms shall not be infringed," it guarantees the right to keep arms to the people, not merely the states. The courts have interpreted the amendment both ways, and the U.S. Supreme Court has studiously avoided making a final definition. It should be mentioned, though, that in the rest of the Bill of Rights, wherever the words "the people" are used, they mean the people, not the states.

The Third Amendment prohibits the quartering of troops on citizens in time of peace. That was one of the causes of the Revolution, but it has not been a burning issue in more than two centuries.

The Fourth and Fifth amendments are those most frequently strained by the War on Drugs. In his *Dead on Delivery*, DEA agent Robert Stutman says that in New York, the custom was to telephone a judge for a search warrant on the way to the site of a raid, instead of attending a formal hearing. That may not violate ". . . no warrants shall issue but upon probable cause, supported by oath or affirmation, and particularly describing the place to be searched, and the persons or things to be seized," but it comes close. "Stop and frisk" laws would seem to clearly violate "The right of the people to be secure in their persons . . ." Since 1969, though, courts have allowed police to search persons without a warrant if they have "probable cause" to think they may be carrying contraband. The Founding Fathers didn't know about automobiles, but it might be supposed that cars would be covered under the protection afforded "their persons, houses, papers and effects." They aren't, though.

The Fifth Amendment's prohibition against seizing property without due process of law raises a question about Drug War tactics. How much process is due process? Under property-confiscation laws, the government can seize the property of a suspected drug violator without having convicted the violator of a crime. The legal process used in these cases is civil, rather than criminal, law. In a civil case, the plaintiff only has to present "a preponderance of the evidence," a far lower standard of proof than criminal law's "beyond a reasonable doubt." Standards of proof in civil forfeiture cases are even lower than in other civil cases. The government must only demonstrate "probable cause"—"more than a suspicion, but less than a fifty-fifty chance," as Benjamin and Miller put it. In some cases, the government has seized property without first holding a hearing or even warning the property owner. We'll look at these questionable police tactics in more detail later in this chapter.

The courts have also held that entrapment, such as the BATF employee persuading and paying Randy Weaver to commit a crime, is a violation of the Fifth Amendment's prohibition of self-incrimination.

Most of the first ten amendments are self-explanatory. The last two, though, seldom receive the emphasis they should. The Ninth says that the rights of the people are not limited to those expressed in the Constitution. The Tenth says the rights of the federal government are.

5

One of the unexpressed rights of the people, according to a series of Supreme Court decisions, is the right to privacy. The federal government, for instance, cannot, without convincing a court it has probable cause to believe a crime is being committed, tap your telephone line or bug your house. Government invasions of privacy have always been considered among the most obnoxious features of life in a dictatorship. During World War II, we heard horror stories about how the Nazis encouraged German children to inform on their parents. The same thing happened regularly in Communist countries from the Soviet Union to Cuba. A few years ago, a little girl in the United States turned her parents in to the police because they used drugs. Was anyone horrified? No. The child was lionized by the U.S. press and hailed as a heroine by the authorities. That was somewhat before the Bush Administration decided to pose as a champion of "family values."

Domestic espionage has been a hallmark of all Communist regimes. Probably the worst are in Cuba and China, where the government appoints informers and holds them responsible for the actions and words of their neighbors and families. Romania, under the bloody Nicolae Ceausescu, relied on volunteers. Anyone who felt that an acquaintance was an "enemy of the state" was encouraged to write his tip—anonymously—on a slip of paper and slip it into one of the drop boxes located all through Romania. It has been estimated that Ceausescu had 20 percent of the population spying on the other 80 percent—and on each other.

Ceausescu's success with his volunteers may arouse some envy among certain U.S. officials. At least, we hope so. At major airports, other Customs Service points of entry, federal buildings—at hundreds of locations around the country—you can find 800 numbers posted with directions on how to use them to make a free phone call reporting anyone involved with drug manufacture, trafficking or consumption. The call will be anonymous. The caller need not give a name, need not present evidence, need not appear in court. But the accused's name will go into a computerized list containing the names of more than a million-and-a-half persons who may—or may not—have had anything to do with drugs. The list will be used to show the government where to direct its surveillance. Callers, according to the government, will be serving their country. There is a difference between Ceausescu's domestic spies and these "concerned citizens." Our informers have better technology.

6

There is little public concern over civil rights violation in the Drug War, because generally the public views drug traffickers with unmitigated horror. That's the result of some seventy years of Dope Fiend propaganda. The horror is so great that even a judge, who could be expected to know better, could say to Desmond Legister, "The crime of selling drugs is just as serious, if not more so, than the crime of murder." Legister's crime, "as serious, if not more so, than . . . murder," was, of course, to take the money of an undercover policeman, go to a drug wholesaler and buy the drugs the cop had ordered.

If efforts to catch drug dealers "inconvenience" innocent persons, well, that's the price you have to pay, the public thinks. Of course, members of the public who think that way are seldom those being "inconvenienced." When in late 1993 the Puerto Rican government posted police and National Guardsmen around a low-income housing unit in San Juan to check the identification of everyone entering and leaving, no middle-class Puerto Ricans protested. National Public Radio even trotted out some residents to say they approved. NPR did admit that a lot of residents protested this violation of their right to enter their own homes, but it didn't give them any live interviews.

"No knock" laws, permitting police to break down doors when they have search warrants, were inspired by "dope fiend" hysteria. Ralph Clifford, a Stamford, Connecticut, lawyer who is chairman of the Fairfield County Civil Liberties Union, told of one black family's experience in Danbury, Connecticut. "There were at least three or four police officers. They yelled at the family. They pointed a gun at one of the kids. He started to protest, and he was picked up and thrown across the room, landing on a coffee table and shattering it. All through this, the mother was asking, 'Why are you here?' Finally, the sergeant said, 'We have a search warrant.' She asked to see it. It was for apartment seven, but the family was in apartment six."

The family filed a complaint with the Danbury police department, but the department said there was no police misconduct. They filed a complaint for federal civil rights enforcement with the U.S. attorney's office. The Justice Department in Washington told the U.S. attorney's office not to prosecute, Clifford said.

The Danbury family was lucky. Glen Williamson, of Plaquemines Parish, Louisiana, was arrested in his own house at 2 A.M. after a "no knock" entry. The police had a warrant to arrest a Glen Williams on a drug charge. When Williamson pointed out that warrant was for someone named Williams, one of the cops simply added the letters "on" to the name and hauled Williamson away. He had to post a $25,000 bond to get out of jail before the charge was dropped.

Bruce Lavoie, of Hudson, New Hampshire, was really unlucky. At 5 A.M., he, his wife and three children were awakened by a loud pounding and a tremendous crash. The police had bashed down his door with a battering ram. They rushed into the house without identifying themselves. Lavoie, unarmed, got out of bed to resist these invaders, and one of them shot him dead. They found a single marijuana cigarette.

Then there was Jeffrey Miles, of Jeffersontown, Kentucky. He was shot and killed by a cop with a search warrant who went to the wrong house.

7

When the Founding Fathers prohibited searches without probable cause, they probably hadn't considered "profiles." Profiles were worked up by FBI psychologists long after the Fourth Amendment was adopted. They describe the appearance, actions and mannerisms of persons who have probably—the psychologists contend—committed various types of crime, including drug crimes. Customs Service officers detain, search and question persons entering the country who fit the "drug courier profile." The searching can be intensive. The U.S. Supreme Court has approved the practice of customs officials of making suspects defecate to see if they have swallowed packages of drugs. It would be interesting to get the opinions of the writers of the Bill of Rights on the reasonableness of this type of search. A few smugglers are caught through these "profile" investigations. Most of the suspects subjected to these degrading searches are innocent.

Now state police also use profiles in their hunt for drug traffickers. Their profiles tend to be looser than the federal ones. In Florida, according to attorney Milton Hersh, "If you look Hispanic and are in a rented car, they'll stop you and ask if you would mind if they search the car." But you don't have to look Hispanic. Sgt. Phil K. Moan, of the Florida Highway Patrol said if your car is "riding low in the back," or if you have an out-of-state license plate but "no luggage or clothing visible," you may be stopped. In New Mexico, you may be stopped if your car has Florida license plates.

Joseph Huberman of Raleigh, North Carolina, didn't even fit a drug profile. He was tending his orchids on October 25, 1989, when six agents of the state bureau of investigation appeared and searched his house. They found nothing more sinister than orchids.

What led them to Huberman?

He had purchased supplies at a garden store that had once placed an ad in *High Times*, a magazine aimed at marijuana users. Police searched the homes of everyone on that store's customer list.

8

Drug War justice is like mercy: It falls like rain on the guilty and innocent alike. In some cases, the authorities don't even try to prove their target is guilty.

Police in Detroit didn't give a reason why they brought drug-sniffing dogs into Joseph Haji's Sunshine Market. Haji does business in a drug-infested area, but nobody has accused the grocer of being involved with drugs. Nevertheless, the cops arrived with their canine search team. One of the dogs found the smell of cocaine on three one-dollar bills in Haji's cash register. The police then confiscated *all* the money in Haji's cash register—$4,384. Haji pointed out that drugs are rife in his neighborhood.

"Seventy-five percent of my business is with dope dealers," he said. "I'm supposed to inspect the money?" He did not, he said, know for certain who the dope dealers were and could not bar people from his store without reason.

The police did not charge Haji with any wrongdoing. They didn't return the money, either. Haji may now be considering laundering his money—literally.

Then there is Willy Jones, who runs a landscaping business in Nashville, Tennessee. Once or twice a year, Jones goes out of state to buy shrubbery. Jones found through experience that he got a better deal on the plants when he paid in cash. So in 1992, he stuffed $9,000 into a money belt and headed for the airport for a trip to Houston, Texas. He never got there. On the way, two cops stopped him, searched him and found the $9,000. They told him they thought he was a drug dealer and confiscated the money. They never arrested him; they never charged him.

Interviewed on CBS News's "60 Minutes," Jones said, "They told me I had not committed a crime, that they didn't have anything to arrest—to arrest me for."

Carrying a large amount of cash is not, of course, a criminal offense. But if the police suspect you're a drug dealer, they can confiscate your money. They only have to have probable cause to believe the money would be involved in a drug deal. Steve Kroft of CBS News explained the probable cause: "Willy Jones was carrying a large amount of cash; he was traveling to Houston, according to the federal government, a source city for drugs; his ticket said he was only going to be on the ground an hour, although Jones was carrying an overnight bag and insists it was a ticketing mistake. Finally, Willy Jones wouldn't or couldn't answer their questions."

Jones says he didn't tell them he was going to Houston or why.

"I didn't feel that it was none of their business," he said. "I had not committed a crime. I had not did anything wrong."

It wouldn't have mattered if he did tell them. Judge Robert Bonner, administrator of the DEA, said the short time his ticket allowed Jones to stay in Houston established probable cause. When Kroft protested that there was no attempt to prove that Jones was a drug trafficker, Bonner brushed off the objection with "You're not a trained narcotics officer, for one thing, Steve."

Then Bonner added, "He was given notice; he could have filed a claim, which would have required the government to go forward and put that proof on in a federal district court before a federal judge or a jury if Mr. Jones wanted a jury trial."

Jones would have liked to go to court. But to file a claim, you have to put up a bond—10 percent of the value of the property seized. Jones didn't have the money. He asked the DEA to waive the bond. The DEA refused.

"So Willy Jones never even got his day in court," Kroft said. "If he had, he would have discovered that unlike criminal cases, where the government has to prove you're guilty, in forfeiture cases, you have to prove you're innocent."

Bo Edwards, a Nashville attorney, took Jones's case. He said, "The Bill of Rights applies to criminal cases. For example, the right to have a lawyer, the right to a trial by jury, that the government must prove its case beyond a reasonable doubt. None of these rights applies in a civil case where the government is bringing a civil forfeiture proceeding against your property."

"Why has it been made so difficult?" Kroft asked.

"To make it easier for the government to keep the property," Edwards said.

The same program aired the case of Billy Munnerlyn, a charter airplane operator. In October 1989, Munnerlyn flew a man he thought was a banker from Little Rock, Arkansas, to Ontario, California. When he landed, federal agents arrested Munnerlyn and his passenger, Albert Wright, who turned out to be not a banker but a convicted criminal. In Wright's baggage was $2.7 million in cash. The charges against Munnerlyn were dropped, but the government kept his plane. So far, Munnerlyn has spent $85,000 in legal fees trying to get it back. He's filed for bankruptcy.

The government decided not to prosecute Wright, but kept the $2.7 million. Munnerlyn's suit to recover his Lear jet got to court in 1992, and the jury found in his favor. The judge overruled the jury and ordered a new trial.

Thanks to Edwards, Jones did get his case into court. In April 1993, a federal judge ordered the government to give back the $9,000. At this writing, Munnerlyn is still waiting.

Donald A. Regan, of Montvale, New Jersey, doesn't have to wait. He knows he won't get his 1986 Camaro back. He's also out $40,000 in legal fees. Regan was a bartender in New Jersey at the time he let a customer ride along with him on an errand into Manhattan. In the city, the passenger asked Regan to stop in a neighborhood where, he said, someone owed him money. Regan stopped. The passenger got out and came back a short time later, presumably with his money. Back in New Jersey, they were stopped by agents of the Bergen County Narcotics Task Force. The passenger had picked up not money but sixteen vials of cocaine. Regan and his passenger were both arrested, but the passenger exonerated Regan of any knowledge of the dope.

Regan was free, but his car wasn't.

"This is an ideal type of car for us to keep, because it's a good undercover car," the prosecutor said. Regan argued, and the police eventually said they'd return the car if he would pay them half its book value. Regan refused and went to court. He lost. Now he's working at three jobs to pay off his legal bills.

The U.S. Supreme Court made several rulings in 1993 that slightly rein in the power of the police to seize property. In February, it ruled that "innocent owners" are exempt from losing property. If you receive property that had been purchased with drug money but you know nothing about the seller's or donor's drug dealings, you can keep the property. In June, the Court ruled that an owner has a constitutional right to challenge the seizure of his home or business as an excessive penalty. The government had contended that the forfeiture suit was against the property, using the legal fiction that property was able to commit a crime. As property has no rights, the owner could not sue. The Supreme Court disagreed. In December, the Court ruled that an owner has a right to prior notice before property is seized. Until then, the government claimed the power to seize property before telling the owner.

"The right to prior notice and a hearing is central to the Constitution's command of due process," wrote Justice Anthony M. Kennedy.

If the government is reluctant to give up property it's seized, it's equally reluctant to recompense owners for property it's damaged during a misdirected search.

The U.S. Coast Guard believed that a 46–foot boat belonging to Robert and Kay Weeks of Charleston, South Carolina, was carrying drugs. Coast Guardsmen boarded the vessel seventeen miles at sea and took it into custody. They "searched" the boat with chain saws, leaving 16–inch square holes in the deck. The damage amounted to $400,000. The Coast Guard refused to pay. The Weeks have filed a lawsuit.

Craig Klein, a professor of journalism, bought a second-hand sailboat and hired a crew to take it from Jacksonville to St. Petersburg, Florida. Customs agents intercepted the boat, and when they couldn't read two of the digits in its state registration number, they boarded it. The ownership papers were not aboard as required. They towed it to a dry dock. There, the inspectors found signs of recent repairs. Believing the patches hid drugs, they drilled holes in the boat and removed panels. There were no drugs, but the inspectors did $4,000 damage. They refused to reimburse Klein, because, the Customs Service said, the search was reasonable.

9

The courts have done something to modify the excesses of the forfeiture law. So far, though, hardly anything has been done to modify the excesses of the police who enforce the laws, especially the drug laws.

Burton Weinstein, a Bridgeport, Connecticut, attorney who took the suit of the misdirected Danbury, Connecticut, "no knock" search mentioned above, said, "The police officers in that suit have been accused of committing outright perjury, but no prosecutor has shown any interest in the case."

In a few highly publicized cases, the U.S. Department of Justice has moved against police officers for violating the civil rights of those they arrest. A recent case was the trial of the four Los Angeles police officers who were videotaped beating up motorist Rodney King. The Rodney King cases, though, are rare.

"Federal [civil rights] enforcement [against police] is virtually nonexistent," New Haven, Connecticut, lawyer John Williams told the author in 1987. "As a matter of fact, you can literally count on the fingers of one hand the number of effective investigations that I've seen in Connecticut in the last twenty years. And almost all of those investigations have taken place because of other factors. There was a case where a motorist was beaten up by a state trooper after he went through a red light. It turned out that the motorist was an FBI agent."

Normally, according to Williams, the FBI agents think they and the police are "all on the same team." That's why the agents who investigated the case of Lorenzo Ricketts (see chapter 17) said they couldn't find any witnesses to Ricketts's beating, although a large crowd was present.

The usual response to police misconduct is to blame it on "a few bad apples."

In a way, that's true. The bullies and sadists are a minority on any police force. But in another way, it's grossly untrue. The bullies and sadists can get away with what they do only because the other cops let them.

John Williams, the New Haven attorney, said that although the sadists are a minority, "they're a powerful minority. Since police work tends to be predominantly male, there's a kind of macho factor that takes control . . . the cops who are disgusted by police brutality tend not to say anything about it for fear of being thought by the others to be wimps. Cops understand that they can do pretty much as they like, because, number one, the department will cover them. Number two, if they get sued, the city and its insurance company will certainly cover them. And if for some reason all that fails, the union will protect them, and they won't get significant punishment."

Perhaps the strongest refutation of the "few bad apples" theory of police misconduct was the 1993 investigation of the felonious activities of a group of New York police officers.

There were bad apples. Michael Dowd, of the 75th Precinct, in Brooklyn, was practically the definition of a bad apple. For six years, Dowd and up to a dozen other cops extorted money from merchants, robbed drug dealers, sold the drugs and guns they stole and snorted the drugs they didn't sell. Dowd confessed to "hundreds" of felonies at a hearing chaired by Milton Mollen, a retired judge. One of Dowd's gang, Bernard Cawley, was nicknamed "the mechanic" by the others for his proficiency in "tuning up"—beating, in NYPD slang—both criminals and ordinary citizens. Cawley admitted he beat up the citizens both to intimidate people in the neighborhood and to rob his victims. According to Kevin Hembury, another of the crooked cops who testified at the hearing, the gang used the police radio net to assemble as many as a half-dozen police cars for illegal raids.

Judge Mollen said he still believes that "bad apples" are in the minority. "I firmly believe that. What I do believe at times does occur is what you might term 'corruption tolerance.' They're reluctant—and this is unfortunate, but it's a fact of life—some were reluctant to go to their superiors and say, 'I think Officer X is corrupt, and you'd better investigate him.' That's not, unfortunately, part of the police culture."

In this case, "corruption tolerance" was matched by "whistleblower intolerance." That's something Sgt. Joseph Trimboli learned.

Trimboli, a field internal affairs investigator, knew about Dowd's activities but was blocked by police brass, as well as rank and file, when he tried to get evidence. He thought he had a break when one of the gang, Walter Yerku, was arrested for shaking down a store owner. He asked to question Yerku in jail. He was forbidden to.

Yerku himself, interviewed by public television's "Frontline" crew, said, "It really looked to me, as it does now, that they were trying to build against an investigation into the 75th Precinct. They wanted to make sure I wasn't going to say anything. . . . They wanted to make sure that the scandal is going to stay quiet."

Trimboli persisted. He was called into Internal Affairs headquarters and accused of drug trafficking. All of the police brass were against him.

He probably would have been driven out of the department. But in 1992, Suffolk County police in Long Island arrested Dowd for drug trafficking, and the Mollen Commission was formed. Trimboli was promoted on the recommendation of the very people who were trying to silence him.

The *New York Times* sent a reporter into another precinct, the 46th, to see if residents in that Bronx neighborhood had seen activities like those described to the Mollen Commission.

They had. Winston Williams, a resident of the 46th, was watching the Mollen hearings on television. One of the cops was telling how he'd beaten up both citizens and drug dealers and stolen drugs and money when he was assigned to the 46th Precinct a few years before.

"That's my precinct! That's one of my cops!" Williams yelled. "You know," he added, "it's what they all do. He did it. They do it every time they make a bust."

The reporter, Craig Wolff, questioned Williams and other residents. Some had seen police misconduct; some hadn't. But all were sure it happens all the time.

One man said he had been beaten up recently when police mistook him for a drug dealer. He said a cop had then urinated on the street and made him lie in it face down.

He said, "Why do I have to put up with that? He shoved the nightstick in my side and pushed me down. I pay my taxes. They should go after the bad guys, not us."

The interviews repeated the same theme over and over: Get rough with the bad guys, the dope dealers, not us. No one cared if the police violated the Constitution when dealing with drug dealers. In fact, they wanted the cops to "get rough" with the bad guys. But they never explained how the cops were to know the bad guys from the good guys. Nor had it ever occurred to them that, as Gerry Spence said, ". . . when the rights of our enemies have been wrested from them, our own rights have been lost as well, for the same rights serve both citizen and criminal."

A woman said she and her neighbors were incensed when two officers were charged with assault after a drug dealer said they had beaten him up. "We want them [the cops] back," she said.

John Brittain, a professor at the University of Connecticut Law School, said that even in minority communities, police misconduct is widely tolerated. Brittain, who is black, added, "The reason seems to be that because there is so much crime in the community that people seek any kind of relief from it."

That toleration has limits, though. Brittain said that policing minority-peopled areas presents special problems. "The policing of the minority community is filled with contradictions. With the majority of police forces being white and often living beyond the urban area they are policing, you largely have almost a foreign police. They must exercise their policing functions in areas that are afflicted with poverty, discrimination and crime. The police become the target of reactions against social conditions. And the police have to operate in a social milieu that's foreign and strange to them."

The police react by closing ranks. Their world becomes composed of two groups—"us," all other police officers, and "them," everyone else.

Walter Yerku, the bent cop convicted of shaking down the merchant, told "Frontline" what it meant to put on the police uniform:

> Your life is now cop. It's going to be cop. It's going to be 100 percent cop. You're going to hang out with cops. You're going to go out with cops. You're going to drink with cops, right? You're going to fool around with cops. You might even marry a cop.
>
> I had a new family. I had a new family with guns and badges and uniforms and I had 30,000 of them to back me up whenever I needed anything. I got a gang of 30,000.

Drugs exacerbate the situation. Illegal drug trafficking, as we've seen, increases both violence and larceny. And because selling and using drugs is itself against the law, it greatly increases the amount of criminality. Some cops succumb to the temptation the Drug War offers—easy riches by ripping off drug dealers. But most cops begin to think of themselves as "the thin blue line," shielding civilization from the criminals who surround them. In most departments, they cruise the streets in patrol cars with the windows rolled up, insulated from the community. They're alert for signs that the kid on the corner may be dealing drugs, that the man strutting down the street may be carrying a pistol, that the flamboyantly dressed woman in the light from the theater marquee may be a prostitute. They dismiss the ordinary citizens they see as persons of no importance to them.

Recently, a new kind of policing is being tried in some cities. Cops operate out of storefront branch stations. They do more foot patrol. They try to get to know the people in the neighborhoods they patrol—the good guys as well as the bad guys. It isn't always easy. Some officers object to what they call "social work." They yearn for the good old days when their job was, as novelist Joseph Wambaugh—a former Los Angeles cop—puts it, to "take names and kick ass."

The state of Connecticut provides a test case for the new approach. Connecticut is a small state—after Hawaii, Rhode Island and Delaware, the smallest state of the union in area. It is, after New Jersey, Rhode Island and Massachusetts, the most densely populated in the union. But it doesn't have any large cities. Three cities, Bridgeport, Hartford and New Haven, have almost the same population, between 100,000 and 150,000.

Several years ago, Bridgeport, the largest of the three, found itself on the edge of bankruptcy for a variety of reasons. It was put under a kind of state-supervised receivership. Municipal services were cut back, and the homicide rate soared. Because of this, comparison of Bridgeport's crime rate with the other two cities is not fair.

Hartford and New Haven make an instructive comparison. New Haven in 1993 was the seventh poorest city of over 100,000 population in the country. Hartford was the tenth. Until the appointment of the current New Haven chief of police, Nicholas Pastore, the police forces of both cities practiced the old-style, hard-nosed law enforcement. Pastore introduced community policing. Hartford introduced "Operation Liberty."

In 1993, Hartford became the center of a war between two large gangs, Los Solidos and the Latin Kings. The city fathers sought aid from the state police, and Operation Liberty was born. City and state police moved in on areas where most gang members lived. A typical Operation Liberty incident was described in a generally favorable article in the *Hartford Courant*:

> A Hartford police cruiser is moving through the Frog Hollow neighborhood when its headlights shine on a familiar Oldsmobile filled with gang members the officers think may be armed.
>
> Knowing little else about the occupants, the police pull

over the car, point pistols and shotguns at the youths inside
and order them, one by one, to get out with their hands in the
air. With guns trained on their heads, the gang members are
handcuffed. Police officers, now five cars strong, pat them
down and rummage through their car.

Finding no drugs, weapons or evidence of any crime, the
police put their guns away after half an hour and let the young
men go.

Operation Liberty got nothing but praise from the Hartford news
media, but it lasted less than two months. The state police needed their
troopers back at their regular jobs. Before it ended, though, Hartford
was the scene of two more gang murders. Operation Liberty, with all
its unprovoked harassing and unreasonable searches, didn't even slow
the Insurance City's homicide rate. The year ended with Hartford
counting thirty-four murders, the highest in four years. Of the thirty-
four, the police said at least fourteen were the result of the gang war;
five of the victims were simply in the wrong place at the wrong time.
There were also about 250 persons wounded in shootings, many of
them drug-related.

In New Haven, the murder rate declined steadily from its 1991 record of thirty-four, and 1993 ended with a total of twenty homicides in
New Haven. Only six were related to drugs.

"If violence is going up in other cities and it's going down here in
New Haven," said Chief Pastore, "we must be doing something right."

The state of the police in the United States is something like the
prevalence of violence. Eliminating the problem is going to take a lot
more than changing our drug laws. But that one step—changing the
drug laws—would be a mighty step forward.

In the next section, we'll see why.

PART FOUR

BURYING THE DOPE FIEND

Reverse: Drug peddler in Bridgeport, Connecticut, negotiates with a customer in a car. Many buyers come from the suburbs.

22

Back in 1934, millions of Americans, deeply disappointed by the failure of Prohibition, were listening to the spellbinding naval hero Capt. Richmond Pearson Hobson. They had lost the war against Demon Rum, but now Hobson was pointing out a new, far worse, demon, the vampire-like Dope Fiend.

The country took the Dope Fiend concept to its heart and waged an increasingly expensive, increasingly violent and increasingly ineffectual war against it. The metaphorical war against the Dope Fiend has become a real war to many. In January 1994, Lee Brown, head of the National Office of Drug Policy, could say, "Legalization is *surrendering* to drugs."

There is reason to doubt, though, that everyone in Washington, or our state capitals, takes the Dope Fiend as seriously as Brown—or most of the American people.

Nelson Rockefeller found that projecting the Dope Fiend image was as good a vote-getter as "waving the bloody shirt" was after the Civil War. Richard Nixon took his cue from Rockefeller, and every succeeding president has, to greater or lesser degree, followed Nixon. Both Rockefeller and Nixon knew that most of their "tough measures" were useless, although they produced good publicity. Nixon bashed the Dope Fiend to show that he was tough. Jimmy Carter wasn't so interested in being tough, so he put the War on Drugs on the back burner. But Ronald Reagan tried to marry drugs and Communism in the public mind. The stance worked for Reagan, so George Bush adopted it too.

But while our presidents were beating drums and clanging cymbals and proclaiming their undying hatred for drugs and drug traffickers, their agents abroad were actively aiding and abetting the enemy.

At the end of World War II, the Office of Strategic Services and the U.S. Army's military government resurrected the Mafia in Sicily. The OSS got a mighty boost in this task from Governor Dewey of New York and the Immigration and Naturalization Service when they deported "Charley Lucky" Luciano, the New York vice lord, as a reward for his alleged wartime service to the government while in prison.

Luciano, with the help of a flock of Italian-American thugs deported at about the same time, took over the Mafia. In a short time, the Lucky One whipped the Mafia into an organization that, for the first time, resembled the vast, secret, sinister Mafia of legend. Instead of relying on the few lira they could extort from peasants, the mafiosi went into the heroin export business. The target of their exports was, of course, the United States. Luciano, no matter what the INS said, was American. All his contacts were American. He knew the country—the biggest, richest potential market for heroin. Before Charley Lucky died, the estimated number of heroin addicts in the United States increased from 20,000 to 100,000.

Luciano's drug-smuggling organization achieved this feat because of further help from the U.S. government. The Central Intelligence Agency, successor to the OSS, poured weapons and money into Marseille, helping the Corsican *milieu* the way its parent had helped the Mafia. Luciano and the head of his American operations, Meyer Lansky, brought the Corsicans into the business. That was a major coup. The Sicilian mafiosi were basically a collection of peasant bully-boys. The Corsicans were sophisticated crooks who could understand Luciano's plans for an enormous heroin empire. Addiction in America zoomed.

Not everyone in government was totally cynical about the War on Drugs. Nixon himself seems to have been more schizophrenic than cynical about drugs. Domestically, he initiated measures that he had to have known would have no real effect on the drug trade but which looked good to the public. Internationally, he allowed the CIA to help traffickers in Southeast Asia to a much greater extent than it had helped them in Europe. But, in fact, there wasn't much the federal government could have done about drugs domestically, and in the cold—sometimes pretty hot—war against Communism, Nixon, like all American presidents, was for any measure he thought would give us an advantage.

For all that, Nixon seems to have sincerely wanted to stop the rise in drug addiction and, if possible, eliminate drugs in American life. He put pressure on Turkey to cut back, then eliminate poppy growing. That resulted in a serious opium and heroin shortage for the European gangsters and for the American Mob they had been shipping to.

The American Mob (the federation Luciano had founded) turned to Southeast Asia. Heroin importation picked up. Ironically, the U.S. government, represented by Nixon's State Department, had dried up opium in Turkey, but the U.S. government, represented by the CIA, nurtured it in Myanmar, Thailand and the old French Indochina. Addiction continued to grow, and the Mob continued to thrive. And, after a little while, Turkey went back to growing opium.

The CIA continued to subsidize opium in the Golden Triangle. The processing of opium, and the exportation of it and heroin, was variously handled by Corsicans in Vietnam, Chinese in Vietnam, Hong Kong and Bangkok, and Thais in Bangkok. Finally, members of the South Vietnam government grabbed much of the trade. The CIA, the State Department and the Johnson and Nixon administrations continued to subsidize our noble allies and protect them from criticism. They protected them even after a cabal headed by the president of South Vietnam launched an aggressive heroin marketing campaign aimed at American GIs fighting the Viet Cong and North Vietnamese. Near the end of the Vietnam War and for a while afterward, heroin use spurted upward on the charts.

Nixon declared a "War on Drugs" that, apart from spending money, accomplished nothing. The U.S. drug policy was settling into what has become a familiar pattern—total ineffectiveness in subduing drug trafficking at home and great effectiveness in fostering it abroad.

When the Soviet Union invaded Afghanistan, the United States, first under Carter, then under Reagan, took measures that opened a whole new source of supply, the Middle East—Afghanistan and Pakistan—to American addicts. David Musto had warned the Carter Administration to avoid the mistakes of Vietnam so that aiding Afghan resistance would not mean increasing the flow of heroin to the United States. He was ignored. All the Reagan Administration did was increase aid to the Afghan producers and the Pakistani middlemen. Heroin consumption in the United States again reached new heights.

Meanwhile, the CIA had been getting increasingly involved with people concerned with another drug, cocaine. The Cuban exile organizations the agency had helped to form after the Bay of Pigs fiasco had gotten into both heroin—by taking over remnants of the old "French Connection"—and cocaine. The prime source of cocaine was South America, a lot closer than either Europe or Southeast Asia. Cocaine gradually became important.

The civil war in Nicaragua resulted in a tremendous spurt in cocaine importation. The CIA was helping one side, the Contras, sometimes secretly, sometimes openly. Either way, "the Company" relied on Cuban exiles to get supplies to the Contras. The Contras also relied on the Cubans. The Cubans would sell cocaine for them in the United States and use the money (some of it, anyway) to buy weapons and ammunition. Heroin use in the United States did not decline, but cocaine use skyrocketed.

While its minions were aiding, protecting and *engaging* in dope trafficking, the Reagan and Bush administrations declared new wars on drugs (as if the old war had ever ended). They spent a lot more money but introduced no new ideas, aside from Reagan's theory that drug trafficking was part of a Communist conspiracy (and even that idea had been around, although somewhat less baldly stated, since Lyndon Johnson and Richard Nixon). After two decades of increasing expenditures and increasing dope addiction, George Bush could declare that "The tools we need are the ones we have now." He could also warn that the country should not give in to what he called "the easy temptation" to concentrate on the "chronic problems of social environment" that "help to breed and spread the contagion of drug use."

Why the temptation to concentrate on the causes of drug addiction and violence is "easy," Bush did not explain. Apparently he thought it's harder for the comfortable majority to require more arrests of inner city drug peddlers and longer incarceration of those convicted than to eliminate poverty and hopelessness among those inner city dwellers.

2

What have "the tools we have now" accomplished?

The War on Drugs, as we know it—more arrests, longer sentences, more minimum mandatory sentences, more seizures of drugs, more seizures of money, more seizures of property, more violations of privacy, more tolerance of unconstitutional acts by government officials and more banal slogans like "Just say no"—has accomplished less than nothing.

It has stimulated the market for drugs. As Judge Knapp wrote, quoting Milton Friedman, "Law enforcement temporarily reduces the drug supply and thus causes prices to rise. Higher prices draw new sources of supply and even new drugs into the market, resulting in more drugs on the street. The increased availability of drugs creates more addicts." Friedman's analysis, of course, leaves out the great help our government's representatives have given to smugglers abroad. And in concentrating on the suppliers, it overlooks the reaction of consumers to the War on Drugs. That was expressed by the "righteous dope fiend" who told researchers Preble and Casey, "Drugs is a hell of a game."

More and more people are learning the game. The rise in arrests due to the War on Drugs—three quarters of them for simple possession—means more and more people are going to prison. There they are getting graduate courses in criminality. They are learning better ways of stealing, more lucrative rackets and more effective ways of evading the law.

To discourage heroin users, the government has made hypodermic needles unavailable to them. The result is not a decrease in drug use but an increase in AIDS. Seizures of real estate where drugs are used has created the "crack house" and the consequent increase in syphilis and tuberculosis.

Because drugs are illegal, users take them in more concentrated form—from cocaine to free-base to crack. Deaths from overdose keep increasing. Prohibition should have been a lesson to us, but we ignored it.

Because drugs are illegal, foreign traffickers have become billionaires. A disgraceful number of police and judges have become affluent from traffickers' bribes. In one year alone, twelve New York police officers were arrested for taking bribes from drug sellers, and seven Miami cops were indicted for the same offense. In 1989, only four months after President Bush declared a new war on drugs, several DEA agents went to jail for corruption. According to a former Miami police chief, 10 percent of his force had been bribed by traffickers. A few street kids like Boy George Rivera and Rayful Edmond III have become, in the eyes of their contemporaries, fabulously wealthy. And their contemporaries think that by going into the drug business, they can become fabulously wealthy too.

Because drugs are illegal, people in the drug trade have no recourse to courts. They settle disputes by murder. Murder is easier, because the drug dealers don't use all their wealth for new sneakers and gold chains. They buy sophisticated weapons. Some of the weapons they buy are no more available to ordinary citizens than heroin by the pound. But people who can bring tons of cocaine into the country have no trouble obtaining machine guns.

Among the benefits of the War on Drugs, then, are: more drug addicts, more disease, more deaths from overdose, a great increase in the size, wealth and power of the criminal class, more corruption in the justice system, and an ever-rising tide of violence.

3

Many people aren't greatly concerned about "dope fiends" dying of disease and overdose. Nor do they worry about drug dealers and their customers shooting each other. But there are ways the War on Drugs affects us all.

Take prisons. The United States has a higher percentage of its population in prison than any country but Russia. And our hard-line drug warriors are constantly demanding more prisons. Prisons are expensive. Prisons are very expensive. And every dollar we spend on a prison is a dollar we can't spend to improve schools, recondition roads or retrain laid-off workers.

Take courts. Our courts are jammed with drug cases. Civil suits are delayed interminably. Each day of delay costs more money. And whether the parties to the suits are government agencies or private businesses, we citizens, either as taxpayers or customers, pay.

Take police. Our police departments are strained to the limit, in money, manpower and time because of the War on Drugs. At the same time, serious crime—some of it completely unrelated to drugs—is increasing. If the cops were allowed to concentrate on crimes more serious than pot smoking and cocaine snorting, our streets might be safer.

Then there is the Constitution of the United States. The many violations and near-violations of the Fourth and Fifth amendments brought on by the War on Drugs diminish us all. We tolerate them because the

Dope Fiend is lurking in the backs of our minds. Anything is all right if it saves us from the dope fiends—the people made inhuman by drugs, the "living dead" of Richmond Pearson Hobson, who, like Satan in the old Catholic prayer, go about the world seeking whom they can devour.

The truth is that by the War on Drugs, we are devouring ourselves. We have to change our drug policy.

But how?

23

Say that our drug laws should be changed, and you may see someone recoil with horror, thinking you mean complete legalization, with three-year-olds toddling into the corner store to get cocaine lollypops. Say the same thing to another, and she may cringe, remembering former Los Angeles police chief Daryl Gates' recommendation for recreational drug users: "They should all be taken out and shot."

Yet you'll look long and hard before you find someone who thinks we're winning the War on Drugs.

Probably the first thing to do when we're thinking about changing our drug strategy is to consider why we're fighting this war at all. There are a variety of answers:

1. *Drugs are evil.* Drug addicts are the "living dead," who'll do anything to get the substance that has enslaved them. They'll not only steal to get money to buy drugs, they'll rob, rape and murder because the drugs deaden their inhibitions and fill them with a lust to do evil. They also have a maniacal desire to corrupt all they meet by introducing them to habit-forming drugs. Those who sell illicit drugs are worse than murderers. Richmond Pearson Hobson popularized this image of the Dope Fiend, and as we've seen, it's still popular. If you hold this view, the prescription of former Chief Gates is rather attractive.

2. *Drugs are not good for people.* Drugs are habit-forming: Drug users become so addicted they can't seem to live without the forbidden substance. They spend more and more money on drugs while they become sicker and waste away because of the drugs.

3. *Drugs are intoxicating.* Drug users are not able to think clearly; they have hallucinations; they are unsafe on the road, and they may

commit crimes when under the influence they would not even consider when sober.

4. *Drug users will steal* to finance their habits. As their drug of choice is the most important thing in their lives, they cannot be trusted to do anything that might jeopardize their access to the drug.

5. *Women who are drug users* have babies that are addicted or otherwise incapacitated.

6. *More people would use drugs* if they were made legal.

There are other reasons given, such as the complaint that drug peddlers ruin a neighborhood or that crack houses spread disease, but they all presuppose the illegality of drugs and the consequent black market.

The first reason, as we have seen, is primarily based on a fantasy. The other five are real. They should be examined closely.

There is no doubt that drugs are a threat to health. How much of a threat depends on both the drug and the person. Some drugs—tobacco and crack, for example—are powerfully addictive. Recently, the Food and Drug Administration has cited evidence that cigarette companies are making their product more addictive by spraying nicotine on the tobacco. Alcohol can also be very addictive, and its hold on the addict may be so tight that withdrawal could be fatal. But not all drug users become addicts. Not everyone who drinks, for instance, becomes an alcoholic. Some persons are more vulnerable to addiction than others. Usually, there is no way a person can discover his vulnerability until he becomes addicted. Carlos Lehder, one of the Colombian "kingpins," tried his own product and decided he could handle cocaine personally as well as in business. For several years, he was right. Then he became addicted. Sigmund Freud was luckier. He quit before the drug got a firm hold on him.

Addiction is a serious matter, not only because illicit drugs are frightfully expensive but because continued use of many drugs, illicit or otherwise, can ruin your health. Cocaine can rot the nasal tissues; alcohol can destroy the liver; tobacco, and apparently marijuana, can cause emphysema; etc.

But drug addiction is not, as Hobson put it, "harder to cure than leprosy." Most addicts are able to cure themselves without help. Witness the decline in heroin addiction during World War II and the legions of smokers who quit tobacco without therapy or seminars. Or consider the study of Vietnam veterans by Lee Robins. A random sample of 400 returning servicemen late in the Vietnam War showed that 43 percent of them had taken drugs, and half of them were addicted. But eight to ten months after their return, only 10 percent of those who used heroin in Vietnam were still taking the drug, and only 7 percent of those—less than 1 percent of the sample—were still addicted. When the supply of cheap, pure heroin disappeared, they simply stopped using. Earlier, Charles Winick, studying the history of 45,000 drug addicts, found that about 7,000 of them dropped out of the drug scene within five years. And many of them were serious heroin addicts—the type thought to be incurable. Winick referred this process as "maturing out."

A minority of addicts apparently need help, and there are a variety of institutions set up to help them.

There are a couple of catches to the cure of addiction, though. One is expressed in a joke:

Q. How many drug counselors does it take to change a lightbulb?

A. Only one, but the lightbulb has to want to change.

The other catch is that those who do want to change currently have a hard time getting help. There are long waiting lines at treatment centers. At one rehabilitation center the author visited, only one of more than a hundred inmates was there entirely voluntarily. The others had been sent there by the courts, having chosen rehabilitation instead of jail. Treatment itself is a complex subject. We'll take a closer look at it later.

Even though drugs are a threat to health, there is the philosophical question of how much society has to protect individuals from themselves. There are no laws against suicide for obvious reasons. Recently, attempts to enact laws against assisting suicide have foundered. It has been argued that because drug addicts may end up as public charges or at least drive up insurance rates by their unhealthy lifestyles, the public has a right to legislate against drug use. But the overwhelming majority of drug users do not end up as public charges. And the cost to the public of the ills caused by illicit drugs doesn't compare with the costs of tobacco and alcohol use. Following this logic, the government should not only ban tobacco and alcohol but arrest those who eat too much red meat and prosecute those too lazy to exercise.

All drug users, of course, do not harm only themselves. All illicit drugs do intoxicate, and intoxicated persons can harm other people.

Intoxication is not a simple matter. Everyone has seen the variety of ways alcohol can affect a person. Some of this is caused by the way the drug affects the body. Alcohol is a depressant: It attacks the nervous system first, slowing reflexes and dulling judgment. It finally puts the intoxicated person to sleep. Some symptoms of intoxication depend on the person's expectation of the way he will behave when intoxicated. In one research project, a group of men was given an alcoholic drink and another group got a placebo the men thought was alcoholic. There is a fairly widespread expectation in the United States that drunks will act aggressively. In the experiment, the group that took the alcohol did become aggressive. But those who drank the placebo acted even more aggressively.

Whether it's because of the physical effect or the expectation, people intoxicated with marijuana are anything but aggressive. Marijuana users claim the drug makes them more sensitive to music and color, which may be why those ancient Scythians howled with pleasure as they inhaled pot fumes in their little tents. Marijuana definitely slows reflexes. Marijuana smokers are over-represented, compared with their proportion of the general population, in automobile accidents.

No matter what the general expectations are, heroin is such a powerful depressant that heroin junkies universally experience a semi-comatose euphoria while they are under the influence.

Cocaine is different. Cocaine users feel euphoria, but it goes along with a sense of power, tirelessness and sharpened mental processes. The drug may also cause irritability and a kind of paranoia. This is especially true if it is combined with that other powerful intoxicant, alcohol. The effects of crack are those of cocaine intensified. In laboratory tests, according to Mark A. R. Kleiman, a former drug-policy analyst at the U.S. Department of Justice, cocaine snorters were unable to tell cocaine from procaine, a non-psychoactive drug. No one, though, has ever said he couldn't feel a high from crack.

LSD, lysergic acid diethylamide, like marijuana, increases sensitivity to light and color. Like peyote, it produces hallucinations. Like cocaine, it produces a feeling of new mental and physical power. Also like cocaine, it can produce paranoia. LSD can produce flashbacks long after use. It can also produce permanent psychosis severe enough to require lifetime confinement in an institution.

PCP, or angel dust, made from phencyclidine, does what LSD does, only more so. PCP users are more likely than LSD users to become violent, but the drug is less likely than LSD to permanently damage the user.

Inhalants such as gasoline or airplane glue produce giddiness and slow the reflexes. They can also kill the user suddenly and without warning.

Theft by drug addicts is also a considerable problem. One major reason for it is that because of drugs' illegality, their prices have been inflated 100 times or more above their true value. The other reason is that people like Finestone's "cat" and Preble's and Casey's "righteous dope fiend" use drugs as an excuse to steal. Without that excuse, they'd find another. They enjoy the game, the hustle. But one reason they got into the game was because there was no way they could get decent jobs.

Crack babies are a serious problem. So are babies afflicted with fetal alcohol syndrome. Use of tobacco too can harm infants before birth.

Probably more people would take drugs if they were legalized. How many more is the question. One answer is to look at Prohibition.

Overall, during the fourteen years it was in existence, Prohibition reduced alcohol consumption about 30 percent. During the last five years, though, it has been estimated that Americans were drinking as much as they had been before. Further, their drinking habits had changed. By the end of Prohibition, they were drinking vastly larger quantities of hard liquor than they had before. Annual per capita consumption of hard liquor in the last year of Prohibition was higher than it had been in the sixty years before or would be in the sixty years after. With that kind of consumption came a startling amount of death from alcohol overdose. No less than 12,000 persons died in 1927 from acute alcohol poisoning. Since Repeal, the death rate from that cause has never approached the Prohibition rate. Mark Kleiman, in presenting the case for Prohibition, notes that in 1929, 8,400 persons died of cirrhosis of the liver; ten years after Repeal, 10,900 died of the same cause, an increase of a bit less than 30 percent. But between 1929 and 1943, the population of the United States had increased by about 18 million, or about 15 percent. The death rate from cirrhosis, therefore, had actually increased about 15 percent, but alcohol poisoning was then quite rare. And in 1929, per capita alcohol consumption was still increasing.

If the experience of Repeal is any criterion, a few more people would use drugs, but they'd be less likely to binge on them and would move from hard to soft drugs. Most people don't use drugs for the same reason they don't kill their neighbors or abandon their children. They don't do those things because they don't want to, not because they're afraid of the law.

2

The evils of the War on Drugs have been covered at some length. All of them, though, stem from the fact that banning some drugs has created a black market.

• The black market put the distribution of drugs in the hands of criminals, people who were ready and willing to use bribery and violence—even murder—to advance their business.

• As the black market is illegal, there is no recourse to the law to settle disputes or to protect the business from predators. All disputes are solved by violence, frequently murder.

• The tendency in an industry like this is for the violent entrepreneurs to wage wars to establish local monopolies.

• The business, from supplier to street retailer, may be characterized as chains of monopolies. Monopolies sell to other monopolies, with the monopolies at the bottom of the chains selling to consumers. These monopolies, using the excuse of the risks they take, have been able to set hugely inflated prices for illegal drugs.

• Because of the inflated prices of drugs, many of the consumers are forced to steal to support their habits.

• With the enormous profits they make, the monopolists are able to arm themselves with a variety of sophisticated and deadly weapons. They are also able to sell or give weapons to their allies in street gangs.

• The homicides perpetrated by those involved in the illicit drug trade have initiated a descending spiral of violence. Their wealth and worldly success has made drug gangsters role models for many young people in America's depressed inner cities. The kids adopt the dress and manners—including the violence—of the mini-kingpins they see. There are more shootings, some of them having nothing to do—directly—with drugs. Then still more shootings. As violence increases, increasing numbers of youths lose their respect for the value of human life and their inhibition against wasting it.

• Weapons are not the only things drug lords—mini and maxi—purchase with their illegal profits. They also buy people—cops, prosecutors and judges.

• The illegality of some drugs and the tactics of the war on those drugs, particularly the forfeiture laws, has created the crack house—the most efficient spreader of disease since Typhoid Mary. Aiding the crack house in promoting plague is the practical prohibition of hypodermic needles, which has been spreading AIDS and hepatitis across the land.

• As in Prohibition, banning some substances encourages binge use, which leads to overdoses. Some overdoses may also be the result of adulteration and variable strength of the street drugs. That too is a product of the black market.

• Between 35 and 40 million Americans are believed to have used illegal drugs. Such widespread law-breaking fosters contempt for all law.

• Such widespread law-breaking has fostered frustration in legislators, judges, prosecutors and police. They have responded with actions that could be called contempt for the Bill of Rights.

• The effort expended to fight the black market in drugs has siphoned off law-enforcement resources sorely needed to stop a rising tide of violent crime. It is filling up prisons with drug offenders, forcing the early release of really vicious criminals. And at the same time, it is bogging down the civil courts.

3

There is no doubt that the homicide, corruption and other crime, as well as the disease, contempt for law and abuses of civil rights created by the War on Drugs, outweigh the evils of the illegal drugs. But those evils too should be addressed. At least we should recognize that intoxicants can cause damage to people other than those intoxicated, and that we should minimize the risk that infants will be born with incapacities caused by their mothers' drug habits. We might well, though, eschew Big Brotherism and let responsible adults decide what to do with their own lives. And we should do something so the "cats" of the inner-city find honesty more attractive than hustling. That, though, is a matter that has little to do with the legality or illegality of drugs.

Clearly, we must change what we're doing about drugs. But how?

The first thing we should do is try to undo the damage caused by seventy years of Dope Fiend-bashing by elected officials willing to deceive the public to get votes. We might begin by getting rid of the foolish laws that prohibit the medicinal use of marijuana and heroin. Is an old person dying of cancer in danger of becoming an addict? Then we might eliminate the minimum mandatory sentences that do no good for anything but the image of certain legislators and do a tremendous amount of harm.

After that, there are a number of possible courses. Kleiman offers what he calls "grudging toleration." That involves keeping all the anti-drug laws on the books, but not going out of the way to enforce such laws as marijuana possession for personal use. It would be somewhat less tolerant than the Netherlands policy, which has the police ignoring drug use and marijuana sales which occur right in front of them. Kleiman's enforcement of drug laws would be less diligent than the Swedish policy, although it seems that "grudging toleration" would rely more on jail and less on fines than the Swedes do. Kleiman does recommend shorter sentences and much more use of involuntary labor under strict supervision, "euphemistically called community service." He also urges heavy use of alternatives to arrest, such as changing traffic patterns to discourage visitors to drug-dealing areas, stopping cars entering such areas to inspect licenses and registration and confiscating cars of drug buyers under civil forfeiture. These measures would economize on what he calls our "valuable prison cells," but some of them also tread heavily on the Bill of Rights. Further, "grudging toleration" is a temptation to selective law enforcement, or rather, to make law enforcement even more selective than it is now—not a good thing. And it does not end the black market.

Sociologist Elliott Currie also suggests more reasonable sentences for drug offenders, with much more use of probation. This might be "strict" probation, with the convict required to visit a probation officer several times a week and be tested for drug use. Currie thinks that the correction systems should put a great deal more effort into providing serious help for convicted offenders. He also thinks law enforcement should shift its emphasis from "crackdowns" and "stings" to cooperation with people in the communities they serve, including the sponsorship of citizen patrols.

One of Currie's suggestions is that the police should concentrate on traffickers rather than consumers. It sounds good, but that's what happened during Prohibition. As long as the demand exists, suppliers will appear to satisfy it. If the demand is for an illegal substance, the suppliers will be criminals. Currie's suggestions also leave the black market in existence. And the black market is the root of all drug-war evils.

Earlier in his book, *Against Excess*, Kleiman introduced some considerably more imaginative ideas that might eliminate the black market and still retain control of dangerous drugs. He dropped them, at least in part, because he felt the public is not yet ready for such abrupt changes. But the public will never be ready for changes unless it knows what they are and what good they will do.

One of Kleiman's most interesting ideas is drug licenses. Basically, each person would get a drug license, something like a driver's license, at a certain age, probably twenty-one. Besides the drugs now considered controlled substances, licenses would be needed to purchase alcoholic drinks and tobacco. Some conditions might be attached for the use of certain drugs. Kleiman suggests that really dangerous drugs might be taken only in special locations and under supervision. Customers could not leave the premises until their intoxication was over. This would be a sort of update of the old Chinese opium den. Persons who commit offenses against public order might have their licenses suspended or confiscated. If the offense concerns a motor vehicle, their driver's licenses might also be suspended. One possibility would be for pregnant women to have their alcohol and cocaine permits suspended during the later stages of pregnancy. One card could cover a variety of drugs. It could be checked by computer much as a credit card is now. It would also be possible to put quantity limits on various drugs. And a person who voluntarily gave up drugs might get a tax break.

Licenses are currently issued to bars and liquor stores. They could also be issued to stores that sell tobacco, so the authorities could prevent the sale of tobacco to persons under twenty-one. As most persons start smoking before the age of nineteen, this could be a powerful deterrent to tobacco use.

At present, not in law but in fact, intoxication is often considered a mitigating factor when judging crimes. It might instead add an additional penalty to the sentence for the offense.

Details of the actual sales organizations distributing drugs could vary. Drugs might be sold by licensed private businesses or they might be sold in state stores, as some states today handle the sale of liquor.

Judge Whitman Knapp and the economist team of Benjamin and Miller suggest that we treat drugs the way Repeal treated liquor—have the federal government remove itself and turn all control over to the states. What is appropriate for New York, Knapp suggested, might not be appropriate for Idaho. The states responded to the end of Prohibition in a variety of ways, ranging from total prohibition in Oklahoma (until the late 40s) to sale in every store, as in Nevada. The states might handle drugs in an even wider variety of ways.

These changes would allow the sale of drugs at a price that reflects their true cost. Such pricing would utterly destroy the vast complex of illicit drug dealers author James Mills calls "The Invisible Empire." People purchasing drugs for sale in the United States could deal directly with the producers and not with the collection of scalawags who now handle exports. Some of the money saved on law enforcement could be spent on treatment centers so that anyone who wanted to quit could enter them immediately. (The rest could be spent on catching the criminals who kill and assault, rob and rape.)

There might be a black market for the sale of drugs that are tightly restricted or for sale to persons who are tightly restricted. It would be miniscule, much smaller than the current black market in moonshine. In the first place, the number of people who would want the really dangerous drugs would be small; so would the number of people who were forbidden drugs. And the black-market prices would be vastly higher than the legitimate market prices.

4

Licensing could be accompanied by the banning of drug advertising, and educational programs on the dangers of drugs in the schools and in public media. The education would have to be honest. There are plenty of good reasons for avoiding drugs. Horror stories based on the imagination of script writers are counterproductive, as Robert Stutman found when he addressed a group of college faculty members, some of whom had practical, as well as theoretical, knowledge of marijuana.

Stutman got to the part in his speech that warned of "marijuana psychosis"—supposedly the result of long marijuana use. Hands went up all over the room.

"Mr. Stutman," someone said. "Look around the room. Many of these people have tried marijuana. Some use it regularly. We are all educated enough to know there is no long-term psychosis attached to the drug."

He was right and I was mortified. I had been caught in a lie and the sermon was over. What I had been feeding the public was disinformation that just didn't jibe with the facts. By overstating the case, I, and the growing cadre of government spokesmen I helped to train, let drug culture advocates have a field day poking holes.

Another ancillary program could be treatment. That would require a lot more time and intelligence, as well as money, than we now expend.

Treatment for drug addiction is a term that's used glibly, with little understanding of what it involves. It is not like a hospital stay to treat a broken leg or pneumonia. Drug addiction is seldom, if ever, a true disease. Although "alcoholism is a disease" is an article of faith at Alcoholics Anonymous, there is some doubt that this statement applies to alcohol any more than to other drugs. Usually, the physical pains of withdrawal from most drugs are easily treated, but the addiction remains. People usually turn to drugs because of something in their personalities or because of apparently unsolvable problems caused by conditions outside themselves.

As there are a variety of causes for addiction, there are also a variety of cures. All approaches, if well done, help some people. No approach helps everyone.

One common type of treatment is the detox center. Inmates get healthy food and heavy counseling for a few days while they abstain from drugs. When they get out, they usually return to their habits.

"When I got home from the detox center," a former drug user said, "I wasn't going to have no more to do with drugs. I done good. I done good: I stayed clean for three weeks. Then I went right back to the block where everybody was dealing, and I started dealing again. And in two or three days, I was using again. . . . After a while, I couldn't get nobody to give me drugs up front to sell, because they seen I was an addict."

Another type of treatment is the "out-patient drug-free" program—extended counseling sessions without any residential requirements. Studies show that better than half of those enrolled have managed to kick drugs. How much of that result is due to the counseling and how much to simply "maturing out" of drug dependence is unknown.

Methadone maintenance treatment is aimed only at heroin addicts, usually those pretty far gone. The addicts take a daily oral dose of methadone, an artificial heroin, to enable them to live normally and hold jobs. At the same time, the good programs include counseling so the patient can eventually kick methadone as well as heroin. Some methadone programs have reportedly cut heroin use by their graduates by almost 75 percent. Of the same graduates, though, only 25 percent have been able to hold steady jobs after treatment.

Therapeutic community programs have received a great deal of publicity in recent years. In TC programs, inmates typically live in dormitories for many months. The program is designed to put the patient under increasing stress and give him or her increasing responsibilities. They are characterized by huge numbers of pettifogging rules it is almost impossible to avoid breaking; hazing; relentless self-exposure; and group encounter sessions characterized by shouting and insults. All of this is designed to eliminate the "drug-dependent" personality. Many patients leave before treatment is completed. More are terminated because they violated the rules too often. In institutions run by the state, that usually means jail, because the inmates have been sent there by the courts. One TC center boasted that 78 percent of its graduates have remained clean. But typically, only 20 percent of a class even graduates.

According to Elliott Currie:

Too much conventional drug treatment is disturbingly disconnected from what we know about the causes of drug abuse and about the factors that encourage addicts to go off drugs—and, more importantly, stay off. As we've seen endemic drug abuse is primarily neither a law-enforcement problem *nor* a medical problem, but a *social* problem. Most addicts enter a career of drugs as one response to a variety of overlapping social deprivations.

Comparing drug addiction to arthritis, Currie says, "Providing someone with a better job or a stable family life will not cure their arthritis; it can, as we shall see, cure their drug abuse."

Clearly, a lot more thought has to go into designing treatments and directing addicts to the appropriate treatment.

5

When Thomas More wrote *Utopia*, everyone knew it was fiction. Too many of us today think Utopia is a reality that can be achieved by passing some laws. If the drug black market were eliminated, life in the United States would be vastly improved. But some problems would remain.

Zeros would still be "beasting" strangers. But with the lucrative drug black market gone, they would no longer be able to afford machine guns to beast with. Fighting gangs would still be fighting, but they'd have to rely more on tire chains than Uzis. Property crimes would decrease, but there would still be thieves, although not as many. Muggers would still be mugging and burglars still burgling, but because the cops didn't have to worry about catching addicts, there would be more police officers to curb the crooks.

There would still be disease, but not as much. Sharing dirty needles would be almost eliminated, crack houses completely eliminated. There would be fewer crack-addicted babies, fewer babies suffering from fetal alcohol syndrome. People would still die from overdoses, but as time went on, these deaths, like those from alcohol overdose, would dwindle down to comparatively few.

Corruption apparently is something that can never be entirely eliminated, but with less drug money around, it would be drastically reduced.

The prison population would go down, although a larger percentage of the truly vicious would be behind bars. We could spend more money on schools and hospitals.

There would still be too many people in prison, though. There would be too much crime, too much poverty and too little hope even without the curse of the drug war. Crime, poverty and hopelessness will continue to increase unless we can do something to make meaningful jobs available to more poor youths. Families will become an increasingly endangered species unless we change the welfare system. Police-citizen relations will continue to be generally hostile in the inner cities unless we can change the "police culture" of "them" versus "us."

None of those changes is likely, though, unless we can first bury the Dope Fiend with a stake through his heart.

NOTES

1. WHAT ARE DRUGS?

As a result of years of study, there is wide agreement on what drugs do to people—far more agreement than on why people do drugs. Richard Lawrence Miller's *The Case for Legalizing Drugs* gives a good summary of the effects of various hard and soft drugs. Alfred McCoy's *The Politics of Heroin: CIA Complicity in the Global Drug Trade* also contains valuable information on cocaine and heroin, and Daniel K. Benjamin and Roger Leroy Miller discuss the effects of everything from coffee to crack in their *Undoing Drugs: Beyond Legalization*. So does Mark A.R. Kleiman in *Against Excess: Drug Policy for Results*. So too, of course, does David F. Musto, a physician and psychiatrist whose main interest in his *The American Disease: Origins of Narcotics Control* is the history of U.S. drug policy. Although these authorities differ strongly about what to do about drugs, none of them endorse the "dope fiend" ideas of Richmond Pearson Hobson explained in chapter 6.

3—"In the country of the Scythians . . ." Herodotus, pages 265–66 (book 4).

4—"According to some experts . . ." Richard Lawrence Miller, p. 3.

4—"According to the Centers for Disease Control . . ." *Richmond Times Dispatch*, Nov. 11, 1993, "Tobacco is Unrivaled Killer, Study Says," by Knight-Ridder Newspapers Syndicate.

7—"Western physicians . . .": Musto, p. 4, quoted from "Address Before the Massachusetts Medical Society, 30 May 1860" in *The Works of Oliver Wendell Holmes*, Boston: Houghton Mifflin, 1892.

2. DRUGS IN AMERICA

Dr. Musto's *The American Disease* is essential reading for anyone interested in the history of drug regulation in the United States. McCoy's *The Politics of Heroin* is also valuable. Edward Jay Epstein's *Agency of Fear* is excellent for what happened during the Nixon Administration and immediately before it.

13—"True, smallpox was . . .": Syphilis, unknown in Europe before the end of the fifteenth century, was called "the French disease" in Italy and Britain. The French called it "the Spanish disease." Its origin is not hard to deduce.

15—"During the Revolution . . .": For an example, see John Bakeless, *Turncoats, Traitors and Heroes*, on the adventures of British spy John Howe, pp. 58–59.

15—"Oliver Wendell Holmes, Sr. . . .": Musto, p. 4, quoted from "Address Before the Massachusetts Medical Society, 30 May 1860" in *The Works of Oliver Wendell Holmes*, Boston: Houghton Mifflin, 1892.

16—" 'If the Chinaman . . . ' ": Musto, p. 17, quoted from *The Proceedings of the American Pharmaceutical Association*, 50, 570 and 572–73, (1902).

16—" 'The use of cocaine . . . ' ": *Ibid*.

17—"But as David Musto . . .": Musto, p. 7.

17—"In 1914, a Georgia . . .": Musto, p. 8.

18—"He wrote that . . .": McCoy, p. 7.

18—"Between 1850 and 1900 . . .": McCoy, pp. 7–8.

19—"It exceeds, in fact . . .": Courtwright's estimate (quoted in McCoy, p. 8) would make the addiction rate in the United States approximately .5%. Musto, pp. 253–4, estimates up to 400,000 in 1900. The population in 1900 was 76,212,000. That would also mean an addiction rate of approximately .5%. Around 1980, in the period when the Department of Justice contends that drug use was at its peak, the number of addicts has been estimated at 450,000 to 500,000. (See McCoy, p. 19.) As the population in 1980 was 226,542,203, 450,000 addicts would mean an addiction rate of .2%; 500,000 addicts, an addiction rate of .22%—a neglible difference. The NIDA estimate (which may be quite high) of 1.7 million addicts in the current population of 255,000,000 would mean an addiction rate of .67%, not much higher than the turn-of-the-century rate.

3. PREPARING THE NOBLE EXPERIMENT

One of the odd things about Prohibition is that two of the best modern books about that strange and uniquely American period are not by Americans. Sean Dennis Cashman, who wrote *Prohibition: The Lie of the Land*, and Andrew Sinclair, who wrote *Prohibition: The Era of Excess*, are both English. Charles Merz's *The Dry Decade* is a classic, but it doesn't cover the whole fourteen years. Everett S. Allen's *The Black Ships: Rumrunners of Prohibition* is a charming account of one of the less sanguinary aspects of Prohibition.

20—" . . . why did the United States, practically alone . . .": Britain and Belgium had a kind of prohibition during the war, and Finland had prohibition into the early 1920s. Some Mexican states were also dry.

22—"People lost interest . . .": Susan B. Anthony later wrote to a friend, "To be successful, a program must attempt but one reform." Sinclair, p. 93.

23—"Oh they say that drink's a sin . . .": Sinclair, p. 126.

23—"On March 10, 1881 . . .": Beebe and Clegg, *The American West*, p. 170.

25—" 'Alcohol is killing our people . . . ' ": Epstein, *Agency of Fear*, p. 24.

4. THE HEATHEN CHINEE

Perhaps the best book anywhere on the complex politics—domestic and international— leading up to the Harrison Act is Musto's *The American Disease*. Among the many books on the Spanish-American War, George O'Toole's *The Spanish War* is as good as any and far better than most.

26—"Opium smoking was not . . .": McCoy details the history of China's drug addiction in pp. 77–89.

26—"In 1906 . . .": McCoy, p. 88, quoting International Opium Commission, *Report*, pp. 44–66.

26—"One mandarin . . .": McCoy, p. 86, quoting Rev. A.S. Thelwall, *The Iniquities of the Opium Trade*, London: 1839.

27—"Dewey wiped out . . .": He also made the commander of a larger German fleet in Manila Bay back down, and through him, the Kaiser's brother, Prince Henry. After repeated German breaches of Dewey's blockade, one of his ships fired across the bow of a German cruiser. The German admiral, Otto von Diedrichs, sent an officer to protest.

Dewey, growing increasingly excited, told the German, "If the German government has decided to make war on the United States, or has any intention of making war, and has so informed your admiral, it is his duty to let me know."

He paused for effect, then added, "But whether he intends to fight or not, I am ready."

The German officer retreated, murmuring, "Mein Gott, mein Gott." Von Diedrichs made no more trouble. Neither did Prince Henry, who had warned Dewey before he set out to "behave himself." Neither did the Kaiser, who made no secret of his designs on the Philippines. O'Toole, pp. 191–92, 223, 634–36.

28—"Secretary of State Elihu Root . . .": Musto, p. 34.

29—"The treaty looked as if . . .": And, in fact, the French and Dutch government opium monopolies were still operating after World War II.

5. THE NOBLE EXPERIMENT

Bill Severn's slender *The End of the Roaring Twenties: Prohibition and Repeal* is very good on the operations of the Anti-Saloon League and other organized Drys. Edward Jay Epstein also has some important information and insights into the campaigns of Richmond Pearson Hobson in his *Agency of Fear*. Frederick Lewis Allen, in both *Only Yesterday: An Informal History of the Twenties* and *The Big Change*, has important information on the history of the dry era. Benjamin and Miller in *Undoing Drugs* have extremely valuable information on the economics of Prohibition and its economic and social aftereffects. Jay Robert Nash in *Bloodletters and Badmen* is very good on the Chicago crime scene in the '20s. Wayne Moquin's *The American Way of Crime*, Gus Tyler's *Organized Crime in America*, and *The Mobs and the Mafia* by Hank Messick and Burt Goldblatt, also give a good picture of the nationwide crime scene in the period covered. The author's *Written with Lead: Legendary American Gunfights and Gunfighters* is recommended for concise views of Chicago in the Capone era, New York in the late Prohibition and post-Prohibition period, the Mafia, the quite different organization the FBI calls La Cosa Nostra and Charley Lucky's "thing."

31—" 'We started off with . . . ' ": Severn, p. 89.

31—"League workers canvassed . . .": *Ibid*.

31—"Meanwhile, 'to let Congress . . . ' ": *Ibid*.

31—"In the election of 1914 . . .": *Ibid*.

33—"Called the Volstead Act . . .": *Ibid*., p. 97.

34—"Portable stills . . .": One has been on exhibit at the Colorado Museum of History, Denver.

34—"The contiguous forty-eight states have . . .": Cashman, pp. 29–30.

35—"The economists . . .": Benjamin and Miller, p. 18.

35—" 'Dion O'Bannion is Chicago's . . .": Nash, p. 410.

36—"That was the origin of Detroit's Purple Gang . . .": Purple in Yiddish slang denoted something that was off-color, wrong, not as it should be. The Purple Gang, ghetto extortionists and loan sharks before Prohibition, fit the description.

37—"A Manhattan syndicate . . .": The careers of O'Bannion, Weiss, Capone, Schultz and Luciano and Luciano's development of a national crime syndicate are outlined in Weir, pp. 199–210 and 249–61.

37—"In the beginning . . .": Benjamin and Miller, pp. 22, 28.

38—"When Prohibition began . . .": *Ibid.*, pp. 21–23.

38—"Prohibition had a profound effect . . .": *Ibid.*, p. 21.

38—"Prohibition contributed . . .": *Ibid.*, pp. 24–25. The author, as a member of the 3420th MP Detachment at Ft. Bragg, N.C., remembers a raid on an illegal still set up in the woods of the military reservation. The bootleggers had been adding bleach to their whiskey to give it an extra kick.

38—"In 1927 alone . . .": *Ibid.*, p. 24; *Cato Institute Policy Analysis*, May 25, 1989, "Thinking About Legalization," by James Ostrowski.

38—"Between 1985 and 1988 . . .": Benjamin and Miller, p. 25; *The Economist*, December 23, 1989, "Russia's Anti-Drink Campaign: Veni, Vidi, Vodka."

38—"The Soviet experiment . . .": Benjamin and Miller, p. 26.

39—" 'Bombay is known . . . ' ": *New York Times*, May 16, 1993, p. A-10.

6. DISCOVERY OF THE DOPE FIEND

Frederick Lewis Allen's *The Big Change* and Sean Dennis Cashman's *Prohibition: The Lie of the Land* are both excellent on the nation's post-Prohibition trauma. Musto's *The American Disease* is the definitive book on American domestic drug policy and was essential to this chapter. Epstein's *Agency of Fear*, although it concentrates on a later time, was also extremely valuable.

40—" 'Every criminal . . . ' ": Cashman, p. 194.

41—"The Klan's method . . .": Allen, p. 68, Cashman, p. 194.

42—" 'To get this heroin supply . . . ' ": Musto, p. 191; also Epstein, p. 28.

42—"Almost every statement . . .": Far from being more incurable than leprosy, most drug addicts have managed to cure themselves without professional help. All records show that the vast majority of violent crimes are NOT caused by heroin. The National Commission on Marijuana and Drug Abuse reported in 1973, "Assaultive offenses are significantly less likely to be committed by . . . opiate users" (Epstein, p. 30). Neither, with one exception, are heroin addicts carriers of disease to a significantly greater extent than the rest of the population. The exception is AIDS (unknown in Hobson's time), which is spread to a large extent by the use of contaminated needles for injecting drugs.

42—"Like alcohol . . .": Epstein, pp. 24–25.

43—"Heroin caused crime . . .": *Ibid.*, pp. 28–29.

43—"Drugs not only . . .": *Ibid.*, p. 27.

43—"The AMA condemned heroin . . .": Musto, p. 200.

43—"Dr. Charles Richardson . . .": *Ibid.*, p. 201.

43—"Dr. Alexander Lambert . . .": *Ibid.*, p. 200.

44—" 'Local police agencies . . . ' ": Epstein, p. 31; *New York Times*, February 23, 1972, "Murphy Attacks U.S. Drug Efforts," by Linda Charlton.

44—"Then in 1920 . . .": Musto, p. 218.

44—" 'Marijuana, perhaps now . . . ' ": *Ibid.*, p. 220.

45—" 'I wish I could show you . . . ' ": *Ibid.*, p. 223.

45—"For years afterward . . .": See short stories and magazine serials during the late '30's and all through the '40's.

45—"In spite of all the horror stories . . .": Epstein, p. 104.

7. CHARLEY LUCKY AND THE FRENCH CONNECTION

All of the volumes used for the previous chapter were helpful. In addition, Alfred Mc-Coy's *The Politics of Heroin: CIA Complicity in the Global Drug Trade*, the product of years of original research on several continents, was absolutely invaluable.

49—"Several of Diamond's hoodlums . . .": Nash, p. 337.

49—"When Charley Lucky excused . . .": Moquin, pp. 89–93; Maas, pp. 103–04.

49—"Having seen Luciano . . .": Messick and Goldblatt, p. 110; Moquin, pp 157–58.

50—"The reason for the pardon . . .": The Office of Naval Intelligence believed the burning of the *Normandie* to be an act of sabotage, although a later extensive investigation proved it to be an accident. Fearing sabotage, they attempted to contact the underworld to get information. They ended up with Meyer Lansky, Luciano's friend and right-hand man. The Luciano-Lansky team reported several times to the ONI, but what, if anything, they reported and what results their reports had are unknown. McCoy, pp. 31–32.

51—"It wasn't that the gangsters . . .": The story is that on a visit to Sicily, Mussolini had patronized a major Mafia leader, treating him like a minor official. In revenge, the don kept everyone out of the plaza where the dictator was to speak except for twenty beggars. Enraged, Mussolini returned to Rome and sent Mori and his troops to Sicily, where they demonstrated that the arts of Torquemada had not been forgotten.

51—" 'It has happened . . . ' ": Tyler, pp. 327–28.

51—"Luciano himself got into . . .": McCoy, p. 29. Unfortunately for Luciano, heroin didn't keep his prostitutes lethargic enough. It was the testimony of several of them that sent him to prison.

51—"Their reasons . . .": It has often been said that the "honor" of the older Italian gangsters forbade them to become involved with prostitution and drugs. They, like Big Jim Colosimo, got into prostitution whenever the opportunities presented themselves.

And it is hard to believe that these specialists in loan sharking, extortion and murder had moral qualms about selling drugs. The exception to Italian non-involvement with drugs is the "cosa nostra" in New Orleans -a descendant of the genuine Sicilian Mafia of old New Orleans. See Scott and Marshall, p. 52.

52—"Vito Genovese . . .": McCoy, p. 35.

52—"In the north . . ." *Ibid.*, p. 36.

52—"At the end of the war . . .": *Ibid.*, p. 38.

53—"By 1952 . . .": *Ibid.*

54—"It began paying . . ." *Ibid.*, p. 59.

54—"The arrest . . .": The SDECE is the French equivalent of the CIA.

55—"By 1965 . . .": McCoy, p. 38.

55—"By 1972 . . .": *Ibid.*, p. 73.

55—"When, in 1957, Albert Anastasio . . .": *Ibid.,* p. 74; U.S. Senate Committee on Government Operations, "Organized Crime," Part 2, pp. 524–25.

8. THE GOLDEN TRIANGLE

The most valuable sources for any discussion of narcotics and politics in Southeast Asia are two books by Alfred W. McCoy. *The Politics of Heroin in Southeast Asia*, written in 1972 when McCoy was a doctoral candidate at Yale University, has to be one of the world's masterpieces of investigative journalism. McCoy studied documents in English and French, interviewed prominent figures in the worlds of drug trading and drug enforcement on three continents and traveled to the Golden Triangle to observe the situation personally. He almost lost his life on several occasions. On returning to the United States, he survived attempts by the CIA to change his facts and to stop the book's publication. In 1991, McCoy published an updated version of his book, *The Politics of Heroin: CIA Complicity in the Global Drug Trade*. The later book has almost all the material of the earlier and includes more explanation of the labyrithine politics of both Southeast Asia and South Asia, as well as developments in the two decades since the first publication. Unless otherwise noted, the McCoy citations below are from *The Politics of Heroin: CIA Complicity*.

56—"Besides the military . . .": One of the gangsters was Frank Furci, son of Dominick Furci, a middle-level boss in Trafficante's organization. He was outmanoeuvered and driven out of Vietnam by a crippled, half-blind "old China hand" named William J. Crum.

56—"Heading the ring . . .": Wooldridge and his associates were investigated by the U.S. Senate in 1971 and were convicted of fraud and larceny by court martial that year.

57—"In Yunnan province . . .": In earlier writings, the Hmong, Yao and other hill tribes are sometimes called Meo, a contemptuous Vietnamese term, or Montagnards, French for mountaineers.

59—" 'For many years . . . ' ": *Practical Anthropology* 4, no. 6 (Nov.-Dec. 1957), "The Hill People of Kentung State," by Elaine T. Lewis, p. 226. Quoted in McCoy, p. 176.

59—"One of them . . .": For a history of the meteoric rise of Khun Sa, see McCoy, pp. 348–49, 355–61 and 424–35.

60—"In 1951, David M. Key . . .": Memorandum of conversation, Deputy Assistant Secretary of State for Far Eastern Affairs (Merchant), Subject: KMT Troops in Burma,

Washington, August 10, 1951 [Top Secret], *Foreign Relations of the United States 1951*, pp. 287–88. Quoted in McCoy, p. 177.

60—"Some Civil Air Transport pilots . . .": McCoy, p. 178; William R.Corson, *The Armies of Ignorance: The Rise of the American Intelligence Empire*, New York: Dial, 1977, pp. 320–22.

60—"While Phao Siyanan . . .": Narcotics became illegal in Thailand with the abolition of the state opium monopoly after World War II.

61—"Foremost among them . . .": In his book *Modern Warfare*, Trinquier advocates, to prevent Communist subversion, a complex system of informers, with agents in each family, each building and each city block, that seems patterned after the system set up in Cuba by Fidel Castro.

63—"Conein was an old Vietnam . . .": For more on OSS operations in Vietnam (at the time, French Indochina), see Bradley F. Smith, *The Shadow Warriors*, pp. 326–28.

63—"Conein, who hung around . . .": McCoy, p. 250, quoting an interview with Conein

63—"When Conein left Vietnam . . .": *Ibid.*

64—"In 1970, the business . . .": *Ibid.*, p. 226.

64—"Later, after the invasion . . .": The invasion may have contributed to the "GI heroin epidemic." The invasion took place in May 1970, when GI heroin use hit its stride. It was easier to move narcotics from Laos, in the Golden Triangle, to Cambodia by land than to carry it over the roadless mountains to South Vietnam. And when the South Vietnamese were in Laos, South Vietnamese planes were able to fly to Laos from Cambodia as well as their own country. See McCoy, pp. 225–26.

64—"A $2 vial in Saigon . . .": One GI being treated for heroin addiction said, "You know, a jug [vial] over here costs only two dollars, but you can get $100 for it back in the world." U.S. Executive Office report, "The Vietnam Drug User Returns: Final Report," p. 57, quoted in McCoy, p. 258.

64—"A CIA report said . . .": McCoy, p. 223.

65—"At first, there were wild rumors . . .": Anslinger was notorious for blaming drug smuggling on Cold War enemies, citing, at various times, Communist China, Cuba and North Vietnam, but he was not the only member of government to do so.

65—" 'The opium-growing areas . . . ' ": Report of the Office of the Provost Marshal, U.S. Military Assistance Command Vietnam (Saigon 1971), "The Drug Abuse Problem in Vietnam, p. 4. Quoted in McCoy, p. 223.

65—" 'Zone I . . . ' ": *Ibid.*, p. 224.

65—"The Americans might be . . .": *Ibid.*, pp. 223–24.

66—"Actually, some GIs . . .": In his biography, *About Face*, Colonel Hackworth writes: "Not only did the buddy help the addict during bad times as he came down, but he also did the honors in Saigon when it came to the now-*ex*-addict's DEROS and piss test. The problem was that since heroin stays in the system for a long time, even after the guy was off the stuff, he could still be found out in Saigon. So we solved this by having both the buddy and the ex-addict piss into the bottles at the overcrowded depot, then just exchange bottles. The buddy would then disappear with the 'smoking gun'; the ex-addict would come out clean, go home, and hopefully start a better life" (p. 804). That procedure took a lot of hope—and a strong belief in the miraculous.

66—"The U.S. Army's . . .": Memorandum for Record from Michael G. McCann, Director, Public Safety Directorate, CORDS, U.S. Military Command, Vietnam, quoted in McCoy, pp. 239–40; McCoy, pp. 255–56.

66—"U.S. Representative Robert Steele . . .": McCoy, p. 256.

66—"The senior U.S. adviser . . .": *Ibid.*, p. 256.

9. HOME FRONT: GANGSTERS AND FLOWER CHILDREN

Herbert Asbury's classic, *The Gangs of New York: An Informal History of the Underworld*, describes urban fighting gangs from colonial times to the early part of this century. T.J. English's *The Westies* contains a quick history of New York's historical gangs. *Deadly Consequences*, by Dr. Deborah Prothrow-Stith, an African-American physician and assistant dean at the Harvard School of Public Health, is outstanding for its analysis of the causes of gang violence. Robert Currie's *Reckoning* has a wealth of material on modern youth gangs and gangsters. And Robert Stutman, in *Dead on Delivery*, has an interesting segment on his experiences as a pseudo-flower child. The "flower children" and the "counterculture" were the subjects of innumerable magazine and newspaper articles in the '60s.

67—"The United States was . . .": Weir, *Fatal Victories*, pp. 220–35 gives a good account of Tet and its aftermath.

67—"The same gangs stayed . . .": Currie, pp. 52–56.

68—"Typically, they were . . .": Prothrow-Stith, pp. 96–98, 108.

68—"Some gangsters carried . . .": A high school classmate of the author made zip guns for his gang in Philadelphia.

69—"Howard Finestone . . .": Currie, pp. 47–54.

69—"Aid to Dependent Children . . .": Typically, ADC is cut off if there is an able-bodied man living in the home.

69—"After a five-year study . . .": Prothrow-Stith, pp. 99–100.

70—"Dr. Terry Williams . . .": *Ibid.*, pp. 101–03.

71—"The flower children . . .": While attendance at college does not necessarily indicate immense wealth, the average college student is far more affluent than the average urban gangster.

71—"Instead, as Robert Stutman . . .": Stutman, p. 68.

72—"They had all the permits . . .": Stutman, p. 68

10. THE BANK FROM HELL AND THE HOLY WARRIORS

Jonathan Kwitny's *The Crimes of Patriots* is practically the definitive book on the infamous Nugan Hand Bank. Alfred McCoy, in *The Politics of Heroin: CIA Complicity in the Global Drug Trade*, summarizes the story neatly. McCoy was able to use some sources that became available after Kwitny wrote his book.

McCoy is also an excellent source of information on the way U.S. policy became entangled with heroin and opium during the Afghan war.

74—"On January 27, 1980 . . .": Kwitny; the entire book covers the Nugan Hand escapade. McCoy, pp. 461–78.

74—" 'The Golden Triangle, that's . . . ' ": Kwitny, p. 59.

74—"His friends Down Under . . .": McCoy, p. 463.

74—"The Nugan Hand Bank opened . . .": Nugan wrote the bank a personal check for $980,000 to purchase 490,000 shares of its stock. He then covered his expense by writing a company check to himself for the same amount. McCoy, p. 464; Australian Royal Commission, *Final Report*, vol. IV, pp. 409–11.

75—"Soon after the bank . . .": Australia-New South Wales Joint Task Force, *Report, Vol. 4, Nugan Hand*, pp. 691–92.

75—"At the time of Nugan's death . . .": McCoy, p. 465, 469.

75—"Prominent among the friends . . .": *Ibid.*, pp. 471–72.

75—"This group . . .": They were sued by Tony Avirgan and Martha Honey in a civil RICO lawsuit handled by Daniel Sheehan, head of the Christic Institute.

75—"Before he died . . .": *National Times*, Feb. 21, 1982, quoted in McCoy, p. 470.

76—"An outraged President . . .": Carter also canceled grain shipments to the Soviet Union. The United States had been arming the anti-Communist rebels before the invasion, but arms deliveries were greatly increased afterwards. See McCoy, pp. 436–37, 447–50.

76—"Dr. David Musto . . .": McCoy, p. 436; *New York Times*, May 22, 1980, "Drug Crisis and Strategy," by Joyce H. Lowinson and David F. Musto.

77—" 'I told the council . . . ' ": McCoy, p. 436.

77—"Drug-related deaths . . .": *Ibid.*, p. 437.

77—" 'Are we erring . . . ' ": *Ibid.*; *New York Times*, May 22, 1980, "Drug Crisis and Strategy," by Joyce H. Lowinson and David F. Musto.

77—"The unsettled conditions . . .": As used here, "Middle East" refers to Iran, Afghanistan and Pakistan, countries which are predominately Muslim and most of whose people speak languages in the Aryan group. "Near East" refers to Egypt, Israel, Lebanon, Syria, Jordan, Saudi Arabia and the Persian Gulf sheikdoms. All of these countries speak Semitic languages (Hebrew and Arabic) and all but Israel are predominantly Muslim. Turkey might be included here, but part of it is in Europe, its language is different and its traditions are at least as bound up with Europe as with the Near Eastern countries. All this, of course, is extremely arbitrary. It's an attempt to avoid the common practice of labeling a country like Morocco (which is farther west than any European country but Iceland) as part of the "Middle East."

77—"At a press conference . . .": McCoy, p. 437.

78—"DEA Special Agent . . .": *Ibid.*

78—"Black syndicates in Harlem . . .": *Ibid.*, p. 438.

78—"By 1983 . . .": Scott and Marshall, *Cocaine Politics*, p. 178, quoting *New York Times*, June 30, 1983.

78—" 'We must grow and sell . . . ' ": McCoy, p. 458; *New York Times*, June 18, 1986.

78—"As an engineering student . . .": McCoy, p. 450.

79—"The DEA refused . . .": *Ibid.*, pp. 454–55.

79—"Pakistani Gen. Fazle Haq . . .": *Ibid.*, p. 456; U.S. State Department Bureau of Narcotics Matters, *International Narcotics Control Strategy Report*, 1990, pp. 290–1.

79—"What might have happened . . .": McCoy, p. 455.

80—"In 1980, there were . . .": *Ibid.*; Pakistan Narcotics Control Board, *National Survey on Drug Abuse in Pakistan*, pp. iii, ix, 23, 308.

80—" 'The government . . . ' ": McCoy, p. 457.

11. NARCOTERRORISM

Two books are outstanding on this subject. The first is *Drugs, Law Enforcement and Foreign Relations*, the report of the Senate Foreign Relations Committee's Subcommittee on Terrorism, Narcotics and International Relations (better known as the Kerry subcommittee). This report, published in December 1988, was largely overlooked by the nation's news media. It details the shocking collusion of the CIA, the State Department and the National Security Council with as evil a group of cutthroats and smugglers as you'll find in any thriller. The other is Scott and Marshall's *Cocaine Politics*, which covers the Latin American drug-smuggling scene in mind-boggling detail. Ideally, both books should be read together: Scott and Marshall seem to expect their readers to have some familiarity with the Kerry report. They refer frequently, for instance, to the Frogman Drug Arrest in San Francisco in 1983 but never explain what happened.

Leslie Cockburn's *Out of Control* contains valuable information on this subject. It was an even more important source for the next chapter, which covers some of the most frightening aspects of narcoterrorism in Central America.

The Christic Institute's *Inside the Shadow Government* is a summary of the plaintiff's case in a lawsuit. It makes no pretence of objectivity. It does, however, present an enormous amount of damning evidence which no one has managed to refute, either in or out of a courtroom.

Also important sources for this chapter were Shirley Christian's *Nicaragua: Revolution in the Family*, a conservative, but fair, account of the Nicaraguan revolution and *Kings of Cocaine: Inside the Medellín Cartel—An Astonishing True Story of Murder, Money and International Corruption*, by Guy Gugliotta and Jeff Leen. Gugliotta and Leen were aided by the Drug Enforcement Administration. In a way, their book is as notable for what it leaves out as for what it says. But what it says, it says very well. Elaine Shannon's *Desperados: Latin Drug Lords, U.S. Lawmen, and the War America Can't Win* focuses primarily on Mexico, but its excursions into the drug scene in Central America and the Caribbean were very helpful. Also very helpful was Michael Levine's *The Big White Lie*, a look at the South American cocaine scene by a DEA agent who was there and who was frustrated by his superiors in Washington. Pete Brewton's *The Mafia, the CIA & George Bush* is mostly about the S&L scandals, but it touches on some drug matters.

82—"But the act did . . .": The war was the Korean War, a relatively short war in a very limited area that was still bloody enough to have killed almost as many Americans in three years as died in the sixteen years covering the Vietnam War and the *Mayaguez* incident. China is a large Communist country. North Vietnam was not. It was not, for example, in a class with the U.S.S.R., East Germany or even Poland.

83—"As Spitz Channell and Richard Miller, two conservative fund-raisers ...": *Action Plan for the 1986 Programs of the American Trust and National Endowment for the Preservation of Liberty*, quoted in the *Iran Contra Report* Appendix A, p. 686. See also Scott and Marshall, p. 23.

83—"In a *Military Review* article ...": *Military Review*, Feb. 1987, pp. 46–47.

83—"The president said ...": Scott and Marshall, p. 23.

83—"The situation began to develop ...": *New York Times*, Feb. 1, 1970, "Illicit Traffic in Cocaine 'Growing by Leaps and Bounds' in Miami," by George Volsky.

83—"Some thirty-three plans ...": Christic Institute, p. 10

84—"In the first ten months ...": Scott and Marshall, p. 30; interview with CORU co-founder Armando Lopez Estrada by CBS News for special report, June 10, 1977.

84—"After he became president ...": Cockburn, p. 100.

85—"Some of the smuggling organizations ...": Scott and Marshall, pp. 30–31, 93; Brewton, pp. 181–83.

85—"On June 21, 1970 ...": Scott and Marshall, pp. 26–27; *Miami Herald*, Nov. 15, 1979.

86—"In October 1972 ...": Conein memo, May 25, 1976, released under the Freedom of Information Act to the National Organization for Reform of the Marijuana Laws and quoted by Scott and Marshall, p. 28.

86—"In 1978, two CNM members ...": Scott and Marshall, p. 33.

86—"Some of the still-unorganized Colombians ...": *Connecticut* magazine, June 1987, "Who Killed Kim Klein?" by William Weir.

87—"When Nicaraguan President ...": He was assassinated in Paraguay a year later. Somoza had been trying to throw his weight around in a country where the only person who had weight to throw was President Alfredo Stroessner. He was blown to bits by an antitank weapon in a country where nobody had as much as an air rifle without Stroessner's permission.

87—"The right-wing military clique ...": Scott and Marshall, pp. 42–46; Levine, pp. 33–76; Shannon, pp. 403–05; Christian, pp. 228–35.

87—"Suárez Mason was one ...": Scott and Marshall, pp. 44–64; Anderson and Anderson, *Inside the League*, p. 147, 204.

87—"The putsch ...": For an inside view of the Cocaine Coup and its aftermath, see Levine, pp. 33–76.

88—"Michael Sullivan ...": Levine, pp. 65–67.

89—"During the revolution ...": Christian, pp. 72–77.

89—"After the Sandinista triumph ...": Cockburn, pp. 22–23; Scott and Marshall, p. 109; *Iran-Contra Report*, p. 32.

89—"Pastora's situation ...": *Iran-Contra Report*, p. 32

90—"In fact, David MacMichael ...": Cockburn, p. 12; *New York Times*, June 11, 1984, "In From the Cold and Hot for the Truth," by Philip Taubman; see also MacMichael, letter dated Aug. 7 to *New York Times*, Aug. 13, 1986 issue.

90—"Even Sen. Barry Goldwater . . .": Cockburn, p. 11; Woodward, *Veil*, p. 322.

91—"Each phase of the Contra operation . . .": Scott and Marshall, pp. 104–06.

91—"Morales later said . . .": Cockburn, pp. 169–71. It had been alleged that Morales confessed to flying drugs to John Hull's ranch in an attempt to get a lighter sentence. Those who believe a convicted drug smuggler could hope for a lighter sentence by testifying against a CIA asset like John Hull must believe the tooth fairy distributes gold pieces. A DEA agent actually did offer Morales a shorter sentence if he *would not* testify before Congress. Morales rejected the offer and testified without immunity (see Cockburn, p. 176). Jonathan Kwitny attempted to disprove some smugglers' tales of landing at John Hull's airstrips by asking aircraft manufacturers if the strips were long enough to permit takeoffs and landings with the loads the smugglers carried. The manufacturers said they were not. This question must be considered while bearing in mind two facts: (1) aircraft manufacturers are not going to endorse any practice even remotely hazardous; (2) Barry Seal did not command a price of $5,000 a kilo because he was a safe-and-sane pilot, nor did ex-crop-duster Gary Betzner follow practices approved by the FAA. In spite of his differences with Cockburn over the airstrips, Kwitny asserts at the beginning of his article that "there is plenty of evidence" linking the Contras and drug smuggling. He says "Interviews suggest that the total amount of drug money that has gone to the *contras'* coffers runs well into the millions." See the *Nation*, Aug. 29, 1987, "Money, Drugs and the Contras," by Jonathan Kwitny; Sept. 19, 1987, "Of Drugs Money and Contras: A Liberal's Dose of Facts," by Leslie Cockburn; and "Kwitny Replies" by Jonathan Kwitny.

91—"All were widely believed . . .": Felipe Vidal Santiago was arrested at least seven times on narcotics and gun charges (*Miami Herald*, Feb. 16, 1987). He helped unload drugs at John Hull's ranch in May, 1985, according to Floyd Carlton Caceres, Noriega's pilot, who testified that he was there. Vidal was arrested with a considerable quantity of drugs in Costa Rica in the summer of 1986. See Cockburn, p. 236.

René Corvo (the "Poison Dwarf") and Vidal had "a problem with drugs," CIA station chief Joe Fernandez reportedly told the Iran Contra Committees in closed hearings. Fernandez said that they had to be protected because they were "our people" (see Cockburn, p. 242). Corvo was the target of a major narcotics investigation which was squelched in 1986 when top levels of the Justice Department became aware of it. See Scott and Marshall p. 120; *Iran-Contra Report*, Executive Session, May 5, 1987, pp. 6, 46–47; *Iran Contra Report*, Appendix B, Vol. 8, pp. 199, 237–38.

Francisco "Paco" Chanes had large quantities of cocaine in his possession, according to both Corvo and Steven Carr, the mercenary. He was a partner of Moises Nuñez in Frigoríficos, a frozen-shrimp importer, which the Costa Rican government called a front for drug smugglers and which the FBI said gave narcotics money to the Contras. Chanes owned a number of companies, most short-lived, and all fronts for drug-smuggling. Cockburn, pp. 157, 160–61.

Moises Nuñez was Chanes's partner in the drug-smuggling enterprises called Frigoríficos and Ocean Hunter. Nuñez is alleged to have been a CIA operative, and there is a strong suspicion (on which Sen. John Kerry refused to comment), that Ocean Hunter was a CIA proprietary company. Jesus García charged that the company was owned by the CIA, a charge "confirmed by several U.S. Government and Contra sources," according to Leslie Cockburn. Cockburn, pp. 157, 161, 163.

SETCO Air, one of the companies picked by the State Department to deliver "humanitarian" aid to the Contras, was partly owned by Mario Calero, Adolfo's brother. According to a U.S. Customs report of 1983, it was actually "headed by Juan Ramon Matta Ballesteros, a class I DEA violator." Scott and Marshall, p. 10; *Kerry Report*, p. 44.

Frank Castro, a business associate of all of these people, had been twice indicted for drug offenses. The first indictment was botched by a crooked DEA agent; the second was dropped for mysterious reasons (Scott and Marshall, pp. 25–32). Rob Owen reported to North that "several sources are now saying Pastora is going to be bankrolled by former Bay of Pigs veteran Frank Castro, who is heavily into drugs" (Owen letter to North, Nov. 4, 1984, discovered by Christic Institute). Less than a year later, Owen wrote to North that Joe Fernandez, CIA station chief in Costa Rica, said that this man who was "heavily into drugs" "can be helpful" (Owen letter to North, Aug. 2, 1985, discovered by Christic Institute).

91—"The protection . . .": *Kerry Report*, pp. 2, 36, 41.

92—"Colombian police . . .": Gugliotta and Leen, pp. 119–37. Ether is used in processing cocaine. When a Colombian named Frank Torres ordered an unusually large quantity of ether from the United States, the DEA installed radio beepers in two of the barrels. Tracking the beepers led the Colombian police to the lab.

92—"The cocaine cartels in the past . . .": Gugliotta and Leen, pp. 91–96; Shannon, pp. 117–18, 158–59.

92—"Several days later . . .": The army reported that it had rescued a group of "cattlemen." It seems that if the traffickers and guerrillas occasionally cooperated, so did the traffickers and the army.

93—"U.S. Ambassador Lewis Tambs . . .": Scott and Marshall, pp. 97–98; Shannon, pp. 144–45; Gugliotta and Leen, pp. 133–34; *Kerry Report*, page 240.

93—"Adler Berriman 'Barry' Seal . . .": Gugliotta and Leen, pp. 145–89; Shannon, pp. 166–83. For Seal's CIA activities, see Brewton, pp. 154–60.

94—"Seal's appeal to Bush . . .": Cockburn, p. 180; see also Cockburn p. 222. According to convicted drug pilot Michael Tolliver, Seal recruited him and other pilots to fly aid to the Contras—more evidence of Seal's long-lasting ties with the CIA. See Christic Institute, p. 106.

94—" 'You're dealing . . . ' ": Gugliotta and Leen, p. 152; Shannon, p. 166. Both quote Seal's testimony before the President's Commission on Organized Crime, Oct. 7, 1985. Seal spoke no Spanish; Ochoa, no English. The English words came from a translator. As Seal remembered it, Ochoa's answer was: "We are not Communists. We don't particularly enjoy the same philosophy that they do. But they serve our means, and we serve theirs." Ochoa undoubtedly spoke good conversational Spanish. But the above is not good conversational English or even, in this context, to the point.

94—"North's propaganda triumph . . .": Scott and Marshall, pp. 98–103; *Kerry Report*, pp. 68–69, 146.

94—"According to authors . . .": Scott and Marshall, pp. 100–101.

94—"Most troubling, the telephone . . .": *Kerry Report*, pp. 68–69

94—"On February 19, 1986 . . .": Shannon, p. 181.

12. THE BIG BANG

Leslie Cockburn's *Out of Control* was the most important source for this chapter, with the Christic Institute's *Inside the Shadow Government* a close second. The first book is by a television journalist who spent a lot of time on the scene and interviewed all the key players. All her quotes were taped, making *Out of Control* a prime source for quotes.

The author of the second book is the public-interest law firm of Daniel P. Sheehan and his associates, which, as we'll see, filed a RICO lawsuit on behalf of Tony Avirgan and Martha Honey against many members of the gun-and-dope smuggling network aiding the Contras.

The report and hearing transcripts of the Senate Foreign Relations Committee's subcommittee investigating the situation in Central America and South America (the Kerry Subcommittee) were invaluable for verifying points made by Cockburn and the Christic Institute. As in the previous chapter, the panoramic view of cocaine in Central America provided by Scott and Marshall's *Cocaine Politics* was essential. The report of the joint House and Senate committees investigating the Iran-Contra scandal was also helpful, even though the House chairman, Lee Hamilton of Indiana, had been embroiled with the President of Costa Rica of behalf of one of the key players in Central America, his fellow Indianan, CIA asset John Hull.

All the previously mentioned books concerned with the Contra War and drugs in Latin America provided valuable information, as did numerous magazine and newspaper articles. So did interviews with several of the players and their lawyers, especially John Mattes and Daniel Sheehan.

97—"He had refused . . .": *New York Times,* May 31, 1984, "Nicaragua Blast Said to Wound a Rebel Leader," by United Press International, and "Efforts on New Alliance," special to *New York Times*; *New York Times*, June 1, 1984, "Costa Rica Holds Nicaraguan Rebel Wounded in Blast," by Stephen Kinzer; *New York Times*, June 2, 1984, "Caracas Takes In Wounded Rebel Chief," by Stephen Kinzer; and *New York Times*, June 14, 1984, "Pastora Vows to Keep Fighting Sandinistas Even Without U.S. Aid," by Alan Riding; *Time*, June 11, 1984, "Starting a New Chapter," by James Kelly; *Newsweek*, June 11, 1984, "An Attack on Commander Zero," by Robert B. Cullen; *Newsweek*, Sept. 3, 1984, "The CIA Blows an Asset," by Harry Anderson; *Kerry Report*, pp. 38, 52.

98—"Peter Torbiornsson . . .": *New York Times*, June 14, 1984, "Attack on Pastora: Much Intrigue but Few Facts," by Richard J. Meislin.

98—"His wallet was always stuffed . . .": *The Nation*, Oct. 5, 1985, p. 315, "The Carlos File," by Tony Avirgan and Martha Honey.

98—" 'It was a human whirlwind . . . ' ": *Time*, June 11, 1984, "Starting a New Chapter," by James Kelly.

98—"Reid Miller of the Associated Press . . .": Cockburn, p. 80; *New York Times*, June 1, 1984, "A Survivor's Story: 'Blinding Explosion' Among Journalists," by Reid G. Miller.

99—" 'Linda Frazier was pulled . . . ' ": Cockburn, pp. 80–81; *New York Times*, June 1, 1984, Miller, *op. cit.*

99—"Tony Avirgan later . . .": Cockburn, pp. 82–83.

99—"Owen later testified . . .": Sworn depositions of Robert Owen, William Crone and Bruce Jones, quoted in the Christic Institute's *Inside the Shadow Government*, p. 75. Holtz, who advised Hull not to go to La Penca, had earlier appeared with Hull and Jones at the scene of a plane crash. The plane, carrying arms for the Contras, had crashed in Costa Rica, and the three Americans got to the scene before Costa Rican authorities. Holtz ordered that the teeth and jaws of the dead be removed and the bodies burned so that nobody could identify them. Christic Institute, pp. 61–62.

100—"Tony Avirgan had . . .": Cockburn, p. 82.

100—"Per Anker Hansen . . .": Cockburn, p. 81; Christic Institute, p. 74.

100—"Before they could even start . . .": Christic Institute, p. 76; Scott and Marshall, p. 68; *Time*, June 11, 1984, "Starting a New Chapter," by James Kelly; *Newsweek*, June 11, 1984, "An Attack on Commander Zero," by Robert B. Cullen. For Noriega's part in the cover-up, see *Kerry Hearings*, Vol. II, p. 204.

100—" 'Other diplomats . . . ' ": Cockburn, note, p. 262.

100—"Later, an unnamed official . . .": *New York Times*, June 14, 1984, "Attack on Pastora: Much Intrigue but Few Facts," by Richard J. Meislin.

100—" 'A year's worth of interviews . . . ' ": *The Nation*, Oct. 5, 1985, "The Carlos File," by Avirgan and Honey, p. 312.

101—"Costa Rican authorities . . .": Cockburn, p. 83; *New York Times*, June 5, 1984, "Imposter is Suspect in Nicaragua Bombing," by United Press International, and June 14, 1984, "Attack on Pastora: Much Intrigue but Few Facts," by Richard J. Meislin. "Hansen" was identified in a sworn statement by Alberto Guevara Bonilla, a former agent of the the DIS, the Costa Rican intelligence service, as a man who had been in the La Penca area two months before the bombing and who had been given special privileges by the DIS. Three weeks before the bombing, he was seen heading for La Penca with John Hull (Cockburn, p. 87). Shortly after Guevara swore to this statement, he was picked up the Costa Rican security forces and disappeared. Cockburn, pp. 245–46; also Christic Institute, pp. 70–74.

On August 1, 1993, the *Miami Herald* reported that the thumb print of a certain Vital Roberto Gaguine, an Argentine leftist killed in 1989, was found on the stolen Hansen passport. The *Herald* further reported that Gaguine had been hired by the Sandinista government to assassinate Pastora. Considering (1) the linguists' identification of "Hansen" as a Libyan or Israeli (Felipe Vidal is reported to said he was a Libyan and also an agent of Mossad, the Israeli secret service), not a native speaker of Spanish; (2) David and Terrell's information about Amac Galil; (3) the fact that fingerprints can easily be lifted and transferred; and (4) the CIA's earlier attempt to blame narcoterrorism on the Sandinistas, this story has the odor of very old fish.

Asked about the story on September 8, 1993, Bill Davis said: "The theory is that the bomber, that is the guy who was using the false Danish passport, was actually Gaguine, from Argentina AND that he was working for the Sandinistas. We think that there are several huge weak links in the daisy chain of evidence. First of all, the fingerprints, they say, match perfectly between one that we got out of Panama that's clearly from the bomber, and they say, 'Oh, the Argentine police just discovered this document that matches perfectly.' Well, it probably does. The question is, how did it get in the Argentine police files? Is it a legitimate document, or is it something planted by the intelligence community? Then secondly, even if it is the bomber's, even if he is this Argentine who is conveniently dead so you can't question him, what is the evidence that he was working for the Sandinistas? It's very thin. They rely on Torbiornsson, the [Swede] who brought the bomber to the press conference, even though he claimed to be a Dane and couldn't speak a word of Danish and didn't recognize the name of the leading beer in Denmark. This guy brings him into the press conference, he sets off a bomb, and ten years later Torbiornsson remembers, 'Oh, yeah, I first saw him at a meeting in Nicaragua.' [Immediately after the bombing, both Torbiornsson and his assistant, Luis Fernando Prado, said they first met "Hansen" at a somewhat rundown hotel in San José, Costa Rica. See *New York Times*, June 14, 1984, "Attack on Pastora: Much Intrigue but Few Facts," by Richard J. Meislin.] Therefore he's working for the Sandinistas. Well, all I can say is, it's weak, at best. It has all the earmarks of disinformation. . . . We think it's a disinformation campaign, geared mainly to getting Costa Rica to drop the charges against Hull, because they're still trying to extradite Hull, and if Hull gets hauled down there and tried, that would reopen the whole can of worms."

101—" 'After analyzing a voice recording . . . ' ": *The Nation*, Oct. 5, 1985, p. 314, "The Carlos File," by Avirgan and Honey. Luis Fernando Prado, Torbiornsson's assistant, told the *New York Times*' Richard Meislin, who interviewed him in a Costa Rican hospital where he was recovering from wounds, that "Hansen" spoke mostly in English "and that 'his Spanish was forced' as if he was trying to disguise an accent." *New York Times*, June 14, 1984, "Attack on Pastora: Much Intrigue but Few Facts," by Richard J. Meislin.

101—"Camper sent them . . .": *Time*, Sept. 17, 1984, "A Mystery Involving 'Mercs,' " by Ed Magnuson; *Newsweek*, Sept. 17, 1984, "The Friends of Tommy Posey," by Russell Watson; *Wall Street Journal*, Aug. 19, 1985, "In Alabama's Woods, Frank Camper Trains Men to Repel Invaders," by Timothy K. Smith.

101—"That boast . . .": Costa Rican officialdom was split between the strongly pro-Contra and the strongly pro-neutrality. This accounts for the seemingly contradictory actions and pronouncements of the Costa Rican government. This situation made things a bit chancy for anyone involved—pro or con—with the Contras. For example, Bill Davis, while investigating the case in Costa Rica, was arrested on the strange (for an American) charge of showing disrespect for a policeman. Fortunately for him, pro-neutrality officials got control of his case.

102—"He said he had met . . .": Cockburn, reporting an interview with Jonathan Winer of Kerry's staff, p. 24.

102—" 'Hull told him . . .' ": Cockburn, p. 43.

103—"Glibbery told CBS . . .": *Ibid.*, p. 44.

103—" 'What's the NSC . . . ' ": Cockburn, p. 33; confirmed by Owen testimony at Iran-Contra hearings, May 14, 1987.

103—"He later told CBS News . . .": Cockburn, p. 150; Carr's account of the call is corroborated by Jonathan Kwitny in *The Nation*, Aug. 29, 1987, "Money, Drugs and the Contras."

103—" 'The thing about John Hull ..' ": Cockburn, p. 33.

103—"Shortly after the La Penca bombing . . .": Sworn deposition of José Coutin for the RICO suit, pp. 57–58.

104—" In 1987, Pat Korten . . .": Cockburn, p. 175.

104—"According to George Morales . . .": Cockburn, p. 172.

104—"Gary Betzner . . .": *Ibid.* On the trips to Hull's ranch, he was paid 20 kilos of cocaine per trip, Christic Institute, p. 103; CBS News, *West 57th*, April 6, 1987.

104—"When he landed . . .": Cockburn, pp. 173–74; CBS News, *West 57th*, April 6, 1987.

104—" 'It wasn't . . . ' ": Cockburn, p. 174; Christic Institute, p. 103; CBS News, *West 57th*, April 6, 1987; *Los Angeles Times*, Feb. 22, 1987, "Committee Probes Reports of Contra Drug Smuggling," by Donald McManus and Ronald J. Ostrow.

104—"The rancher told . . .": Cockburn, p. 65; Christic Institute, p. 88.

104—"Hull added . . .": Cockburn, p. 48.

105—"Of Vidal . . .": *Ibid.*; CBS News, *West 57th*, June 26, 1986, "John Hull's Farm: Bordering on War."

105—"Hull had transported . . .": Cockburn, p. 48.

105—"Joe Fernandez . . .": *Ibid.* Fernandez also told Jeffrey Feldman that Hull was a CIA operative, according to a deposition Feldman made for the Joint Iran-Contra Committees. José Blandón, former Panamanian chief of civil intelligence, swore he knew Hull was CIA as early as 1981. Deposition of José Blandón in RICO suit, quoted in Christic Institute, p. 58, 78.

105—"But the evidence mounted up . . .": Cockburn, p. 47.

105—" 'They came to me . . . ' ": *Ibid.*, page 56; Christic Institute, pp. 86–87; interview with John Mattes, July 19, 1990.

106—"García was happy . . .": Cockburn, p. 56; Christic Institute, p. 87; interview with John Mattes, July 19, 1990.

107—" 'We turned all that . . . ' ": Cockburn, p. 64; interview with John Mattes, July 19, 1990.

107—"Two days later . . .": Cockburn, p. 65; interview with John Mattes, July 19, 1990.

107—"The government postponed . . .": *New York Times*, Dec. 13, 1986, "2 Aides in Miami Report Order to Stop an Inquiry," by Joseph B. Treaster.

108—" 'That would be like me . . . ' ": Cockburn, p. 69.

108—"Hull flew into a rage . . .": Scott and Marshall, p. 127; Cockburn, p. 56; Terrell testimony in *Hull v. Avirgan and Honey* libel case, May 22, 1986, quoted in Christic Institute, pp. 86–87; Terrell statement to Ben Bradlee, Jr., quoted in *Guts and Glory*, p. 261.

109—". . . Aristides Sánchez, a high-ranking Contra (and drug smuggler) . . .": Scott and Marshall, p. 104, 107–09.

109—"Vidal said . . .": Scott and Marshall, p. 130. The Christic Institute (p. 85) says Vidal also told Terrell that Galil was a Mossad agent.

109—"During the meeting . . .": Scott and Marshall, p. 130.

109—"While Terrell and the Contras . . .": A somewhat sanitized version of this affair appears in the *Iran-Contra Report*, pp. 106–09. The report claims, for instance, that "Terrell admitted that most, and perhaps all, of his information was based on hearsay rather than on his direct participation and observation." As Terrell swore that he was a participant in the conspiracy to murder Pastora, the statement is simply untrue. The *Iran-Contra Report* similarly glosses over the way the Department of Justice later frustrated Jeffrey Feldman's efforts to call a grand jury.

109—" 'You must help me . . . ' ": *The Nation*, Oct. 5, 1985, page 312, "The Carlos File," by Avirgan and Honey.

109—"David believed . . .": Christic Institute, p. 89.

111—"On August 25, 1985 . . .": Owen memo, Aug. 25, 1985, quoted in Cockburn, p. 88.

111—" 'We specifically asked to talk . . . ' ": Cockburn, p. 89.

112—" 'I was a carpenter . . . ' ": *Ibid.*, p. 51.

113—"Five months after the trial . . .": *New Haven Register*, July 27, 1990, "Hasenfus Testifies on Capture by Sandinistas in Nicaragua," by Associated Press; *New York Times*,

July 27, 1990, "Testimony Begins in Lawsuit Over Effort to Aid Contras," by Associated Press; *New Haven Register*, July 27, 1990, "Nitty-Gritty of Iran-Contra Affair Aired in Hasenfus Suit Over Wages," by *Washington Post* syndicate.

113—"The Kerry subcommittee . . .": *New York Times*, Oct. 31, 1987, "A Contra Supplier in Costa Rica Got $375,000, U.S. Agency Says," by Martin Tolchin.

113—"Two and a half years . . .": *New York Times*, Feb. 7, 1989, "Costa Rica Struggles With Enigma: Is Local Hero Also a U.S. Warlord?" by Mark A. Uhlig.

113—"But the next year . . .": *Miami Herald*, Jan. 6, 1990, "Costa Rican Prosecutor Links Two Americans to Fatal Bombing," by John McPhaul.

113—"It issued an extradition . . .": SE ORDENA DETENCIÓN Y EXTRADICIÓN DE IMPUTADA . . . el imputada John Hull Clarke . . . (ARREST AND EXTRADITION OF IMPUTED IS ORDERED . . . the imputed John Hull Clarke . . .)—the Costa Rican extradition order for John Hull, dated Feb. 2, 1990.

113—"Before John Hull left . . .": *The Nation*, Aug. 29, 1987, "The Case of 'Mr. Glenn,' " by Jonathan Kwitny.

13. THE BIG MUFFLER

The main sources for this chapter were the Kerry Subcommittee Report, Leslie Cockburn's *Out of Control*, and *Cocaine Politics* by Peter Dale Scott and Jonathan Marshall. Very helpful too were the Rev. Bill Davis, S.J., and Bill Taylor, private investigators; Daniel Sheehan, founder of the Christic Institute; John Mattes, a Miami lawyer who has been investigating the drugs-and-guns network for years; Anthony Lapham, who once represented the CIA; Thomas Green, who represented defendants Secord, Hakim, Quintero and Clines in the Christic RICO suit; Thomas Spencer, who represented defendants Singlaub and Hull in the same suit; Michael Withey, who represented the Trial Lawyers for Public Justice in the RICO suit; and Morton Staves, who worked on the same suit on behalf of the Center for Constitutional Rights.

115—" 'I have . . . ' ": Interview with Bill Taylor, June 4, 1990, and with Bill Davis Sept. 8, 1993.

115—"The Christic Institute . . .": Sheehan and the Christic Institute case became the target for a large segment of the liberal press during the '80s. Much of the criticism was specious. For example, an article in *Mother Jones* (Feb.-March 1988) ridicules the idea that the "Enterprise" is responsible for "the tide of cocaine that has washed up on American shores since the early 1980s." The trouble with the criticism is that Sheehan never said it was. It has become obvious, though, that the Contras and the CIA did much to increase the flow of cocaine, and statistics on cocaine seized show a huge increase in the drug during the Contra War. *Mother Jones* quotes Tony Avirgan as saying, "The Medellín cartel is bigger than any government in Central America. They didn't need John Hull. They didn't need Costa Rica." That reasoning depends on what is meant by bigness. The oil companies operating in Libya are certainly bigger in monetary resources than the Libyan government. But does anyone believe that one platoon of Qaddafi's infantry couldn't take over the Libyan headquarters of the biggest oil company in the world? Anyone who may think so certainly is not part of any oil company in Libya. Neither the Medellín cartel nor the bigger Cali cartel could supply drug traffickers with anything like the protection they got from the CIA for cooperating with the likes of John Hull. *Mother Jones* also quotes Susan Morgan, a *Newsweek* stringer who was injured at La Penca, as saying some of Sheehan's informants are "compulsive liars." That may be true, but we know that almost all of the people they're accusing are liars. Oliver North admitted he lied—and to Congress, which makes it a felony. And all CIA officers are professional liars by definition.

116—"During the Silkwood case . . .": The people in the Christic Institute named their organization after an essay by the French anthropologist Teilhard de Chardin. "He wrote an essay called 'The Christic,' " said Father Bill Davis, Sheehan's assistant. "Basically it's sort of a hopeful view that evolution is moving toward some kind of higher consciousness and higher unity. Teilhard called it the Christic Force mainly because he was a Christian. He says you can call it evolution or you can call it anything you want, but the idea is that evolution is not random and is moving toward some sort of higher unity. So we took the name from that." See also the *New York Times*, July 20, 1987, "A Liberal Group Makes Waves With Its Contra Lawsuit," by Keith Schneider.

116—". . . Sheehan received a disturbing report . . .": Information on the plot is taken from the affidavit of Daniel P. Sheehan filed Dec. 12, 1986, revised April 1, 1987, supplemented by interviews with investigators William Taylor and William Davis and Daniel P. Sheehan.

117—" 'This investigation . . . ' ": Sheehan affidavit, p. 8.

118—"Sheehan began . . .": *New York Times*, April 30, 1987, "Testimony of a Top Bush Aide Conflicts With North's Notes," by Stephen Engelburg; *New York Times*, March 1, 1989, "Trial of North Stalled Again; Defense Moves for Dismissal," by David Johnson.

119—" 'It took five hours . . . ' ": Cockburn, p. 149.

119—" 'Just found out today . . . ' ": Letter from Carr given to Leslie Cockburn. Cockburn, p. 236.

120—"The police officer . . .": LAPD report dated Dec. 13, 1986, quoted in Cockburn, p. 237.

120—"In April 1987 . . .": Glibbery telephoned Mattes from his prison with the information. Mattes informed Leslie Cockburn. Cockburn, p. 238.

120—"He said he 'learned . . . ' ": Scott and Marshall, pp. 130–31; National Public Radio, "All Things Considered," May 5, 1986; *Kerry Report*, p. 438.

120—"On May 13, 1986 . . .": North Diary; *Kerry Report* pp. 150, 160.

121—"According to the sworn testimony . . .": Scott and Marshall, p. 141; *Iran-Contra Report*, Appendix B, Vol. 20, pp. 837–38.

121—" 'SUBJECT: Terrorist Threat . . . ' ": Scott and Marshall, pp. 142–43; Poindexter deposition, exhibit 44, *Iran-Contra Report*, Appendix A, Vol. 2, p. 1321.

122—"He later told . . .": Scott and Marshall, p. 145; *Iran-Contra Report*, Poindexter deposition, exhibit 45, Appendix A, Vol. 2, p. 1322.

123—"It was a staff memo . . .": Scott and Marshall, p. 151.

123—" 'an ongoing . . . ' ": *Ibid.*, p. 151; *Kerry Report*, pp. 861–63.

124—" 'What the judge did . . . ' ": Interview with John Mattes, July 19, 1990.

125—" 'He [Judge King] entered . . . ' ": Interview with Daniel Sheehan, July 20, 1990.

125—" 'He was clearly convinced . . . ' ": *Ibid*.

125—"Sheehan said . . .": See *New York Times*, March 17, 1989, "Giving Law Teeth (and Using Them on Lawyers)," by Felicity Barringer.

125—"In August 1993, Judge King . . .": *New Haven Register*, October 12, 1993, "Cuban Exiles Arm, Wait for the Day," by Associated Press.

127—" 'It generally turns out . . . ' ": CBS News, "Eye to Eye with Connie Chung," June 17, 1993, " 'Who Killed Colonel Sabow?' "

127—"Navy and marine investigators . . .": *Ibid*.

127—" 'Utter BS . . . ' ": *Ibid*.

127—" 'If all the naval . . . ' ": *Ibid*.

127—"Flights were made . . . ' ": *Ibid*.

128—" 'They never went in . . . ' ": *Ibid*.

128—" 'They not only supply . . . ' ": *Ibid*.

129—" 'The decision to designate . . .' ": *Iran-Contra Affair*, p. 9.

14. THE POLITICIAN AS TOUGH GUY

Agency of Fear by one of America's greatest investigative reporters, Edward Jay Epstein, provided most of the information for this chapter, supplemented by Peter Collier's and David Horowitz's account of an American dynasty, *The Rockefellers*. *Drugs in America: The Case for Victory* by the well-known attorney and writer Vincent T. Bugliosi was another major source. Because so much of the information in this chapter was recorded in the news media, the *New York Times* was also an important source.

136—"The governor's great-grandfather . . .": Epstein, p. 35; Collier and Horowitz, p. 8.

136—"When the government . . .": Epstein, p. 36; Collier and Horowitz, pp. 36, 40–43.

136—"Although a Republican . . .": Epstein, pp. 36–37; Collier and Horowitz, pp. 2–4, 228–43.

137—"As Rockefeller later told . . .": Epstein, p. 38.

138—"If he wanted to terrify . . ." *Ibid*., pp. 40–41.

138—"At one time, he estimated . . .": *Ibid*., p. 42.

138—"In his 1966 . . .": Collier and Horowitz, p. 470.

138—"He pushed a law . . .": *New York Times*, Feb. 24, 1966, "Confinement of Addicts Proposed by Rockefeller," by Bernard Weinraub.

138—"Even Rockefeller's allies . . .": Epstein, p. 42.

138—"That there were practically no . . .": Epstein, p. 39; Collier and Horwitz, pp. 470, 475–76.

138—"When O'Connor called . . .": *New York Times*, Sept. 26, 1966, "O'Connor Assails Narcotics Plan," by Peter Kihss.

138—"Frank O'Connor's election . . .": Epstein, pp. 39–40.

139—"As a Democratic leader . . .": *New York Times*, Nov. 14, 1966, "A 'Major Error' Laid to O'Connor," by Sydney H. Schanberg.

139—"Under the plan . . .": Epstein, p. 43.

139—"In 1973, Rockefeller . . .": *New York Times*, Jan. 4, 1973, "Governor Asks Life Term for Hard-Drugs Pushers and for Violent Addicts," by William E. Farrell; "Rockefeller Cites Need of 'Decisive' Steps to End Lawlessness," by Francis X. Clines; " 'Tough' Stand Stirs Fear on Fate of Civil Liberties," by Lesley Oelsner.

140—"Known as the 'Attila the Hun' law . . .": Epstein, p. 43; Collier and Horowitz, p. 476; *New York Times*, January 4, 1973, "Hard Line in Albany."

140—"Rockefeller, testifying . . .": Epstein, p. 44.

141—" 'Narcotics are a modern curse . . . ' ": *Ibid.*, p. 61.

141—"Egil Krogh, who was to become . . .": *Ibid.*, pp. 65–66.

141—"In 1962, for instance . . .": *Ibid.*, p. 69.

141—"The FBI, he said . . .": *Ibid.*

142—"According to Krogh . . .": *Ibid.*, p. 67.

142—"President Clinton . . .": "Clinton/Gore on Crime and Drugs," position paper published by the Clinton/Gore '92 Committee.

143—"Although President Bill Clinton . . .": *Hartford Courant*, Oct. 8, 1993, Editorial: "Drug War Continues Off Course."

143—"On June 15, 1988 . . .": Bugliosi, pp. 36–37.

143—"Barry Seal testified . . .": *Ibid.*, p. 34.

143—"And California Bureau of Narcotics Enforcement Special Agent . . .": *Ibid.*, p. 32.

15. U.S.A.: THE SMUGGLERS' DELIGHT

Four books were especially helpful in preparing this chapter: Edward Jay Epstein's *Agency of Fear*, which covers the Nixon Administration's early interdiction efforts, including its pressure on Turkey to eliminate the opium poppy; *Undoing Drugs*, Daniel K. Benjamin's and Roger Leroy Miller's treatise on the economics of drug trafficking; Elliot Currie's *Reckoning*, which, among its other virtues, has reliable statistics on drug use and its consequences; and *Cocaine Politics* by Peter Dale Scott and Jonathan Marshall, which had been so helpful in previous chapters.

144—"If you consider . . .": See Weir, *Written with Lead*, pp. ix-xi, for a discussion of the U.S. homicide rate.

144—"The Bureau of Narcotics and Dangerous Drugs . . .": Epstein, pp. 109–10.

144—" 'The estimate makes . . . ' ": *Ibid.*, pp. 174–77.

145—"In 1970, New York Police Commissioner . . .": Epstein, pp. 175–76; *New York Times*, Oct. 1, 1973, "Narcotics Arrests Drop 75% in City," by M. A. Farber.

145—"Dr. Richard S. Wilbur . . .": Epstein, p. 176.

145—"In 1985, before the flow of drugs . . .": Currie, p. 28.

146—"In 1981, for instance . . .": Bugliosi, p. 28.

146—"The street value of a kilo . . .": *Ibid.*, p. 29.

146—"Just what the rate . . .": Musto discusses estimates of the addiction rate. He says:

Narcotics are assumed to cause a large percentage of crime, but the political conve-
nience of this allegation and the surrounding imagery suggest fear of certain minorities and make one suspicious of this popular assumption. During the last seventy-five
years, responsible officials have stated that narcotics caused between fifty and seventy-
five percent of all crime, especially in large cities like New York. Narcotics have been
blamed for a variety of America's ills, from crime waves to social disharmony. Their
bad effects have been given as the excuse for certain minorities, as evidence for stopping legal heroin maintenance in 1919, and as evidence for starting legal heroin maintenance in 1972.

Like the speculated percentage of crimes caused by narcotics use and sales, the
number of addicts estimated for the nation appears often to have been exaggerated.
Peaks of overestimation have come before or at the time of the most repressive measures against narcotics use, as in 1919 when a million or more addicts and five million
Parlor Reds were said to threaten the United States. Both groups were the object of
severe penalties, although in retrospect both figures appear to have been enormously
inflated (p. 246).

And again:

The number of addicts in the U.S. is a very difficult figure to arrive at. One problem
is the definition of an addict, for there are at least two major categories of those who
use narcotics in a regular fashion, the hard-core addict who requires daily opiates to
hold off abstinence symptoms, and the occasional users who can stop without any
significant symptoms. There is another category of "addict" composed of individuals
who are not taking enough opiates to create the possibility of an abstinence syndrome
but who believe they are. These individuals are dependent on addict life style or even
simple needle injections, although physiologically they could not be classified as addicts.

Given these qualifications, most authors who have closely studied the question of
addict-population in the past (Wilbert, Terry, Pellens, Kolb, DuMez, Lindesmith) tend
to agree that there was a peak in addiction around 1900 and that in the teens of this
century the number began to decrease and reached a relatively small number (about
100,000) in the 1920s. The peak might be 200,000 to 400,000 in 1900. A peak of drug
use in 1919 reported by New York City and Federal officials which estimated the total
in the U.S. seems highly unlikely. It seems reasonable to maintain that the decline in
opiate use after 1900 continued. What actually increased was the fear directed at addiction by officials and the public. In general, exaggerated fear of the number of narcotics addicts have reflected public concern rather than actual numbers. Nevertheless,
the number in the U.S. seems to have exceeded in the twentieth century the per capita
rate in other Western nations and without question was so perceived by the Federal
government until the 1920s, when the admission became an embarrassment (pp.
253–54, note 13).

147—"Every year . . .": Benjamin and Miller, p. 38.

147—"Heroin is worth . . .": *Ibid.*, p. 36.

147—"The plan, devised by . . .": *Ibid.*, pp. 81–85.

148—"It arrives . . .": Bugliosi, p. 31.

148—"Take a typical . . .": Benjamin and Miller, p. 37; see also *New York Times*, April
29, 1990, "Bypassing Borders, More Drugs Flood Ports," by Joseph B. Treaster.

149—"In the late '80s . . .": Benjamin and Miller, p. 37.

149—"One expert . . .": Benjamin and Miller, p. 38; *Wall Street Journal*, Aug. 10, 1989, "Federal War on Drugs is Scattershot Affair, With Dubious Progress," by Paul M. Barrett.

149—"A veteran customs agent . . .": Benjamin and Miller, p. 38; *Miami Herald*, Dec. 18, 1989, "In Drug War, Crafty Smugglers Stay a Step Ahead."

149—"According to Anthony Bocchichio . . .": Benjamin and Miller, p. 38; *Ibid.*

149—" 'There are places . . . ' ": Benjamin and Miller, p. 39.

149—"An ounce of cocaine . . .": *Ibid.*, p. 36.

150—" 'To show you how . . . ' ": Epstein, p. 91.

150—"Turkey, though, produced . . .": *Ibid.*, p. 86.

151—"Twenty-five square miles . . .": Benjamin and Miller, p. 32.

151—"At present . . .": Benjamin and Miller, p. 31; *The Drug Policy Letter*, No. 3, "Dire Economics Drive Cocaine Production," by Susan Hamilton Saavedra.

151—"But because no one . . .": Most poppy producers and coca cultivators depend on the plant to prevent starvation. From Pakistan to Peru, they will fight to the death to protect their crops.

151—"In 1986, President Ronald Reagan . . .": *New York Times*, June 8, 1986, "Bush Discloses Secret Order Citing Drugs as Security Peril," by Neil A. Lewis.

152—"Defense Secretary Dick Cheney . . .": Scott and Marshall, p. 2; *Los Angeles Times*, Dec. 15, 1989.

152—"This yearning . . .": and all quotations from Representative Solarz and Senators Cohen and Kerry; Scott and Marshall, pp. 2–3.

153—" 'Getting help from the military . . . ' ": Scott and Marshall, p. 3; *Los Angeles Times*, Dec. 15, 1989.

153—" 'Whatever the merits . . . ' ": Bugliosi, p. 78.

154—"As a precedent . . .": For a brief history of the Villa raid and the subsequent pursuit, see Weir, *Written With Lead*, pages 171–87.

155—" 'Traffickers in Cali . . .": Scott and Marshall, p. 81.

156—"At present, the most potent . . .": Benjamin and Miller, p. 33, quoting Mark A. R. Keiman, *Marijuana: Costs of Abuse, Costs of Control*, New York, Greenwood Press: 1989. Sinsemilla (without seeds) marijuana is the female plant which has been kept isolated from the male plant so there is no fertilization.

156—"Even in the present . . .": *New Haven Register*, Oct. 9, 1993, syndicated column by Jack Anderson.

157—"Heroin addicts also . . .": Benjamin and Miller, p. 44; *New Haven Register*, July 19, 1993, "New 'Killer' Heroin Hits State," by Associated Press; *New York Times*, Oct. 24, 1989, "Effort to Control Use of Chemicals for Illegal Drugs," by Malcolm W. Browne.

16. STIMULATING THE MARKET

Two books were most valuable sources for this chapter. *Reckoning*, by Elliott Currie, takes a long look at the causes of the drug problem in America's inner cities. It's particularly valuable because it is based on the work of social scientists who have lived with, and studied close-up the various types of addicts and traffickers in impoverished sections of large cities. *Undoing Drugs*, by Daniel K. Benjamin and Roger Leroy Miller, is bursting with facts about the drug situation in the United States.

The U.S. Justice Department's Bureau of Justice Statistics publishes annually *The Sourcebook of Criminal Justice Statistics*, an invaluable tool for anyone studying crime in the United States. It was most helpful in this and following chapters. Robert Stutman's *Dead on Delivery*, concentrating as it does on recent cases, was also very helpful. Readers will have noticed that the subject matter of the chapters is gradually becoming more contemporary. As it progresses, therefore, newspapers, magazines and television documentaries are becoming more important sources.

158—"In the '60s . . .": Currie, pp. 60–63.

158—" 'They are actively . . . ' ": *Ibid.*, p. 61.

159—"One addict . . .": *Ibid.*

159—"The lure of heroin . . .": *Ibid.*, p. 62.

159—" 'Given the social . . . ' ": *Ibid.*, p. 63.

159—" 'Drugs,' one druggie told . . .": *Ibid.*

160—"A gang of Dominican . . .": Benjamin and Miller, pp. 90–91; *New York Times Magazine*, Oct. 1, 1989, "Crack's Destructive Sprint Across America," by Michael Massing.

161—"In 1986, according . . .": Benjamin and Miller, p. 122; *U.S. News and Word Report*, Oct. 1, 1990, "More Unsafe Sex and AIDS."

161—"Hong Kong . . .": Benjamin and Miller, p. 122.

162—"Crack babies . . .": *Ibid.*, p. 126; *New York Times*, June 17, 1990, "How Much is a Baby Worth?" by A. M. Rosenthal.

162—"According to the National Institute . . .": Currie, pp. 22–27; also Bureau of Justice Statistics, *Fact Sheet: Drug Data Summary*, p. 3.

163—". . . 'mainstream Americans . . . ' ": Currie, p. 24.

163—"Another survey . . .": Bureau of Justice Statistics, *Fact Sheet: Drug Use Trends*, p. 3, table 2.

163—"In 1989, about 40 percent . . .": Benjamin and Miller, p. 47; *U.S. News and World Report*, Sept. 18, 1989, "Drugs and White America," by David R. Gergen.

164—"Monsignor Joseph Potter . . .": *New York Times*, Feb. 14, 1993, "Drug Trade Links Bridgeport and Its Suburbs," by Fred Musante.

164—"In 1982 . . .": Bureau of Justice Statistics, *Fact Sheet: Drug Data Summary*, p. 1.

164—"When George Rivera . . .": See Stutman, pp. 194–205, for a history of Boy George.

164—"Arrested the same year . . .": Benjamin and Miller, pp. 48, 100–02; *Wall Street Journal*, Nov. 13, 1989, "How a 24–Year-Old Became a Local Hero Until His Drug Arrest," by Joe Davidson.

166—"Three quarters of all . . .": Benjamin and Miller, p. 3.

167—"According to Dan Stebbins . . .": *Connecticut* magazine, Jan. 1994, "Life with the Latin Kings," by Karon Haller, p. 49.

17. DRUGS AND VIOLENCE

Dr. Deborah Prothrow-Stith, whose greatest interests are public health and the welfare of people in the inner cities, was particularly helpful here. Her *Deadly Consequences* presents the viewpoint of ordinary people—not gangsters—particularly minority people, who live in the middle of big cities. Elliott Currie's *Reckoning* covers much the same ground from a slightly different viewpoint. *Gun Control*, edited by Charles P. Cozic, looks at that one issue from about every possible viewpoint. *The Samurai, the Mountie and the Cowboy*, by David R. Kopel examines gun laws in several countries and how they reflect each nation's culture. The Bureau of Justice Statistics' *Sourcebook* and bulletins were invaluable.

168—"The August 2, 1993 . . .": *Time*, Aug. 2, 1993, "A Boy and His Gun," by Jon D. Hull, pp. 20–24.

169—"In 1964 . . .": *Sourcebook*, p. 381, table 3.133.

169—"If I'd have gone to jail . . .": Interview with inmate of rehabilitation center, Aug. 1988.

170—"A study of murders . . ." *Sourcebook*, page 387, table 3.140

170—"The statistics on murder . . .": *Sourcebook*, pp. 386–87, table 3.139.

171—" 'I believe that if all . . . ' ": Prothrow-Stith, p. 157.

172—"Dr. Brandon S. Centerwall . . .": *American Rifleman*, July 1993, "TV Violence: Does It Cause Real-Life Mayhem?" by Susan R. Lamson, pp. 32–33.

173—"Further, there is . . .": Kopel, pp. 20–58, 413.

174—"Britain also had . . .": "Gun Control in Other Nations: An Overview," by Charlotte A. Carter-Yamauchi in *Gun Control*, pp. 240–41. See also Kopel, pp. 59–135.

174—"Switzerland and Israel . . .": *Ibid.*; also "Israel Has a Successful Gun Control Policy," by Abraham N. Tennenbaum in *Gun Control*, pp. 248–51; Kopel, pp. 278–302.

175—"The study compared . . .": "Gun Control Wouldn't Reduce Crime," by Robert W. Lee in *Gun Control*, p. 51; Kopel, pp. 151, 153–55, 182–83.

175—" 'Criminal Activity' . . .": *Sourcebook*, p. 387, table 3.140.

176—"Nevertheless, blacks . . .": *Ibid.*, p. 390, table 3.143.

176—"Dr. William Julius Wilson . . .": Prothrow-Stith, p. 17.

176—" 'If you've got an individual . . . ' ": *Connecticut* magazine, Jan. 1994, "Inside the Latin Kings," by Karon Haller, p. 50.

177—"In the early part . . .": Prothrow-Stith, pp. 71–72.

177—"Here's how the percentages . . .": *Hartford Courant*, Nov. 1, 1993, "Illegitimate Births are a Major National Tragedy," by George F. Will.

177—"In *Manchild in the Promised Land* . . .": Prothrow-Stith, p. 53.

177—"In Boston . . .": *Ibid.*, p. 122.

178—" 'The police are . . . ' ": *Ibid.*, p. 87, quoting from an essay by a student at Boston's Burke High School.

178—"In 1989, a black . . .": *Ibid.*, p. 122.

178—"Then there was Lorenzo Ricketts . . .": *Connecticut magazine*, April 1989, "A Black and White Affair," by William Weir, pp. 152–58.

179—"There has always been an underclass . . .": For a history of the underclass in the largest U.S. city, see *The Gangs of New York*, by Herbert Asbury.

180—"The average ghetto resident . . .": The word "ghetto" as used in this book does not refer to the walled areas of European cities used to confine Jews, but to urban areas predominantly inhabited by a single ethnic group, usually African-Americans.

180—"Sociologists Roderick and Deborah . . .": Cited in Curry, pp. 141–42.

181—" 'If somebody messes . . . ' ": Currie, p. 175.

181—" ' . . . don't care about nothing . . .": *Ibid.*

181—" 'I likes to bust . . . ' ": *Ibid.*

182—"In the fourteen-to-seventeen . . ." *Sourcebook*, p. 392, table 3.147.

182—"Medical examiners in Washington . . .": Prothrow-Stith, pp. 117–18.

182—"In New York . . .": *Ibid.*, p. 118.

183—" '*First*, criminals . . .' " *Ibid.*

18. GANGLAND REVISITED

As might be expected, information on a subject as fast-changing as "gangland" came mostly from newspapers and magazines. Benjamin and Miller, however, also have excellent information on the background of such organizations as the Jamaican posses and the Los Angeles-based Crips and Bloods federations.

184—"On November 1, 1993 . . .": *New York Times*, Oct. 31, 1993, "Modern 'Fagins' Admit to Series of Bank Robberies," by Robert Reinhold.

185—"One such gang . . .": *Hartford Courant*, Nov. 21, 1993, "A Corner Where Crack is King," by Edmund Mahony.

188—"In 1980, Jamaica . . .": Benjamin and Miller, pp. 92–94. Seaga has been denounced by his opponents as CIAga, Kopel, p. 268.

189—"Today they control . . .": Benjamin and Miller, p. 93; *New York Times Magazine*, Oct. 1, 1989, "Crack's Destructive Sprint Across America," by Michael Massing.

189—"According to the U.S. Bureau . . .": Benjamin and Miller, p. 93; *New York Times Magazine*, Oct. 1, 1989, *op. cit.*

190—"These 'trademark' murders . . .": Benjamin and Miller, p. 93.

190—"In 1986, a federal organized crime . . .": *Ibid.*, p. 95; also *Police Chief* 55 (1), "The Kansas City Experience: 'Crack' Organized Crime Cooperative Task Force," by David Barton, pp. 28–31.

191—"Today, kids born and raised . . .": *New York Times*, Jan. 31, 1993, "Teenage Gangs are Inflicting Violence on Small Cities," by Erik Ekholm.

192—"To complicate things . . .": *Ibid.*

19. THE TROUBLE WITH TOUGHNESS

As this is being written, President Clinton's crime bill with its emphasis on "tougher" penalties and law enforcement has just been signed into law. For most of 1993 and the beginning of 1994, crime has become a major media topic—even though there was less serious crime in 1993 than in the previous year.

Consequently, "getting tough" on crime is currently a very hot topic, and the sources most used for this chapter are newspapers and magazines. Thanks to national wire services and syndicates, a reader gets almost the same news everywhere. The papers most used here are those regularly read by the author: the *New York Times*, the *Hartford Courant* and the *New Haven Register*.

195—"On April 16, 1993 . . .": *New York Times*, April 17, 1993, "Two Federal Judges in Protest," by Joseph B. Treaster.

195—" 'People think . . . ' ": *Ibid.*

195—"Judge Weinstein . . .": *Ibid.*

196—"One of these . . .": *Ibid.*

196—"At the federal . . .": *Ibid.*

196—" 'Each year . . . ' ": *New York Times*, April 24, 1993, "Dethrone the Drug Czar," by Whitman Knapp.

197—"If drugs were federally . . .": *Ibid.*

198—"For example, a formula just recommended . . .": Interview with William Flower, spokesman for the Connecticut Department of Correction, Jan. 31, 1994.

198—"In Florida, almost 2,000 . . .": *New Haven Register*, Aug. 23, 1993, "Mandatory Sentences Filling Jails," by Jack Anderson.

199—"A few years ago . . .": Benjamin and Miller, p. 78, quoting U.S. Sentencing Commission, *Supplementary Report on the Initial Sentencing Guidelines and Policy Statements*, p. 72.

199—"In 1991 . . .": *Hartford Courant*, Jan. 24, 1994, "Begin the Debate on Legalization of Drugs," by Jerry V. Wilson (former Washington, D.C., police chief).

199—" 'Early in the year . . . ' " *New Haven Register*, Aug. 23, 1993, "Mandatory Sentences Filling Jails," by Jack Anderson.

199—"Pat Sullivan, sheriff . . .": *Denver Post*, March 13, 1993, "Sentencing Bill's Death Riles Sheriff."

199—"Sullivan said . . .": *Ibid.*

200—"An American Bar Association . . .": *New York Times*, Feb. 14, 1993, "Bar Group Sees Overemphasis on Drug Cases," by Associated Press.

200—"The number of adults . . .": *Ibid.*

200—"Sheriff Sullivan has . . .": *Denver Post*, March 12, 1993, "Education Programs Cut at County Jail."

200—" 'While many Democrats . . . ' ": *New Haven Register*, Aug. 23, 1993, "Mandatory Sentences Filling Jails," by Jack Anderson.

200—"Texas senator . . .": *Ibid.*

201—"He wrote . . .": *Hartford Courant*, Sept. 12, 1993, "Federal Sentencing Rules Often Judged Unfair," by Matthew Kauffman.

201—"Then there's Tonya Drake . . .": *Time*, Feb. 7, 1994, ". . . And Throw Away the Key," by Ann Blackman, Cathy Booth, Jon D. Hull, Sylvester Monroe and Lisa H. Towle, p. 55.

202—"Nicole Richardson . . .": *USA Weekend*, Jan. 14–16, 1994, "Debate: Throw Out the Key? No: 'Cookie Cutter' is Counter Productive," by Victor Kamber.

202—"At least two countries . . .": Benjamin and Miller, pp. 56–57.

202—" 'The joint? . . . ' ": Currie, p. 160.

203—"Another dealer . . .": *Ibid.*, p. 161.

203—" 'You have to realize . . . ' ": *Connecticut* magazine, Jan. 1994, "Inside the Latin Kings," by Karon Haller, p. 49.

203—"Sociologist Jeffrey Fagan . . .": Currie, p. 158.

203—" 'They learn this trade . . . ' ": *Time*, Feb. 7, 1994, " . . . And Throw Away the Key," by Ann Blackman, Cathy Booth, Jon D. Hull, Sylvester Monroe and Lisa H. Towle, p. 55.

204—"Robert Gangi . . .": *Ibid.*

204—"There's another practical objection . . .": *The New Yorker*, Jan. 24, 1994, "Comment: A Minium of Sense," p. 7.

204—"The maximum penalty . . .": Currie, p. 191.

205—"One solution . . .": *New York Times*, Dec. 18, 1993, "As Boot Camps for Criminals Multiply, Skepticism Grows," by Adam Nossiter.

205—"One of these, Governor Zell Miller . . .": *Ibid.*

206—"A study by Doris L. MacKenzie . . .": *Ibid.*

206—"But according to William Jenkins, Jr. . . .": *Ibid.*

206—"The recidivism rates . . .": *Ibid.*

207—"As Benjamin and Miller point out . . .": Benjamin and Miller, pp. 108, 86–87.

207—"In Texas, it's . . .": *New York Times Index*, 1969, chart, p. 554.

20. CLOGGING THE WHEELS OF JUSTICE

Once again, Benjamin and Miller's *Undoing Drugs* proved invaluable. The authors, conservative economists, have a keen appreciation of how much damage the War on Drugs is doing to the civil-justice system of this country and how this is hurting not only all business but all taxpayers.

The other invaluable source was the U.S. Department of Justice's Bureau of Justice Statistics. The Bureau's periodic bulletins and its *Sourcebook* give an unmatched picture of the whole U.S. criminal justice system.

208—"In 1990 . . .": Bugliosi, p. 21.

208—"Individual prosecutors . . .": Benjamin and Miller, p. 83; *New York Times*, Aug. 24, 1990, "Volunteer Prosecutors and Backlog of Drug Cases," by Robb London.

208—"King County . . .": Benjamin and Miller, pp. 83–84; *New York Times*, Aug. 24, 1990, "Volunteer Prosecutors and Backlog of Drug Cases," by Robb London.

209—"In some urban centers . . .": Benjamin and Miller, p. 86.

209—"In Manhattan . . .": *Ibid.*, p. 82.

210—"A decade ago . . .": *Ibid.*

210—"In some federal courts . . .": *Ibid.*

210—"Benjamin and Miller cite . . .": *Ibid.*, p. 81.

210—"Nationwide . . .": *Ibid.*, p. 86.

210—"A survey by . . .": Bureau of Justice Statistics, *Fact Sheet: Drug Data Summary*, p. 1.

211—"Benjamin and Miller cite . . .": Benjamin and Miller, pp. 80–81.

212—"According to the Bureau . . .": Bureau of Justice Statistics, Bulletin: *Census of State and Local Law Enforcement Agencies, 1992*, p. 1.

21. THE POLICE STATE AND THE STATE OF THE POLICE

The Branch Davidian case is probably too recent to have resulted in a book-length analysis. The other two incidents that start this chapter, the siege of Randy Weaver and the burning of MOVE, have not been popular subjects for books. One exception is the account of the Weaver case *From Freedom to Slavery*, a *cri de coeur* from one of the nation's most distinguished lawyers, Gerry Spence.

There are probably a number of reasons for the national tendency to overlook atrocities committed in the name of law enforcement.

One may be the prevalence of cop shows on television, which often show the heroes taking the law into their own hands and ending up with their ill-grounded suspicions justified.

Another may be the national infatuation with spectator sports. People identify with the police the way they identify with their favorite football teams. The fans hop up and down in the stands chanting "We're number one!" Actually "we" (the fans) have done nothing but buy tickets to see their hired gladiators confront someone else's hired gladiators. When they see the police chastising dirty, disrespectful or antisocial oddballs, they feel that they are doing it too.

A third reason, almost certainly, is that the victims of this abuse are usually associated in the popular mind with that boogeyman, the Dope Fiend.

At any rate, most of the information in this chapter came from newspapers, magazines and television documentaries, all of which presented the information either as the action was happening or fairly soon after, or from interviews.

214—"On Sunday, February 28 . . .": Information on the Branch Davidian raid and siege came principally from accounts in the *New York Times*, the *New Haven Register* and the *Hartford Courant* between March 1 and Oct. 9, 1993, and accounts of the trial of the survivors beginning Jan. 13, 1994.

215—"According to Charles Richards . . .": *New Haven Register*, March 1, 1993, "Agents Killed in Gun Battle with Texas Cult," by Charles Richards.

215—"Months later . . .": *New York Times*, Jan. 30, 1994, "Lift For Defense in Cultists' Trial."

215—"At the trial . . .": *Ibid.*

216—"It turned out . . .": *New York Times*, March 28, 1993, "U.S. Agents Say Raid on Sect in Waco was Full of Miscalculations."

216—"Six of the survivors . . .": *New Haven Register*, April 23, 1993, "Cult Failed to Realize its Danger," by Associated Press.

216—"But Dr. Nizam Peerwani . . .": *Ibid.* Later, other officials claimed to have seen bullet wounds on the bodies, and Peerwani's initial statement was forgotten.

217—" 'I guess what it does . . . ' ": *New Haven Register*, May 13, 1993, "Cult Member's Lawyer Objects to Bulldozing," by Associated Press.

217—"Attorney General Janet Reno . . .": *New Haven Register*, April 22, 1993, "40 Bodies Found in Compound," by Associated Press.

218—"The earlier raid . . .": Information on the Randy Weaver incident came from Gerry Spence in his book, *From Freedom to Slavery*; the *American Rifleman*, Nov., 1993 article, "The Randy Weaver Case," by Jim Oliver; and from *The New York Times* issues of March 13, Aug. 22–31 and Sept. 1 and 17 of 1992, and of July 7, 9 and 12 of 1993.

218—"They're not uncommon . . .": the author, federal beat reporter for the old *Topeka State Journal* in 1954–55, recalls several sawed-off shotgun cases.

220—"According to Sara Weaver . . ." *American Rifleman*, "The Randy Weaver Case," by Jim Oliver, p. 43, quoting Sara Weaver's account in the Moscow, Idaho, *Spokesman Review*.

220—" 'My name is . . . ' ": Spence, p. 4.

221—"After the trial . . .": Oliver, p. 43.

224—"Spence put it . . .": Spence, p. 7.

224—"In his *Dead on Delivery* . . ." Stutman, p. 149.

225—". . . more than a suspicion . . .": Benjamin and Miller, p. 146.

226—"It has been estimated . . .": *Ibid.*, p. 134.

227—" 'The crime of selling drugs . . . ' ": *Ibid.*, p. 87.

227—" 'There were at least . . .": Interview with Ralph Clifford, March 1987.

227—"Glen Williamson . . .": Benjamin and Miller, p. 137.

228—"Bruce Lavoie . . .": *Ibid.*

228—"Then there was Jeffrey Miles . . .": *Ibid.*

228—"The U.S. Supreme Court . . .": Benjamin and Miller, p. 139, paraphrasing *U.S. v. Hernandez*, 473 U.S. 531 (1985).

228—"In Florida . . .": Benjamin and Miller, p. 136.

228—"In New Mexico . . .": *Ibid.*; *U.S.A. Today*, Nov. 15, 1989, "Some Worry Police 'Out of Control,' " by Tony Mauro.

228—"Joseph Huberman ...": Benjamin and Miller, p. 138; *New York Times*, April 5, 1990, *"Marijuana McCarthyism,"* by Peter Gorman.

229—"Police in Detroit ...": Benjamin and Miller, pp. 143–44; *U.S.A. Today*, Nov. 15, 1989, "Some Worry Police 'out of Control,' " by Tony Mauro.

229—"Then there was Willy Jones ..." CBS News, "60 Minutes," Aug. 8, 1993, "You're Under Arrest," from Burrelle's Information Service Transcripts.

231—"The same program ...": *Ibid.*

231—"Donald A. Regan ...": *New Haven Register*, Feb. 6, 1993, "The Innocent As Well As the Guilty are Snared by Civil Forfeiture Statutes," by Jack Anderson.

231—"In February, it ruled ...": *Hartford Courant*, Dec. 14, 1993, "Court Again Limits Seizures in Drug Cases," by David G. Savage, *Los Angeles Times* Syndicate.

232—" 'The right to prior notice ... ' ": *Ibid.*

232—"The U.S. Coast Guard ...": Benjamin and Miller, p. 139; *Wall Street Journal*, April 30, 1990, "Searches for Drugs Roil Boaters," by Arthur S. Hayes.

232—"Craig Klein ...": Benjamin and Miller, p. 140; *Wall Street Journal*, April 30, 1990, "Searches for Drugs Roil Boaters," by Arthur S. Hayes.

233—"Burton Weinstein ...": Interview with Burton Weinstein, March 1987.

233—"Federal [civil rights] enforcement ...": Interview with John Williams, March 1987.

233—"John Williams ...": *Ibid.*

234—"There were bad apples ...": PBS "Frontline," Dec. 14, 1993, "Behind the Badge," Journal Graphics transcript.

234—"Judge Mollen ...": *Ibid.*

234—"Yerku himself ...": *Ibid.*

235—"The *New York Times* sent ...": *New York Times*, Oct. 10, 1993, "Tales of Police Corruption Not Surprising, 46th Precinct Residents Say," by Craig Wolff.

235—" 'That's my precinct ...": *Ibid.*

235—"He said, 'Why ... ' ": *Ibid.*

235—"John Brittain ...": Interview with John Brittain, March 1987

236—"Walter Yerku ...": PBS "Frontline," Dec. 14, 1993, "Behind the Badge," Journal Graphics transcript.

237—"A typical Operation Liberty ..." *Hartford Courant*, Oct. 2, 1993, "Fighting the Gangs by Any Means," by Matthew Kauffman.

238—" 'If violence is going up ... ' " *New Haven Register*, Jan. 3, 1994, "Murder Rate Plunges," by Thomas Pelton.

22. LOOKING BACK

This chapter is a summary of the earlier chapters, so almost all of the sources have already been listed. Two small pieces of new information appear in the second section.

245—"In one year alone . . ." Benjamin and Miller, p. 69.

245—"According to a former . . ." Bugliosi, pp. 195, 269.

23. LOOKING FORWARD

Against Excess by Mark A.R. Kleiman was particularly helpful for this chapter. Kleiman is associate professor of public policy at the John F. Kennedy School of Government of Harvard University and a former drug-policy analyst at the U.S. Department of Justice. Perhaps because of his background, he favors the legal prohibition of all drugs on the Controlled Substances Act list, even though some, by his own showing, are less dangerous than two legal drugs, alcohol and tobacco. He does, however, know a lot about drugs, and he mentions some very imaginative answers to the country's drug problem.

The other important source book was *Reckoning* by Elliott Currie. Currie is a sociologist, and he recommends treating addiction as a social problem. That approach has much to be said for it, as no other approach seems to give generally satisfactory results. The trouble with the "social problem" approach is that it is expensive, hard and slow. So much so that it's been little used. But if getting rid of the drug problem were easy, it would have been done long ago.

249—"Carlos Lehder . . .": Gugliotto and Leen, *Kings of Cocaine*, pp. 48–49.

250—"Or consider . . .": Currie, pp. 234–35.

250—"Earlier, Charles Winick . . .": Currie, pp. 232–33.

250—"Q. How many drug counselors . . .": Kleiman, p. 164.

251—"In one research project . . .": *Ibid.*, pp. 216, 434.

251—"In laboratory tests . . .": *Ibid.*, p. 295.

258—"Stutman got to . . .": Stutman, p. 85.

259—" 'When I got home . . . ' ": Interview, Aug. 1988.

259—"According to Elliott Currie . . .": Currie, pp. 214–15.

260—"Comparing drug addiction . . .": Currie, p. 216.

BIBLIOGRAPHY

BOOKS

Allen, Everett S. *The Black Ships: Rumrunners of Prohibition*, Boston: Little, Brown, 1979.

Allen, Frederick Lewis. *The Big Change*, New York: Harper & Brothers, 1952.

———. *Only Yesterday: An Informal History of the Nineteen-Twenties*, New York: Blue Ribbon Books, 1931.

Anderson, Scott and Anderson, Jon Lee. *Inside the League: The Shocking Expose of How Terrorists, Nazis and Latin American Death Squads Have Infiltrated the World Anti-Communist League*, New York: Dodd, Mead, 1986.

Asbury, Herbert. *The Gangs of New York: An Informal History of the New York Underworld*, New York: Dorset Press, 1989.

Ashmore, Harry S. and Baggs, William C. *Mission to Hanoi: A Chronicle of Double-Dealing in High Places*, New York: G. P. Putnam, 1968.

Bakeless, John. *Turncoats, Traitors and Heroes*, Philadelphia: J. P. Lippincott, 1959.

Barry, Tom and Preusch, Deb. *The Soft War: The Uses and Abuses of U.S. Economic Aid to Central America*, New York: Grove Press, 1988.

Beebe, Lucius and Clegg, Charles. *The American West*, New York: E. P. Dutton, 1955.

Benjamin, Daniel K. and Miller, Roger Leroy. *Undoing Drugs: Beyond Legalization*, New York: Basic Books, 1991.

Bradlee, Ben, Jr. *Guts and Glory*, New York: D.I. Fine, 1988.

Brewton, Pete. *The Mafia, CIA & George Bush: The Untold Story of America's Greatest Financial Debacle*, New York: Shapolsky Publishers, 1992.

Buckley, Kevin. *Panama: The Whole Story*, New York: Simon and Schuster, 1991.

Bugliosi, Vincent T. *Drugs in America: The Case for Victory, A Citizen's Call for Action*, New York: Knightsbridge, 1991.

Burdick, Thomas and Mitchell, Charlene. *Blue Thunder: How the Mafia Owned and Finally Murdered Cigarette Boat King Donald Aronow*, New York: Simon and Schuster, 1990.

Bureau of Justice Statistics, U.S. Department of Justice. *Sourcebook of Justice Statistics—1992*, Washington: U.S. Government Printing Office, 1993.

Cashman, Sean Dennis. *Prohibition: The Lie of the Land*, New York: Macmillan, 1981.

Christian, Shirley. *Nicaragua: Revolution in the Family*, New York: Vintage Books, 1986.

Cockburn, Leslie. *Out of Control: The Story of the Reagan Administration's Secret War in Nicaragua, the Illegal Arms Pipeline, and the Contra Drug Connection*, New York: Atlantic Monthly Press, 1987.

Cohen, William S. and Mitchell, George J. *Men of Zeal: A Candid Inside Story of the Iran-Contra Hearings*, New York: Penguin, 1989.

Colby, William with Peter Forbath. *Honorable Men: My Life in the CIA*, New York: Simon and Schuster, 1978.

Collier, Peter and Horowitz, David. *The Rockefellers: An American Dynasty*, New York: Holt, Rinehart and Winston, 1976.

Cooke, Alistair, ed., *The Vintage Mencken*, New York: Vintage Books, 1955.

Corson, William R. *The Armies of Ignorance: The Rise of the American Intelligence Empire*, New York: Dial, 1977.

Cozic, Charles P. and Wekesser, Carol, ed. *Gun Control*, San Diego: Greenhaven Press, 1992.

Crittenden, Ann. *Sanctuary: A Story of American Conscience and Law in Collision*, New York: Weidenfeld & Nicolson, 1988.

Currie, Elliott. *Reckoning: Drugs, the Cities, and the American Future*, New York: Hill and Wang, 1993.

Curry, Cecil B. *Edward Lansdale: The Unquiet American*, Boston: Houghton Mifflin, 1988.

Dickey, Christopher. *With the Contras: A Reporter in the Wilds of Nicaragua*, New York: Simon and Schuster, 1985.

Draper, Theodore. *A Very Thin Line: The Iran-Contra Affairs*, New York: Simon and Schuster, 1991.

Duster, Troy. *The Legislation of Morality: Law, Drugs and Moral Judgment*, New York: Free Press, 1970.

Effros, William G., ed. *Quotations Vietnam: 1945–1970*, New York: Random House, 1970.

English, T. J. *The Westies: Inside the Hell's Kitchen Irish Mob*, New York: G.P. Putnam's Sons, 1990.

Epstein, Edward Jay. *Agency of Fear*, New York: G.P. Putnam's Sons, 1977.

———. *Deception: The Invisible War Between the KGB and the CIA*, New York: Simon and Schuster, 1989.

Farwell, Byron. *Queen Victoria's Little Wars*, London: W.W. Norton, 1972.

Fitzgerald, Frances. *Fire in the Lake: The Vietnamese and the Americans in Vietnam*, New York: Random House, 1973.

Fried, Arthur. *The Rise and Fall of the Jewish Gangster in America*, New York: Holt, Rhinehart and Winston, 1980.

Gentry, Curt. *J. Edgar Hoover: The Man and the Secrets*, New York: W.W. Norton, 1991.

Gettleman, Marvin E., Lacefield, Patrick, Menashe, Louis and Mermelstein, David, eds. *El Salvador: Central America in the New Cold War*, New York: Grove Press, 1987.

Gettleman, Marvin E., ed. *Viet Nam: History, Documents, and Opinions on a Major World Crisis*, Greenwich, CT: Fawcett Publications, 1965.

Golden, Renny and McConnell, Michael. *Sanctuary: The New Underground Railroad*, Maryknoll, NY: Orbis Books, 1986.

Goodrich, L. Carrington. *A Short History of the Chinese People*, New York: Harper & Row, 1959.

Goulden, Joseph C. *The Death Merchant: CIA Intrigue, International Terrorism, Multimillion Dollar Weapons Deals—The Violent and Shadowy World that Saw the Rise and Fall of Edwin P. Wilson, Master Dealer in Illicit Arms*, New York: Simon and Schuster, 1984.

Graham, Hugh Davis and Gurr, Ted Robert. *The History of Violence in America: A Report to the National Commission on the Causes and Prevention of Violence*, New York: Bantam Books, 1969.

Gugliotta, Guy and Leen, Jeff. *Kings of Cocaine*, New York: Simon and Schuster, 1989.

Hackworth, David H. and Sherman, Julie. *About Face: The Odyssey of an American Warrior*, New York: Simon and Schuster, 1989.

Halper, Albert, ed. *The Chicago Crime Book*, New York: World Publishing Company, 1967.

Herodotus. *The Histories*, translated by Aubrey de Selincourt, Baltimore: Penguin, 1960.

Honegger, Barbara. *October Surprise*, New York: Tudor Publishing Company, 1989.

Hougan, Jim. *Spooks: The Haunting of America—The Private Use of Secret Agents*, New York: William Morrow, 1978.

Johnson, Loch K. *America's Secret Power: The CIA in a Democratic Society*, New York: Oxford University Press, 1989.

Kates, Don B., ed. *Restricting Handguns: The Liberal Skeptics Speak Out*, Croton-on-Hudson, NY: North River Press, 1979.

Kirkham, James F., Levy, Sheldon G. and Crotty, William J. *Assassination and Poltical Violence: A Staff Report to the Naional Commission on the Causes and Prevention of Violence*, New York: Bantam Books, 1970.

Kleiman, Mark A.R. *Against Excess: A Drug Policy for Results, Alcohol, Cocaine, Heroin, Marijuana, Tobacco*, New York: Basic Books, 1992.

Kohn, Howard. *Who Killed Karen Silkwood?*, New York: Summit Books, 1981

Kopel, David B. *The Samurai, the Mountie and the Cowboy: Should America Adopt the Gun Controls of Other Democracies?* Buffalo, NY: Prometheus Books, 1992.

Kwitny, Jonathan. *The Crimes of Patriots: A True Tale of Dope, Dirty Money and the CIA*, New York: Simon and Schuster, 1987.

——. *Endless Enemies: The Making of an Unfriendly World*, New York: Congdon & Weed, 1984.

Levine, Michael. *Deep Cover: The Inside Story of How DEA Infighting, Incompetence and Subterfuge Lost Us the Biggest Battle of the Drug War*, New York: Delacorte Press, 1990.

Levine, Michael, with Laura Kavanau-Levine. *The Big White Lie: The CIA and the Cocaine/Crack Epidemic*, New York: Thunder's Mouth Press, 1993.

Maas Peter. *The Valachi Papers*, New York: G.P. Putnam's Sons, 1968.

McClintick, David. *Swordfish: A True Story of Ambition, Savagery and Betrayal*, New York: Pantheon, 1993.

McCoy, Alfred W. with Cathleen P. Read and Leonard P. Adams II. *The Politics of Heroin in Southeast Asia*, New York: Harper & Row, 1972.

McCoy, Alfred W. *The Politics of Heroin: CIA Complicity in the Global Drug Trade*, Brooklyn, NY: Lawrence Hill Books, 1991.

McGarvey, Patrick J. *C.I.A.: The Myth and the Madness*, Baltimore: Penguin Books, 1973.

McGehee, Ralph W. *Deadly Deceits: My 25 Years in the CIA*, New York: Sheridan Square Press, 1983.

Marchetti, Victor and Marks, John D. *The CIA and the Cult of Intelligence*, New York: Dell, 1975.

Martin, David C. and Walcott, John. *Best Laid Plans: The Inside Story of America's War Against Terrorism*, New York: Simon and Schuster, 1988.

Mayer, Jane and McManus, Doyle. *Landslide: The Unmaking of the President, 1984–1988*, Boston: Houghton Mifflin, 1989.

Merz, Charles. *The Dry Decade*, Garden City, NY: Doubleday, 1931.

Messick, Hank and Goldblatt, Burt. *The Mobs and the Mafia*, New York: Galahad Books, 1972.

Miller, Richard Lawrence. *The Case for Legalizing Drugs*, New York: Praeger, 1991.

Mills, James. *The Underground Empire*, Garden City, NY: Doubleday, 1986.

Moore, Robin. *The French Connection*, Boston: Little, Brown, 1969.

Moquin, Wayne, ed. *The American Way of Crime*, New York: Praeger, 1976.

Morgan, Edmund S., *Inventing the People: The Rise of Popular Sovereignty in England and America*, New York: W.W. Norton, 1988.

Morison, Samuel Eliot. *The Oxford History of the American People*, New York: Oxford University Press, 1965.

Musto, David F., M.D. *The American Disease: Origins of Narcotics Control*, New Haven: Yale University Press, 1973.

————. *The American Disease: Origins of Narcotics Control* (Expanded Edition), New York: Oxford University Press, 1987.

Nash, Jay Robert. *Bloodletters and Badmen*, Philadelphia: M. Evans and Company, 1973.

National Advisory Commission on Civil Disorders. *What Happened? Why Did It Happen? What Can Be Done?* New York: Bantam Books, 1968.

National Commission on the Causes and Prevention of Violence, Final Report. *To Establish Justice, to Insure Domestic Tranquility*, New York: Bantam Books, 1970.

Newton, George D. and Zimring, Franklin E. *Firearms and Violence in American Life: A Staff Report to the National Commission on the Causes and Prevention of Violence*, Washington: U.S. Government Printing Office, 1969.

O'Toole, G. J. A. *The Spanish War: An American Epic 1898*, New York: W. W. Norton, 1984.

Padover, Saul K. *The Living U.S. Constitution*, New York: New American Library, 1953.

Parkman, Francis *The Oregon Trail*, Garden City, NY: Doubleday, 1946.

Powell, William. *The Anarchist Cookbook*, Secaucus, NJ: Lyle Stuart, 1976.

Powers, Richard Gid. *G-Men: Hoover's FBI in American Popular Culture*, Carbondale IL: Southern Illinois University Press, 1983.

Prothrow-Stith, Deborah, M.D., with Michaele Weissman. *Deadly Consequences: How Violence Is Destroying Our Teenage Population and a Plan to Begin Solving the Problem*, New York: HarperCollins, 1991.

Raskin, Marcus G. and Fall, Bernard B. *The Viet-Nam Reader: Articles and Documents on American Foreign Policy and the Viet-Nam Crisis*, NY: Random House, 1965.

Rather, Dan and Gates, Gary Paul. *The Palace Guard*, New York: Harper & Row, 1974.

Schoenbrun, David. *Vietnam: How We Got In, How to Get Out*, New York: Atheneum, 1968.

Scott, Peter Dale and Marshall, Jonathan. *Cocaine Politics: Drugs, Armies and the CIA in Central America*, Berkeley: University of California Press, 1991.

Severn, Bill. *The End of the Roaring Twenties: Prohibition and Repeal*, New York: Julian Messner, 1969.

Shannon, Elaine. *Desperados: Latin Drug Lords, U.S. Lawmen and the War America Can't Win*, New York: Penguin, 1989.

Sheehan, Daniel P. *Affidavit*, filed Dec. 12, 1986, revised April 1, 1987, Washington: Christic Institute, 1987.

Sheehan, Neil. *A Bright Shining Lie: John Paul Vann and America in Vietnam*, New York: Random House, 1988.

Sheehan, Neil, Smith, Hedrick, Kenworthy, E. W., and Butterfield, Fox. *The Pentagon Papers*, New York: Bantam Books, 1971.

Sinclair, Andrew. *Prohibition: The Era of Excess*, Boston: Little, Brown, 1962.

Skolnick, Jerome H. and Fyfe, James J. *Above the Law: Police and the Excessive Use of Force*, New York: Macmillan, 1993.

Smith, Bradley F. *The Shadow Warriors: O.S.S. and the Origins of the C.I.A.*, New York: Basic Books, 1983.

Spence, Gerry. *From Freedom to Slavery: The Rebirth of Tyranny in America*, New York: St. Martin's Press, 1993.

Stutman, Robert M. and Esposito, Richard. *Dead on Delivery: Inside the Drug Wars, Straight from the Street*, New York: Warner Books, 1992.

Swisher, Karin, ed. *Drug Trafficking*, San Diego: Greenhaven Press, 1991.

Trinquier, Col. Roger. *Modern Warfare*, translated by Daniel Lee, New York: Praeger, 1964.

Tyler, Gus. *Organized Crime in America*, Ann Arbor, MI.: University of Michigan Press, 1962.

Weir, William. *Fatal Victories*, Hamden, CT: Archon Books, 1993.

Weir, William. *Written with Lead: Legendary American Gunfights and Gunfighters*, Hamden, CT: Archon Books, 1992.

Wells, Tim and Triplett, William. *Drug Wars: An Oral History from the Trenches*, New York: William Morrow, 1992.

White, Theodore H. *Breach of Faith: The Fall of Richard Nixon*, New York: Atheneum, 1975.

Wills, Garry. *Reagan's America: With a New Chapter on the Legacy of the Reagan Era*, New York: Penguin, 1988.

Woodward, Bob. *Veil: The Secret Wars of the CIA 1981–1987*, Simon & Schuster, New York: 1987.

PERIODICALS

American Rifleman, July 1993. "TV Violence: Does It Cause Real-Life Mayhem?" by Susan R. Lamson.

———, Sept. 1993. "President's Column" (questions about raid on Branch Davidians in Waco), by Robert K. Corbin.

———, Nov. 1993. "The Randy Weaver Case: Another Federal Fiasco," by Jim Oliver.

———, Dec. 1993. "President's Column" (more about about Randy Weaver and the Branch Davidians), by Robert K. Corbin.

American Spectator, May 1988. "Christic Mystics and Drug-Running Theories."

Atlanta Constitution, Nov. 10, 1993. "It's Not the People—It's the Guns," by Arthur L. Kellerman.

Better Health, May–June 1993. "TV Violence—What Influence on Young Minds?" by Robert A. Hamilton.

Cato Institute Policy Analysis, May 5, 1989. "Thinking About Legalization," by James Ostrowski.

Columbia Journalism Review, May/June 1990. "A Twice-Told Tale Puts the Press to Sleep."

Connecticut magazine, June 1987. "Who Killed Kim Klein?" by William Weir.

———, Oct., 1988. "No Pain, No Gain," by William Weir.

———, April, 1989. "A Black and White Affair," by William Weir.

———, Jan. 1994. "Life With the Latin Kings," by Karon Haller.

Conservative Digest, Oct. 1988. "Christic Conspiracy."

Denver Post, March 12, 1993. "Education Programs Cut at County Jail."

———, March 13, 1993. "Sentencing Bill's Death Riles Sheriff."

Drug Policy Letter, No. 3. "Dire Economics Drive Cocaine Production," by Susan Hamilton Saavedra.

The Economist, Dec. 23, 1989. "Russia's Anti-Drink Campaign: Veni, Vidi, Vodka."

Fortune, July 4, 1988. "Lions in Winter."

Hartford Advocate, Aug. 1, 1991. "Blood in the Water," by Melinda Tuhus.

Hartford Courant, April 17, 1988. "Probation Office Struggles Amid a Rising Flood of Cases," by Jon Elson.

——, Nov. 15, 1992. "Drug Abuse Fuels Hartford Area's Demise," by Christopher Merrow and David C.-H. Johnston.

——, Feb. 23, 1993. "Stalking a 'Serial Killer' Narcotic," by Edmund Mahony.

——, Feb. 25, 1993. "State Trooper, Officer the Focus of Grand Jury," by Lynne Tuohy and Blanca M. Quintanilla: "Court Bans Seizures of Drug Dealers' Gifts," by combined wire services.

——, May 12, 1993. "Russian-Colombian Drug Link a Worry," by Associated Press.

——, May 23, 1993. "Add the Voices of Recovering Addicts to the Drug Debate," by Maia Szalavitz.

——, June 10, 1993. "Measures Sought to Stop Salary of Judge Jailed in Bribe-Taking" by Knight-Ridder Syndicate.

Hartford Courant's magazine, *Northeast*, June 20, 1993. "Matters of Substance," interview with Dr. David F. Musto.

Hartford Courant, Aug. 26, 1993. "Drug Penalty Said to Target Blacks," by Associated Press.

——, Sept. 12, 1993. "Federal Sentencing Rules Often Judged Unfair," by Matthew Kauffman.

——, Sept. 19, 1993. "Gang Violence Has Roots Behind Prison Walls," by Carmine R. Fragione.

——, Oct. 1, 1993. "Errors Led to Waco Raid Disaster," by *Los Angeles Times* syndicate.

——, Oct. 2, 1993. "Fighting the Gangs by Any Means," by Matthew Kauffman; "Waco Probe Faults ATF," by Pierre Thomas, *Washington Post* syndicate.

——, Oct. 8, 1993. Editorial: "Drug War Continues Off Course."

——, Oct. 10, 1993. "Gang Strife Spreading to Towns," by Tom Puleo.

——, Oct. 16, 1993. "Meese Made Up 'False Account' of Arms Deal, Prosecutors Say," by Pete Yost, Associated Press.

——, Oct. 19, 1993. "Gangs Aren't Families; They Are Criminal Enterprises," by Stanley Wasilewski, Hartford P.D.

——, Oct. 26, 1993. "Weicker Favors Ban on Handguns," by Mark Pazniokas.

——, Oct. 27, 1993. "Wider Gun Ban Weighed," by Mark Pazniokas.

——, Oct. 30, 1993. Editorial: "Strong Medicine for Gangs in Prison."

——, Nov. 1, 1993. "Illgitimate Births Are a Major National Tragedy," by George F. Will.

——, Nov. 21, 1993. "A Corner Where Crack is King," by Edmund Mahony.

——, Nov. 23, 1993. "Anti-Drug Laws Promote a Crime Wave," by Paul Craig Roberts.

——, Nov. 28, 1993. "Escobars Leave Medellin; Surrender May Follow," by Associated Press.

——, Nov. 30, 1993. "Report Questions Value of Employee Drug Tests" by Ronald J. Ostrow of *Los Angeles Times* syndicate.

——, Dec. 1, 1993. "Time for an Urgent, Public Discourse on Legalizing Drugs," by Don Noel.

————, Dec. 2, 1993. "Grand Juror Details Police Abuse of Power" by Lynne Tuohy.

————, Dec. 5, 1993. "Solutions Lie in the Causes of Gang Violence," by Tom Condon; "Pills and Pressure: An Officer's Addiction," by Mike McIntire.

————, Dec. 6, 1993. "Serious Crime in U.S. Declines Slightly," by Associated Press.

————, Dec. 9, 1993. "President Says Time Has Come to Consider Strengthening Gun Controls," by *Los Angeles Times* syndicate.

————, Dec. 10, 1993. "Clinton Seeks 'Action Plan' to Stop Crime," by Robert A. Rankin, Knight-Ridder syndicate; "Legalizing Drugs Wouldn't Get at Root of Problem," by Denis Horgan.

————, Dec. 12, 1993. "Cali Cartel is New Front in Drug War," by Andrew Selsky, Associated Press; "Clinton Urges Nation to Begin Fight Against Violence with Values," by Associated Press.

————, Dec. 14, 1993. "Court Again Limits Seizures in Drug Cases," by David G. Savage, *Los Angeles Times* syndicate.

————, Dec. 17, 1993. "Gun Laws Penalize Honest People, Not Criminals," by Bill Clede; "Probing Web of Drugs, Money," by Maxine Bernstein and Dave Drury.

————, Dec. 18, 1993. "Keep an Open Mind About Legalizing Drugs," by Robert M. Yoder.

————, Dec. 22, 1993. "Boot Camp," by Rick Green; "Proposed Institute Would Target Violence," by Katherine Farrish; "GOP Anti-Crime Package Targets Gangs, Gun Use," by Larry Williams.

————, Dec. 31, 1993. "When Neighbor Spied on Neighbor," by Tyler Marshall, *Los Angeles Times* syndicate.

————, Jan. 1, 1993. "Legalizing Drugs Will Exacerbate Social Problems, Not Alleviate Them," by Michelle A. Cretella.

————, Jan. 6, 1994. "Officials to Review Ban on Medicinal Marijuana," by Associated Press.

————, Jan. 7, 1994. "Military Repression in Haiti," letter by Sister Kathryn Wrinn.

————, Jan. 13, 1994. "Prosecutor Says Cult Carried Out 'Acts of an Army,' " by *Washington Post* syndicate.

————, Jan. 17, 1994. Editorial: "A Cancer in the Streets . . . Continues to Take Its Death Toll."

————, Jan. 23, 1994. "Court Testimony of Innocence Lost," by Edmund Mahony.

————, Jan. 24, 1994. "Begin the Debate on Legalization of Drugs," by Jerry V. Wilson; "Federal Agents Testify About Deadly Waco Raid," by Associated Press.

————, Jan. 26, 1994. "Smokers Losing Refuge," by Associated Press.

————, Jan. 29, 1994. "Agent Testifies Federal Officials Had Lied About Surprising Koresh," by Associated Press.

————, Feb. 1, 1994. "Hartford Crimes Down," by Maxine Bernstein; "Teenage Drug Use on Rise," by Pierre Thomas, *Washington Post* syndicate; "Boot-Camp Prisons May Sound Good, but the Idea is Flawed," by Jefferson W. Chase.

——, Feb. 16, 1994. "Prosecutors Rest Case Against Koresh Cult," by Associated Press.

——, Feb. 24, 1994. "Branch Davidians' Trial Goes to Jury," by Associated Press.

——, March 8, 1994. "Treat Drugs as a Health Issue, Not a Crime," by Richard R. Brown.

——, March 8, 1994. "Guns, Gangs and Tough Times," by Kathryn Kranhold.

——, March 15, 1994. "Locking 'Em Up Won't Reduce Crime," by Joseph D. McNamara, former police chief of San Jose, CA.

Los Angeles Times, Feb. 22, 1987. "Committee Probes Reports of Contra Drug Smuggling," by Donald McManus and Ronald J. Ostrow.

Miami Herald, Dec. 18, 1989. "In Drug War, Crafty Smugglers Stay a Step Ahead."

——, Jan. 6, 1990. "Costa Rican Prosecutor Links Two Americans to Fatal Bombing," by John McPhaul.

Military Review, Feb., 1986.

Mother Jones, Feb./March 1988. "The Law and the Prophet," by James Traub.

The Nation, April 5, 1971. "Detention Camps."

——, May 20, 1978. "The Terrorist as Scapegoat," by Frank Donner.

——, July 1, 1978. "The FBI's Forty-Year Plot," by Robert Justin Goldstein.

——, Aug. 31, 1985. "Conspiracies from Costa Rica."

——, Oct. 5, 1985. "The Carlos File," by Martha Honey and Tony Avirgan.

——, Jan. 31, 1987. "The CIA's War in Costa Rica," by Tony Avirgan and Martha Honey.

——, Aug. 29, 1987. "Money, Drugs and the Contras," by Jonathan Kwitny; "The Case of 'Mr. Glenn,' " by Jonathan Kwitny.

——, Sept. 12, 1987. "Leaning on Arias," by Martha Honey and Tony Avirgan.

——, Sept. 19, 1987. "Of Drugs, Money and *Contras*: A Liberal's Dose of Facts," by Leslie Cockburn; "Kwitny Replies," by Jonathan Kwitny.

National Review, March 4, 1988. "Mob Rule."

New England Journal of Medicine, Oct. 7, 1993. "Gun Ownership as a Risk Factor for Homicide in the Home."

New Haven Advocate, May 21, 1990. "The Great Savings and Loan Robberies," by David Armstrong.

New Haven Register, April 17, 1988. "Former CIA Operative Blasts Covert Actions," by Associated Press.

——, May 18, 1988. "Drug Dealers Helped Obtain Arms for Contras, Congressman Claims," by Associated Press.

——, Oct. 28, 1988. "FBI Knew of Group Illegally Aiding Contras, Reports Say," by Associated Press.

——, March 30, 1990. "Casolo's Home Burglarized, Files Ransacked," by Associated Press.

——, April 14, 1990. "Register Closes Its Eyes to One Drug Story," letter from Anne Schalet.

————, July 27, 1990. "Hasenfus Testifies on Capture by Sandinistas in Nicaragua," by Associated Press.

———— July 29, 1990. "Nitty-Gritty of Iran-Contra Affair Aired in Hasenfus Suit Over Wages," by *Washington Post* syndicate; " 'Coverup' Lays Out Evidence in Credible Documentary," by Steven Rea.

————, April 26, 1992. "U.S. Plane Failed to Answer Military Warnings, Peru Says," by Associated Press; "Drugs Keep Circling from Fame to Infamy," by Abram Katz.

————, Nov. 29, 1992. "U.S. Losing Ground Against African Heroin Smugglers," by Associated Press.

————, Dec. 10, 1992. "Sniffing Whiteout brings Ban in 3 Schools," by Lorna Grisby.

————, Feb. 6, 1993. "The Innocent as Well as the Guilty Snared by Civil Forfeiture Statutes," by Jack Anderson.

————, Feb. 25, 1993. "Gangs Make Headway in Farm Belt," by Associated Press.

————, Feb. 25, 1993. "Court Protects Innocent Owners Against Forfeiture," by Associated Press; "Agents Killed in Gun Battle with Texas Cult," by Charles Richards, Associated Press.

————, March 28, 1993. "U.S.-Funded Drug Policy in Andes Called a Failure," by *Washington Post* syndicate.

————, March 28, 1993. "Substance Abuse Blamed for Increase in Kids on Disability," by Associated Press.

————, April 22, 1993. "40 Bodies Found in Compound," by Associated Press.

————, April 23, 1993. "Cult Failed to Realize Its Danger," by Associated Press.

————, May 13, 1993. "Cult Member's Lawyer Objects to Bulldozing," by Associated Press.

————, May 18, 1993. "Tribesmen Protect Poppy Fields," by Associated Press.

————, June 16, 1993. "Alliance Seeks Reform of Feds' Forfeiture Law," by Scripps Howard News Service.

————, June 29, 1993. "Racial Gerrymandering Voided by Court," (containing paragraph on Supreme Court decision limiting government civil forfeitures) by Scripps Howard News Service.

————, July 19, 1993. "New 'Killer' Heroin Hits State," by Associated Press.

————, Aug. 23, 1993. "Mandatory Sentences Filling Jails," by Jack Anderson.

————, Sept. 30, 1993. "Corruption Inspiring, Rogue Cop Testifies," by Associated Press.

————, Oct. 4, 1993. "Inspectors Fleeced in Drug Sting," by Associated Press.

————, Oct. 6, 1993. "Big Pot Find Reflects Popularity, Cops Say," by Allan Drury.

————, Oct. 7, 1993. "Government Defends Surprise Assets Seizures," by Associated Press.

————, Oct. 9, 1993. " 'Cat' More Dangerous than Cocaine," by Jack Anderson.

————, Oct. 10, 1993. "Latest Scandal has Many Asking Whether NYPD Has Any Soul to Save," by Tom Hayes, Associated Press.

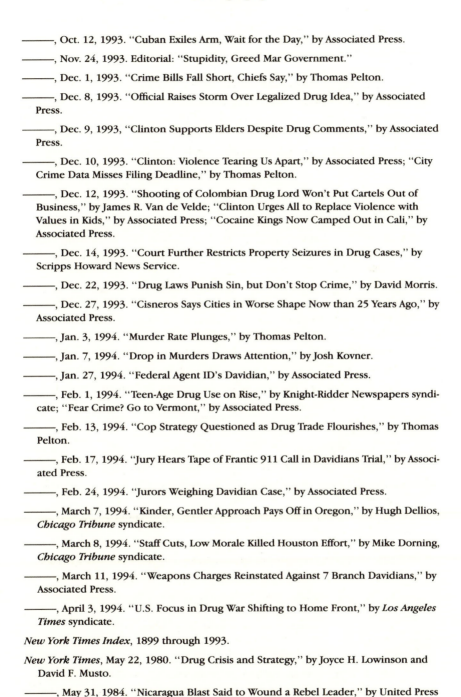

———, Oct. 12, 1993. "Cuban Exiles Arm, Wait for the Day," by Associated Press.

———, Nov. 24, 1993. Editorial: "Stupidity, Greed Mar Government."

———, Dec. 1, 1993. "Crime Bills Fall Short, Chiefs Say," by Thomas Pelton.

———, Dec. 8, 1993. "Official Raises Storm Over Legalized Drug Idea," by Associated Press.

———, Dec. 9, 1993, "Clinton Supports Elders Despite Drug Comments," by Associated Press.

———, Dec. 10, 1993. "Clinton: Violence Tearing Us Apart," by Associated Press; "City Crime Data Misses Filing Deadline," by Thomas Pelton.

———, Dec. 12, 1993. "Shooting of Colombian Drug Lord Won't Put Cartels Out of Business," by James R. Van de Velde; "Clinton Urges All to Replace Violence with Values in Kids," by Associated Press; "Cocaine Kings Now Camped Out in Cali," by Associated Press.

———, Dec. 14, 1993. "Court Further Restricts Property Seizures in Drug Cases," by Scripps Howard News Service.

———, Dec. 22, 1993. "Drug Laws Punish Sin, but Don't Stop Crime," by David Morris.

———, Dec. 27, 1993. "Cisneros Says Cities in Worse Shape Now than 25 Years Ago," by Associated Press.

———, Jan. 3, 1994. "Murder Rate Plunges," by Thomas Pelton.

———, Jan. 7, 1994. "Drop in Murders Draws Attention," by Josh Kovner.

———, Jan. 27, 1994. "Federal Agent ID's Davidian," by Associated Press.

———, Feb. 1, 1994. "Teen-Age Drug Use on Rise," by Knight-Ridder Newspapers syndicate; "Fear Crime? Go to Vermont," by Associated Press.

———, Feb. 13, 1994. "Cop Strategy Questioned as Drug Trade Flourishes," by Thomas Pelton.

———, Feb. 17, 1994. "Jury Hears Tape of Frantic 911 Call in Davidians Trial," by Associated Press.

———, Feb. 24, 1994. "Jurors Weighing Davidian Case," by Associated Press.

———, March 7, 1994. "Kinder, Gentler Approach Pays Off in Oregon," by Hugh Dellios, *Chicago Tribune* syndicate.

———, March 8, 1994. "Staff Cuts, Low Morale Killed Houston Effort," by Mike Dorning, *Chicago Tribune* syndicate.

———, March 11, 1994. "Weapons Charges Reinstated Against 7 Branch Davidians," by Associated Press.

———, April 3, 1994. "U.S. Focus in Drug War Shifting to Home Front," by *Los Angeles Times* syndicate.

New York Times Index, 1899 through 1993.

New York Times, May 22, 1980. "Drug Crisis and Strategy," by Joyce H. Lowinson and David F. Musto.

———, May 31, 1984. "Nicaragua Blast Said to Wound a Rebel Leader," by United Press International; "Efforts on New Alliances," special to the *New York Times*.

————, June 1, 1984. "Costa Rica Holds Nicaraguan Rebel Wounded in Blast," by Stephen Kinzer; "A Surviver's Story: 'Blinding Explosion' Among Journalists," by Reid G. Miller.

————, June 2, 1984. "Caracas Takes In Wounded Rebel Chief," by Stephen Kinzer.

————, June 5, 1984. "Imposter is Suspect in Nicaragua Bombing," by United Press International.

————, June 11, 1984. "In From the Cold and Hot for the Truth," by Philip Taubman.

————, June 14, 1984. "Pastora Vows to Keep Fighting Sandinistas Even Without U.S. Aid," by Alan Riding; "Attack on Pastora: Much Intrigue but Few Facts," by Richard J. Meislin.

————, June 8, 1986. "Bush Discloses Secret Order Citing Drugs as Security Peril," by Neil A. Lewis.

————, Dec. 13, 1986. "2 Aides in Miami Report Order to Stop an Inquiry," by Joseph F. Treaster; "U.S. Says it Briefly Delayed Contra Case Over Hostages," by Philip Shenon.

————, April 30, 1987. "Testimony of a Top Bush Aide Conflicts with North's Notes," by Stephen Engelberg.

————, July 20, 1987. "A Liberal Group Makes Waves with its Contra Lawsuit," by Keith Schneider.

————, Oct. 31, 1987. "A Contra Supplier in Costa Rica Got $375,000, U.S. Agency Says," by Martin Tolchin.

————, Jan. 14, 1989. "U.S. Expatriate Held by Costa Rica as a Spy," by Reuters.

————, Feb. 6, 1989. "Defendants Win Fees in Suit on Contra Aid," by Associated Press.

————, Feb. 7, 1989. "Costa Rica Struggles with Enigma: Is Local Hero Also a U.S. Warlord?" by Mark A. Uhlig.

————, March 1, 1989. "Trial of North Stalled Again; Defense Moves for Dismissal," by David Johnston.

————, March 8, 1989. "Dispute with Arias," by David Johnston and Stephen Engelberg.

————, March 12, 1989. "Hull Bailed Out in Costa Rica," by Associated Press.

————, March 17, 1989. "Giving Law Teeth (and Using Them on Lawyers)" by Felicity Barringer.

New York Times Magazine, Oct. 1, 1989. "Crack's Destructive Sprint Across America," by Michael Massing.

New York Times, March 25, 1990. "CIA Shedding Reluctance to Join War on Drugs," by Jeff Gerth; "Drug Cartels, Squeezed, are Turning to Ecuador," by Richard L. Berke.

————, April 5, 1990. "Marijuana McCarthyism," by Peter Gorman.

————, April 9, 1990. "Tough Call for Bush: A Presidential Pardon for Poindexter?" by David Johnston.

————, April 29, 1990. "Bypassing Borders, More Drugs Flood Ports," by Joseph B. Treaster.

————, June 17, 1990. "How Much Is a Baby Worth?" by A. M. Rosenthal.

————, July 29, 1990. "Testimony Begins in Lawsuit Over Effort to Aid Contras."

————, Aug. 23, 1990. "World Court Heard the Truth on Nicaragua," letter by David C. MacMichael (former CIA analyst).

————, Aug. 24, 1990. "Volunteer Prosecutors and Backlog of Drug Cases," by Robb London.

————, April 26, 1992. "Peru Jet Attacks U.S. Air Transport," by Nathaniel C. Nash.

————, June 14, 1992. "20 Years of War on Drugs, and No Victory Yet," by Joseph B. Treaster.

————, Jan. 31, 1993. "Teen-age Gangs Are Inflicting Violence on Small Cities." by Erik Ekholm.

————, Feb. 14, 1993. "Drug Trade Links Bridgeport and its Suburbs," by Fred Musante; "Bar Group Sees Overemphasis on Drug Cases," by Associated Press.

————, March 28, 1993. "Patients in Pain Find Relief, Not Addiction, in Narcotics," by Elisabeth Rosenthal; "U.S. Agents Say Raid on Sect in Waco was Full of Miscalculations."

————, April 11, 1993. "Chileans Baffled by Briton's Death," by Nathaniel C. Nash.

————, April 17, 1993. "2 Federal Judges in Protest, Refuse to Accept Drug Cases," by Joseph B. Treaster.

————, April 24, 1993. "Sharp Rise in Hospital Visits by Heavy Drug Users is Seen," by Joseph B. Treaster.

————, May 8, 1993. "Reno Questions Drug Policy's Stress on Smuggling," by Stephen Labaton.

————, May 9, 1993. "Dethrone the Drug Czar," by Whitman Knapp.

————, May 16, 1993. "Bombay Bombings: So Far, Trail Leads Nowhere."

————, June 20, 1993. "Mexico's Drug Habit is Giving It Shivers," by Tim Golden.

New York Times Magazine, July 4, 1993. "Lawrence Walsh's Last Battle," by Scott Spencer; "Oliver North's Next War," by Philip Weiss.

New York Times, Aug. 8, 1993. "Costa Rica Reopens Inquiry in 1984 Bombing," (special to the *New York Times*).

————, Oct. 2, 1993. "Report on Siege to Blame Agents, Law Officials Say," by Stephen Labaton.

————, Oct. 9, 1993. "Reno Contradicted in New Report On Decision to Attack Waco Cult", by Stephen Labaton.

————, Oct. 10, 1993. "Tales of Police Corruption Not Surprising, 46th Precinct Residents Say," by Craig Wolff.

————, Oct. 31, 1993. "Modern Day 'Fagins' Admit to Series of Bank Robberies," by Robert Reinhold.

————, Nov. 13, 1993. "Save the Children," by John J. DiIulio Jr.

————, Nov. 14, 1993. "CIA Formed Haitian Unit Later Tied to Narcotics Trade," by Tim Weiner with Howard W. French and Stephen Engleberg; "Healing Herb or Narcotic? Marijuana as Medication," by Joseph B. Treaster; "Clinton Delivers Emotional Appeal on Stopping Crime," by Douglas Jehl; "Excerpts From Clinton's Speech to Black Ministers."

————, Nov. 20, 1993. "Anti-Drug Unit of CIA Sent Ton of Cocaine to U.S. in 1990," by Tim Weiner.

——, Nov. 21, 1993. "When Only Monsters are Real," by Brent Staples; "U.S. Aid Hasn't Stopped Drug Flow from South America, Experts Say," by James Brooke; " 'If I Had Known,' " by Bob Herbert.

——, Dec. 12, 1993. "Surgeon General Proposes, The White House Disposes And a Debate Continues," by Stephen Labaton.

——, Dec, 18, 1993. "As Boot Camps for Criminals Multiply, Skepticism Grows," by Adam Nossiter.

——, Dec. 19, 1993. "It's Not Legalization, but a User-Friendly Drug Strategy," by Joseph B. Treaster.

——, Jan. 15, 1994. "Cult Had Illegal Arms, Experts Say."

——, Jan. 27, 1994. "More Arrests, More Therapy in Drug Plan," by Joseph B. Treaster; Editorial: "Tough and Smart on Crime?"

——, Jan. 28, 1994. "Agent Explains Why Cult Raid was Moved Up," (special to *New York Times*).

——, Jan. 30, 1994. "Lift for Defense in Cultist Trial," (special to *New York Times*); "Truth and Justice: Why the Best Hope In a 'War' on Crime May be a Stalemate," by Charles E. Silberman.

——, Feb. 5, 1994. "21% of U.S. Inmates are Called Nonviolent," by Associated Press.

——, Feb. 6, 1994. "Death and Domesticity Mix at Trial of 11 Cult Members," (special to *New York Times*); " 'Pot Surges Back, but It's, Like, a Whole New World," by Melinda Henneberger.

——, Feb. 13, 1994. "Grisly Testimony in Cultists' Trial," (special to *New York Times*).

——, Feb. 20, 1994. "Drug Case Derails U.S.-China Law Tie," by Constance L. Hays; "Colombians Press for Legalization of Cocaine," by James Brooke.

——, Feb. 26, 1994. "U.S. Agency Suggests Regulating Cigarettes as an Addictive Drug," by Philip J. Hilts; "Hardly Mentioned at Cultists' Trial: Their Leader," by Sam Howe Verhovek; "Police Raid Wrong Man's House and Kill His Dogs," by Associated Press.

——, Feb. 27, 1994. "11 in Texas Sect are Acquitted of Key Charges," by Sam Howe Verhovek; "The Useless War," by Gabriel Garcia Marquez.

New York Times Magazine, March 13, 1994. "Blowback From the Afghan Battlefield," by Tim Weiner.

The New Yorker, Oct. 25, 1993. "Exit El Patron," by Alma Guillermoprieto.

——, Dec. 6, 1993. "The Truth of El Mozote," by Mark Danner.

——, Dec. 27, 1993. "Ollie's Next Mission," by Jeffrey Toobin.

——, Jan. 24, 1994. Comment: "A Minimum of Sense."

Newsweek, June 11, l984. "An Attack on Commander Zero," by Robert B. Cullen, Ron Moreau and John Walcott.

——, Sept. 3, 1984. "The CIA blows an Asset," by Harry Anderson, Robert Rivard and Nicholas M. Horrock.

——, Sept. 17, 1984. "The Friends of Tommy Posey," by Russell Watson, Kim Willenson and Ron Moreau.

Parade, Feb. 27, 1994. " 'None of This Had to Happen,' " by Peter Maas.

The Police Chief, 55 "The Kansas City Experience: 'Crack' Organized Crime Cooperative Task Force," by David Barton.

The Progressive, May 1985. "The Take-Charge Gang," by Keenan Peck.

———, March 1987. "The Contras' Little List."

Richmond Times-Dispatch, Nov. 11, 1993. "Tobacco is Unrivaled Killer, Study Says," by Knight-Ridder Newspapers.

Rolling Stone, Nov. 17, 1988. "Jackson Browne No Longer Running on Empty."

Scientific American, July, 1991. "Opium, Cocaine and Marijuana in American History," David F. Musto.

Time, May 8, 1984. "The Freedom We Have Lost," by Anthony Burgess.

———, June ll, 1984. "Starting a New Chapter," by James Kelly, David DeVoss and Johanna McGeary.

———, Sept. 17, 1984. "A Mystery Involving 'Mercs,' " by Ed Magnuson, Jerome Chandler and Ross H. Munro.

———, Aug. 2, 1993. "A Boy and His Gun," by Jon D. Hull.

———, Nov. 29, 1993. "Drugs: Confidence Games," by Elaine Shannon.

———, Dec. 13, 1993. "Escobar's Dead End," by Kevin Fedarko.

———, Dec. 20, 1993. "The Political Interest: Clinton's Drug Policy is a Bust," by Michael Kramer.

———, Feb. 7, 1994. "The Political Interest: Tough. But Smart?" by Michael Kramer; "Lock 'Em Up!" by Ann Blackman, Cathy Booth and Janice C. Simpson; ". . . And Throw Away the Key," by Ann Blackman, Cathy Booth, John D. Hull, Sylvester Monroe and Lisa H. Towle.

———, Feb. 28, 1994. "Kicking the Big One," by Barbara Ehrenreich.

———, March 14, 1994. "The Political Interest: Frying Them Isn't the Answer," by Michael Kramer.

U.S.A. Today, Nov. 15, 1989. "Some Worry Police 'Out of Control,' " by Tony Mauro.

USA Weekend, Jan. 14–16, 1994. "Debate: Throw Out the Key? Yes: It's Time to Get Very, Very Tough," by Bradley S. O'Leary and "No: "Cookie Cutter" is Counter Productive," by Victor Kamber.

U.S. News and World Report, Sept. 18, 1989. "Drugs and White America," by David R. Gergen.

———, Oct. 1, 1990. "More Unsafe Sex and AIDS."

Wall Street Journal, Aug. 19, 1985. "In Alabama's Woods, Frank Camper Trains Men to Repel Invaders," by Timothy K. Smith.

———, Aug. 10, 1989. "Federal War on Drugs Is Scattershot Affair, with Dubious Progress," by Paul M. Barrett.

———, Nov. 13, 1989. "How a 24-Year-Old Became a Local Hero Until His Drug Arrest," by Joe Davidson.

————, April 30, 1990. "Searches for Drugs Roil Boaters," by Arthur S. Hayes.

————, Feb. 11, 1992. "How to Win the Drug War Quickly," letter from Mark R. Carter.

————, Dec. 23, 1992. "How to Reduce Drug Crimes," letter by Philip D. Harvey

————, Feb. 18, 1993. "To Save Lives, Raise Funds and Cut the Deficit: Tax Tobacco," letter from Jimmy Carter.

REPORTS

Commonwealth of Australia-New South Wales, Joint Task Force, *Report, Volume 4, Nugan Hand*, part 1, Canberra: Australian Government Printer, June, 1982.

Commonwealth of Australia, Royal Commission of Inquiry into the Activities of the Nugan Hand Group, *Final Report, Volume 1*, Canberra: Australian Government Publishing Services, 1985.

Connecticut Alcohol and Drug Abuse Commission, *Building for the Future*.

Connecticut Alcohol and Drug Abuse Commission, *Building for the Future*, Information Appendix to the CADAC Three Year Policy Plan, 1987.

Institute for Health Policy, Brandeis University, prepared for the Robert Wood Johnson Foundation, Princeton, New Jersey, *Substance Abuse: The Nation's Number One Health Problem*, Princeton: October 1993.

Pakistan Narcotics Control Board, *National Survey on Drug Abuse in Pakistan*, Islamabad: 1986.

U.S. Congress, House of Representatives Select Committee to Investigate Covert Arms Transactions with Iran and U.S. Senate Select Committee On Secret Military Assistance to Iran and the Nicaraguan Opposition, *Report of the Congressional Committees Investigating the Iran-Contra Affair: With Supplemental, Minority and Additional Views*, Washington: U.S. Government Printing Office, 1987.

U.S. Congress, Senate, Committee on Government Operations, *Organized Crime and Illicit Traffic in Narcotics*, 88th Congress, First and Second Sessions, Washington: U.S Government Printing Office, 1964.

U.S. Congress, Senate, Foreign Relations Committee, Subcommittee on Terrorism, Narcotics and International Operations of the Committee on Foreign Relations, United States Senate, *Drugs, Law Enforcement and Foreign Relations*, Washington: U.S. Government Printing Office, 1988.

U.S. Department of Justice, Office of Justice Programs, Bureau of Justice Statistics, *Drugs and Crime Facts, 1991*, Washington: U.S. Government Printing Office, 1992.

U.S. Department of Justice, Office of Justice Programs, Bureau of Justice Statistics, *Drugs & Crime Data Center & Clearinghouse*, Washington: U.S. Government Printing Office, 1992.

U.S. Department of Justice, Office of Justice Programs, Bureau of Justice Statistics, *State Drug Resources: 1992 National Directory*, Washington: U.S. Government Printing Office, 1992.

U.S. Department of Justice, Office of Justice Programs, Bureau of Justice Statistics, *Fact Sheet: Drug Data Summary*, Washington: U.S. Government Printing Office, 1992.

U.S. Department of Justice, Office of Justice Programs, Bureau of Justice Statistics, *Fact Sheet: Drug Use Trends*, Washington: U.S. Government Printing Office, 1992.

U.S. Department of Justice, Office of Justice Programs, Bureau of Justice Statistics, *Special Report: Murder in Large Urban Counties, 1988*, Washington: U.S. Government Printing Office, 1993.

U.S. Department of Justice, Office of Justice Programs, Bureau of Justice Statistics, *Bureau of Justice Statistics Bulletin, Crime and the Nation's Households, 1992*, U.S. Washington: Government Printing Office, 1993.

U.S. Department of Justice, Office of Justice Programs, Bureau of Justice Statistics, *Census of State and Local Law Enforcement Agencies, 1992*, Washington: U.S. Government Printing Office, 1993.

U.S. Department of Justice, Office of Justice Programs, Bureau of Justice Statistics, Bulletin: *Jail Inmates 1992*, Washington: U.S. Government Printing Office, 1993.

U.S. Department of Justice, Office of Justice Programs, Bureau of Justice Statistics, Special Report: *HIV in U.S. Prisons and Jails*, Washington: U.S. Government Printing Office, 1993.

U.S. Department of Justice, Office of Justice Programs, Bureau of Justice Statistics, Bulletin: *A National Crime Victimization Survey Report: Criminal Victimization 1992*, Washington: U.S. Government Printing Office, 1994.

U.S. Department of Justice, Office of Justice Programs, Bureau of Justice Statistics, Special Bulletin: *Federal Offenses and Offenders: Prosecuting Criminal Enterprises*, Washington: U.S. Government Printing Office, 1994.

U.S. Department of Justice, Office of Justice Programs, Bureau of Justice Statistics, Bulletin: *Capital Punishment 1992*, by Lawrence A. Greenfield and James J. Stephan, Washington: U.S. Government Printing Office, 1994.

U.S. State Department, Bureau of International Narcotics Matters, *International Narcotics Control Strategy Report, March 1990*, publication no. 9749, Washington: U.S. State Department, March, 1990.

MISCELLANEOUS

Avirgan, Tony, et al., Plaintiffs vs. John Hull et al., Defendants, *RICO Conspiracy Suit filed in United States District Court, Southern District of Florida*

CBS News, "West 57th Street," June 26, 1986, "John Hull's Farm: Bordering on War."

CBS News, "Eye to Eye with Connie Chung," June 17, 1993, "Who Killed Colonel Sabow?," transcript from Burrelle's Information Services.

Christic Institute, "Inside the Shadow Government: Declaration of Plaintiff's Counsel filed by the Christic Institute U.S. District Court, Miami, Florida, March 31, 1988."

Poder Judicial, Republica de Costa Rica, *Se Ordena Detencion y Extradicion de Inputado* . . . (Order for the extradition of John Hull Clarke for "Hostile Acts and Qualified Homicide").

National Public Radio, "All Things Considered," May 5, 1986.

National Public Broadcasting System, "Frontline," Nov. 17, 1992, "JFK, Hoffa and the Mob," transcript from PBS Transcript.

National Public Broadcasting System, "Frontline," Dec. 14, 1993, "Behind the Badge," transcript from Journal Graphics.

INTERVIEWS

Lorenzo Ricketts, victim of police brutality, in person and by telephone at various times between Nov. 1987 and Aug. 1993.

Bernard Sullivan, then Hartford police chief, in person and by telephone, several times in March 1987.

Wesley Spears, Ricketts's attorney, in person and by telephone several times in March 1987.

John (Jack) Bailey, then Connecticut state's attorney for Hartford, now Connecticut chief state's attorney, March 1987.

Stanley Twardy, then U.S. attorney for Connecticut, by telephone to New Haven, Feb. 1987.

John Williams, attorney, by telephone to New Haven, Connecticut, March 1987.

Ralph Clifford, attorney, by telephone to Stamford, Connecticut, March 1987.

Burton Weinstein, attorney, by telephone to Bridgeport, Connecticut, March 1987.

John Brittain, professor at University of Connecticut Law School, by telephone to Hartford, Connecticut, March 1987.

Sally Kruel, head of the Berkshire Woods narcotics treatment center; two staffers, Dennis Buffard and Henry Buxton; and three inmates, Aug. 1988.

William J. Taylor, March 20, 1990, April 16, 1990, April 25, 1990 and June 4, 1990 in Danbury, CT. Taylor, a private investigator, worked with Daniel Sheehan on the Avirgan-Honey lawsuit.

Daniel P. Sheehan, April 9, 1990, May 3, 1990, June 5, 1990, and July 20, 1990 by telephone to Washington, DC. Sheehan, head of the Christic Institute, was the principal counsel for Avirgan and Honey.

Federal Judge James Lawrence King's secretary on July 3, 1990, and July 17, 1990, by telephone to Miami. (King refused to return calls.) King was the judge at the Avirgan-Honey suit.

Anthony Lapham, July 3, 1990, by telephone to Washington. Lapham had been chief counsel for the CIA in the Avirgan-Honey suit. He resigned after learning that his fee came from the sale of arms to Iran.

Thomas Green of Sidley and Austin, Chicago, by telephone to S&A's Washington branch, July 3, 1990. Green represented Contra-supporters Secord, Hakim, Quintero and Clines.

Thomas R. Spencer, Jr., July 17, 1990, by telephone to Miami. Spencer was a member of Lapham's firm and was representing General John Singlaub and John Hull.

Michael Withey by telephone to Seattle, July 18, 1990. Withey worked on the Avirgan-Honey lawsuit on behalf of the Trial Lawyers for Public Justice.

John Mattes, July 19, 1990, by telephone to Miami. Mattes represented Jesus Garcia who revealed the plot to bomb the U.S. embassy in Costa Rica.

Morton Stavis by telephone to New York, July 20, 1990. Stavis worked on the Avirgan-Honey lawsuit on behalf of the Center for Constitutional Rights.

Adria Henderson by telephone to Bridgeport, CT, August 19 and 26, 1993. Ms. Henderson is a private investigator employed by the William J. Taylor agency.

Rev. William Davis, S.J. by telephone to Los Angeles September 8, and September 16, 1993. Father Davis is a legal investigator for the Christic Institute.

William Flower, spokesman for the Connecticut Correction Department, by telephone to Hartford, January 30, 1994.

INDEX